KNIGHTS OF THE GREEN CLOTH

University of Oklahoma Press: Norman

KNIGHTS OF THE GREEN CLOTH

The Saga of the Frontier Gamblers

By Robert K. DeArment

Part-title drawings by Joan DeArment Hall

Books by Robert K. DeArment

Bat Masterson: The Man and the Legend (Norman, 1979)
Knights of the Green Cloth: The Saga of the Frontier Gamblers (Norman, 1982)

Library of Congress Cataloging in Publication Data

DeArment, Robert K., 1925–
  Knights of the green cloth.

  Bibliography: p.
  Includes index.
    1. Gambling—West (U.S.)—History.   2. West
(U.S.)—Social life and customs.   3. Gamblers—
West (U.S.)—Biography.   I. Title.
HV6721.W38D42   306'.4   81–16196
                              AACR2

To
ROSE
My Partner

CONTENTS

ILLUSTRATIONS

MAPS

ACKNOWLEDGMENTS

The following people were of great assistance to me in gathering the material and illustrations for this book, and to them all I owe a debt of gratitude:

Dennis Anderson, University of Washington, Seattle, Washington.

Ron Brey, Montana Historical Society, Helena, Montana.

Emory Cantey, Jr., Fort Worth, Texas.

Patrice E. Carlson, State Historical Society of Missouri, Columbia, Missouri.

John E. Carter, Nebraska State Historical Society, Lincoln, Nebraska.

Cathy Cooper, Keeneland Library, Lexington, Kentucky.

Jim Davis, Idaho State Historical Society, Boise, Idaho.

Lori Davisson, Arizona Historical Society, Tucson, Arizona.

Jack DeMattos, Foxboro, Massachusetts.

Bonnie Gardner, South Dakota State Historical Society, Pierre, South Dakota.

Roslyn Goodman, Alaska Historical Library, Juneau, Alaska.

Marion W. Hagerman, Vancouver Public Library, Vancouver, British Columbia, Canada.

Opal Harber, Western History Department, Denver Public Library, Denver, Colorado.

Michael Harrison, Fair Oaks, California.

Joan Heida, Yuma City-County Library, Yuma, Arizona.

John Warren Hunter, San Antonio, Texas.

Mary C. Johnson, Spokane Public Library, Spokane, Washington.

Judith Kremsdorf Golden, Colorado Historical Society, Denver, Colorado.

Emily M. Myers, Western History Collections, University of Oklahoma Library, Norman, Oklahoma.

Patricia S. Preate, Auctions by Therault, Waverly, Pennsylvania.

William M. Roberts, Bancroft Library, University of California, Berkeley, California.

Brenda S. Robertson, University of Wyoming, Laramie, Wyoming.

June Sampson, University of South Dakota, Vermillion, South Dakota.

William B. Secrest, Fresno, California.

Nancy Sherbert, Kansas State Historical Society, Topeka, Kansas.

C. L. Sonnichsen, Tucson, Arizona.

Harold D. Wilson, Seattle Public Library, Seattle, Washington.

and

Joan DeArment Hall, who drew the part-title card illustrations.

ROBERT K. DEARMENT

KNIGHTS OF THE GREEN CLOTH

From Soda to Hock

The first card out of a faro box was called the "soda" and did not count in the betting. The last card in the deck, the "hock," was also dead. Thus derived the expression, "from soda to hock," meaning from beginning to end, one of many idiomatic terms that came into the language from the frontier's most popular game.

Soda

In the story of the Old West he is a familiar figure, as instantly recognizable as those other stock characters, the reckless cowboy, the painted Indian, the steely-eyed lawman, the desperate outlaw, the shaggy mountain man, the grizzled prospector, the seductive dance hall girl, the brawny mule skinner, and the virginal schoolmarm.

We recognize *him* at a glance. He is tall and thin, almost emaciated. His hair is dark and he is clean-shaven except for a drooping mustache that adds to his saturnine appearance. He is dressed in black and his mien matches his attire. His pale, somber features could have been carved in ivory. Only his eyes move. They flick over everything, ignoring nothing. Jewels flash at his hands and breast. He is not visibly armed, but it is certain that several weapons are concealed on his person. We know that he can be extremely dangerous when angered, that he lives by taking the wealth of others and can be ruthless in the taking. We also know that he is fearless and willing to risk all he owns to achieve his ends. He can be generous to the unfortunate. He is at all times courteous and protective to women, children, and other defenseless critters.

He is the Frontier Gambler and we know so much about him because we were introduced to him more than a hundred years ago by Bret Harte, who called him at times "John Oakhurst" and at other times "Jack Hamlin." In song and story, stage melodrama and novel, motion picture and television play, we have seen him countless times. He is as ubiquitous as he is unchanging.

That stereotype figure lives on as a character of popular imagination. Long since vanished, though, are the historical frontier gamblers, those very real human beings who, between the years 1850 and 1910, were to be found plying their trade in every mining camp, cattle town, railhead, and army cantonment that sprouted during those years between the Gulf of Mexico and the Klondike.

The frontier gambler of history was not always tall and thin; he was often short and sometimes quite stout. His hair was frequently fair rather than dark, and sometimes he wore a full beard. There were some gamblers who neglected to shave and still others were beardless because they were women. Some of the professional gamblers of the western frontier were scrupulously honest and some were as crooked as a Colorado creek bed. There were the generous and the niggardly, the courageous and the cowardly, the intelligent and the stupid. They were, in a word, human, with all the virtues and vices of any other segment of mankind.

The great popularity of gambling games in the frontier West and the perceived need for the professional gambler were inevitable and predictable. In that historical time and place everyone was to some extent a gambler. All who sought fortunes in the West were betting on the land, the future, and themselves. It was a period of great enthusiasm and optimism, for all were convinced that huge rewards awaited those with nerve enough to take a risk. For those too impatient to wait for the claim to produce a bonanza in gold, the cattle to multiply, or the town to develop, the gambler's table offered an opportunity for instant riches. It was a time of almost unlimited personal freedom and it was a loose, tolerant society with few to say that gambling was a sin, a crime, or a folly. Of course, the professional gambler himself was a product of the same nineteenth-century American influences; he had simply turned to the tables earlier and had made a profession of seeking his fortune there. Not many gamblers found a fortune, but there were those who discovered at the tables an exciting way of life, a calling as true and as real for them as law, medicine, or the clergy was for others.

Among the thousands of adventurers who gambled professionally during these years on the frontier, a few had outstanding careers and became a kind of royalty of the sporting gentry—the court cards of the deck. This book is a recounting of the stories of some of those who were famous in their time, familiar names in gambling dens from Bannack to El Paso.

Some were loners, unusual men of great card skill who were viewed by their peers with a kind of awe—the Aces.

There were others who achieved economic or political power through the gambling profession and to some extent became—the Kings.

The few hardy females who gained proficiency and notoriety in the masculine world of gambling were—the Queens.

And perhaps the most colorful, as well as the most numerous, were the crooked gamblers—the Knaves.

ACES

Gambling was not only the principal and best-paying industry of the town at the time, but it was also reckoned among its most respectable.

W. B. ("Bat") Masterson
"Famous Gunfighters of the Western Frontier: Doc Holliday," *Human Life* (May, 1907)

1

I have a son, and I had rather follow him to the grave than see him contract the habit of gambling. Yet I continue in that line of life . . . which I will probably follow until I am dead.

Ben Thompson
William M. Walton, *Life and Adventures of Ben Thompson*

On December 28, 1849, the sidewheeler *California* anchored in San Francisco Bay, having made the voyage from Panama in twenty-three days. Built to carry 250 passengers, the vessel was jammed with almost twice that number, all tense with excitement and burning to set foot on the new El Dorado, the fabled California land of gold. Back in the States they had heard the stories of golden nuggets lying on the ground and how fortunes could be made almost overnight by dipping a pan in the California streams or scratching the ground with a shovel. Many of these new arrivals to the scene of the great excitement of 1849, however, had no intention of touching pan or pick. They were professional gamblers who had left comfortable facilities in New Orleans, Memphis, or Natchez to seek gold in El Dorado, not from the earth but from across the green cloth of the poker table or the painted oilcloth of the faro spread.[1]

One of the sporting men who disembarked from the little sidewheeler was a tall, olive-skinned Italian-American with coal-black hair and mustache and dark, flashing eyes. At thirty-three years of age, Charles Cora had already achieved renown among the southern gambling fraternity as a veritable demon of the faro table, whose winnings had been calculated in the hundreds of thousands. For six years he would enhance that reputation in San Francisco and in the mountain mining camps of California. Those who challenged him at faro would retreat poorer in pocket and pronounce him the luckiest of men.

The city that Cora found when he landed was like nothing he had ever seen before; it presented a spectacle that must have started a sporting man's blood pounding. San Francisco was a town gone gambling mad. It would set a pattern for innumerable western mining boomtowns to follow, but none ever

9

equalled it for sheer quantity of gambling opportunity or excitement of the play.

The exact number of gambling houses that blossomed in the first flush of the wild stampede to the California goldfields is not known, but there were several hundred, at least, and perhaps as many as a thousand. Wrote an argonaut who arrived the same month as Cora:

It was a Sunday morning in December, 1849, when landing from the Panama steamer I wended my way with the throng to Portsmouth Square . . . mostly occupied by buildings which served the double purpose of hotels and gambling houses, the latter being regarded at the time as a very respectable profession. . . . It was a scene I shall never forget. On all sides . . . were gambling houses, each with its band of music in full blast. Crowds were going in and coming out; fortunes were being lost and won; terrible imprecations and blasphemies rose amid the horrid wail, and it seemed to me pandemonium was let loose.[2]

Everybody gambled. In 1854 the authors of the *Annals of San Francisco* wrote of those early days:

Gambling was *the* amusement—*the* grand occupation of many classes—apparently the life and soul of the place. . . . The extensive saloons, in each of which a dozen . . . tables might be placed, were continually crowded, and around the tables themselves the players often stood in lines three or four deep, everyone vying with his neighbors for the privilege of reaching the board, and staking his money as fast as the wheel and ball could be rolled or the card turned. . . . Judges and clergymen, physicians and advocates, merchants and clerks, tradesmen, mechanics, laborers, miners and farmers, all adventurers in their kind—every one elbowed his way to the gaming table, and unblushingly threw down his golden or silver stake.

Even the few children of the town burned with the fever. Little boys of ten or twelve years were to be seen wiggling their way to the tables, "smoking cigars as big as themselves . . . and losing their hundred dollars at a pop with all the nonchalance of an old gambler."[3]

It was here that the American expression "You bet!" came

into being. It derived from the gambling table as a shortened form of the commonly heard dealer's question, "How do you bet?" or "Do you bet?" By the 1860s a New York correspondent would report that "You bet" was the most popular and most used expression heard in San Francisco. A new gold camp that sprang up eight miles east of Nevada City in 1860 was named You Bet. Bret Harte, who has been called "the Homer of Gamblers," recalled standing at the doorway of a San Francisco gambling hall and overhearing the following conversation as an entering miner met one who was just leaving:

"Hello! When did you come down?"
"This morning."
"Made a strike on the bar?"
"You bet!"

An hour later Harte observed the same two miners meeting again:

"Hello! What now?"
"Back to the bar."
"Cleaned out?"
"You bet!"[4]

The first of the great gambling houses of San Francisco was the Parker House, which had been built as a hotel by Robert A. Parker early in 1849. Parker's ambition had been to own the biggest and best hotel west of the Mississippi River, but when the gamblers began pouring into town from the ships and flashing their bankrolls, he leased the place out as a gambling establishment. The main room downstairs rented for $10,000 a month. Here were installed three faro tables, two monte tables, a roulette table, and a seventh reserve table held open for the use of anyone who desired a different game. A smaller room behind the bar brought $3,500 a month. The gamblers paid $3,500 each for three apartments on the second floor, and two other rooms upstairs were rented out by the hour or day for private poker games. Later a syndicate headed by the appropriately named Colonel Jack Gamble leased the entire second floor at $60,000 a year. Dealers in the Parker House often had as much as $40,000 in gold stacked on each of their tables. It has been estimated that at the peak of the

The Bella Union, Verandah, and El Dorado gambling halls look down on the northeast corner of Portsmouth Square, San Francisco, about 1856. Courtesy The Bancroft Library, University of California.

gold rush there was half a million dollars on the Parker House tables at one time.

Samuel Dennison built a gambling house immediately adjoining the Parker House and called it Dennison's Exchange. He made a lot of money very quickly and moved on, selling the building to Tom Bartell, who was not so fortunate. Shortly after Bartell acquired the place a fire broke out, destroying both his building and the Parker House. A new Parker House, built at a cost of $40,000, was completed May 3, 1850. The following day it too went up in smoke.

Flanking the Parker House on the other side was the famous El Dorado Gambling Saloon, owned by James McCabe and

Thomas J. A. Chambers. When it was only a canvas tent, covering an area fifteen by twenty-five feet, the El Dorado rented for $40,000 a year. Later, a wooden building was erected on the site. It consisted of one large room and several private nooks partitioned off for the convenience of those few men fortunate enough to have mistresses they wished to entertain. Paintings of nudes covered the rough boards of the walls. Musical groups performed on a platform at one end of the hall, providing continual entertainment. At the other end was an elegant mahogany bar backed by fine cut-glass mirrors. Bayard Taylor described the scene in 1850:

The greatest crowd is about the Eldorado; we find it difficult to effect an entrance. There are about eight tables in the room, all of which are thronged; copper-hued Kanakes, Mexicans rolled in their serapes, and Peruvians thrust through their ponchos, stand shoulder to shoulder with the brown and bearded American miners. The stakes are generally small, though when the bettor gets into a "streak of luck" as it is called, they are allowed to double until all is lost or the bank breaks. Along the end of the room is a spacious bar, supplied with all kinds of bad liquors, and in a sort of gallery, suspended under the ceiling, a female violinist tasks her strength of muscle to minister to the excitement of the play.[5]

The musical entertainment provided by the houses was diverse and in some cases quite unusual. The Verandah, across the street from the El Dorado, featured a one-man band, a musical oddity who blew on a set of pipes tied to his chin while beating a drum on his back with sticks on his elbows. His hands held cymbals which he crashed frequently, and all the while he kept time by stamping his feet on the floor. What his performance lacked in artistry it made up for in sheer volume. A black chorus was the attraction at the Aguila de Oro, and the Bella Union offered a Mexican string quintet composed of two harps, two guitars, and a flute. The Bella Union also featured for several years the celebrated singer and violinist, Charlie Schultze, who introduced the tune "Aloha" into the United States. Schultze sang the plaintive refrain, "You Never Miss Your Sainted Mother Till She's Dead and Gone to Heaven," to the Hawaiian melody.

Other houses on or near Portsmouth Square, the very heart of the rapidly expanding city, were the Empire, the Mazourka, the Arcade, the Varsouvienne, the Ward House, La Souciedad, the Fontine House, the Saint Charles, the Alhambra, and the Rendez-vous. French syndicates owned and operated many of these houses and outfitted them in grand style, with great glass chandeliers and floor-to-ceiling mirrors so that "entering at night from the unlighted street . . . was like passing from the dark depths to celestial brightness."

Most of the men who ran these elaborate temples of chance had, like Charles Cora, arrived early on the scene by avoiding the slower routes, either the long sea journey around South America or the trek overland by wagontrain. They had sailed to Panama and braved the steaming jungles of the Isthmus. By dugout canoe and mule-back they had traversed the swamps to Panama City and boarded another ship for San Francisco. So many sporting men came this way that in California the Panamanian passage was commonly called "The Gamblers' Route."

One of the first to arrive had been James McCabe, an imposing figure of a man with a handsome mane of hair and a full beard of which he was inordinately proud. A native of Pittsburgh, Pennsylvania, he had gambled extensively on Ohio and Mississippi River steamboats and had been a part owner of various gambling establishments in the South. When he appeared on the Pacific Coast in April, 1849, he was accompanied by a feisty paramour named Mrs. Irene McCready. McCabe and Tom Chambers opened the El Dorado, and several months later Mrs. McCready began operation of a brothel in a small one-story building not far from her lover's gambling house. Both establishments were destroyed in the first of the famous fires that swept San Francisco later that year. The conflagration, originating in Dennison's Exchange, caused property destruction estimated at one million dollars.

Rebuilding began before the smoke had cleared and Jim McCabe was back in business within a few days. Noted a local paper twelve days after the disaster: "Last evening a band played, coins chinked, glasses clinked, in the rebuilt El Dorado."[6] The paper did not mark the reopening of Irene Mc-

Cready's bagnio, but it must have been shortly afterward. Several months later, on May 4, 1850, the second of Mrs. McCready's whorehouses was destroyed by fire. Her third and final establishment was a brick two-story parlor house, which she operated through the year 1856.

This was long after she and McCabe had terminated an association that had been notable for the frequency and violence of its storms. An extremely jealous woman, Irene had on several occasions publicly accused McCabe of infidelity. When she finally badgered him in his own establishment, he beat her severely and sent her packing with a warning never to return. Later he attempted a reconciliation. Weighted down with gifts and apologies, he went to her house. Irene seemed equally contrite and suggested that they toast their rekindled love with a drink before indulging in activities of a more intimate nature. Shortly after partaking of a concoction that Irene had carefully doctored, McCabe collapsed on the floor in a state of unconsciousness. Chuckling to herself, Mrs. McCready then stripped him, lathered his body from crown to sole, and shaved every hair from his body.

Shorn by his Delilah, his head and body as smooth and white as a keno ball, Jim McCabe skulked around San Francisco. "I came across him one night in my meanderings, disguised in a slouch hat pulled down over his ears," a friend later recalled. "He did not appear in his usual haunts until his hair had grown out. . . ."[7] And when he did appear, it might have been added, it was not in the company of Irene McCready.

Another early arrival was Bill Briggs, who ran a house on Montgomery Street. A gambler noted for his charity, Briggs was said to have given away thousands of dollars to miners and small-fry tinhorns down on their luck.[8] He was convinced that coins of denominations amounting to less than a dollar were unlucky. Every morning at four o'clock he gathered up all the small change taken in over his tables during the night. Opening the front door of his establishment, he would fling the coins into the street where they were fought over by a crowd of small boys who were waiting for this largesse.

Bill Briggs operated gambling houses in San Francisco for

thirty years, openly during liberal times and clandestinely during periods of reform. He banked his last game in 1880, eleven years before his death.

The Pacific Club on Commercial Street was operated by Steve Whipple who, for a change of pace, sometimes plied his trade on the steamboats that ran to Sacramento. A plunger—a reckless gambler—named Jim Rynders once won $89,000 in three grueling days of play at Whipple's faro table but a week later returned and dropped the $89,000 and an additional $11,000.

Rynders's gambling was spectacular, but Ed Moses indulged in the greatest faro bank plunge in the history of San Francisco, and perhaps of the United States. Moses, who owned interests in several San Francisco emporiums, was determined to break the faro bank at the El Dorado. At his request, Chambers and McCabe removed the limit on the table and the highroller went to work. He won at first, but his luck changed and he went deeper and deeper in the hole. After eight hours of play he was heavily in debt to the bank. He wrote a marker for $60,000 and played it on a single card. The card was a loser and Ed Moses rose from the table poorer by $200,000.

Forty years later he was still in San Francisco, old and bent, his hands swollen to enormous size by arthritis. In the early nineties he was a fixture in the lobby of the Palace Hotel, where he was pointed out to visitors as a relic of the great sporting days of the gold rush.

Jack Gamble had been one of the first of the big-time professionals to arrive in San Francisco and, with Bill Briggs, was one of the last to knuckle under to the pressures exerted by the later reformers. A state law making gambling and the keeping of a gambling house a felony was passed by the California legislature in 1854. Gamble led a lobby in Sacramento for repeal of the law and was successful in having it repealed in 1859. Another law, passed in 1873, finally defeated him and all open gambling in the city by the Golden Gate.

Of all the topflight sporting men in California during the early gold rush days, none was more successful or well known than Colonel J. J. Bryant, a verteran of twenty years of high-stakes play in the Mississippi River country. Charles Cora knew him well, having tried unsuccessfully for fifteen years to collect a debt of $35,000 from the self-styled colonel.

When Bryant arrived in San Francisco a few months before Cora, he opened a monte bank and within a few weeks had accumulated winnings of $75,000.[9] He sent a third of this amount back to his wife in Mississippi and with the remainder of his capital purchased the Ward House, a hotel he converted into a fine, well-equipped gambling house. As the majordomo of this establishment, renamed the Bryant House, he quickly became one of the most prosperous and influential men in the city.

When the first election for sheriff of San Francisco was scheduled in 1850, the local Democrats chose Bryant as their candidate. His opponents in the race were Colonel John E. Townes, a Whig who had held the sheriff's office by appointment for a year, and Jack Hays, a famous Indian-fighting former Texas Ranger who was running as an independent. During the campaign Bryant festooned his gambling resort with flags and bunting and dispensed free drinks to all who would listen to his oratory. On election day he led a grand parade of bankers around Portsmouth Square, marching to the music of a brass band riding atop a huge wagon. Crowds of miners lined the square and cheered Bryant, but they cast their ballots for Jack Hays, who appeared alone, decked out in his Mexican War uniform, sitting tall and straight astride a spirited jet-black stallion. Hays won the election handily, and Bryant, who had spent $50,000 on his campaign and had bet another $10,000 that he would win, found himself in financial difficulty. He sold the Bryant House to acquire working capital, and, embarrassed by his political failure in San Francisco, left the city to tour the mining towns of the mother lode.

His sojourns at Columbia, Nevada City, Marysville, and other goldfield camps proved lucrative, and later he returned to San Francisco to invest in a faro bank operation in the El Dorado. In 1854 he left California to return to his family in Mississippi. He confided to friends that during his five-year

California stay he had sent a total of $110,000 home to his wife, at the same time maintaining himself in the finest style available.

His subsequent gambling operations were confined primarily to New Orleans until the beginning of the Civil War, when he transferred his interests to Mobile, Alabama. He reappeared in New Orleans in 1866, having won more than a million dollars at Mobile. The winnings, unfortunately, were all in worthless Confederate currency, and Bryant was reduced to "roping suckers" for Allen Jones, an old crony of his who ran a gambling establishment across the street from the Saint Charles Hotel. In 1868, Bryant steered a visiting Texan to Jones's game and helped relieve the Texan of his cash. The Texan left markers for an additional one hundred dollars. Several days later Bryant approached the Texan in the lobby of the Saint Charles and attempted to collect on the markers. A heated argument ensued, during which Bryant made a quick move toward his pocket. The Texan, believing that the gambler was about to draw a gun, whipped out his own pistol and shot Bryant dead. Although it was later shown that Bryant had nothing in his pocket more deadly than a handkerchief, it was reckoned that he had used poor judgment and the killing was deemed justifiable.

Although Charles Cora had never seen so many quality gambling houses in operation in one city nor such an aggregation of first-rank professionals as he found in San Francisco, he was no stranger to high-stakes play with the best men in the business. For seventeen years he had been courting Dame Fortune on riverboats and in river towns of the antebellum South.

Born in Genoa, Italy, in 1816, he had been brought to the United States as an infant and raised by the madam of a bordello at Natchez-Under-The-Hill, at that time probably the wildest, most lawless town in America. Cora was gambling professionally at sixteen years of age and within two more years had sufficiently mastered the intricacies of the popular games to take on the most skillful dealers of Natchez for heavy stakes. He early acquired the reputation of a faro fanatic and, although he dealt the game very successfully, taking on all

Charles Cora, demon of the faro table, whose phenomenal luck suddenly deserted him in San Francisco in 1856. Courtesy The Bancroft Library, University of California.

comers, his great delight was attacking the tiger in another man's lair.[10] His luck was phenomenal and there were those who believed he possessed a sixth sense that enabled him to know whether a given card would win or lose. During one six-month period he was said to have taken $85,000 from faro banks at New Orleans, Vicksburg, and Natchez. It was generally believed that he had won $300,000 from his fellow professionals, raking in his winnings over their own oilcloth layouts.

Early in 1835, at the age of eighteen, he went to Vicksburg with a stake of $10,000 he had won at Natchez. Within a couple of months he had added $40,000 to his bankroll, most of it taken from faro banks backed by J. J. Bryant, the same man who was to make a flamboyantly unsuccessful bid for the office of sheriff of San Francisco years later.

Bryant was at this time the most famous gambling man on the lower Mississippi. Originally from Lynchburg, Virginia, he had run away from home at the age of eighteen to join a traveling circus where he became a sword swallower and slack wire performer. In his early twenties he married and settled in Jackson, Mississippi, where he ran a hotel and dealt in slaves,

but all his enterprises ended in failure. During these years he
was an inveterate gambler, spending much time at the tables.
Finally, he turned to gambling on a professional basis. He
worked the riverboats, where he was considered a wizard at
brag, poker, all fours, and old sledge, his favorite card games.
He backed faro games in the towns along the river and sometimes dealt the game, but he was never considered a topflight
faro expert. It was acknowledged all along the river, however,
that he had few equals at poker and other short-card games.
By 1832 he had bestowed the southern gentleman's title of
"Colonel" upon himself and had settled at Vicksburg, where
he became the successful owner of interests in a number of
different games.

When the young Charles Cora plundered Bryant's games in
1835, Bryant became perturbed about his losses and especially
about the audacity of the young upstart. He resolved to get his
money back from Cora and to do it in a way that would serve
as an object lesson to the Italian smart aleck. He began to
curry favor with the young man, buying him expensive meals,
plying him with cigars and drinks, and introducing him to
beautiful women. Cora was understandably flattered by the
attention lavished on him by one of the South's most famous
and successful sporting men, and when the Colonel offhand-
edly mentioned that he was a little short of money and could
use a loan, the young gambler quickly came up with $10,000.
Bryant had a confederate open a faro bank with the $10,000
and persuaded Cora to get into the game, hoping to break him
with his own money. To the contrary, the young man won the
$10,000 in a few deals. A day or two later Bryant borrowed
another $10,000 from Cora, and Cora won that also. A week
later $15,000 made the same triangular route: Cora to Bryant
to Bryant's dealer and back to Cora. The Colonel was now in
Cora's debt to the tune of $35,000, and still the brash young
high roller had not learned his lesson. In disgust, Bryant
washed his hands of the whole project, removing himself so
completely that he failed to pay back the borrowed money,
then or ever. The subject was a sore point between the two
gamblers fifteen years later when both were in the California
goldfields.

For ten years Vicksburg had been a mecca for the premier sporting men of the Mississippi River, but by mid-1835 the town had become so infested with cutthroats, footpads (high-waymen), cheap prostitutes, and tinhorn sharpers and their ilk that an irate citizenry felt the time had come for a general housecleaning. A meeting of the Vicksburg Volunteers, the local militia company, was held on July 4, 1835, resulting in a series of riots lasting several days. On July 6, five gamblers were lynched by the enraged mob. By this time Charles Cora, J. J. Bryant, and other intelligent gamblers who had early recognized the seriousness of the situation had departed.

Bryant went to Huntsville, Alabama, where he participated in a game with a poker player of local renown named Allen Jones and cleaned him of property and cash. Jones, fascinated by Bryant's skill, begged his conqueror to instruct him in the higher techniques of the game. Jones was an apt pupil, and the two men became partners. The team of Bryant and Jones was a terror to poker players from Saint Louis to New Orleans until 1849, when Bryant dissolved the partnership and left for California.

After leaving Vicksburg, Charles Cora was active in New Orleans and Mobile, where he was preceded by his fame as the youngster who had bested the great Colonel Bryant. Many faro dealers barred him from their games because of his uncanny skill, and he turned to the steamboats of the Mississippi for his action.

The golden age of riverboat gambling lasted from about 1835 until the beginning of the Civil War. For a quarter of a century some six to eight hundred professionals worked the paddleboats that plied the Big Muddy from Saint Louis to New Orleans. The riverboat gamblers established their own style of dress during those years and were acknowledged to be, as a class, the best-dressed men in the country.

Black was always the dominant color in the gambler's attire: black broadcloth suit, soft black hat, black high-heeled boots of high quality leather, and flowing black tie. In vivid contrast to this somber basic background were the flamboyant accessories that distinguished the gambler. A snowy white shirt adorned with overlapping layers of ruffles covered the chest

Towns and Cities where the frontier gamblers flourished, 1850–1910.

and disappeared in an embarrassment of inadequacy beneath a garish flowered vest. The prosperous professional wore the symbols of his affluence like the medals of an Austrian duke. The gaudy vest was studded with buttons of gold, pearl, or diamond. Rings with precious stones sparkled on his fingers, and one very large stone, called the "headlight," gleamed in a stickpin on his chest. A huge gold pocket watch, usually festooned with gems, was worn in a pocket of the vest, and trailing from it was a long golden chain that looped behind the gambler's neck and hung in glittering drapes across the brocaded vest.

Jimmy Fitzgerald was considered the most resplendent of the riverboat gamblers. His boots were custom-made in Paris, and when he boarded a sidewheeler he was followed by three slaves lugging a wardrobe that included four overcoats and two dozen expensive suits. The watch chain hanging in golden cascades at his chest was said to be almost a rod long and as big around as his little finger. Fitzgerald took great pains never to fall overboard; with such a golden anchor at his neck he would have disappeared like a stone into the Mississippi mud. He made a fortune at poker and faro on the river during the 1840s but lost most of it in the gambling houses ashore.

Vying with Fitzgerald as the epitome of sartorial elegance was Colonel Charles Starr, a tall, handsome man famous among the fraternity as the biggest liar on the river. Although he was an inveterate braggart, Starr was popular because of his distinguished appearance and marvelous wit. Like his rival, Fitzgerald, Starr lost in the gambling halls of New Orleans and Saint Louis the fortune he had made on the river. By 1860 he was ill, penniless, and bereft of friends. He went to a New Orleans restaurant that had catered to his every whim during the great years of his prosperity and ordered dinner. The manager demanded payment in advance. Starr departed, pawned his overcoat for five dollars, and returned. Ostentatiously producing the five, he ordered the finest meal the money would buy, and then when it was served, deliberately turned over every dish on the tablecloth and stalked out. The next morning he was found dead in his bed.

Other famous riverboat dandies included Jim McLane, the scion of a wealthy family, whose mother sent him $10,000 a year to stay away from home, and his partners, Gib Cohern, Dock Hill, and Tom Mackey; Star Davis, for whom a famous racehorse was named and who became a heavy drinker and finally broke his neck in a fall down a flight of stairs in a Saint Louis hotel; and Major George M. White.

White was twenty years old when he played his first game of faro in New Orleans in 1825, and for sixty-two years he made his living with cards. So great was his fame as a master of faro that New Orleans houses paid him $400 a week to deal the game. Like Charles Cora and J. J. Bryant, he answered the call to the California goldfields where he dealt his last game in 1887. He died in 1900 at the age of 95.

Another gambler, one Napoleon Bonapart ("Poley") White, turned to professional gambling after serving a brief apprenticeship on the Mississippi River as a steamboat engineer. Poley White ran a gambling house in New Orleans after the Civil War and was highly respected, but his two sons brought disgrace to his name. One son died of alcoholism while awaiting trial for a shooting, and the other became a fugitive, disappearing after murdering two men. In 1889, Poley White called on each of his friends, bade them goodbye, went home with a pistol and an ounce of sulphate of morphine, and killed himself.

Perhaps the most dashing and romantic of the riverboat gamblers was John Powell, a tall, handsome, well-educated Missourian whose personal charm made him an intimate of the most affluent and influential men of the South. He was a welcome visitor in the finest homes along the river. A close friend of Andrew Jackson and Stephen A. Douglas, Powell was offered a nomination for a seat in Congress but refused.

John Powell was conceded by his peers to be one of the cleverest poker players in the South. After taking to the river in 1845, he enjoyed great success for some thirteen years. In the year 1858 he participated in a memorable poker game aboard the steamer *Atlantic*, involving two other professionals and a wealthy planter named Devereaux. When the game broke up after three days and nights of continuous play, the four players owed a bar bill of $791.50, Devereaux was $100,000 poorer, and Powell had pocketed something in excess of $50,000. Shortly after this extraordinary game, Powell relieved a young English traveler of his $8,000 bankroll and all of his luggage. The distraught Englishman went to his stateroom and shot himself in the head. Learning of the suicide, Powell was shattered with guilt. Sending the money and baggage to the young man's family in England, he retired from gambling for a year. He was fifty years old at this time and financially well off. He owned a theater and other real estate in New Orleans, a farm worth $100,000 in Tennessee, and a number of properties in Saint Louis. Still he could not resist the lure of the riverboat gambling tables. He returned to the old life, but some part of his former skill and boldness was gone. Within a year he had lost his entire fortune. He went to Seattle during the Civil War and died there, a pauper, in 1870.

In 1846, Charles Cora, thirty years old and a veteran of fourteen years' play on the river, met Arabella Ryan, the young daughter of a Baltimore clergyman, whose life was to be entwined with Cora's for the remainder of his days. Arabella, or Belle as she was more commonly called, had been seduced at the age of seventeen by a young man who, upon learning that she was pregnant, skipped town, leaving Belle to the mercy of her minister father. That Christian gentleman promptly threw her into the street, where she wandered, penniless and friendless. Her baby died at birth, and Belle turned to the only livelihood available to a girl in her situation in mid-nineteenth-century America—she became a prostitute.

Cora found her working in a fancy New Orleans parlor house and immediately fell victim to her charms. By all accounts she was a beautiful woman, with dark hair, hazel eyes, a flawless complexion, and a gorgeous figure. "She was," said San Francisco Police Detective Ben Bohen to a newsman years later, "a voluptuous creature." There is a story that another New Orleans gambler also coveted the beautiful Belle, and that he and Cora flipped a coin to see who would have the honor of taking her out of the parlor house. Cora, with his usual luck, won the toss.[11]

In the fall of 1849, Cora and the woman who was now known as "Belle Cora," although no matrimonial vows had ever been exchanged, embarked from New Orleans on the steamship *Falcon*, bound for Colón, Panama. They made the difficult Isthmus crossing and sailed for San Francisco on December 5 aboard the *California*. The rigors of the Panamanian journey and the cramped conditions aboard ship apparently had an ill effect upon Cora, who had become accustomed to the finest traveling accommodations available during his years on the Mississippi. A young passenger aboard the *California* named Edward Williams recorded in his journal that Charles Cora and two other gamblers became obstreperous during the voyage and intimidated the other passengers. The ship's captain finally had to put the three gamblers in irons until they gave their word that there would be no more trouble. Noted Williams in his journal: "It was reported that they had with them 40 thousand dollars and intended to start a gambling bank at San Francisco."[12]

Charles Cora and Belle remained in San Francisco for the first few months of the year 1850 and then moved on to Sacramento, where there was said to be plenty of lively action. Later that year at Marysville, Cora ran the New World gambling house in partnership with J. Y. McDuffie. Although faro was still his favorite game, Cora could win at other games and he had lost none of his zeal for high-stakes play. A forty-niner named Edward McIlhany remembered seeing him win a $10,000 bet at poker in a game at the New World gambling house.

Always restless, Cora soon disposed of his interest in the New World and left to tour the mining camps of the mother lode. Some of the towns that sprang into existence around the mining sites offered fertile ground for the professional sporting men. One of the first buildings erected was invariably a saloon, and every saloon had its gambling tables. As the towns grew, the gambling houses gained in number and opulence in direct proportion to the prosperity of the surrounding mining district. Where gold was plentiful the gambling men spared no expense to outfit their houses in the grandest style possible, and the ornate interiors of these establishments bedazzled the miners, who generally were living in tents and squalid shacks.

After spending the day in Nevada City, an argonaut wrote in his journal on February 8, 1852:

Nevada . . . is getting to be quite a big town. . . . Saturday night and Sundays . . . are the lively days. Then there are two or three thousand miners in town, the majority drinking, gambling and carousing. . . . If you see anybody dressed up it's a sure thing he is either a gambler or a lawyer. What beats me is the craze the miners have for gambling. Every saloon has some sort of game running, and the big ones have a dozen. "Monte," "Red and Black," "Chuck-a-luck," "Twenty-one," "Rondo," and "Fortune Wheels" are the banking games, and they play Poker and "Brag" for big stakes. The fool miners work hard all the week and then lose their dust at these games of chance. . . . I suppose they are looking for excitement—anything to break the monotony—and this is the way they get it.[13]

Of all the towns of the mother lode, the largest and liveliest was Columbia, called "the gem of the southern mines." During the mid-1850s, promoters at Columbia attempted to have the state capital moved from Sacramento to Columbia, boasting that their town contained thirty saloons, a stadium for bull and bear fights, a brewery, and 143 faro banks with a combined capital of almost $2 million.

The largest gambling house in Columbia was a place called the Long Tom, a low building extending from one street to another with a doorway at either end. Flanking the wide aisle between the doors were twenty-four gambling tables, twelve to each side. Three huge, whale-oil lamps with bucket-sized bowls and wicks two inches thick were suspended from a beam over the aisle and brilliantly lighted the room. Proper decorum was maintained by guards stationed at each doorway and by two floormen who patrolled the aisle. These housemen all wore pistols prominently displayed and were called upon to settle disputes that arose at the tables. Their decisions were final with no appeal.

"The gamblers, you know, they wouldn't tolerate cheating from nobody," testified one Columbia old-timer:

The minute they discovered that a man was cheating, the game was going to end right there. If the dispute got hot, and it began to look like trouble, the floormen would pull out their guns and "Bang" would go this light, and "bang" would go that light, and "bang" would go the other light, and the whole place would be dark. At the same time the doormen would lock the doors. Then the floormen would take dark lanterns that would just throw a beam like a flashlight—they would take one of these lanterns in one hand[,] a gun in the other and would go to the table where the dispute was and find out what the trouble was about. . . . The fellow that was caught cheating always had to pay back before they'd let him go. Then the floormen would rig up new lights and the games would go on as usual.[14]

Some high-stake games were played in the Long Tom during Columbia's boom period, and many times there was as much as $100,000 on the tables at once. Chips were not used and the cash was almost always in the form of gold, either dust or coin—eagles, double eagles, and $50 slugs.

The Long Tom was owned by the three Mitchell brothers, who did not directly enter into the play. They rented out the tables to professional gamblers like Charles Cora and sold drinks and cards. So many new decks were sold to cold streak players trying to change their luck that when the place was swept out each morning, the discarded pasteboards were often ankle-deep in the center aisle. Young boys would be waiting at dawn outside the doors to sift through the sweepings. Often they would find silver coins and $2½ and $5 gold pieces that players had dropped and hadn't bothered to pick up.

A professional named Lou Alverson presided over a table in the Long Tom for several years and was considered to be the top gambler in the house. Others of note were Ad Pence, Doc Johns, Jack White, Charlie Karp, and Governor Hobbs.

Another dealer in the establishment, a man named John Milton Strain, had a touch of prospecting fever in his blood. He would work his table all night, sleep in the morning, and then roam the surrounding hills in the afternoon with a burro, a pan, and a pick and shovel. One day he found a nugget roughly the size and shape of an adobe brick. About twelve inches long, ten inches wide, and five inches thick, it contained a little quartz but was almost all high-grade ore. Strain took some specimens from the nugget and melted the rest

down into a bar weighing 33½ pounds that brought him
$7,438.50 at Sleeper's Gold Exchange.

In partnership with a faro dealer named Bailey, he left Columbia and for several years in the late 1850s toured the California and Nevada camps. About 1860 he returned to Columbia, penniless and disenchanted with the gambling life. He
moved into a cabin near the site of his fabulous find and spent
years in a futile search for the vein that had yielded his golden
nugget. One day another prospector entered the cabin and
found him dead. Said the old-timer who recounted Strain's
tale: "How the coroner wrote down his death I don't know, but
I saw the body and have no doubts. John Milton Strain died of
starvation."[15]

By 1857, Columbia was the third largest city in California.
On August 24 of that year a fire broke out in the north part of
town. The fire destroyed the entire section and then spread
south, destroying twelve square blocks in the business district.
It took two days to extinguish the flames in the south end of
town, and by that time most of the north end was back in
business. The Long Tom had been one of the first buildings to
go, burning completely to the ground, but by four o'clock the
next afternoon, while the conflagration still raged to the south,
the Mitchell brothers had a new building up and were open for
business as usual.

Ten years later another fire destroyed the Long Tom, but by
1867 the Mitchell brothers knew that Columbia was a dying
town and did not rebuild the place. Former dealer Jack White
mined the site of the gambling house and today in Columbia,
now a ghost town, only a hole in the ground remains to mark
the memory of the famous Long Tom.

While Charles Cora was working the mining camps, Belle,
using the name Arabella Ryan and the know-how acquired
during her New Orleans brothel days, had opened a sporting
house in Sonora. Late in 1852 she moved to San Francisco
where she established a first-class bordello on Dupont Street.
Cora, who was now said to be worth some $400,000, joined
her there soon afterward. In the spring of 1855, Belle moved
to newer and finer quarters, a brick two-story edifice on Pike

Street (later Waverly Place), which offered the most beautiful and accomplished females of any of the city's more than one hundred bagnios. The Coras were regarded as the elite of the sporting gentry and were well acquainted with many of the political and professional leaders of the city.

Charles and Belle were thus at the pinnacle of their respective professions on the evening of November 15, 1855, when they attended the American Theater to see a new play performed by the Ravel family troupe called "Nicodemus; or The Unfortunate Fisherman." As was their custom, the Coras took their seats in the first balcony, the most expensive section. During an intermission, men in the seats below turned and, looking up into the balcony, recognized the madam of their favorite parlor house. They laughed, waved, and gestured in a manner some observers might have considered obscene. It happened that immediately in front of the Coras sat United States Marshal William H. Richardson and his wife. Mrs. Richardson found the laughter and joking remarks offensive and asked her husband to put a stop to the vulgar display. Descending to the pits, Richardson learned the true source of the rowdies' interest. He then demanded that the Coras leave. The gambler and his mistress refused and the two couples exchanged angry words. Richardson then sought the theater manager, insisting that the Coras be ushered out. The manager also refused to comply with the demand, and the marshal and his wife stalked from the theater.

The following evening, Cora and Richardson happened to be in the Cosmopolitan Saloon. A Doctor Mills, who was acquainted with both men and knew of the unpleasantness at the theater the previous night, attempted to patch up the difference. He brought the two together and they discoursed and drank for a time with no animosity evident. Outside the saloon later, however, the two men argued again and insults were hurled. Cora reentered the Cosmopolitan and told Mills that Richardson had threatened to slap his face, but that he, Cora, had broken off the confrontation because he did not want to draw on a drunken man.

At 6:30 on the evening of November 18, Charles Cora was in the Blue Wing Saloon on Montgomery Street when he was informed that someone wanted to see him outside. He found Marshal Richardson waiting for him. The two talked quietly for a time and then walked together down the street. Suddenly Cora grabbed Richardson with his left hand and pulled a derringer with his right. Firing it at point-blank range, he shot the marshal through the heart, killing him instantly.

Within minutes a large crowd gathered at the scene. Cora was seized and there were cries of "Hang him! Hang him!" from the more bloodthirsty of the mob. A voice vote was called for; the "noes" outshouted the "ayes" by a narrow margin, and the prisoner was turned over to the police.

Charles Cora had chosen a particularly unfortunate time to gun down a prominent personality. San Francisco was in the throes of a crime wave of epidemic proportions and there was building a wave of reaction more than a little tinged with hysteria. Shortly after Cora was locked up, Morman church elder and city pioneer Sam Brennan exhorted a crowd outside the Oriental Hotel to take the gambler from the authorities by force and hang him at once. Brennan was arrested, charged with inciting to riot, and the mob dispersed with much grumbling.

The newspapers reporting the killing added fuel to the fires of popular anger.[16] "Gen. William H. Richardson was assassinated in the streets of this city last evening, under circumstances particularly atrocious," fulminated the *Alta California*. "Murders have been committed for robbery or from motives of revenge but this one appears to have no inciting cause but an unnatural thirst for blood. . . ."

The *San Francisco Herald* was no more objective:

The truth is that, from all accounts, we have come to the conclusion that the killing of General Richardson was a most atrocious murder. He was assassinated in cold blood, without a single effort at resistance. Those who have known him as we have, must be assured he would have sold his life dearly if he had the slightest chance. The deceased gentleman was of a most kind, generous and noble nature. That such a man should fall by such a hand is to be everlastingly deplored.

When the rumor spread that the jailer, Billy Mulligan, was

a close friend of Cora and would undoubtedly release him, James King, publisher of the *Bulletin*, screamed from the pages of his paper: "Hang Billy Mulligan! That's the word! If Sheriff Scannell does not remove Billy Mulligan from his present post as keeper of the county jail, and Mulligan lets Cora escape, hang Billy Mulligan, and if necessary to get rid of the sheriff, hang him—hang the sheriff!"

Fifty armed deputies guarded the jail while the mob awaited the outcome of the legal proceedings. On the morning after the shooting, a coroner's jury heard sixteen witnesses and viewed the physical evidence, three derringer pistols. Two of these, one fired, the other loaded, were identified as belonging to Cora and on his person at the time of his arrest. The third weapon, loaded but uncocked, had been picked up near Richardson's body. The coroner's jury found that the shooting had been "premeditated, and that there was nothing to mitigate the same."[17]

Charles Cora was bound over to the grand jury, which was to meet in a few days. Asked if he wished to appear with counsel at the grand jury proceedings, the gambler stared icily at his questioner. "I don't wish to appear at all," he answered. On November 24 an indictment charging Cora with premeditated murder was brought in by the grand jury.

Belle Cora engaged a battery of prominent attorneys to represent her lover, headed by Colonel E. D. Baker, a nationally renowned courtroom strategist and orator who would later become a United States senator from Oregon. Baker demanded $30,000 as his fee to defend the gambler. Belle gave him $15,000 in cash and promised to deliver the balance in a few days. The same night Baker sat down at a faro table and lost the entire retainer. Working now with only half his stated fee, and acutely aware of a storm of public indignation building against Cora and his defenders, Baker tried to withdraw from the case, but Belle would have none of that. She was adamant in her insistence that he continue, and Baker reluctantly agreed.

Cora's trial opened on January 3, 1856, and lasted until January 15. The prosecution produced witnesses who claimed to have seen the shooting and who testified they saw Cora grasp Richardson suddenly around the body with his left arm, pinning the marshal's arms down, as he, Cora, drew his derringer with his right hand. Richardson, according to several of these witnesses, cried out, "Don't shoot! I am unarmed!" just before Cora fired the fatal shot. Cora's attorneys attempted to show a clear case of self-defense by producing witnesses who swore that the gambler seized Richardson by the collar, whereupon the marshal reached in his pocket for his pistol, and Cora simply outdrew him.

After forty-one hours of deliberation, the jury reported that it was hopelessly deadlocked. The prisoner was returned to jail to await a second trial that few believed would ever be held.

James King's *Bulletin* was laden with vitriol:

Rejoice, Ye gamblers and harlots! rejoice with exceeding gladness! Men were placed upon that jury who should never have been there. They went upon it to defeat the ends of justice, in other words, to "tie" the jury. This they effectually did. It is not pleasant for us to comment upon the depravity which has been brought to light in the trial. It is not very agreeable to state that the conviction is almost universal, that crime cannot be punished in San Francisco. . . .[18]

In the ensuing weeks King continued his diatribes against Cora in the pages of his paper. King, in turn, was attacked by James P. Casey, a political enemy, who was on the city's board of supervisors and who also edited a weekly political sheet. King and Casey fired salvo after salvo of vituperous broadsides at each other in the pages of their respective publications. Cora, who still languished in jail, was scarcely mentioned as the editorial attacks became increasingly personal in nature. Finally, on May 14, 1856, King asserted in his paper that Casey deserved "to have his neck stretched" for obtaining his post as supervisor by fraudulent means. As King was leaving his office that afternoon, he was met by Casey who shouted: "Draw and defend yourself!", at the same time leveling and firing a Navy Colt revolver.

King stumbled and fell, seriously wounded. Casey gave himself up to the police. Again San Francisco was in turmoil as word of the shooting spread like one of the city's famous

James P. Casey, who used the Cora case to attack an enemy. The quarrel led to murder and cost him his life. Courtesy The Bancroft Library, University of California.

fires. Crowds of glowering men formed on every street corner. When Casey was taken to the county jail and placed in a cell adjacent to Cora's, the gambler regarded him sadly for several moments and then said quietly, "You have put the noose about the necks of both of us."

Five years before these events, the famous San Francisco Vigilante Committee, usurping all legal authority in the city, had arrested, tried, convicted, and executed several felons, and had sent hundreds of others scurrying to the hinterlands. Since 1851 the committee had not met, although violent street crime had been increasing again at an alarming rate. A New York newspaper reported in January, 1856, that during the previous year a total of 489 murders had been committed in California, of which about two-thirds had been perpetrated in San Francisco. Not one murderer had been punished in San Francisco, declared this paper, while in the outlying districts six had suffered official execution and forty-six had been lynched by mobs.

On the morning of May 15, the day after Casey's attack on King, a notice appeared in the city's papers calling all members of the committee together for a meeting. William T. Coleman, who had headed the 1851 clean up, was again chosen to lead the 1856 committee. By the end of the day two thousand men had offered their services to the vigilantes. Two troops of militia had been assigned by the governor the previous night to guard the jail against mob action. The next day the militiamen left their posts and marched en masse to join the committee. All weapons in the state armory were seized, including two cannon.

For three days the committee organized its forces and awaited word from some twenty doctors attending James King as to the condition of the wounded man. On the night of Saturday, May 17, a rumor spread that friends of Casey and Cora were planning a rescue attempt the next day. At the same time the doctors reported that King's life was slipping away and they could offer no hope for his recovery. The next morning William T. Coleman led an army of 2,600 armed men to the jail. Deploying his forces on all sides and training his cannon on the gates, Coleman demanded custody of Cora and Casey. Sheriff Scannell, with less than forty deputies to defend the jail, promptly surrendered. The prisoners were taken in chains to committee headquarters, a commandeered warehouse on Sacramento Street, and held in cells guarded by three hundred vigilantes.

On Tuesday, May 20, Charles Cora was put on trial before the vigilante committee. The presiding judge was William T. Coleman. John P. Manrow, who had acted as judge during the vigilante trials of 1851, served as prosecutor. Two members of the committee were assigned as defense counsel. Cora was advised that a simple majority of signed ballots cast by the jury, composed of members of the executive committee, would be sufficient to convict or acquit.

The trial began shortly before noon. At 1:30 P.M. the proceedings were interrupted by the announcement that James King had died. If there had been any hope for the gambler before, the emotion that surged through the crowd upon receiving that news sealed his fate. By four o'clock the trial was concluded and a guilty verdict rendered. Casey was tried that evening with the same result. Sentence in both cases was death by hanging.

When Charles Cora reached the end of his rope. Courtesy The Bancroft Library, University of California.

On May 22, as James King's funeral procession moved through the streets, preparations were made for the executions. Two planks were extended from second-story windows of the vigilante headquarters and held by ropes running to the roof. Directly above the planks heavy beams were affixed to the roof. At the end of each beam dangled a noose.

Belle Cora was permitted to see Charles in his cell that morning. Shortly before noon the gambler and his mistress were joined in holy matrimony by a Catholic priest. The couple had one hour together as man and wife. At one o'clock the sobbing woman was torn from her husband. He was blindfolded, tied hand and foot, heaved onto a platform, and a noose tightened around his neck. Casey was treated similarly, but he demanded an opportunity to make a statement. For seven minutes he harangued the crowd in the street below, protesting his innocence and damning those who were taking his life. Throughout this ordeal Cora stood quietly, awaiting death. Finally, Casey ceased his tirade, his eyes were covered, the noose was adjusted, and, at a signal, the ropes supporting both platforms were released. Simultaneously, the bodies of Charles Cora and James P. Casey plunged six feet and their souls continued on to whatever reward awaited them.

There is a persistent legend that Belle Cora mourned alone in her room for a month after the death of her husband, that she then sold her parlor house and devoted the rest of her life to good works, dying in poverty in 1862. In truth, Belle's "good works" were confined to a six-year campaign of vengeance against the leaders of the Vigilante Committee of 1856, a remarkably successful vendetta, and during this time she maintained operation of her bordello on Pike Street. She died of pneumonia in February, 1862, and today her remains and those of the gambler Charles Cora lie together beneath a common headstone in San Francisco's Mission Dolores Cemetery.

2

There was a time in this country when men could be found who would bet their eyeballs out and yours too, on what they believed to be an even thing, but that was before barbering came into vogue. Now our big operators want a flash at your hole card before loosening up.

W. B. "Bat" Masterson
New York Morning Telegraph (September 14, 1921)

Charles Cora is today the best remembered of the California gold rush gamblers because of his dramatic death, but of the hundreds of sporting men who worked the gambling dens of San Francisco and the mining towns, many acquired fame later in other locales.

J. Ferdinand Patterson and Sumner Pinkham, veterans of a dozen California camps, were the best-known gambling men in Idaho ten years later when they became involved in a bitter feud that culminated in a celebrated gunfight.

John J. Cozad, like Cora a wizard at breaking faro banks, was so feared in gambling houses throughout the West that many places barred him. In 1872 he founded a town in Nebraska that still bears his name.

A gold rush gambler named Henry Plummer, after the California excitement, became Montana's most notorious outlaw chieftain.

Eleanore Dumont dealt her first game of *vingt et un*[1] in San Francisco in 1850 and for thirty years, as "Madame Mustache," was the best-known female gambler on the frontier.

A famous mother lode thimblerigger, "Lucky Bill" Thornton, ended his career dancing at the end of a vigilante rope in Nevada.

The gold rush gambling graduate with the most spectacular later career was probably John Morrissey. In 1851, when Morrissey arrived in San Francisco, he was a nineteen-year-old New York tough with a barrel chest, brawny shoulders, hands the size of hams, and thirteen dollars in his pocket. Opening a brace faro game with a stranded artist as a partner, he prospered quickly. One of his victims, a man named Jim Hughes, upon finding that he had been fleeced, challenged Morrissey to a duel and gave the New Yorker his choice of weapons. Hughes blanched and fled the field of honor when Morrissey appeared at the appointed place carrying two meat cleavers. In 1852, Morrissey fought his first professional bare-knuckle prizefight, winning over George Thompson, billed as "Pete Crawley's Big 'Un," in nineteen minutes in a bout held on Mare Island. His effort won for him a purse of $4,000 and a side bet of $1,000. After making his stake in California, this brawling, rough-and-tumble ruffian, who could not write his own name until he was grown up, returned to New York where he became the recognized heavyweight champion of America, a member of the New York Senate and later a United States congressman. He was one of the Tammany Hall bosses, the gambling czar of New York, a close associate of Cornelius Vanderbilt, and a millionaire many times over.

The hanging of Cora and Casey by the Second Vigilante Committee in 1856 precipitated an exodus of gamblers from San Francisco. It has been estimated that five hundred to eight hundred gambling men felt they were no longer welcome in the city by the Golden Gate and departed for friendlier climes. One of them was a man named Charley Harrison, a gambler who was destined to play a leading role in the early history of another great western city.

Little is known of Harrison's early life. Although his soft drawl and outspoken secessionist beliefs suggested southern state origins, he appears to have begun gambling profession- ally in New York City in the 1840s. Some people believed he was the son of a man named Jack Harrison who ran a famous gambling house in Park Place during this period. Charley dealt faro in New York for several years and went to the West Coast about 1854. After leaving California in 1856, he drifted through a number of mining towns in Montana and Idaho and in the summer of 1859 was in Salt Lake City.

A fellow gambler named Tom Hunt had gotten himself in trouble with the Mormons of Salt Lake City and was about to be the star attraction at a lynching party when Harrison went

into action. Astride a stolen racehorse named Border Ruffian
and with Hunt's mount trailing behind, Harrison rode to the
scene of the lynching. Holding the Mormons at bay with leveled pistols, he snatched Hunt from under the hangman's
noose. The two gamblers fled east with the mob at their heels,
but Harrison, on the swift Border Ruffian, and Hunt, on his
sorrel stallion, soon outdistanced their pursuers. Later they
were attacked by an outlaw gang, and in a running fight in the
mountains Hunt's big sorrel was hit. Harrison doubled back,
Hunt swung up behind his friend, and, double-mounted on the
powerful Border Ruffian, they managed their escape.

After a long, hard mountain journey, they finally arrived at
their destination, a new boomtown called Denver City that had
sprung up at the confluence of the South Platte River and
Cherry Creek. Here squatted several hundred rude buildings,
thrown together by gold seekers caught up in the "Pike's Peak
or Bust" excitement of 1858. Although there was little gold to
be found in the nearby mountains, and ready cash never was
available in huge amounts as it had been in San Francisco a
decade before, the gamblers were on hand in force. Writing
from Denver City in January, 1859, one early arrival noted:
"In the last two months this has grown to be an almighty fast
country, owing to the number of fast men that have emigrated
here."[2] Wrote another in March:

We have six good trading houses, two blacksmith forges in full blast,
and grog shops without number. The gamblers are very numerous,
and [have] got most of the gold in their possession. They have come
from Salt Lake, New Mexico and the various forts through the country until the place is full of them. They brought money and horses
with them, and many of them are quite rich for men in this country. . . .[3]

A month later another Denver pioneer wrote to his home in
Kansas City: "There is more drinking and gambling here in
one day than in Kansas City in six—in fact about one-half of
the population do nothing else but drink whiskey and play
cards."[4]

By San Francisco standards, the saloon and gambling facilities of Denver in 1859 were crude indeed. The best accom-

modations were at the Denver House, the town's first hotel. A long, low building constructed of logs, this edifice had neither ceiling nor floor. A huge canvas stretched from wall to wall kept out most of the rain and snow, and the bare earth, sprinkled occasionally to hold down the dust, served as a floor. Holes in the log walls, covered by pieces of canvas, were the only windows. Canvas partitions separated the "rooms," where men slept on the ground for fifty cents a night, or on straw pallets for a quarter more. The saloon, at one end of the building, was dominated by the bar, which was simply the sideboard of a wagon mounted on boxes. Rough tables and chairs for the convenience of the gamblers were the only furniture, and meager light was provided by a few flickering candles and lamps.

Horace Greeley, famous editor of the *New York Tribune*, and A. D. Richardson, one of Greeley's journalists, stayed at the Denver House in the summer of 1859, and Richardson described the experience in his book, *Beyond the Mississippi*, published in 1869. One of the favorite amusements of the rough characters who frequented the saloon, said Richardson, was taking potshots at the bartender. "At first he bore it laughingly, but one day a shot grazed his ear, whereupon, remarking that there was such a thing as carrying a joke too far and that *this* was 'about played out,' he buckled on two revolvers and swore he would kill the next man who took aim at him. He was not troubled afterward." Greeley stood in the center of this saloon and delivered a speech denouncing the prevalent vice. Said Richardson: "On one side the tipplers at the bar silently sipped their grog; on the other the gamblers respectfully suspended the shuffling of cards and the counting of money from their huge piles of coin, while Mr. Greeley, standing between them, made a strong anti-drinking and anti-gambling address, which was received with perfect good humor."

Of the motley assortment of frontier personages who made up Denver society, "Americans from every quarter of the Union, Mexicans, Indians, half-breeds, trappers, speculators, gamblers, desperadoes, broken-down politicians and honest men," Richardson was most impressed by the gamblers.

As a class the gamblers were entertaining in conversation, had curious experiences to relate, evinced great knowledge of human nature,
and were specially kind to each other in misfortune. Some were
gentlemanly in manners. Like all men who gain money easily, they
were open-handed and charitable. I never saw a place where more
dollars could be obtained in less time for a helpless woman or orphan
than among those gaming tables.

From the day that he rode into Denver and opened a monte
game in the Denver House, Charley Harrison was the undisputed leader of the gambling element. He was a clever and
fearless gambler, as most of those who tried his game learned
to their sorrow, but there was something in the manner of the
man that commanded respect. He was a born leader. A com-
pactly built, balding man with a silky, carefully trimmed
beard, Harrison was about forty years of age in 1859. Always
fastidious of appearance, he usually dressed in black. At his
hips were a pair of pearl-handled 41-caliber Colt revolvers. Well-groomed and quiet, almost courtly of manner and
speech, Harrison stood in marked contrast to the roughs who
comprised most of the town's population. Gene Teats, a
youngster whose father purchased the Denver House about the
time of Harrison's arrival, worshiped the gambler as a hero.
"He would give his last dollar to a friend," Teats said. "Often
I would find myself short of funds, and only a hint was sufficient. He would generally ask how little I could get along
with. If I said a couple of dollars, it was likely to be twenty."[5]
In addition to his outstanding generosity, gambling ability,
and leadership qualities, Charley Harrison was renowned for
his skill with the fancy cap-and-ball pistols he always wore
and which he called his "pets." Gene Teats in his time had the
opportunity to see a number of celebrated gunfighters in action, but he always claimed that Harrison was the best of the
lot. Teats spent many hours on the banks of the Platte with
Harrison, who kept his hand and eye sharp by constant practice. They boy would toss a can into the air and watch the
gambler draw and put two or three bullets through the can
"with either hand or with the two guns at once."
Legend has it that the handle of one of Harrison's pistols

was notched eleven times on one side for the men he had killed
and three times on the other for the women who had fallen
before his smoking gun. He is supposed to have said that,
counting the three women as equal to one man, he would have
a full jury to try him in hell. Another version of this fanciful
tale has him walking down the street in Leavenworth, Kansas,
ticking off on his fingers the eleven men he had killed. "By
God!" he cried, "I'll have a jury of my own to try me in Hell!"
and he drew and shot to death an old German shoemaker
working at an open window across the street.

These are, of course, examples of the apocryphal tales that
attached to the famous gunmen of the West. It is not known
how many fatal encounters Harrison had during his career, but
it is a safe bet that he never notched his guns or shot down
innocent shoemakers; it was not in the nature of the man, as
was well evidenced by the history of his two years in Denver
City.

Gene Teats said that during those two years Harrison shot
three men dead and hanged one. The first of these, he said,
took place one morning when

some fellow from the gold fields with an overload of booze pulled
his gun and began popping it off in the street. Leaning against the
porch posts of the Elephant Corral was the colored cook of the Ford
brothers' gambling saloon. . . . One of the stray bullets found a vital
spot in his frame, and he was a cook in our town no longer. The
rowdy mounted his pony and started up the street with a number of
men shouting, "Stop him! Stop him!"

Just then Harrison came walking along, quite early for him, and
noticed the fellow. Realizing that he was the man wanted, Charley
pulled his old reliable, and although he was quite a distance away,
dropped the rowdy from the pony with one shot. . . .[6]

This incident may have happened, for the usually reliable
Teats claimed to have seen it, but, strangely, no mention of it
can be found in the pages of the *Rocky Mountain News*, which
began publication shortly before Harrison's arrival at Denver
City. The other two shootings and the hanging were well publicized, however, and Harrison's difficulties in Denver City
furnished much material for the pages of the *News*.

Harrison ran his monte game only a few months in the saloon of the Denver House, renamed the Elephant Corral by Gene Teats's father. He soon bought into the Criterion Saloon, a new establishment opened by Ed Jump in 1859. This two-story frame building on Larimer Street provided Denverites the best sleeping, dancing, dining, drinking, and gambling facilities in town. Harrison managed the saloon and gambling rooms in partnership with Jump, who took care of the restaurant and hotel accommodations. The Criterion quickly became the most popular club and meeting place in Denver.

There were, of course, many other gambling places. One of the earliest was Reid Hall, a place on Ferry Street constructed by James Reid, a former Missouri River steamboat pilot. James Gordon and several other gamblers later bought into this establishment, refurbished it, and renamed it Cibola Hall. Near the Cibola was the Louisiana Saloon, where Gordon, the blacksheep son of a respected rancher, went on a drunken, homicidal tear and coldbloodedly murdered a harmless and aged German immigrant. Gordon fled, and after an extensive manhunt was brought back by Sheriff William Middaugh to Denver, where he was tried and hanged.

Other early establishments included Ackey's Saloon; Apollo Hall, which boasted the finest theater in the area; Cannon's Saloon on Blake Street; Stag Hall; the Eldorado, owned by a wealthy black from Cincinnati named J. G. Sims; Alexander Bennett's Denver Hall; the Mountain Boys Saloon; the Iambian Saloon on Larimer Street; Poland Exchange; Dick Doyle's Club House Saloon; old frontiersman "Uncle Dick" Wootton's Western Saloon; and "The House That Jack Built," later renamed the Capitol Saloon, owned by Jack O'Neil.

The proprietor of the Capitol had been the first professional gambler to settle in Denver. There were not more than half a dozen buildings on the site when Jack O'Neil built a cabin for himself and his mistress, a Mormon girl known as Salt Lake Kate, and opened a card game in the town's first saloon, the Hote de Dunk. A handsome giant of a man, standing six-feet, four inches tall and weighing over two hundred pounds, former New Yorker O'Neil always dressed well, even in the raw

early days before the introduction of any of civilization's re-
finements. Courteous, even-tempered, and amiable, O'Neil
was well liked by the men and greatly admired by the women
of early Denver. He and Charley Harrison were close friends;
the two leading gamblers of the town may well have been
acquainted previously, both having operated in New York and,
more recently, in Salt Lake City.

Early in the spring of 1860, O'Neil had a run-in with John
Rooker, ne'er-do-well son of Samuel Rooker, another Denver
pioneer. The Rooker women, John's mother and sister, were
the first white women to settle in the new community, and
Samuel Rooker was a prominent property owner. John, however, had taken to running with the "Bummers," a scurvy
crowd of cheap gamblers and saloon loafers. At the season's
first horseraces, O'Neil interfered with Rooker and a group of
Bummers who were pestering an old miner. Harsh words were
exchanged between Rooker and O'Neil. Finally, the gambler
made a comment concerning the Rooker women that John
considered slanderous. He demanded an immediate apology
and O'Neil refused. Rooker insisted on an apology or satisfaction. O'Neil suggested that Rooker might attempt to find his
satisfaction by meeting him with bowie knives in a dark room.
At this, Rooker's anger cooled noticeably and O'Neil turned
his back, calling him a coward.

There was, therefore, bad blood between the two as they sat
together in a poker game several weeks later in Dick Wootton's Western Saloon. It was late on the night of March 29
when O'Neil and Rooker became embroiled in a five-card
draw hand with a sizable pot at stake. Both had raised several
times and driven the other players out of the hand. Finally
O'Neil called Rooker's last bet. "Two pairs of pictures," said
Rooker.

"Three jacks," said O'Neil, reaching for the pot.

"Hold it!" snapped Rooker, and then, grinning: "Both my
pairs are kings," and he spread the four kings dramatically on
the table. As he started to rake in the pot, O'Neil grabbed his
wrist. "You did not call your hand right. The money is mine,"
he said.

Rooker protested violently and the two men were soon on

their feet, leaning over the table, exchanging insults. Again O'Neil made a snide remark about the Rooker women. Rooker paled. It was well known that he feared the tall gambler, but now he must stand up to him or admit to being the coward O'Neil had branded him. "Arm yourself," Rooker said, his voice tight. "Either it's you or me, should we meet again."

Word of the imminent clash spread throughout the town and wagering on the outcome was heavy. John Rooker looked up his friend George Steele and borrowed his horse, a strong, fleet animal. He then stole back to the Western Saloon, which by this time was closed. Slipping into the rear of the building, he took up a position near the front door from which he had a clear view of O'Neil's cabin.

While Rooker was making his preparations, Jack O'Neil had simply walked to his home a block away and gone to bed. He arose about ten the next morning, an unusually warm day for March, and, in his shirt-sleeves, walked up Ferry Street toward the hardware store.

John Rooker followed him every step of the way, squinting through the sights of a double-barreled shotgun. When the big gambler was directly in front of the Western Saloon, Rooker shouted: "You son of a bitch, I got you now!"—at the same time pulling both triggers. Thirteen shot plowed into O'Neil's body and he pitched headlong into the street. Rooker raced out the back of the Western, leaped to the back of George Steele's horse, and galloped out of town.

Jack O'Neil was the most prominent person to die in Denver up to that time, and most of the town was in attendance the following day when he was buried in a tiny graveyard on a knoll southeast of town. The site came to be called "O'Neil's Ranch," and the term was later picked up and attached to cemeteries in other frontier communities. At one time, "O'Neil's Ranch" was a more frequently heard colloquialism for a border town graveyard than the better-remembered "Boot Hill." Those who "died with their boots on" were well represented in Denver's first cemetery, however. Of the first dozen recorded burials at O'Neil's Ranch, only a third of the deaths were attributed to natural causes. Two of the dead were executed for murder, five had been shot, and one was a suicide.

Charley Harrison and other friends of Jack O'Neil grumbled, but exactly nothing was done to bring O'Neil's killer to justice. No officer pursued him and the majority of townfolk seemed content to shrug the incident off as just another gambler's quarrel that did not concern them. William Byers, editor of *The Rocky Mountain News*, deplored this apathetic attitude, writing in the issue of April 4: "It is high time that the citizens of Denver should show enough interest in their own welfare to right public wrongs, and not leave it to every individual who feels himself aggrieved to take vengeance into his own hands, and deal out retribution according to his own will—even to the taking of human life."

A few months later Byers, the outspoken and courageous newspaperman, and Harrison, the town's leading gambler, were to become the major figures in a controversy that would bring Denver to the verge of anarchy.

On July 12, Charley Harrison stood at the bar of Cibola Hall having a drink with three prominent local figures, Postmaster Park McClure, Probate Judge Seymour Waggoner, and attorney J. Bright Smith. At a nearby poker table sat a Negro blacksmith known as "Professor" Charles Stark. A former slave, Stark was well liked in Denver. He had purchased his freedom and spent some time working the Mississippi riverboats before operating a barbershop in Omaha for several years. In Denver he had worked as a bullwhacker and a mule skinner when not practicing his blacksmith trade. He was a large man and his powerful body filled out well the expensive clothes that were his pride. This penchant for fancy raiment had earned him the nickname, "Professor."

In the poker game Stark was losing. Noticing Harrison at the bar, he called: "Hey, Charley, let's me and you have a game. I know you to be honest, but these here fellers are swindlers."

Harrison returned the black man's white-toothed smile with a look of disdain, his southern blood brought to a quick boil.

"Who the hell are you to address me as Charley and these gentlemen as swindlers?" he snorted.

For a moment the big black man was rendered speechless

William N. Byers, editor of the Rocky Mountain News, *who was rescued from the "Bummers" by Charley Harrison. Courtesy Denver Public Library, Western History Department.*

by the unexpected retort. Then he jerked to his feet and lumbered toward the gambler.

"I'll show you who I am, damn you!" he roared. As he advanced, he drew a bowie knife from his belt. Harrison backed away.

"Put it down!" he warned.

Instead, Stark lunged with the blade. Harrison's hand flashed to his hip and came up with a pistol. Three shots followed in quick succession. Stark went down with .41-caliber holes in his thigh, shoulder, and chest. He would fight for life for more than a week before the onset of mortification and eventual death on July 21.

"A damn fool and nothing more," was the way Gene Teats, who witnessed the shooting, sized up Professor Stark. Apparently those officers charged with maintaining order held the same view, for Charley Harrison was not even arrested after the Stark shooting.

William Byers had a contrasting opinion he expressed in his newspaper four days after Stark's demise:

From the facts that transpired since the shooting, we are led to think that the act was wanton and unprovoked, in short, a cold-blooded murder. . . .

The man who has shot down an unarmed man, and then repeats his shots, while his victim writhes at his feet, until the charges of his pistol are exhausted—even if justified in the first act, is unfit to live in . . . a civilized community.

After denouncing Harrison, Byers went on to castigate the "rowdies, ruffians, and bullies" who he said infested the town, and he issued a stern warning: "One more act of violence will at once precipitate the inevitable fate; and the terrors that swept over the fields of California at various times, and first purified its society, will be reenacted here with terrible results to outlaws and villains. . . ."[7]

As soon as the paper appeared, the Bummers, those black-leg tinhorns and carousers who had made the Criterion their unofficial headquaters, were in an uproar. They were for marching in a body to the offices of the *News* and burning the building to the ground, preferably with William Byers in it. They were held back, however, by a calm and unperturbed Charley Harrison, who was not one of them, but to whom they looked for leadership. Harrison advised restraint. He was soon to have a meeting with Byers, he announced.

When the paper was published, Seymour Waggoner, the

probate court judge, a representative to the First Territorial Constitutional Convention, and a friend of both Harrison and Byers, had recognized the seriousness of the situation and the very real possibility of an imminent bloodbath. He immediately talked to Harrison and got his promise to take no action until he, Waggoner, had arranged a meeting between the editor and the gambler. Harrison had agreed to wait two hours and to see that the Bummers made no attack on the *News* during that period.

Before the time was up Waggoner was back at the Criterion. Soon he, Harrison, and attorney J. Bright Smith were headed for the *News* building. Behind them trailed a delegation of Harrison adherents that included locally prominent citizens and saloon toughs.

In Byers's office, Waggoner spoke for Charley Harrison. He described the Stark shooting and the events leading up to it as he himself had seen them. He presented a number of other eyewitnesses who corroborated his version of the incident. Finally, he demanded that Byers publicly apologize to Harrison and issue a retraction. This Byers agreed to do, and that same night he had printed and circulated a handbill entitled "Justice." Under the judge's account of the circumstances of the shooting, Byers wrote:

From two conversations with Judge Waggoner, and one with Mr. Smith . . . both of whom were in the immediate vicinity at the time of the killing, we learn unmistakably that the first insult was given by Stark and that he was the first to draw arms and make an attack. We had before understood that Stark was unarmed, but such was not the case. He drew a heavy bowie knife and made two or three lunges at Harrison before the latter fired. Stark continued his attack until the knife was knocked from his hand by the pistol of Harrison. Mr. Harrison himself tells us that he was then, and is yet, anxious to have an investigation before the people's tribunal, and stands ready at any moment to vindicate his cause. We had hoped that such a trial would have been given, but the public seems so well satisfied of justification of Mr. Harrison that we presume nothing will be done. . . .

In justice to Mr. Harrison, we will say that the statement above, made by Judge Waggoner, presented quite another complexion to the unfortunate transaction on the 12th inst. We await the result of the investigation instituted today, hoping Mr. Harrison will be acquitted of all blame. . . .[8]

The investigation alluded to was a meeting of a newly formed Denver vigilance committee that held its first meeting on July 26 and unanimously voted to exonerate Harrison of any wrongdoing.

Editor Byers had issued his retraction and Charley Harrison had apparently been vindicated, but the Bummers in the Criterion were unmollified. For a week they nursed their grievances, taking on huge quantities of Criterion whiskey and grumbling over Byers's attack on their "old pal Charley." Finally, five of the worst malcontents—tinhorn gamblers Carl Woods and Jim Innis; John Rooker, who had slipped back in town after his murder of Jack O'Neil; Bill ("Chuck-a-luck") Harvey; and George Steele, who ran a three-card monte skin game in the Elephant Corral—decided to launch an attack on the *News* and deal with Editor Byers. They invaded Byers's office and threatened to kill him on the spot. After some deliberation, they marched him at gunpoint back up the street to the Criterion. In their alcohol-sodden minds was some vague plan to hold court in the saloon and try Byers for unjustly accusing their friend Harrison. During the two-block walk to the Criterion the Bummers continually jabbed their pistols at Byers's head and threatened him with instant death.

Reaching the saloon, the Bummers confronted Harrison with their prisoner. The gambler, who had no foreknowledge of the Bummer's intentions, immediately took charge of the situation. He told the gun-waving toughs to wait while he had a talk with the editor. He then took Byers through a doorway into the kitchen of the Criterion, out a back door, and started with him toward the offices of the *News*. They were some distance away when they were spotted by the Bummers, who shouted and cursed and ordered them to stop. Harrison and Byers walked on, never looking back. The Bummers leveled their guns but withheld their fire for fear of hitting Harrison. At Byers's office Harrison advised the newsman and his employees to arm themselves against another attack. Byers agreed and thanked Harrison profusely for his help. There was never any doubt in Byers's mind, then or later, that the gambler had saved his life that day.

Back in the Criterion, Charley Harrison did his best to quiet the Bummers, but their blood was up now and nothing would appease them but William Byers's scalp. Later that day they mounted another assault on the newspaper office. The newsmen were ready this time, however, and in an exchange of gunfire George Steele received a minor buckshot wound and the gang dispersed. By this time the town's police and the vigilantes were out in force. George Steele and Marshal Tom Pollock, both mounted and carrying shotguns, suddenly confronted each other at the corner of Blake and G streets. Steele threw up his gun, but Pollock was a little faster. His shotgun blast took off most of Steele's face.

Innis, Harvey, and Rooker made their escape and were seen no more in Denver City. Carl Woods was apprehended, tried by the people's court, and sentenced to immediate banishment from the territory. A secret group of vigilantes known as "The Stranglers" moved on other Bummers. A month later Jim Latty, a red-bearded gambler who had been George Steele's partner, and five other undesirables were found hanging in a cottonwood grove ten miles from town.

Throughout all these events, Charley Harrison's stature in Denver had actually been enhanced. His disavowal of the Bummers, and particularly his quick and courageous action in saving Byers's life, had won for him the respect and admiration of the town's better element. His Criterion Saloon soon was enjoying the patronage of a better clientele and he wasted little time capitalizing on the change. He and Ed Jump remodeled the second floor of the Criterion, turning it into a theater seating 650. Harrison then inveigled a troupe called the Converse and Petrie Ethiopian Minstrels away from Apollo Hall for an opening night performance that was so successful that Harrison immediately signed the "sable harmonists" to a longterm contract.

When representatives to the Jefferson Territorial Provisional Legislature met in Denver City to elect officers and establish a temporary organization, the town's leading entertainment establishment, the Criterion, furnished the necessary accommodations. Meetings were held upstairs and informal convivial gatherings took place downstairs. The amiable Charley Harrison made a perfect host, and the money poured in.

There were some persons who coveted the windfall that Harrison was reaping. A group from Golden City lobbied through a proposal to adjourn the assembly to Golden and several of the Goldenites celebrated their coup at the Criterion bar. Harrison, understandably miffed at the turn of events, became irritated by the gloating of one loudmouthed Golden City boomer named A. B. Riley and had him thrown out.

The following day two of Riley's friends called on Harrison and presented him with a challenge: "Sir: I demand from you an apology by the hands of the bearers of this note, or by some other friend whom you may select; for the ungentlemanly manner in which you treated me yesterday. Believing myself to be entirely justified in my course, I do hereby pronounce and post Charles Harrison a liar and a coward. (Signed) Riley."[9]

Harrison's answer, accepting the challenge and setting the weapons and conditions, was not long in coming. It was delivered that afternoon by his friend and fellow southerner, the postmaster of Denver, "Bold Thunder" McClure:

Friday, November 23, 1860

Mr. Riley: It is my pleasure to reply in request to the challenge forwarded by your friend to me this very day.

As I see no reason for making any public apology in your behalf at this time or any other time, for this matter, I accept your challenge on the following terms:

Tomorrow, November 24, Saturday morning at ten o'clock at a point one-half mile south of Warren's ferry along the north bank of the Platte River. Both parties to be armed with heavy duty Navy Colt revolvers and a bowie knife; to be placed only ten paces asunder; to advance and fire until all six shots are exhausted, and if neither has fallen, the bowie knife is to finish the work.

W. P. McClure
for
Charles Harrison[10]

Denver was soon buzzing with talk of the impending duel

and the next morning, hours before the appointed time, hundreds of spectators had gathered at the river. At 9:30 A.M. Sheriff Ned Wynkoop rode his horse into the assembled throng, held up his hand for quiet, and announced that Harrison and Riley had reconciled their differences and the duel had been called off. Said Wynkoop, "Mr. Riley has publicly proclaimed that he was wholly in the wrong from the beginning and has asked Mr. Harrison to disregard any remarks he may have made."

The duel had been averted, but in frontier Denver such an incident often began a chain of events culminating in further violence. Harrison's shooting of Stark had led directly to the near-assassination of William Byers and the killing of George Steele. In this instance, the scheduled duel with Riley set the stage for another shooting involving Harrison.

James Hill was a rancher who had come to town Saturday morning to see the Harrison-Riley duel. Disappointed in that objective, he had begun a two-day binge, drinking and gambling in a succession of saloons. A bear of a man, Hill stood six feet, two inches tall and weighed well over two hundred pounds. His hair was long and matted and a bushy black beard concealed most of his face. In a heavy ankle-length coat trimmed in mangy wolf fur, he was a formidable figure indeed. He was known in Denver as a rugged pioneer who minded his own business but brooked no interference in his own affairs and feared neither man nor devil.

Late Sunday night Hill was in the Criterion, bellied up to the bar. Harrison was standing nearby, engaged in conversation with several men. Also in attendance was Sheriff Ned Wynkoop. Suddenly loud and angry voices drew everyone's attention. Harrison's bartender, Rocky Thomas, had denied Hill another drink, saying the rancher had had enough, and Hill was denouncing him in derogatory terms and stentorian voice. Harrison and Wynkoop both moved toward the source of the commotion. The sheriff attempted to calm Hill, but the rancher jerked away and drew his pistol. Before he could raise it he found himself looking into the barrel of Wynkoop's leveled revolver. The two men stared at each other for several seconds, and then Hill let his hand drop to his side.

Charley Harrison stepped between the two. Motioning Wynkoop away, he put his arm around Hill, gently guided him to the bar, and offered to buy him a drink.

The hulking rancher seemed to be settling down, lulled by Harrison's southern drawl. Then Rocky Thomas suggested that he should step outside for some air.

"I don't need to go anywhere for you or any other sonofa-bitch!" snorted Hill.

"Hold on," said Harrison, tensing. "I'll have no man calling my employees a sonofabitch!"

"I'll call him as I please," snarled Hill, pushing away, "and you ain't no better. . . ."

Hill's gun hand was coming up filled as he spoke. Harrison grabbed at the rancher's gun as he went for his own weapon. The gambler ripped off four shots in rapid succession. Hill pitched forward to the floor.

Sheriff Wynkoop leaped forward and threw his arms around Harrison, who surrendered his pistol, mumbling, "He shouldn't have called my man a sonofabitch." Doctor William Bell, who had been standing at the Criterion bar conversing with Harrison when the trouble began, attended Hill, but the rancher died several hours later.

When word of the shooting spread through town the following morning, angry, gesturing knots of men began to form on street corners. Hill had many friends and they were talking lynch-law retribution. Within an hour the small groups were beginning to coalesce into a mob. Harrison's friends read the signs and hurried to the Criterion, carrying rifles and shotguns. The situation was ominous when City Marshal Bill Middaugh drove his rig up in front of Harrison's saloon. He pleaded with the crowd to let him arrest the gambler and deal with him legally, but his entreaties had little effect. Middaugh, realizing that he could not appeal to the mob's reason, worked on its emotion. Harrison and a bunch of his very tough friends were forted up in there, he warned, and if an attempt was made to rush the place, blood would flow in the street.

Where reason had failed, fear prevailed. The crowd slowed its surge and then stopped. Middaugh was permitted to enter the Criterion to attempt Harrison's arrest. He was accompanied only by his twenty-year-old son, Asa. Inside Middaugh found a force of seventy-five determined looking men. Heavily armed with rifles, shotguns, and handguns, they were four-deep at every window and doorway. Any attack on the building would have exacted a terrible price in lives.

Marshal Middaugh and Harrison conversed briefly. The gambler agreed to surrender his guns and accept arrest if Middaugh would personally guarantee him protection from the mob. Middaugh pledged his life and that of his son, and Harrison handed over his weapons. He walked out the doorway flanked by the Middaughs. The crowd, which had grown to several hundred, again pressed forward, but the stern-eyed father and son, their prisoner between them, strode resolutely on, and a lane opened for them.

After a day in custody, Harrison was released under $1,000 bond. The wheels of justice moved swiftly in frontier Denver. Within two hours of the gambler's arrest, a coroner's jury had determined that Hill had died from the effects of a gunshot wound "inflicted upon his person at the hand of Charles Harrison," and that same day a grand jury was impaneled and brought in an indictment charging Harrison with first degree murder. Trial was set for one week later.

There had been many witnesses to the shooting, but at the trial there was little agreement in their testimony as to what had happened. Some saw no pistol on Hill's person at any time; others said he wore a pistol but never drew it; and still others swore he pulled his gun and pointed it at Harrison, whereupon the gambler pulled his own iron and fired. The jury was understandably confused by this conflicting testimony and, after fourteen hours of deliberation, reported that they stood ten to two for acquittal and were hopelessly deadlocked. The prosecution deemed it folly under the circumstances to ask for a new trial and dropped the charges. Harrison was dismissed.

There was general rejoicing in the Criterion, but editor Byers was dissatisfied with the outcome. The taking of a human life "just because a boisterous drunken man used profane epithets," he deemed wholly unjustified. "We are told . . . that before firing, Harrison caught Hill's right hand and immediately began firing. . . . Now was Mr. Harrison's life in jeopardy after he caught Hill's pistol arm? Was it necessary for him to take Hill's life to save his own, and if not, how was the killing justifiable?"[11]

These questions were answered by Harrison himself in a letter to Byers, which the editor published in the next day's edition. He was pleased to help Harrison state his case, said Byers, and, alluding to the incident when Harrison had rescued him from the Bummers, added: "It would enable us to discharge an obligation we owe Mr. Harrison for a service rendered us on a former occasion. . . ."

Wrote Harrison:

On my coming to Mr. Hill, I told him I did not allow any man to call my barkeeper a sonofabitch, for I kept no such men in my employ. Mr. Hill said if I took his part, I was not better than him, and shoved me off with one hand and raised his pistol in range of my body. I grabbed his pistol and tried all in my power to get it away from him, but he tried to get it in range with me, and I shall always believe when this was done he meant to fire at me. My fingers caught before the trigger and behind the guard of his pistol, and when he let go of it my finger was benumbed, and all the skin rubbed off by the guard. I had no use of my finger for some time. . . .

When I went up to Mr. Hill, I had no intention of killing him, nor did such a thought enter my brain for one moment, until I saw he was determined on killing me if he could. Then I commenced shooting at him, but for the smoke I could not tell whether I hit him or not, until just as I was going to shoot the fourth time, Mr. Hill let go of his pistol and fell, as my pistol went off. . . .

Now, Mr. Editor, let every man that is a man, put himself in my place at the time of my seizing Mr. Hill's pistol, and when they can see by his motion that he wanted to bring the pistol in range of their body, what would they do? I will leave this for you all to answer.[12]

Harrison's explanation seemed to satisfy Byers, but many other Denverites would always feel that he had gotten away with wanton murder. The report spread that the hung jury had resulted from the judicious distribution of $5,000 in cash by Harrison's mistress, the beautiful Ada Lamont.

At twenty-one years of age, Ada Lamont was the town's leading madam. Two years before, in the fall of 1858, she had appeared in Denver with one of the first wagon trains bringing gold seekers to the new bonanza. Other arrivals on that train would tell her strange story. At seventeen she had married a young minister back in the middlewest and had cheerfully followed her husband westward when he decided to take the word of God to the Rocky Mountain gold regions. During the journey the minister suddenly was missing, and disappearing on the same night was a woman of dubious virtue. The wagon train stopped for a full day while a fruitless search was made for the missing couple. When no evidence of foul play was found, the natural assumption had been that the two had run off together. The nineteen-year-old wife was inconsolable and was rarely seen outside of her wagon for the remainder of the journey.

When the train reached the raw new gold camp at the foot of the Rockies, the young girl emerged from her wagon and announced that from that day on her name would be Ada LaMont and she intended to open the town's first whorehouse. She began in a rough shack in Indian Row, a collection of log buildings along the South Platte River, with her own charms the sole attraction, but within a year she had moved to a large two-story house on Arapahoe Street and had a number of "soiled doves" in her employ.

Almost from the day that Charley Harrison arrived in Denver it was understood that Ada LaMont was his woman and he was her man. The two attended theatrical and sporting events together, and no longer was she available to other men. All agreed they made a very handsome couple.

In December, 1860, the very month that Charley Harrison stood trial for the killing of James Hill, he figured in another murder case, but this time his role was that of one who helped bring the accused killer to justice.

On December 5, while the Harrison trial was in progress and the attention of most of Denver's citizenry was riveted upon it, a local rancher named Tom Freeman was reported missing. His abandoned wagon, stained with blood, had been found about thirty miles from town, and the report spread quickly that he had been killed by Pat Waters, a handyman on Freeman's ranch, with whom he had last been seen. Freeman was a member of the Masonic Lodge, as were Harrison, William Byers, and many other prominent Denverites. After Waters was apprehended near Cottonwood Springs, Nebraska, and returned to Denver, a posse of Masons, which included Harrison, Byers, Judge John Wanless, and Sheriff Ned Wynkoop, set out in search of Freeman's body. The suspect Waters, protesting his innocence, was taken along to the point where the wagon was found. Here he was given a chance to pray while a rope was attached to a cottonwood limb. Harrison placed the noose over the man's head and was adjusting the knot under his ear when Waters suddenly broke down and offered to show where the body was hidden. He then took the posse to a site six miles farther away where the body was recovered from a thicket along the river.

Back in Denver, Waters was indicted for murder, and, since the town lacked a jail, was confined in a room over the Criterion. Here Harrison interviewed the prisoner in private and managed to elicit a complete confession. The gambler testified at the trial, which proceeded briskly, and a jury of distinguished Denverites took just ten minutes to bring in a verdict of guilty. The next day Waters was taken in chains from the Criterion to a new scaffold and legally hanged. Although Harrison had played a leading part in this case, the assertion of Gene Teats and others that "Charley Harrison hanged a man in Denver" is somewhat of an overstatement of the facts.

Excitement of a different kind gripped Denver in May of 1861. A few months earlier Congress had approved the formation of a new territory to be called Colorado, with Denver as the capital. In May the town was visited by William Gilpin, the newly appointed governor. A week of festivities was planned, to be capped by a race featuring the two most famous horses in the region, Border Ruffian and Rocky Mountain Chief. Charley Harrison, who was primarily responsible for arranging the race, asked for donations in gold for a winner's purse. Gold dust, coins, and nuggets flowed into the Criterion. Harrison took it all to the Clark and Gruber Mint and had it melted down into a nugget valued at $95,000.

It will be remembered that Harrison had appeared in Denver astride Border Ruffian, having stolen the racehorse in Salt

Lake City to effect the rescue of Tom Hunt. The horse was now owned by Colonel A. B. Miller, a gambler with extensive holdings in Denver. His rider in the great match race was to be Jim McNassar, son of James McNassar, owner of the Planter House.

Border Ruffian had saved Harrison's life once, but the gambler would not allow sentiment to influence his betting; he had his money down on Rocky Mountain Chief, a fine piece of horseflesh owned by Bill Greer, a gambler from Saint Joseph, Missouri. Gene Teats was to ride Chief, and Bill Greer had hired as trainer for the animal one Tom Hunt, the same man who had ridden into Denver with Harrison on the back of Border Ruffian.

The race was to be run in three heats of one mile each with the winner of the $95,000 nugget to be the owner of the horse that won two of the three heats. Of course, there were many side bets, and it was estimated that as the trainers led the horses to the starting line there was at least $100,000 wagered on the result of the first heat. Tom Hunt, Chief's trainer, had secretly bet his bankroll on the other horse, and when the starter's gun sounded, he held onto Chief's bridle. Border Ruffian got away to a flying start, and by the time Hunt released his hold, had taken a lead that Rocky Mountain Chief could not overcome.

The backers of Chief set up a howl when Border Ruffian was declared the winner. There were calls to lynch Hunt right on the spot, but cooler heads prevailed and he was ordered to get out of town before nightfall.

As preparations were being made for the second heat, odds of twenty to one against Rocky Mountain Chief winning the best-of-three competition were being quoted. Harrison, taking the odds, warned Gene Teats not to spare the whip if it became necessary. He had everything riding on the last two heats, he said, and the boy had better boot Chief home in front.

Both horses got off to a good start and were neck and neck at the half-mile marker. Still Teats had not whipped his horse. Charley Harrison felt it was time to act. Mounting up, he galloped to the final turn, swung his horse in alongside the racers as they took the turn head-to-head, and entered the stretch with them. Pulling a six-gun, he roared at Teats: "Whip that horse *now*!"

One glance at the yawning muzzle of Harrison's gun convinced young Teats, and he went to the whip. As Chief started to move away, Jim McNassar lashed out with his own whip, striking Teats across the face. Teats hung on, however, and Rocky Mountain Chief crossed the finish line in front.

It was now the turn of Ruffian's supporters to rant and rave. Harrison had interfered, they claimed, and the heat should be disallowed. After much argument it was agreed by both sides to abide by the decision of the judges who, after conferring, ruled that Harrison's action had not affected the outcome of the heat, that McNassar had fouled Teats in any event, and that the winner was Rocky Mountain Chief.

The heats now stood at one each for the horses, and the betting was reaching a peak of feverish activity when the owner of Border Ruffian, A. B. Miller, dropped a bombshell. So enraged was he by the ruling of the judges that he was withdrawing his horse from the competition. Teats ran Chief all alone around the track, and Bill Greer claimed the great gold nugget. Charley Harrison and the other backers of Greer's horse went about collecting their bets.

That night in the Criterion, Bill Greer and Charley Harrison sat down to a game of high-stakes poker. When Greer rose from the table the next morning, he left behind his $95,000 gold nugget. The day of the great race was over and Charley Harrison had picked up just about all the marbles. It was to be the high point of his gambling career, for stirring events were transpiring in the East that would soon bring his Denver period to a close and change the course of his life.

A month before, on April 18, 1861, the *Rocky Mountain News* had carried the banner headline: "Most Exciting News! Commencement of Hostilities! Batteries Open on Sumter!" The populace of Denver City, composed almost equally of northerners and southerners, began drawing into two camps of armed and suspicious men. On the morning of April 24, the town awoke to find the Confederate flag flying above the general store next door to the Criterion. The threat of armed conflict hung ominously over the town before the banner was taken down. Throughout the summer of 1861 there were numerous clashes between unionists and secessionists. All Denver knew that the Criterion was the headquarters of the southern sympathizers and its owner was their leader. The situation worsened on August 21 when Company B of the First Colorado Volunteers, recruited in the mountain mining camps, arrived in town and took quarters in a building directly behind the Criterion.

Violence erupted that very night. It started with a brawl in Ada LaMont's sporting house between soldiers from Company B and several southerners. The secessionists, outnumbered, took a thorough beating. Later, a group from the Criterion, out to even the score, mauled a sentry just a block from the saloon. The soldier claimed he had been pistol-whipped by Charley Harrison and John Cody, uncle of the yet-to-be-famous Buffalo Bill. Harrison and Cody were arrested and released after posting bond.

For three days the town was tense as squads of soldiers patrolled the streets and the southerners eyed them darkly from Harrison's saloon. On the night of August 24 a gang of soldiers attempted to crowd into the Criterion. Harrison ordered them out, and a group of his friends moved to eject the unwelcome patrons. A chair-swinging, bottle-throwing melee developed. Before it was over the gambling house was a shambles. Later that night someone in the Criterion began firing a rifle, pumping bullets into the nearby barracks. Two Colorado Volunteers suffered minor wounds. The soldiers leaped to their rifle racks and soon a full-scale fire fight was in progress. The company bugler blew "assembly" and quickly the Criterion was surrounded. A cannon was drawn up Larimer Street and wheeled into position in front of the saloon, its muzzle leveled at the main entrance.

City officers arrived and, after two hours of negotiations, placed Charley Harrison and several of his friends under arrest. They were taken in chains to await trial but were soon freed on writs of habeas corpus drawn by Harrison's lawyers. Under bonds of $1,000 each they returned to a warm reception at the Criterion. Harrison's trial on a charge of rebellion was slated for September 3.

Wild rumors swept the town. It was said that rebel forces were gathering in Pueblo and plans were being laid to drive north to Denver, join Harrison's crowd, and burn Denver to the ground. Another report had Company A of the First Colorado Volunteers, then marching under orders to New Mexico, being called back to defend the town.

Harrison's trial lasted two weeks. He could have been convicted of treason and conspiracy to overthrow the government by force—offenses punishable by death. He was, instead, found guilty of the lesser crime of obstructing the proper officers of government in the discharge of their duties. Benjamin F. Hall, recently appointed chief justice of the territory by Abraham Lincoln, set Harrison's fine at $5,000 and gave him two days to settle his affairs and to depart the territory, never to return in his lifetime.

Within the allotted time Harrison had paid his fine and sold the Criterion to the firm of Rice and Lewis. On the morning of the nineteenth of September, 1861, he rode out of Denver on the eastbound stage. He would never return, but he would make one spectacular attempt.

Ada LaMont continued to maintain her popular brothel on Arapahoe Street after Harrison's departure. One day a friend came to see her after a trip to Kansas. He had, he said, accidentally come upon a human skeleton out on the prairie. A hole in the skull and a bullet within it were stark testaments to a tragedy that had been enacted there years before. From the remnants of clothing remaining around the bones the man had extracted a pocket Bible. Faded, but still legible, was an inscription written on the flyleaf by a young bride to her minister husband. The truth was plain; the young man had not run off with another woman but had been gunned down by a hostile Indian or a renegade white.

Ada LaMont's fortunes changed drastically from the day that she held that Bible in her hand and gazed at the familiar script. She began to drink heavily and her business suffered. Finally, she closed her house and went to Georgetown, then in the midst of a boom. Nothing, however, could halt her downhill slide. Her beauty gone, her health ravaged by whiskey and drugs, she died in abject poverty, unloved and unmourned.

Two months after Denver City's most famous gambler departed, the *Leavenworth* (Kansas) *Daily Times* noted that "Charles Harrison, of Denver notoriety, is in town and rejoiceth in the title of Captain Charles Harrison."[13] The title was not an honorary one that Harrison had conferred upon himself in the custom of the times, but a military rank, for he was now an officer in the Army of the Confederacy, commanding Company A of Colonel Emmett MacDonald's Fourth Missouri Cavalry.

Harrison's military career was exemplary and MacDonald commended him to his superior, General Marmaduke, on several occasions. After the November 29, 1862, battle at Cane Hill, Arkansas, MacDonald reported: "During the entire engagement Companies A and B fought nobly. No company of officers and men ever fought better. Capt. Harrison . . . and the lieutenants in both companies deserved much praise."[14] Harrison took part in the battles at Reed's Mountain and Prairie Grove, Arkansas, in December, 1862. His company captured 40 supply wagons, 200 horses, about 200 prisoners, including a Union major, and 450 stands of arms. It was Harrison's company that rescued Colonel Shelby and his battery of light artillery after they had been captured by the Yankees.

On January 6, 1863, Harrison was promoted to lieutenant colonel. Shortly thereafter, he attacked and burned Fort Lawrence in Missouri. At the head of a cavalry unit of less than two hundred men, he routed a force of more than 250, captured 200 horses, 300 stands of arms, and 10 supply wagons. He served at the siege of Springfield, Missouri, and when General Marmaduke ordered a withdrawal, took a heavy toll of Union forces on the way out. He and MacDonald drove through the fortified town of Marshfield and burned the fort at Hartville. When MacDonald fell, Harrison became a full colonel and assumed command of the Fourth Missouri Cavalry. For three months in early 1863, his command of six hundred veteran cavalrymen, organized into guerrilla bands of sixty to eighty men each, raised havoc with an opposing army of five thousand.

In April, Harrison's horse was shot from under him during

an exchange of prisoners under a flag of truce. In May he was involved in a skirmish at Center Creek and was reported to have been killed. Charley, however, was not dead yet.

He had long entertained the notion that a raid into Colorado Territory by a small, fast-moving force of plains-wise fighting men could be successful and perhaps extremely profitable for the Confederacy. There was booty to be taken at Denver City: arms and ammunition, horses and wagons, and a stockpile of the item most sorely needed by the Confederacy, gold. Nothing stood in the way of a raiding party between Missouri and Denver but a few wild Indians. Harrison finally convinced his superiors that such a raid was feasible and he was given permission to organize a force and lead it to Denver.

One of the first to volunteer for the mission was an old pal from Denver, Bold Thunder McClure, now a captain. Another was Colonel Warner Lewis, nephew of Meriwether Lewis. Others in the party were another full colonel, B. H. Woodson, a lieutenant colonel, one major, three captains besides McClure, and eleven lieutenants—a force of twenty officers in all. On May 16, 1863, Charley Harrison led his raiding party away from the bivouac at Center Creek and turned his mount west, toward Denver City.

In the first days of the Civil War on the border, Confederate guerrillas had driven the Osage Indians from their homes in Texas and Arkansas. Now, in the spring of 1863, Osage hunting parties criss-crossed the Kansas plains. They had no real interest in the white man's war in the East, but out of bitterness toward the men who had forced them from their ancient homes, they swore allegiance to the Union and attacked with a vengeance any man in a gray suit.

On Lightning Creek, a tributary of the Verdigris River in southeastern Kansas, a band of Osage warriors under Chief Little Bear surprised Harrison's party. Most of the officers were hit in the first volley of rifle fire and shower of arrows. Harrison was struck in the face by a bullet and tumbled from his horse. He was on his knees on the ground, blazing away with his Colt revolvers, when an Osage lance skewered him.

Eighteen of the officers died in the attack. Only Colonel Lewis and Lieutenant John Rafferty escaped. Without food or horses, they hid in the river thickets by day and traveled by night. After three nights they managed to reach the Missouri border, eighty miles from the site of the massacre.

A patrol of cavalrymen from the Ninth Kansas came upon the scene of the slaughter several days later. The eighteen Confederate officers lay where they had fallen. Some had been beheaded by the Indians, others scalped. The brave who counted coup on Charley Harrison had apparently scorned the sparse hair on his balding head and had taken his trophy from Harrison's luxuriant black beard. The beard-scalp was later seen in proud display hanging from a lance in an Osage village.

3

A gambler is possessed of some rights, if not under and by the law, certainly from his fraternity, and those who consort with him. It is a sorry dog, indeed, that will eat dog.

Ben Thompson
William M. Walton, *Life and Adventures of Ben Thompson*

During the reign of Charley Harrison as Denver City's premier sporting man, there arrived in the Colorado boomtown a newcomer who was destined to become one of the best known and widely respected professional gambling men in the West.

Richard Brinsley Sheridan Clark, born April 15, 1838, at Cayuga, New York, moved with his family to Saginaw, Michigan, from whence he departed late in 1858 to seek fame and fortune in the great Wild West. Dick Clark was not quite twenty-one when he reached Denver early in 1859. Like most of the other Pike's-Peak-or-Bust enthusiasts, he tarried but a short time in the little town on Cherry Creek and soon hurried on to the mining camps in the mountains. A few months of hard-rock mining convinced the young Clark that this was not the life for him, and he was soon spending most of his time in the saloons of Denver and the outlying settlements. He was fascinated by the gambling games and particularly by the nimble-fingered gentry who directed the activity at the tables. By the time he turned twenty-one Dick Clark had determined to pattern his life after the style of Charley Harrison and Jack O'Neil, both of whom he greatly admired.

The Civil War interrupted his education at the Colorado gaming tables. On September 1, 1861, he enlisted in Company H of the First Colorado Infantry where he attained the rank of corporal. At war's end he was mustered out but reenlisted as a Veteran Volunteer. He left the army for the second time on October 28, 1865, with the rank of quartermaster sergeant.

The military left its mark on Clark; for the rest of his life he carried himself ramrod-straight like a drill sergeant. More important, in the army he learned dicipline and self-control, essential attributes of the successful high roller. He was a tall, thin man with a naturally pallid complexion. The pallor of his skin was accentuated by the contrast with his dark, carefully barbered whiskers.

He had, of course, gambled during all his years in the army and had sharpened his skills in his chosen profession. From the beginning Clark prided himself on being a "square" gambler, and throughout a thirty-year career and extensive travel in the West, he maintained that reputation. Gambling was his life; he was totally devoted to it. All other areas of human thought and activity seemed to hold little interest for him. He was a true professional, a kind of genius in his line.

Late in 1865 he headed for Kansas City, Missouri, and spent more than a year in the city, which at this time was as lively a town for the man of sporting blood as could be found in the country. During the fifteen years following the Civil War, Kansas City became something of a playground for the restless adventurers of the Great Plains. Here came the Texas cattlemen after their trail drives, pockets bulging with the proceeds of their beef sales; army officers on leave from a dozen scattered frontier outposts, back pay smoldering in their billfolds; bearded hunters from the buffalo ranges of western Kansas, receipts from the sale of thousands of hides hot in their horny hands. With them, like flies after honey, came the gamblers to vie for a share of his bonanza.

Gambling had been a key industry in Kansas City from its earliest days. When Horace White, later editor of the *New York Evening Post*, stopped in the town of "Kanzas" in 1857, he thought that the principal business seemed to be "gambling, selling whiskey and running dives." One of the most impressive buildings of the town during this period was a three-story gambling place kept by a Colonel Titus.

By the mid-1860s, Kansas City had entered its golden era of gambling and local citizens were claiming that in the six-block area called "Old Town" more gambling houses were in operation than in any city in America. It was this section that became the mold from which were patterned the wild sporting districts of towns all along the line of the Kansas Pacific Railroad. The west side of Main Street between Fourth Street and

Missouri Avenue was lined with first-class establishments, while cheaper, more disreputable places were situated on Fifth Street between Walnut and Main. Wrote an early city historian: "Games of chance, cards, keno, faro, roulette, dice, cock-mains, dog-fighting and kindred means of hazarding money flourished day and night."[1]

The leader of the toughest element of the gambling fraternity in the years immediately following the war was a hard character known as Jim Crow Chiles. Christened James J. Chiles, he had been nicknamed "Jim Crow" at an early age because of the gay abandon with which he performed the popular dance of that name. He had been a member of Quantrill's Raiders during the war. With the end of hostilities he had turned to gambling for a career, as did former fellow raiders Jim Bruce, Johnny Owens, and others. At Kansas City he opened a large gambling house called the Headquarters. Chiles was a big, powerful fellow with long, flowing black hair and dark eyes, and he cut a dashing figure on the streets of Kansas City astride his black stallion, John Morgan. He always went heavily armed, wearing a pair of long-barreled dragoon cap-and-ball revolvers at his waist and keeping a brace of derringers secreted as backup weapons. He had often demonstrated his skill with pistols, both on inanimate targets and on men. When liquored up, he was a terror to all who crossed his path. Finally, in September, 1872, he ran up against a man he could not bulldoze. Jim Peacock, deputy city marshal of Independence, Missouri, killed Jim Crow in a wild melee during which Peacock was shot in the back by Chiles's fourteen-year-old son Elijah, and the Chiles boy was shot and killed by Peacock's fifteen-year-old son Charlie.

Another Kansas City gambling house proprietor of renown was the imposing Major James S. Showers, who ran a Main Street resort in partnership with Doc Frame. A dignified-appearing old gentleman more than six feet tall and weighing three hundred pounds, Showers dated his gambling history back to the famous Hall of the Bleeding Heart in Washington, D. C., where he claimed to have dealt faro for Henry Clay and Daniel Webster.

Of the thirty or forty houses operating, the best were Bob

Potee's Faro Number Three, on Missouri just off Main Street; the Marble Hall, run by Joe Bassett and Colonel Rickets; the Senate, kept by the Findlays, father and son; and the establishments of Hank Teas, John Evans, Clayton Maltby, Jake Forcades, George Frazier, and Tom Wallace. Most of these places enjoyed a high turnover of customers who generally played for relatively low stakes. During one month Clay Maltby maintained a close record of all chips purchased at his tables. The total for the month was $63,843.75, although only one man purchased as much as $100 worth of chips at one time. Maltby estimated that about two-thirds of the $63,000 remained in his till, and he projected a total gross income for the year at more than half a million dollars.

Potee's Faro Number Three was famous for its opulent appointments. Situated over Strein's restaurant and saloon, it was resplendent with rich carpeting, elaborately carved mahogany furniture, lace and damask curtains, and silver and gold bric-a-brac. The softly lighted entrance hall was guarded by life-size statues of nude maidens. It was said that an entering player could increase his chances of winning at the tables if he caressed his favorite "Lady Luck," and he was almost certainly assured a success if he tossed a token, a twenty-dollar gold piece, perhaps, at the lady's feet.

Bob Potee, the proprietor of this elaborate temple of chance, was tall and slender, with gold-rimmed spectacles and a neatly trimmed van dyke beard. He was always meticulously attired in black long-tailed coat and ruffled white shirt. On the street he was never seen without his high silk hat and gold-headed cane. He was proud of his reputation as a southern gentleman and a square gambler.

One night his honesty was challenged by a hot-headed tinhorn who lost his bankroll and his composure at Potee's faro table. Whipping out a pistol, the red-faced man pushed the muzzle at Potee's face and accused him of cheating.

"You are mistaken, my friend," drawled Potee, carefully spreading both hands, palms down, on the table. "Please sit down."

"Like hell I will!" blurted the tinhorn, thumbing back the hammer of his six-gun.

Eyewitnesses were not entirely sure what happened next because they were busy getting away from the table, but all agreed that two shots were fired in rapid succession, the lamp over the table was shattered, and darkness enveloped the room. When a new lamp was brought in, Bob Potee still sat straight in his chair, his hands flat on the faro layout. Sprawled across the table was the body of the tinhorn, a bullet through his heart and the fully loaded pistol clutched in his hand.

"We will start with a fresh deck when the layout is cleared," said Bob Potee.

In 1881 an antigambling act was passed by the Missouri legislature and the great days were over for the sporting gentry of Kansas City. Gus Galbaugh, Clay Maltby, Joe Bassett, and others moved across the state line to Kansas City, Kansas, and opened up new places. Here gambling was prohibited by local ordinance but was in effect licensed by the imposition of periodic fines. Reformed gambler John Philip Quinn, writing in 1890, said there were seven houses still open on the Kansas side, most of them operated by former Missourians Maltby, Frazier, Galbaugh, and Bassett.

This group of veterans was later joined by Jack Dugan who came into the business rather suddenly. Dugan had been a pig-sticker at the Armour Packing Plant and a compulsive faro plunger. One night he hit a hot streak and couldn't be stopped. He broke the bank and the owner put up the house against Dugan's winnings. By morning Jack Dugan was a gambling house proprietor.

Bob Potee had refused to join the exodus. He chose to wait and watch Old Town die. One day in 1883 he penned a note for his old friend Joe Bassett, dressed up in his finest togs and favorite silk hat, tucked his gold-headed cane under his arm, and walked up Main Street for the last time. Nodding and smiling to friends, he strolled casually to the Missouri River and walked until his hat floated.

"Plant me decently, Joe," his note to Bassett had said.

Bassett did as asked. The body was recovered, church services were held, and six tall gamblers, as in the old song, bore Potee's remains in a mahogany casket to the hearse and on to the cemetery.

Joe Bassett's fortunes turned in later years, and when he died in 1907 he was blind and paralytic, without a dime to his name. Clay Maltby, the last of the high rollers from Kansas City's salad days, was still prosperous and provided Bassett with an elaborate funeral.

Dick Clark had moved on from Kansas City long before this, of course. As the 1860s waned there was in development the phenomenon of the Kansas cattle towns, the storied sin-cities that sprang up at the termini of the railroad tendrils then creeping across the Plains. To these dusty, wind-swept rail-heads squatting on the prairies of western Kansas came tens of thousands of Texas longhorns to be shipped to the beef-hungry masses of the eastern cities. Arriving with them were hundreds of young cowboys, eager for fun after three months on the trail, flush with back pay. Waiting for the cowboys was the sporting horde.

Between 1867 and 1885 the towns of Abilene, Newton, Ellsworth, Wichita, and Dodge City followed one another as claimants to the title, "Queen of Cattle Towns." If veteran drovers could find little to distinguish one town from another, it is understandable, for the names of the saloons, dance halls, and gambling dens of the currently popular town were often the same as the deadfalls of the town of the previous season. There were Alamo and Lone Star saloons, obviously named to curry the favor of the Texas men, in each succeeding town. There was a Bull's Head in Abilene and another in Newton, and Gold Rooms in Newton and again in Wichita. The build-ings themselves might very well look familiar, for they were often loaded on flatcars, lock, stock, and whiskey barrel, and moved to the next town.

Dick Clark saw service in all the cattle towns. He conducted a faro game in Abilene during the shipping seasons of 1867 through 1871 and was a familiar figure in such garden spots as the Alamo, the Lone Star, the Old Fruit and the Applejack saloons. In the Bull's Head Tavern he often locked horns in high-stake poker games with Texas ranchers, in town to meet their herds.

Other frequent participants in these games were Texas gamblers Phil Coe and Ben Thompson, coowners of the Bull's Head, and James Butler ("Wild Bill") Hickok, city marshal of Abilene. Nationally renowned for his exploits as a Union spy, Indian-fighting scout, and premier pistoleer, Hickok had accepted appointment as marshal after the murder of his predecessor, Bear River Tom Smith. Wild Bill was a professional gambler by natural inclination and took on jobs of law enforcement as an income-augmenting measure and as a means of controlling the play in town.

In 1871, Dick Clark moved on to Newton, which, during its big seasons of '71 and '72, boasted twenty-seven saloons and eight gambling houses open around the clock. There were at least eighty professional gamblers in town during Newton's heyday and they literally controlled law enforcement—or the lack of it. The police force, which included a tough frontier knockabout named Billy Brooks and Tom Carson, nephew of the famous Kit, was paid from a fund raised and maintained solely by the gambling fraternity.

Clark dealt faro in the Gold Rooms, Newton's largest gambling hall, run by Isaac ("Doc") Thayer and Bill Pierce. Thayer, in the tradition of top-notch gambling men, was a meticulous dresser. His shirts were always spotless, he wore a suit coat even on the hottest of Kansas dog days, and he kept his pant legs outside of his polished boots. He was often mistaken by strangers for a preacher. Bill Pierce was a popular, open-faced fellow who had tried his hand at mining and cattle ranching before joining the sporting brethren. The Gold Rooms, situated on Main Street in the heart of town, contained at least six tables open for play at all times of day or night, a long bar, and music and sideshows were frequently provided. It was said that every male in Newton stopped into the establishment sometime during the course of a day.

Another popular Newton resort was the Bull's Head Saloon. The proprietor, Tex Bruton, was described by a Topeka reporter who visited Newton in September, 1872, as "a longhorn who wears a hat wide enough to deal a game upon, and a face that seems to scintillate sparks of good nature."

Big money poker games were sometimes played in Newton, and Dick Clark was usually present to take a hand. Of Clark,

*Dick Clark, for thirty years an imposing figure on the Western gam-
bling scene. From* Billy King's Tombstone. *Courtesy C. L. Sonnichsen.*

the Topeka newsman wrote: "He is widely known and has the reputation of being one of the best hearted and cleverest poker players in the country. His face, while engaged in play, is one of the most impassive I ever saw."[2]

The big event of the 1871 cattle season in Newton was the gunfight that erupted the night of August 19 in Perry Tuttle's saloon. Mike McCluskie was seated at a faro table when attacked by Hugh Anderson. All hell broke loose and when the smoke lifted, five men were dead or dying and several more were wounded. Most of those who were shot had no part in the quarrel that triggered the cannonade, proving once again what a dangerous place a gambling table could be in a frontier town loaded with short-fused, gun-toting characters.

One such character was a powerfully built former Union soldier named Jim Moon who partnered Clark for a time in Newton, keeping cases at Clark's faro game, but Clark soon realized that Moon was cursed with a volcanic temper that would eventually get him and probably his partner, too, into deep trouble, so he broke up the team and moved on.

Between 1871 and 1875 the towns of Ellsworth and Wichita competed for the cattle trade, and Clark divided his time between the two. At Ellsworth he dealt his game in Joe Brennan's saloon, dubbed by the locals the "Gamblers' Roost." At Brennan's, or at an occasional game in Jake New's saloon or in Nick Lentz's, he took on the Texas cowboys or parried the wagering attacks of Ben Thompson, one-legged Jim Goodwyn, and John Sterling, the other leading professionals in town. Sterling was an Indiana gambler who was described by an associate as "a good-natured, warm-hearted man always ready to help the needy or skin a sucker." After a sojourn on the frontier, Sterling returned to Fort Wayne, Indiana, where for several years he operated a profitable gambling house called the Lodge.

In 1872, Doc Thayer and Bill Pierce moved their Gold Rooms from Newton to Wichita. Major competition for them in Wichita was Keno Hall, operated by W. W. ("Whitey") Rupp. Situated on the northwest corner of the town's main intersection, Douglas and Main streets, Keno Hall was for several years acknowledged to be one of the finest gambling emporiums west of Kansas City.³ Rupp, a born showman, brought in a brass band, ensconced it on the second-floor veranda of his establishment, and provided Wichita with a free concert every evening.

Like most gamblers, Rupp was of a generous nature. When drought and a grasshopper plague devastated the plains of Kansas in the summer of 1874, the gamblers of Wichita were quick to donate for the relief of the unfortunate pioneer sodbusters, and, as reported in the *Wichita Eagle*, "Mr. Whitey Rupp, the popular proprietor of the Keno House, started the ball rolling . . . with a contribution of $250."⁴

The most infamous member of the sporting brotherhood in Wichita was a beefy, mustachioed hustler named Joe Lowe, who, early in his lurid career, had been tagged with the cognomen "Rowdy Joe." A native of Florida, Lowe was in Missouri when the Civil War broke out and enlisted in the Second Missouri Light Artillery. After his discharge in 1865, he served for a time as a civilian scout with the army. In the cattle towns of Kansas he ran a series of disreputable gambling saloons and dance halls, enterprises in which he was ably assisted by the first of his seven wives, a tough vixen known as "Rowdy Kate." In 1873, Rowdy Joe shot and killed "Red" Beard, his chief competitor in Wichita. He was arrested for murder, jumped bail, and, with Rowdy Kate, fled to Luling, Texas, where he opened another dance hall and sporting house. He operated similar establishments in Dallas, Fort Worth, San Antonio, Leadville, and Denver for a quarter of a century. In 1899 he was shot to death in a Denver saloon by a former city police officer.

Dodge City was the last and most notorious of the Kansas cow towns. Founded in 1872 at the end-of-track of the west-building Atchison, Topeka & Santa Fe Railroad, Dodge was the major shipping point for hides during the great buffalo slaughter of the 1870s. By 1875, Texas longhorns were being driven up the Western Trail to Dodge, and for ten years the town gloried in the title "Cowboy Capital," and its reputation as the "beautiful, bibulous Babylon of the frontier." As the little town's notoriety spread from Canada to Mexico, gambling men from all over the West made an appearance. There

Rowdy Joe Lowe, who ran a succession of disreputable saloons, dance halls, and gambling dens in the border towns. Courtesy Kansas State Historical Society.

were times in the late seventies when the sporting men in the gambling halls of Dodge—the Crystal Palace, the Alhambra, the Lady Gay, the Junction Saloon, the Alamo, the Lone Star, the Oasis, the Green Front, and the Long Branch—almost outnumbered the cowboys who were their prey.

Dick Clark was there, of course, a fixture sitting tall and

dignified behind his faro spread, long white fingers snapping the cards from the box, deep voice intoning the winning and losing cards. Working Dodge at one time or another were other veterans of earlier cattle towns, including "Pony" Reid, a monte dealer from Texas whose ubiquitous high-crowned white hat contrasted handsomely with his black hair and beard; "Trick" Brown, another Texan; hot-tempered Jim Moon; Joe Lowe, the rowdy one; J. J. Harlan, powerful as a mule and nicknamed "Offwheeler"; Jim Bush, sometime associate of Rowdy Joe; and Johnson Gallagher, known variously as "Corn-Hole Johnny," "Three-Card Johnny," and "Chuck-Luck Johnnie." Gallagher, though still a young man during the halcyon days of the Kansas trail towns, was a seasoned veteran of the gambling wars, "having taken to the cards," according to one contemporary, "as soon as he could distinguish between the spots."

Arriving in Dodge from Cheyenne and Albuquerque, Denver and El Paso, Tucson and Omaha, were other well-known gambling men: Luke Short, Nat Kramer, Charlie Ronan, Ed Ryan, Walter Hart, "Doctor" Neil, Tom O'Brien, Jack Regis, John Sheridan, Lon Hyatt, Johnny Green, Tom Lane, Dave St. Clair, W. H. Bennett, "Cock-eyed Frank" Loving, and "Colonel" Charlie Norton.

Norton's most celebrated feat while in Dodge was separating a former governor of the state from all he owned. In March, 1877, Thomas Carney of Leavenworth, who had served as governor of Kansas during the turbulent war years, came to Dodge City as a buyer of buffalo hides for a Saint Louis firm. In a short time he found himself in a poker game with Norton, Charlie Ronan, and a tinhorn named Robert Gilmore, known more commonly as Bobby Gill. In due course Carney found himself in possession of what appeared to be an unbeatable hand, four kings and the "cuter" or joker, which he took to be the ace of spades. He wagered heavily on this once-in-a-lifetime hand, of course, and tried mightily to conceal his delight when Colonel Norton repeatedly raised his bets. Gill and Ronan were long gone from the hand, but Norton was still persisting when Carney threw his last dollar into the huge pot and added his gold watch and chain, shirt studs, cuff links, and money clip. Triumphantly he spread his four kings upon the table.

"But at that moment," according to an account of the game in the pages of the *Dodge City Times*, "a sight met the old Governor's gaze which caused his eyes to dilate with terror, a fearful tremor to seize his frame, and his vitals to almost freeze with horror." Laid before Norton were "four genuine and perfectly formed aces."

That night the eastbound freight train out of Dodge bore a broken old man, "without shirt studs or other ornament, apparently bowed down by overwhelming grief," and, concluded the *Times*'s story: "Gov. Carney is not buying bones and hides in this city any more."[5]

Most of the gunmen who gave Dodge City its first notoriety and whose real and fancied adventures spawned countless dime novel tales, books, slick magazine articles, and motion picture and television dramas, were professional gamblers. Many served as law officers in Dodge and elsewhere, but their first allegiance was always to the gaming table. The progression usually went as follows: A young gambler, in order to protect himself among hard-bitten, gun-toting frontiersmen, practiced daily the fine art of the draw-and-shoot; inevitably he was challenged at his game and downed his man; a reputation as a fast man with a gun was attached to him; a job riding herd on troublemakers in a border town was offered, and he accepted because a marshal's position afforded him a steady income while still providing time to pursue his first calling of gambling.

Some sporting men, when play slowed or they experienced long runs of bad luck, turned to other fields. They worked as bartenders, stagecoach drivers, teamsters, hunters, guides, undertakers, and whoremongers. They peddled real estate, patent medicines, mining stock, and gold bricks. They practiced law, turned outlaw, opened banks, and held up banks. Some practiced dentistry and pulled out teeth; others hired out as bouncers and knocked out teeth.

But it was in the role of the quick-shooting frontier lawman that many western gamblers gained renown, and the names of some who opted for this job are well known today, a hundred years later. Bat Masterson, Wyatt Earp, and Doc Holliday gained a kind of immortality as frontier lawmen, and all three were gamblers by profession. Other sporting men who operated in Dodge during its bravura period and wore the tin star there or elsewhere included Ben Thompson, Josh Webb, Al Updegraff, Nat Haywood, Joe Mason, Mysterious Dave Mather, Charlie Bassett, George Goodell, Jack Allen, Billy Brooks, and Jack Bridges.

Bat Masterson, whose nickname derived from a shortening of his given name, Bartholomew, was a Canadian-born farm boy who left home as a teenager to hunt buffalo on the plains of western Kansas, fought Indians as a scout under General Miles, and drew his fame as a peace officer primarily from a two-year stint as sheriff of Ford County, headquartered at Dodge City. Less well-remembered were four other Masterson brothers, Ed, Jim, Tom, and George, all of whom saw service at the Dodge City tables during these years and who were sometime law officers in Kansas, Colorado, New Mexico, and Oklahoma. Ed Masterson, the oldest brother, lost his life in a fracas with drunken cowboys while acting as city marshal of Dodge.

There were five Earp brothers also; James, Virgil, Wyatt, Morgan, and Warren. Originally from Illinois, they were prominent in Wichita sporting circles before moving on to Dodge and points west. All of the brothers, with the exception of James, were destined to become deeply involved in the violent history of Tombstone, Arizona.

Doc Holliday was a Georgian who drifted west and turned to professional gambling when his dental practice suffered as a result of his consumptive cough. He was an undistinguished house dealer in Dallas and Denver before meeting Wyatt Earp at Fort Griffin, Texas. For some reason Earp took a liking to the pale, cadaverous Holliday who, by all accounts, was an ill-tempered sort. Doc followed Earp to Dodge City and later to Tombstone.

Of all gambling men operating in Dodge in its heyday, however, none perhaps was more famous at the time than English-

Ben Thompson, respected in the cowtowns as equally dexterous with a deck or with a gun. Courtesy Western History Collections, University of Oklahoma Library.

born and Texas-reared Benjamin F. Thompson. A medium-sized man with dark curly hair, waxed mustaches and small goatee, Ben Thompson is best remembered today for his six-shooter exploits, but for twenty years he was one of the most popular gambling men in the West. The cattlemen who favored his table found him to be a straight-dealing, intelligent, congenial, generous gambler, albeit a dangerous man to cross.

Born at Knottingly, England, November 11, 1843, he came to Texas with his parents and was throughout his lifetime militantly pro-Texan. In his early teens he apprenticed as a printer's devil at Austin, but the fascination of the gambling tables soon caught him and by the time he was eighteen he was gambling professionally. His reputation as a dangerous and efficient man-killer was established early. At the age of eighteen he is reported to have killed a Frenchman named Emil DeTour in a knife duel at New Orleans.

With the outbreak of the Civil War he enlisted in the Second Regiment, Texas Cavalry. Two of his comrades-in-arms were his younger brother Billy and a very tall, handsome young man named Phil Coe, both of whom were to be associated with Ben in cow town gambling during the postwar years.

Gambling was not entirely unknown to the rebel cavalrymen, of course, and Ben managed to keep his hand in while serving the Confederacy. His unit was deployed for some time along the Rio Grande, and Thompson opened Spanish monte banks at several locations. At first he allowed only "Americans" to play at this game, barring those he called "Mexicans," although all were Texans serving in the same regiment. This discrimination was not so much because of Thompson's ethnic bias as it was respect for the ability of the Mexicans at the game of Spanish monte. "Mexicans are inveterate monte players and perhaps the shrewdest in the world." Thompson was quoted by his lawyer, friend, and biographer, Buck Walton. "When they think they have the advantage they bet very high and will risk not only their money but their clothing and their very liberty."[6]

At Eagle Pass, after cleaning out the Americans in camp, he reluctantly opened his game to the Mexicans, later reporting ruefully:

In less than five hours I did not have a cent. I even put up my silver spurs and gold cord that ornamented my hat. It was of no use, money, spurs, hat, cord, and all went, and the cigarette-smoking devils grinned as they won. A picked chicken, a scalded cat, a Georgia major, each was better fitted to walk abroad than I was. When that hatless, barefooted, one gallus thing called luck frowns, a man sins against good gambling if he don't quit.[7]

Later at Laredo he opened another game with a $300 stake advanced him by a friend. His luck had changed and he won $1,200 in an evening. The next night the Mexicans were back at him again. When they ran out of cash, Thompson permitted them to bet their revolvers. He allowed $22.00 for a Colt, $18.50 for a Remington, and $16.00 for a double-action pistol. By midnight the Mexicans were without sidearms and Thompson had an arsenal of twenty-three revolvers.

With the close of the war, Thompson returned to Austin but was soon in trouble with the "blue-belly" Union troops who had imposed martial law in the Texas towns. He enlisted as a mercenary in the forces of Emperor Maximilian, then struggling to retain his rule in Mexico. In 1867, Thompson was back in Austin where he opened a gambling room in a fine saloon owned by his old friend Phil Coe and the latter's partner, Tom Bowles.

By 1868 he was ready for greener fields. He went to Bryan, Texas, and faced a man named King in a memorable monte game. King was the owner of the leading saloon in Bryan, the Blue Wing, and was renowned as a plunger. Thompson challenged him to a no-limit monte game and King accepted. With Thompson dealing and King betting, the game went on through the early afternoon, continued through that evening and night, the next day and night, and finally ended on the morning of the third day, with neither player, it is said, having stopped the game once for food, drink, or rest. When the final card was turned and King lost, Thompson was the owner of the Blue Wing and all its stock and furnishings.

He was not to run the saloon for long, however. Several nights later, three embittered gamblers who had lost heavily at Thompson's tables, returned to the Blue Wing after closing hours. They knocked the heads from the whiskey barrels, smashed the glassware, and scattered cigars over the whiskey-flooded floor. Thompson disposed of the vandalized saloon for what he could get and returned to Austin.

During the war Thompson had married an Austin girl named Catherine Moore. He had never liked Catherine's brother James and on several occasions the brothers-in-law had exchanged heated words. Finally, on September 2, 1868, Thompson shot and wounded James Moore. In October he was tried and found guilty of assault with intent to kill and was sentenced to four years at the Texas State Penitentiary at Huntsville.

Pardoned by President Grant in 1870, he left Texas to ply his gambling trade in the Kansas cow towns. He arrived in Abilene in the spring of 1871 as the town was preparing for the summer invasion of Texas drovers. Low on funds when he struck town, Thompson was forced to play a conservative game, waiting for a streak of luck. Three times he had to pawn his revolver to obtain working capital. Finally, he felt fortune moving his way and pushed it for all he could. When he arose from the table he was $2,583 ahead. About that time Phil Coe showed up in Abilene with several thousand dollars in his poke. The two Texans pooled their resources and opened a gambling saloon on First Street which they called the Bull's Head. From its opening this place was a favorite of the Texas cattlemen, and for several months the partners enjoyed a bonanza. There was some talk around town of trouble brewing between the two former Confederates and City Marshal Wild Bill Hickok, the former Yankee scout and spy. There were those, no doubt, who would have enjoyed seeing a showdown gunfight between the premier pistoleers of North and South, Hickok and Thompson, but they were to be disappointed. Thompson was on his good behavior in Abilene and welcomed Union veterans like Hickok, Dick Clark, and Jim Moon to his tables.

There was one confrontation between the two gunmen, with overtones more comic than tense. Marshal Hickok called on Thompson and informed him that there had been complaints by townsmen about the sign on the front of the Bull's Head, a painted representation of a bull with all anatomical features included. The organs that made the bull a bull had been greatly exaggerated, Hickok said, and some folks found the picture offensive. Thompson laughed and reminded the marshal that this was a Texas bull and everything grew big in Texas, but Hickok was adamant and would not leave until the offending parts were painted out.

Business was going well for the firm of Thompson and Coe, and believing that the gambling operation in Abilene would continue to prosper for some time to come, Ben sent for his wife and small son to join him in the Kansas cow town. For some reason, though, tragedy was always hanging low over Ben Thompson's head. In Kansas City where he went to meet the train bringing his family, there was a buggy accident. Ben's leg was broken, his son's foot was crushed, and Kate Thompson suffered the loss of an arm. Sadly, Thompson took his family back to Austin.

Meanwhile, in Abilene, Ben was losing his business partner. On the night of October 5, Wild Bill Hickok shot Phil Coe dead in front of the Alamo Saloon. There was talk that the two men had been rivals for the affections of a woman of the town named Jessie Hazel, but it was clear that the Texan and the Yankee required no romantic triangle to precipitate their gunfight; they had been natural enemies from the start.

Deeply depressed by the double shock of his family's misfortune and the death of his friend and partner, Ben Thompson remained in Austin for almost a year, passing up the cattle shipping season of 1872 in the Kansas cow towns. In 1873 he went north again, this time to Ellsworth. He was joined there by Billy Thompson, who was perhaps even more trouble-prone than his elder brother. One day in mid-August at the height of the season, Ben got into a dispute with gambler John Sterling over the division of the spoils of a game. The local police interfered, Ben thought unfairly, and threats and challenges were made. Ben, who was unarmed at the time, retired to strap on his iron. He was joined by brother Billy, sodden with liquor and carrying Ben's shotgun. Billy was ready to take on the whole town. In the street the brothers were approached by Sheriff Chauncey Whitney, who was friendly to the Thompsons and was playing the role of peacemaker. In the excitement Billy's shotgun discharged accidentally, killing Whitney.

The town was in an uproar. Billy rode out while Ben forted up at the Grand Central Hotel, anticipating an attack by his enemies and the Ellsworth constabulary. Finally emotions cooled and Ben gave up his guns.

Billy Thompson made good his escape to Texas but was outlawed in Kansas for several years. Late in 1876 he was arrested in Texas and extradited to Kansas, where, at a trial in 1877, he was acquitted of the murder of Sheriff Whitney.

During the cattle-shipping season of 1874, Ben Thompson dealt a game in Whitey Rupp's Keno Hall in Wichita. He was the house dealer at Dodge City's Long Branch in 1875. Somehow his proclivity for violence was kept under control in Kansas but surfaced again back home in Austin. On Christmas Day, 1876, he shot and killed the proprietor of the Capital Theatre in Austin, Mark Wilson, and seriously wounded Wilson's bartender. The following May he stood trial for this killing and was found not guilty of murder.

During the years of the great cattle drives, the Kansas cow towns were, to the gamblers working them, places of either feast or famine. In the summer when the cattlemen were on hand, money was plentiful and action at the tables almost nonstop. With the coming of fall and the departure of the cowboys, the sporting life slowed to a crawl. Most gamblers left for warmer and friendlier climes, but some wintered in the trail towns and their plight was amusingly depicted in the *Dodge City Times* of February 23, 1878:

The festive sportsman is as keenly sensitive to the stringency in the money market as the merchant or mechanic. . . . His bank roll which last summer he flashed on every available occasion, now scarce ever sees the light of day, and when it does its diminished proportions frighten his landlord, his washer-woman and even himself, stern and bold as he is. In the place of 20's and 50's he has ones and twos, and only occasionally does a "five-caser" meet his piercing eye. . . . Time is more plentiful with him than anything else. He sits around in the sun during the day, or near some friendly stove by night, he relates to his comrades the thrilling scenes and incidents of his past chequered career—tells of the days when he won and lost by the thousands and wore a diamond pin. At the recollection of those past flush times he says, "d——n such country as this, the Black Hills for me." But after a second thought he takes it all back and concludes to wait for the cattle trade.

The summer of 1878 was the high point of Dodge City's reign as the queen of cow towns. The gambling fraternity, including both Thompson brothers, was there in force, but by the fall of that year the talk among sporting men was all of Leadville, the new bonanza camp high in the Colorado Rockies. Ben Thompson made several trips to the mining town that winter, partnered by Frank Cotton and others. He was looking for investment opportunity and in a letter to an Austin newspaper in March described the town of Leadville:

It is a city of 10 or 15 thousand inhabitants, of which 2500 are ladies. . . . One variety man pays for his house seventeen hundred dollars per month rent and at least two thousand a week for performers. He takes in about six or seven hundred a night for drinks at $5 a bottle in the conversation parlors, where the visitors are entertained by the lady performers. Of gambling houses it is useless to speak as there are so many and all so crowded that you cannot pass through them from morning to morning; they never close. Houses for sporting and saloon business rent for 5 to 10 hundred per month. . . . Drinks are 25 cents, 25 cents for a shave, water is 50 cents a barrel. Bedrooms, 10 by 12 in size, scantily furnished, rent for 60 dollars a month.[8]

Ben found that most faro banks in Leadville ranged in amount from $500 to $2,000, and dealers limited single card bets to $25, but there were proprietors who would take the limit off for the real high rollers and bets of $10,000 on the turn of a card were not unknown. Faro banks in Leadville averaged $1,000 profit per month.

During the town's peak years more than one hundred fifty assorted resorts—saloons, dance halls, restaurants, theaters, and concert halls—provided gambling opportunities for patrons. Some of the better known were the Olympic, the Opera House Club, the Little Casino, Coleman's Place, the Canterbury, the Grand Union, Louie Mitchell's, the Coliseum, the Belle Union, Cole and Alexander's Dance Hall, the Chestnut, and the Little Globe. At the Comique, the Grand Central

Theater, and Miss Mable Rivers' Gaiety Theater, burlesque skits, vaudeville acts, and minstrel shows entertained customers between bouts with the tiger. In 1879, Eddie Foy was the headliner at Tom Kemp's Dance and Gambling Hall. St. Anne's Rest offered variety, with tables running around the clock for faro, keno, paddle-wheel, and chuck-a-luck.

Some of the houses, in an effort to attract a high-class clientele, strove to achieve an atmosphere of taste and elegance. The Church Casino featured a Gothic window, and the Carbonate Concert Hall had living pines within its walls providing "cozy arbors and grottos," and on a small stage Miss Mollie Newton, billed as "the most perfectly formed woman in America," presented a "series of tableaux representing Greek and Roman statuary." On the other hand, down-to-earth Pop Wyman, proprietor of the Great Saloon, hung a large sign over his bar that read: "Don't Shoot the Pianist—He's Doing His Darndest."

The most popular places were the Board of Trade Saloon, the California Concert Hall, and the Texas House. George W. Silks, tall and dark, with cavernous eyes and a magnificent longhorn mustache, presided over the Board of Trade where high-stake stud-horse poker was the house specialty. Jeff Winney's California Hall featured beautiful Kitty Crawhurst, lady faro dealer. Bailey Youngston and "Con" Featherly, late of Galveston, were the owners of the Texas House, where a dozen faro tables were available twenty-four hours a day. Floor manager at their place was John Pentland, veteran of Virginia City, Nevada, who would take over the dealer's box for the serious gamblers. It was said that Pentland won more than $80,000 for the house during the first few months of his employment.

Ben Thompson did not find the business opportunity he sought in any of these places, but, not surprisingly, he did find trouble in Leadville. One night he dropped more than $3,000 in a faro game. Infuriated, he turned over the table, unlimbered his Colt, and shot out the lights. In seconds he stood alone in the darkened room, the crowd having vacated the premises in a rush. Thompson sauntered across the street to a saloon, ordered a drink, and remarked that some sort of commotion seemed to have transpired across the way. When city officers placed him under arrest, he went along without argument, paid the fine, and settled for the damages.

While in Colorado, Thompson became involved in the Royal Gorge War, a struggle between the Denver & Rio Grande Railroad and the Atchinson, Topeka & Santa Fe for the rights to build a line through the Royal Gorge of the Arkansas River to the new silver fields at Leadville. While the battle was being fought in the courts, officials of both railroads enlisted fighting men to take and hold strategic positions along the line. A corps of gunmen recruited in the saloons and gambling halls of Dodge City, led by Bat Masterson and Ben Thompson, entered the field for the Atchinson, Topeka & Santa Fe. In the end the dispute was settled with little bloodshed, but Ben Thompson was reported to have been paid $5,000 for his services. Back in Austin he used the money to buy the gambling concession in the rooms above John Neff's Iron Front Saloon at Sixth and Congress streets and to buy into various gambling houses in other Texas towns.

His gaming interests prospered, but Ben Thompson began to drink more heavily and his wild shooting sprees became more frequent. One night while in his cups he wandered into the faro room of the Iron Front where his house dealer, a man named Lorraine, was methodically cleaning out all challengers. Thompson watched for a few moments and then suddenly jerked his pistol and shot each stack of chips off the

This elaborate "Monkey Magician Gambling Device" was featured in the Iron Front Saloon in Austin, Texas, when Ben Thompson held sway there. Created in France by skilled automaton artisans, it enabled gamblers to bet on the dice as thrown by a mechanical monkey garbed as a magician. Fortunately for collectors, Thompson spared it in his shooting sprees and today it is highly valued as a unique curiosity of the period. Courtesy of Auctions by Theriault, Waverly, Pennsylvania.

table. He then blasted the dealer's box and emptied his weapon into the hanging lamps. When the startled players regained some of their composure, Thompson explained: "I don't think that set of tools is altogether honest, and I want to help Mr. Lorraine buy another."

The incident seemed to whet Thompson's appetite for more target practice. Reloading his six-shooter, he went next door to Solomon Simon's keno establishment and shot the "goose," the cage containing the ivory keno balls. He shot out the lamps and laughed as the patrons scurried for cover. Following them outside, he marched down the center of the street, shooting out streetlights as he went. He didn't stop until his ammunition was exhausted. The next morning he appeared at the mayor's office, apologized for his behavior, and paid his fine.

The most notorious escapade of this kind perpetrated by Thompson was the violent disruption of a dinner meeting of the Texas Live Stock Association in Austin. Enraged because of an affront to one of his friends by the members of the association, Thompson stormed into a Congress Street restaurant where Seth Mabry, Alonza Millett, Abel H. ("Shanghai") Pierce, and others, the foremost cattle ranchers of Texas, were gathered. Flourishing his pistol and breaking crockery, Ben cleared the room in a matter of seconds. Only Captain Lee Hall of the Texas Rangers remained in his chair. It was said that the six-feet, four-inch Shanghai Pierce exited through a window, taking the sash with him. Ben never fired his gun and the only casualties were a few dishes and the dignity of the dignitaries. The following day, when asked by a newsman to comment upon Thompson's behavior, Seth Mabry said, "I always thought, until last night, that Ben Thompson was a brave man, but I have changed my mind. If he had been a brave man, he would have attacked the whole convention when we were together and three thousand strong, but instead, he let nearly all of them get out of town, and cut off a little bunch of about forty of us, and jumped onto us."[9]

Despite his tantrums, Thompson was well liked in Austin and at an election in December, 1880, became city marshal of the town, running first in a field of five candidates. He proved to be a popular and efficient peace officer, his reputation as a swift and deadly pistoleer acting as a major deterrent to would-be badmen. During his term as chief lawman in the city of Austin, there were no cases of murder, burglary, or assault with intent to kill.

The year 1880 was notable also in the career of Ben Thompson as the year in which transpired the first of a connected series of incidents that culminated ultimately in his death. At the Vaudeville Theatre and Gambling Saloon, a notorious San Antonio resort, Ben got into a dispute with Joe Foster, the faro dealer. There are several versions of this incident, but most accounts agree that there was an argument over the value of some diamonds Thompson had risked in the game, and that Ben accused Foster of having cheated him.

The owner of the Vaudeville Theatre was a man named Jack Harris, as celebrated a figure in frontier sporting circles as Thompson himself. Harris had run away from his Connecticut home at the age of twelve and gone to sea. He turned up on the California coast in 1855 and joined William Walker's filibustering expedition into Nicaragua. There he almost met death before a firing squad but was saved by a timely rescue party. Harris settled in San Antonio and served as a city police officer. With the outbreak of the Civil War he joined the Second Texas Cavalry and saw action in a number of border clashes. His most notable exploit during the war was participation in the capture of a Union schooner off Galveston. Harris and four others boarded the vessel at night, overpowered the crew, and gorged themselves on the fine food and wines in the ship's stores before sailing her into port.

Returning to San Antonio after the war, Harris acquired interests in a number of the town's gaming establishments, finally opening the Vaudeville Theatre and Gambling Saloon on Commerce Street in January, 1869.

When Jack Harris learned of the difficulty between his faro dealer and Thompson, he let it be known that Thompson was banned from his establishment and that if he set foot inside he would be shot on sight. The two men met some time later in San Antonio's Green Front Saloon. Witnesses to that meeting would testify that Thompson confronted Harris and demanded to know if the report was true.

Jack Harris, who barred Ben Thompson from his gambling house and as a result fell victim to Thompson's quick gun. Courtesy Western History Collections, University of Oklahoma Library.

Jack Harris's Vaudeville Theatre and Gambling Saloon was housed in this building in San Antonio. The site came to be called "Fatal Corner." Courtesy Western History Collections, University of Oklahoma Library.

"Do you mean to say that I can't come in your house down there?"

"Ben," said Harris, "if you had a house and forbade me to go in it, I would not go around it."

That really did not answer the question and Thompson wanted it spelled out plainly.

"Do you say I can't go in your house?"

"No, you can't," replied Harris.

"Well," said Ben Thompson, "I'm coming to your house and if your doors are closed I am going to kick 'em down!"

He did not make good on his threat at that time, but a few months later he was again in San Antonio and headed for the Vaudeville. Harris was warned of his approach and took up a position just off the barroom, a shotgun in his right hand, the barrels resting in the crook of his left arm. During one of his earlier adventures he had suffered a crippling injury to his left hand but had shown on several occasions that he could make deadly use of a shotgun held in this fashion.

When Thompson entered the barroom, several patrons scurried out the back, one calling out a warning that Harris was waiting with a gun. A venetian blind screen across the room hid the proprietor from Thompson's view. Thompson stepped close to the screen and, peering through, made out the form of Harris, shotgun in hand. Ben called out and the San Antonio gambler hurled back a challenge. Thompson drew and fired through the blinds. Jumping to the side, he pumped two more bullets in the direction of Harris, but his first shot had done the work. Harris managed to stagger up the stairs to the theater before collapsing. He died later that night.

The following day Thompson surrendered to the authorities and at a trial in January, 1883, was found not guilty of murder.

The death of Jack Harris only intensified the hatred that had developed between Ben Thompson and the crowd at the San Antonio Vaudeville Theatre. Joe Foster and a former Austin gambler named Billy Simms took over the management of the establishment after the demise of Harris. Simms had once been a protege of Ben Thompson, and Thompson bitterly resented Simms's defection to the camp of his enemies, Harris and Foster.

In March, 1884, Thompson once again traveled from Austin to San Antonio, this time in the company of a former rustler turned lawman, Uvalde County Deputy Sheriff King Fisher. Having concluded some official business in the state capital, Fisher talked Thompson into taking the train with him back to San Antonio and making a call at the Vaudeville Theatre. Fisher was known to be friendly with both Joe Foster and Billy Simms, and although he and Thompson had had some disagreements in the past, these had been patched up and he was evidently on cordial terms with the Austin gambler. Perhaps Fisher was playing the role of peacemaker, bringing his pals together to settle their differences amicably.

Word of their coming preceded them and before the two gunmen reached San Antonio, Billy Simms had contacted the police chief and told him to expect trouble. Simms greeted Thompson and Fisher, shook hands, and had a drink with them

John King Fisher, shot dead in the Vaudeville Theatre with Ben Thompson. Courtesy Western History Collections, University of Oklahoma Library.

at the bar. The three men then went upstairs to the theater area where they were joined by Joe Foster and a special policeman in the employ of the house, Jacob Coy. The conversation was quiet and friendly at first but soon the men's voices began to rise angrily. Simms, Foster, and Coy stepped back from Thompson and Fisher. A fusillade of shots rang out. The room was suddenly filled with smoke as women screamed and men

W. H. "Billy" Simms, a principal in the Thompson and Fisher assassinations, later became a prominent San Antonio gambling figure. Courtesy Western History Collections, University of Oklahoma Library.

leaped from the balcony and tumbled down the stairs in their panic.

Captain Shardein of the San Antonio police was outside the building when he heard the shots. Running in, he met Simms, Foster, and Coy on the stairs. Simms was supporting the other two. Coy had taken a bullet in the hip and Foster was bleeding profusely from a leg wound. At the top of the stairs Ben Thompson and King Fisher lay in a pool of blood. Fisher had been struck by thirteen bullets and Thompson had been hit nine times. Both died instantly.

The following day a coroner's jury found that the deaths had resulted "from pistols held in and fired from the hands of J. C. Foster and Jacob S. Coy." It was further found that the killings were justifiable and done in self-defense. Ignored was an autopsy report disclosing that the dead men had received both rifle and pistol fire simultaneously from at least five different persons who were positioned above and to the left of them. Thompson's friends would always be convinced that he had been lured to the theater and there brutally murdered by hidden assassins. It was small comfort to them when the man they held most responsible for the outrage, Joe Foster, died a few days later after amputation of his shattered leg. Jacob Coy was permanently crippled by his hip wound and received financial help from Billy Simms until Coy's death in 1907.

William H. Harris, who partnered Dick Clark and Luke Short in gambling ventures in Tombstone and Dodge City. Courtesy Kansas State Historical Society.

Sooner or later, however prosperous a gambler may be, he meets with an untimely death; if not from the pistol or danger, then from fatal disease contracted by dissipation. . . . Every time a man sits down to a card game to gamble he takes his life in his hands and lays it between him and his adversary.

Ben Thompson
William M. Walton, *Life and Adventures of Ben Thompson*

By the close of the decade of the 1870s the greatest days of the Kansas cow towns as sporting men's centers had passed. Newton and Ellsworth, Abilene and Wichita were fast becoming stodgy farm communities, populated on a Saturday night by hay-balers rather than high rollers. Dodge City would enjoy a few more years as a cattleman's playground, and itinerant gamblers would try to make at least one stop in Dodge each summer as late as the mid-eighties, but it was clear to most of the sporting clan by late 1879 that the consistent big action would take place farther west, in the new mining camps of Colorado, New Mexico, and Arizona.

Dick Clark was one of the first to hear the call from a brand-new mining camp deep in the wilds of Arizona, a place called Tombstone. By early 1880 he was settled in the town that was to be his base of operations for the remainder of his life. In partnership with Lou Rickabaugh, a well-known San Francisco sporting man, and Bill Harris, formerly of the Long Branch in Dodge City, Clark leased the gambling rooms in the Oriental Saloon and Gambling Hall at the corner of Allen and Fifth streets in Tombstone.

When the Oriental opened for business in July, 1880, a writer for *The Epitaph*, one of the town's papers, described the scene in terms of rapture:

Last evening the portals were thrown open and the public permitted to gaze upon the most elegantly furnished saloon this side of the favored city of the Golden Gate. Twenty-eight burners suspended in neat chandeliers afforded an illumination of ample brilliancy, and the bright rays reflected from many colored crystals on the bar sprinkled like a December iceling in the sunshine. The saloon comprises two apartments. To the right of the main entrance is the bar, beautifully carved, finished in white and gilt and capped with handsomely polished top. In the rear of this stand a brace of sideboards which are simply elegant and must be seen to be appreciated. . . . The back apartment is covered with a brilliant body brussels carpet, and suitably furnished after the style of a grand club room with conveniences for the wily dealers in polished ivory. . . ."[1]

A number of former Dodge City luminaries dealt for Clark in the Oriental, including Bat Masterson, Luke Short, Wyatt Earp, and Doc Holliday. Masterson and Short did not stay long in Tombstone, but Earp and Holliday remained to become embroiled in the highly publicized vendetta that enlivened the history of the town during its early years.

Arrayed on one side were the Earp brothers and their pal Doc Holliday. The Earps held appointments as local peace officers and were supported by Mayor John Clum, his newspaper, *The Epitaph*, and many businessmen of the town. Because of their history of involvement with the sporting gentry, the Earps and Holliday were often referred to derisively as "the fighting pimps" by their enemies, who were for the most part men with cattle interests in the hills surrounding Tombstone. Foremost of these were the Clanton family, the McLaury brothers, "Curly Bill" Brocius, and John Ringo. Friends of these fellows called them "cowboys"; the Earps called them "rustlers." County Sheriff John Behan was sympathetic to the cowboy faction, as was the town's other paper, *The Nugget*.

The reasons for the feud were many. Politics certainly played a large part, as Behan and *The Nugget* were Democrats and Clum and the Earps were Republicans. Sectionalism was involved; the cowboys were southerners and the Earp brothers were northerners, and Civil War animosities still rankled. There was even a romantic triangle in the plot—Wyatt Earp and John Behan were rivals for the affections of a beautiful girl named Josephine Sarah Marcus. She had come to Tombstone to live with Behan but switched her affections to Wyatt and eventually married him. Finally, the gambling ambitions of John Behan and Wyatt Earp were a root source of their mutual antipathy.

The owner of the Oriental was a man named Mike Joyce who leased the gambling concession to the Clark-Rickabaugh-Harris combine. The gaming rooms of the establishment became so popular that other gamblers in town were aware of a noticeable decline in business. A group of them, led by Johnny Tyler, who sported a quick-gun reputation, began to disrupt the decorum of the Oriental on a nightly basis in an attempt to intimidate the clientele. The managers of the rooms, not known as gunmen, offered Wyatt Earp a quarter interest in the business if he would take care of Tyler and his friends. Earp leaped at the chance to get in on the bonanza at the Oriental, and the first time Tyler stepped out of line Wyatt threw him into the street with a warning not to return. Doc Holliday, following Wyatt's lead as always, tried to force a gunfight with Tyler, backed him down, and humiliated him to such an extent that he left town.

Mike Joyce, owner of the Oriental, was a political cohort of John Behan, which naturally put him at odds with Wyatt Earp and his shadow, Holliday. Any disagreement with the volatile former dentist usually meant gunplay, and Holliday unlimbered one evening, shooting Joyce in the hand and one of the bartenders in the foot. This disturbed Joyce, of course, and when the lease on the gambling rooms expired at the end of 1881, the firm of Clark, Rickabaugh, Harris, and Earp was requested to vacate. It came as no great surprise to the ousted gamblers to learn that the new manager of the Oriental gaming rooms was Sheriff John Behan.

Clark and Earp received information that the new operation was undercapitalized, with Behan's bankroll amounting to only $5,000. One night the two entered the hall and took seats at the faro table, which was presided over by a dealer named Fries. John Behan slid into the lookout's chair.[2] Earp exchanged $1,000 for chips and Clark kept cases. Other players withdrew to watch Wyatt buck the tiger. For an hour neither player nor house gained an advantage. Then Earp won ten straight turns. He pushed back his chair and announced that he was cashing in his checks.

"What's the matter?" asked Behan.

Wyatt tapped a finger on his stack of chips. "There's $6,000

John Behan, whose clashes with rival Wyatt Earp were political and economic but also involved a woman. Courtesy Library Archives and Public Records Division, State of Arizona.

here," he said. "I put a thousand into your cash drawer and you only had $5,000 to begin."

"That's all right, I'm good for anything you win," Behan said.

"I'll take mine in cash," Earp insisted. "Your credit with me doesn't cover a white chip."

Behan was forced to empty every money drawer and the safe in order to settle up with Earp and then watched as Wyatt divided the money with Dick Clark.

As a result of this loss, it was necessary for Behan to close down his tables until he could find some financial backing. His Oriental venture never turned much of a profit for the sheriff, and he always blamed Earp for getting him off to a bad start.

By late 1881 the bitterness between the two factions had grown to the point where something had to give, and give it did. In rapid succession came the famous fight at the O.K. Corral in which the two McLaury brothers and one Clanton were shot and killed by the Earps and Holliday, followed by the ambush of Virgil Earp on a Tombstone street that crippled him for life. Then came the assassination of Morgan Earp, and Wyatt's cold-blooded stalking of those he held responsible for Morgan's death, backed by Holliday and a coterie of gunmen. Quick victims of Wyatt's wrath were Frank Stilwell, a man known as "Indian Charlie," and Curly Bill. Some time later Johnny Ringo was killed mysteriously, but few in Tombstone doubted that Wyatt had called in his final debt.

Murder warrants were issued for Wyatt Earp and Doc Holliday and they were outlawed in Arizona after this sanguinary episode. They fled to Trinidad, Colorado, where Wyatt's old pal Bat Masterson was maintaining a gambling room and wearing the badge of city marshal. There Earp and Holliday finally parted company, Wyatt going to the Gunnison country, and Doc going to Denver, where a few days later he was arrested and held for extradition to Arizona. Masterson took the first train north, stopped over long enough in Pueblo to work up a fictitious bunco charge against Holliday with the local constabulary, and went on to the state capital. There he obtained an audience with the governor, convinced him that his

This is said to be a likeness of dentist-gambler-gunman John H. Holliday. If this isn't "Doc," it certainly is his double. Courtesy Jack DeMattos Collection.

trumped-up Pueblo bunco charge took precedence over a mere Arizona murder warrant, and got Holliday released.

For five more years the consumptive dentist drifted through the Colorado mining camps, getting into minor gun scrapes from time to time and eking out a bare subsistence at the tables. By 1887 his frail body was completely ravaged by tuberculosis and alcoholism, and in November he died at a sanitarium at Glenwood Springs. He was thirty-five years old.

Wyatt Earp, after parting from Holliday at Trinidad, went to Gunnison where he banked a faro game in Charlie Biebel's saloon. An incident that took place in Gunnison is illustrative of the kind of man Earp was and the way he dealt with hardcases. A gambler in camp named Ike Morris had a local reputation as a mean man with a gun. One day while Earp was absent, Morris sat down at his table, placed a pile of bills on a card, and told Wyatt's dealer to turn. After a few turns the card won for the bank and the dealer picked up the wagered money. Morris immediately set up a howl, claiming the cards were crooked, and demanded his money back. The dealer replied that he was not authorized to return the bet, that he only worked for wages, and that Morris must see Wyatt Earp if he had a complaint. When Earp returned, Morris confronted him, insisting that he had been cheated and demanding restitution. Wyatt heard him out and said that he would talk to his employee about the problem. He conferred with the dealer and was assured that the cards were honest and Morris had been given a square deal. By now the word had spread that a showdown was imminent between the two gunmen, with fireworks likely, and a large crowd had gathered.

Wyatt walked back to where Morris waited. "You were right," he said. The dealer had admitted cheating, continued Earp, and for that reason he felt very much like returning Morris's money. "However," he went on, "you are looked upon in these parts as something of a bad man, and if I give you back your money it will be said that you made me do it. Therefore, I am going to keep it."

The next move was clearly up to Morris. He stared at Earp for a few moments, then laughed nervously and offered to buy the drinks. His reputation destroyed, and unable to cope with this obloquy, Morris vanished from Gunnison a few days later.[3]

For about a year Earp operated his faro games in the Colorado mining towns of Gunnison, Ouray, Silverton, and Aspen. He was at Silverton when Bat Masterson showed up with the news that Luke Short was in trouble back in Dodge City and could use a little help from his friends.

Luke Short, a soft-spoken, dapper little man, had been born in Mississippi and raised in Texas. As a teenager he had driven longhorns to the Kansas railheads, where he became fascinated by the nimble-fingered, well-dressed sporting men behind the gambling tables in the saloons. He had early resolved to become one of them. For a few years most of the wages he earned as cowpuncher, scout and dispatch-runner for the army, and whiskey peddler, disappeared over the tables as Short paid his dues to learn the trade. By the late 1870s, however, he was a house dealer for Chalk Beeson and Bill Harris, the owners of the Long Branch Saloon in Dodge City. In 1881 he was at Tombstone, dealing his game in the Oriental, and it was here that he had his first serious six-gun encounter of record.

His adversary was gambler Charlie Storms, a seasoned veteran of thirty years on the frontier and a dozen border hellholes. Born in New Orleans, Storms had been in on the California gold rush and had made a great deal of money on the Pacific Slope in the 1850s by means of a crooked faro box. Back in the eastern states he proceeded to dissipate the fortune in a life of debauchery. Returning to the frontier, he became a familiar figure in Cheyenne, Deadwood, Leadville, and Denver. During these years he had been involved in several celebrated gunfights and, having survived them all, was considered a very dangerous man to cross.

Storms attempted to bully the diminutive Short one morning in the Oriental and pistols were about to be drawn when Bat Masterson jumped between the two and attempted to cool the situation. He led Storms back to his hotel room and had just returned to the saloon when Storms suddenly reappeared. Storms grabbed Short by the arm, at the same time clawing for his pistol. Luke Short got his weapon into action first, and

Diminutive, sartorially elegant Luke Short, a dangerous gambler to cross as several men learned too late. Courtesy Kansas State Historical Society.

Storms was dead when he hit the ground. Short was cleared of murder charges at a hearing in Tucson, and soon thereafter went back to Dodge City.

Bill Harris also had returned to the Kansas cow town after the dissolution of his partnership with Dick Clark, Lou Rickabaugh, and Wyatt Earp in the Oriental gambling rooms. Harris renewed his association with Chalk Beeson in the Long Branch Saloon, taking on Short as chief house dealer. In February, 1883, Beeson sold out his interest to Short, and for the first time the little Texan had a piece of the action.

Two months later Bill Harris was defeated in his bid for the office of mayor of Dodge and within a matter of days the new mayor, Larry Deger, elected on a reform ticket, began a campaign to run Luke Short out of town. Three female entertainers in the Long Branch were arrested and charged with prostitution. Luke paid their fines but noticed that women working in saloons kept by Deger's political cronies were not molested by the city police. He went looking for the city officials and the first he found was police officer Lou Hartman, who had assisted in the arrests of the Long Branch women. Short accosted the officer and shots were fired. Hartman, in his rush to leave the scene, tumbled into the street. Short thought he had killed the man. He returned to his saloon and forted up with a shotgun. He was finally talked into surrendering when he learned that Hartman was unhurt, but once he gave up his guns he was marched to the railroad station by a large body of armed men and given his choice of eastbound or westbound trains. Banished from Dodge at the same time were fellow gamblers Tom Lane, W. H. Bennett, Doc Neil, Johnny Gallagher, and L. A. Hyatt.

Short chose the eastbound train and went to Kansas City, where he placed a wire to Bat Masterson in Denver. Masterson hurried to Kansas City, and at Joe Bassett's Marble Hall the two gamblers discussed the unfair treatment Short had received at Dodge. Bat, remembering the success of his appeal to the governor of Colorado on behalf of Doc Holliday, suggested that Short go to Topeka and plead his case before Kansas Governor George Washington Glick. While Short was in Topeka, Bat scurried around Kansas and Colorado, rounding up fighting men to help take Dodge by storm if necessary to establish Luke Short's rights.

Glick fired off a series of telegrams to the officials at Dodge City and received a number in return, but the situation was hopelessly unclear to him when he was called upon again by Short, accompanied by Masterson who had joined his friend in the state capital. Wrote Bat of that meeting some years later: "We stated to the Governor that we believed we were able to rehabilitate ourselves in Dodge, but didn't care to run afoul of state authorities. . . . The governor told us to go ahead and re-establish ourselves, if we could; that he would keep off, and wished us luck."[4]

So it was that Wyatt Earp's aid was enlisted and he found himself a few days later in Caldwell, Kansas, meeting in a council of war with other members of the sporting brethren who were known to be adept with a sixshooter. Besides Bat Masterson and Luke Short, there were Charlie Bassett, Johnny Green, Texas Jack Vermillion, Dan Tipton, Johnny Millsap, Neal Brown, Shotgun Collins, and Frank McLain.

Kinsley, a town just east of Dodge City, was selected as the forward staging area from which the attack on Dodge would be mounted. Earp, backed by Green, Vermillion, Tipton and Millsap, was to enter the town by train. Bassett, Collins, Brown, and McLain would approach from different directions on horseback. Short and Masterson would remain at Kinsley, awaiting word from the forward elements that the town was secured before coming in.

The entire affair of Luke Short versus Dodge City had received considerable attention in the Kansas papers, which were calling it the "Dodge City War." Reports in these papers of an army of murderous cutthroats descending on the cow town had many of the citizens of Dodge in a near-panic. Wyatt Earp and company met no resistance on their arrival and, at a meeting with Mayor Deger and other city officials, were assured that Luke Short could return to his place of business any time he so desired. Short and Masterson came into town the next day and, surrounded by backslapping well-wishers, strode triumphantly to the Long Branch, where peace reigned supreme and drinks were had all around.

Five months after the bloodless "Dodge City War," Luke Short and Bill Harris sold the Long Branch. The glory days of the queen of cow towns were drawing to a close, and as in all frontier communities that turned humdrum, the gamblers were the first to sense the change. Short and Harris sold out on November 19, 1883. The *Dodge City Times* of November 22 noted, "The business of gambling is shaky in Dodge and is almost shook out entirely."

Luke Short returned to Texas and bought an interest in the White Elephant Saloon in Fort Worth. He maintained the gambling rooms on the second floor of this Main Street establishment, managed by Jake Johnson.

In February, 1887, Jim Courtright, a former city marshal of Fort Worth and a gunslinger of wide reputation, was operating a private detective agency in the city. He was using this agency as a front to shake down saloon and gambling house owners for "protection." Luke Short refused to pay for this protection, telling Courtright that he could provide his own. The dispute culminated in a gunfight on the sidewalk a few doors away from the White Elephant. After the two had exchanged harsh words Courtright went for his gun, but Short got his pistol out of his specially designed leather-lined pocket first and Courtright was a dead man. Short spent one night in jail after this killing, was released on $2,000 bond, and the matter, a clear case of self-defense, never came to trial.

Luke Short was undisputed top dog of square, high-stakes gambling in Fort Worth and operated several clubrooms "uptown" where he catered to professional and civic leaders of the city who liked to match their luck and skill against Short and other gambling celebrities. Reformers were constantly applying pressure on city officials to suppress gambling, and Short, feeling his business threatened, tended to vent his indignation on the operators of the crooked houses "downtown." Foremost of these was a man named Charlie Wright who had run brace games in Omaha, Dodge City, and Las Vegas, New Mexico, before opening a skinning house for suckers over the Bank Saloon in Fort Worth.

One night in December, 1890, Short went down to Wright's place, showed his pistol, and ordered the dealers and patrons to "skin out." The little man turned over tables, smashed wheels, broke up the furniture, and was standing alone amid the debris, everyone having "skinned," when he was shot from behind by a shotgun in the hands of Charlie Wright. Buckshot struck his left leg and took away part of his left thumb, but Short wheeled and snapped off a shot at the retreating form of Wright, fracturing his wrist.

This was to be Luke Short's last hurrah. Shortly after the Wright fracas he developed dropsy, which grew progressively worse. On September 8, 1893, at the age of thirty-nine, he died at a health spa at Geuda Springs, Kansas.

Wyatt Earp and Bat Masterson, after the Dodge City war of 1883, resumed their travels along the pathways of the western gamblers' circuit, which was in full flower in the decade of the eighties. Scattered throughout the West at this time were dozens of "good" towns, wide-open new communities where money was plentiful and "true-blue sports" abounded who were willing to take a risk on the turn of a card. From Dead-wood in South Dakota to San Antonio in Texas, and from Virginia City, Nevada, to Omaha, Nebraska, the Great Plains and mountain region of the West was studded with "wide-awake" towns: Cheyenne in Wyoming; Denver, Leadville, Pueblo, and Trinidad in Colorado; Dodge City, Wichita, and Kansas City in Kansas; Albuquerque, Taos, Silver City, Santa Fe, and Las Vegas in New Mexico; Tucson, Tombstone, Phoenix, Globe, and Prescott in Arizona; and in Texas, San Antonio, Tascosa, El Paso, Austin, Dallas, and Fort Worth.

The riders of the circuit moved from one to another, gener-ally with the seasons; the northern mining camps got the big play in the summer, the southern towns in the winter months. But news of unusual activity—a cattlemen's convention in Dallas, perhaps, or a new rich ore strike in the Leadville dis-trict—would bring them hustling from a thousand miles away. They were known by sight wherever they went and were wel-comed enthusiastically by the townsmen, for it was an article of faith on the frontier that the degree of prosperity of a town was in direct proportion to the number of high-rolling gam-blers on hand at a given time.

W. B. "Bat" Masterson, circuit gambler, was said to be "the best known man between the Mississippi and the Pacific Coast." Courtesy Kansas State Historical Society.

Wyatt Earp played the circuit for several years in the mid-eighties before settling down, more or less permanently, in San Diego, where he had interests in three gambling houses. In partnership with Eli Gifford, a noted Tucson gambler, he acquired a stable of Thoroughbreds, and in the late eighties and early nineties was a prominent figure in Pacific Coast racing circles. In 1896, Earp refereed the Bob Fitzsimmons–Tom Sharkey prizefight in San Francisco, which ended in uproar when Wyatt stopped the bout in the eighth round and awarded the victory to Sharkey—who had been given little chance to win—on a low blow foul. Those who had bet on Fitzsimmons set up a howl that the fight was fixed, and their suspicions turned to certainty when high-rolling gambler Riley Grannan contended that he had personal knowledge that Earp had wagered a bundle on Sharkey. Wyatt himself had little to say, but his wife later insisted that his decision cost him money because he had bets placed on Fitzsimmons that he was unable to cancel after being selected as referee. Grannan had lost a great deal of money to Wyatt at cards previously, she said, and spread the story out of spite. Bat Masterson defended Earp in this controversy, both at the time and later, and his testimony carried weight, for it was known that he had lost heavily on the fight.

Late in 1897, Earp joined the rush to the Klondike. At Nome, in partnership with Charlie Hoxie, he opened the Dexter Saloon, which he advertised as "The Only Second-Class Saloon in Alaska." In 1901 he sold out his interest to Hoxie and returned to the States, bringing back with him net profits amounting to some eighty-five thousand dollars.

In 1902 he was in the new mining camp of Tonopah, Nevada, where he opened the Northern Saloon. He was at Goldfield, Nevada, in 1905, and this was to be his last boomtown. A year later he settled down in Los Angeles, where he lived out his last years quietly, dying in 1929 at the age of eighty.

Bat Masterson, Wyatt's lifelong friend, had also dealt in the Oriental Saloon in Tombstone back in 1880. He left the Arizona mining town suddenly in 1881 in response to an urgent message from Dodge City that brother Jim was in trouble with two saloonmen named A. J. Peacock and Al Updegraff and that powder was about to be burned. By stage and by rail Bat hurried back to Kansas, and as he swung down from the train at Dodge he came face to face with his brother's enemies. Somebody pulled a gun, and in seconds lead was flying in the Dodge City Plaza. When the smoke cleared, Updegraff was down with a bullet through the lungs. Masterson and Peacock were unhurt. Bat was arrested and ordered out of town. He went to Trinidad, Colorado, accepted an appointment as city marshal, and opened up a faro game. A year later he transferred his base of operations to Denver after being defeated for reelection. He was still persona non grata in Dodge City when he received Luke Short's appeal for help after being ousted from the cowboy capital, and, by getting Short back in, Masterson reestablished himself also. Bat was in and out of the cow town often during the eighties and, at a Fourth of July celebration in 1885, was voted the most popular man in Dodge and awarded a gold-headed cane and a gold watch chain.

About this time the editor of a Dodge City paper was calling Masterson "The Boss Gambler of the West."[5] This may have been an exaggeration, but it is true that Bat was as celebrated and respected as any follower of the gamblers' circuit. The *New York Times* would report at the time of his death that during these years he "was said to have been the best known man between the Mississippi and the Pacific Coast."[6] As for his success at the tables, in 1890 in a letter to Frank D. Baldwin, with whom he had served in the Red River Indian War of 1874, Bat wrote:

I can't say that I have been prosperous, although I have not suffered much from adversity. . . . I have been connected nearly all the time . . . in the gambling business and have experienced the vicissitudes which has always characterized the business. Some days—plenty, and more days—nothing. . . . I came into the world without anything and I have about held my own up to date.[7]

Several years earlier, Masterson had acquired the Palace, a combination gambling saloon and vaudeville theater that had been something of a Denver institution for over twenty years.

About 1890 a group of reformers, led by the Reverend

Henry Hart, mounted one of their periodic campaigns against vice in Denver. Hart singled out the Palace for his fulminations, calling it a "death-trap to young men, a foul den of vice and corruption." Masterson, at the moment disillusioned with Denver, sold the Palace and, in 1891, moved on to Creede, a new boom camp sprouting high in the San Juan Mountains. There he managed the gambling rooms of the Denver Exchange, a saloon, gambling house, and restaurant complex.

When the Creede boom cooled, he returned to Denver and dealt in several resorts during the nineties. Masterson had always been an avid follower of pugilism and had witnessed most of the important heavyweight prizefights in America dating back to the 1882 bareknuckle title fight in New Orleans when John L. Sullivan took the crown from Paddy Ryan. In the late nineties he operated a fight club in Denver and wrote a sports column for a newspaper called *George's Weekly.*

By 1902 Masterson had completely soured on Denver and the entire West and moved to New York City, where he accepted President Theodore Roosevelt's appointment as a deputy United States marshal. Soon he was writing a column primarily concerned with fistic events for *The Morning Telegraph* and was nationally recognized as a leading authority on boxing. In 1921 he was at his desk, turning out a column, when he suffered a heart attack and died at the age of sixty-seven.

Another follower of the gambling circuit who was active in Tombstone during that camp's salad days was Dave Neagle, who, like so many of the fraternity, was a sometime peace officer. In Tombstone, Neagle served as deputy sheriff under John Behan and succeeded Virgil Earp as town marshal. His association with Behan automatically made him an adversary of the Earp brothers and their friends. To his biographer Wyatt Earp characterized Neagle as honest and courageous but thought he was "not very shrewd." Wyatt would undoubtedly have rated Neagle's mental powers of a higher order had Dave lent his gun to the Earp faction rather than to the hated opposition. Neagle's life was fully as exciting and eventful as that of Wyatt Earp, and, had he found a clever writer to record his history as Wyatt did, his name today would be as familiar as Earp's.

In 1868, Dave Neagle was twenty-one years old, a student at Santa Clara College in California. This was the year of the White Pine madness when thousands heard the call of silver from a mountain in the Nevada wilderness and stampeded to the new eldorado. Neagle joined the rush with no intention of mining the mountain but with high hopes of mining the pockets of the silver seekers as a professional gambler. White Pine was a mining district composed of a galaxy of boomtowns: Hamilton, Treasure City, Shermantown, Eberhardt, Swansea, Menken, White Pine City, Monte Cristo, California, Mammoth City, Greenville, and Babylon. Neagle hit them all, learning his trade. He worked his way across Utah and Colorado into Kansas and back again. At Pioche he was involved in a wild fracas during which he shot gambler-gunman Jim Levy in the face. The bullet passed through both of Levy's cheeks, shattering his jaw, and leaving him with a sinister scar which added to his baleful reputation.

In 1873 the discovery of rich silver ore outcroppings in the Panamint Mountains, high above the floor of Death Valley, California, signaled the birth of a new camp called Panamint City. Dave Neagle was one of the first up Surprise Canyon to the site of the boomtown, dubbed by a Wells Fargo agent "a suburb of Hell." Setting up two whiskey barrels at opposite ends of a tent and bridging them with a plank, Neagle declared the Oriental Saloon open and ready for business. Later he put up a frame building and installed fixtures worth $10,000. The new Oriental featured a billiard table, a black walnut bar, a number of large studies of the undraped female form, and two cardrooms. Flanking Neagle's establishment were Joe Harris' Occidental Saloon and the Dexter, run by Fred Yager. Neagle maintained order in his place, but so frequent were the gunfights in the neighboring gin mills that he bullet-proofed his walls with sheets of corrugated iron to protect his customers from stray slugs.

Another leading Panamint emporium was the Dempsey and Boultinghouse Saloon where Jim Bruce presided over the faro table. A squat, swarthy Kentuckian, Bruce had toured the boomtowns for ten years after seeing considerable guerrilla action on the Missouri-Kansas border as a rider with Quantrill. Like most gamblers, Bruce had another trade on which to rely when play slowed or Fortune frowned. He was an undertaker, and in the towns he visited his talents were often in demand.

After dropping his roll at Bruce's table in Panamint, a man named Bob McKenny nursed a grudge against the dealer. Shortly thereafter, he met Bruce on the street and greeted him with a fusillade of shots. One bullet slammed into Bruce's left wrist and spun him around. Another caught him in the back. As Bruce slumped to the ground, he got his own gun out and working. He put four bullets into his attacker. McKenny died and Bruce was taken by wagon to San Francisco for treatment.

Said the *Panamint News*: "We are pained to record that during an unfortunate affair which occurred at the express office, one of our esteemed citizens was compelled to resort to violent measures to protect his person. His opponent will be buried tomorrow in the little cemetery in Sour Dough."[8]

Jim Bruce survived and returned to Panamint, his faro bank, and his embalming fluids. He was warmly welcomed back by Martha Camp, the leading madam of the town and Bruce's inamorata. He was sharing Martha's bed one night when a terrible pounding and cursing at the door demanded his attention. Ed Barstow, who seemed to consider Miss Camp *his* inamorata, was tearing down the door. Bruce rolled over, picked up his revolver, and waited. With a crash the door came off the hinges and Barstow hurtled into the room. Bruce raised his six-gun and shot him dead. Everyone agreed that Ed Barstow looked very natural laid out in his casket and that Jim Bruce's work as funeral director was of the highest quality.

The owner and top gambler of Panamint's Independent Saloon was Ned Reddy, another veteran of the Nevada camps. Reddy also had proven himself in several six-shooter battles. In 1871, at his gambling house in Cerro Gordo, he had shot and killed a man named Tom Dunn, and at Columbus in 1873, Bulger Rains had gone down before his smoking iron. In all, it was said, there were six notches on that gun when Reddy arrived in Panamint. In spite of his reputation for violence, or perhaps because of it, Reddy did not have to unsheath his Colt while in Panamint, but he was remembered as a participant in one of the biggest poker games in the camp's short history. There was $10,000 in the pot when the final bet was called, and the holder of aces over sixes raked the table.

Five years after the first boomers struggled up Surprise Canyon to establish the "Suburb of Hell," a deluge suddenly struck the Panamints and a flash flood washed away most of Panamint City. Neagle's Oriental, the Dexter, the Occidental, the Snug Saloon, the Arcade, Martha Camp's bordello, Jack Lloyd's stage office, and more than a hundred other buildings went tumbling down the five-mile-long canyon to be scattered over a wide area of Panamint Valley. The townsmen had been warned of impending disaster by the shrieking stamp mill whistle and had fled to higher ground, but Panamint City was gone forever.

Dave Neagle moved on to Bodie, California. In 1878, Bodie was at its peak, its inhabitants boasting of two banks, four daily newspapers, three breweries, and six hotels. It was said to have "the widest streets of any Western mining town, the wickedest men and the worst climate." Neagle gambled at the Bonanza, the Rifle Club, the Champion, and other saloons. He may have played poker with Charlie Curran, constable of Bodie and considered by many of the fraternity to be the clumsiest tinhorn ever exposed. Charlie would slyly place a stacked deck of cards between his legs when he sat down to play and cover it with a bandanna. When he got behind in the game, as he invariably did, he would slip in the cold deck in an effort to recoup.

Before one game some of the boys fixed up a deck, gluing all the cards together except for a few loose tickets on the top and bottom. During the game a diversionary commotion was created, causing Curran to jump up, spilling his bandanna. The stuck-together cards were then swiftly substituted for Charlie's stacked deck. When the time came for Curran to make his big switch, he dipped under the bandanna and started to deal. One, two, three cards were distributed and then the fourth would not move. Charlie fumbled desperately with a deck that apparently was not just cold but frozen solid. He finally threw down the cards in disgust and stormed from the room.

It is more likely that while in Bodie, Dave Neagle played against Pat Reddy, the brother of Ned Reddy, Dave's competitor back in Panamint. Pat, a handsome man with silky muttonchops, had started out with his brother as a professional gambler. Then, in Virginia City, Nevada, he had his right arm shot off in a dispute over a game. During his long recuperation he began the study of law and eventually became the most sought after criminal lawyer in the Southwest.

Pat Reddy was famous for employing whatever means were required to defend a client, legal or extralegal. In Bodie he was hired to defend a man accused of rustling. The star witness for the prosecution was a gunman and desperado named Pearly Plane. In Bodie's saloons Plane made it clear that this was one case Reddy had better lose. When the trial began in Aurora, Reddy noted that Plane had posted three or four gunslicks around the courtroom. Before Plane was to take the stand, Reddy requested a recess and whispered to an assistant, who quietly slipped from the courtroom and rode fast for Bodie, fourteen miles away. Shortly after court resumed, a wagon pulled up outside and eight of Bodie's toughest gunslingers sauntered into the room. Outmanned and outgunned, Pearly Plane was destroyed on the stand by Reddy. The jury's verdict of not guilty was anticlimactic, but Ed Loose, a giant of a man and a great admirer of Reddy's, was so excited he turned handsprings out of the room, his bootheels punching holes in the wooden floor wherever his big feet came down. The patches covering these holes were known for years as "Loose's Trail" and were felt to symbolize the path to freedom for the falsely accused.

Pat Reddy's services were in great demand but he came high. When a man named DeRoche was accused of murder in Bodie and asked Reddy his fee for defending him, the one-armed lawyer said simply, "All you've got." The owners of the promising Yellow Aster mining property became involved in litigation and retained Reddy. He asked for and received an interest in the mine as his fee. The Yellow Aster proved to be a bonanza, and Reddy was a very wealthy man when he died in 1900.

For Dave Neagle the Tombstone excitement followed Bodie. There he served as both a city and county law officer while pursuing his primary vocation as gambler. In the mid-nineties he returned to California and accepted appointment as deputy United States marshal. He was acting in this capacity in 1889 when he became involved in one of the most bizarre and notorious scandals of the period.

The story began in 1883 when William Sharon, a financial giant and a United States senator from California, initiated legal action to force Sarah Althea Hill to desist from her claim that she was his wife. She filed a counteraction for divorce and alimony. Before either case was brought to final settlement, Sharon died. Sarah Hill continued to fight for Sharon's estate. Her attorney was David S. Terry, former state chief justice and a man of passion and violence. Years before, Terry had killed Senator Dave Broderick in a duel, and on numerous occasions had demonstrated his vicious temper and utter fearlessness when aroused. While preparing the briefs for Miss Hill—or, as she wished to be called, Mrs. Sharon—Terry convinced her that she should be his bride.

It was two years after this marriage that Stephen J. Field, associate justice of the United States Supreme Court, came from Washington to hand down the final decision in the Hill-Sharon litigation. Field ruled against the Hill woman, declaring that the papers purporting to prove her marriage to Sharon were forged. Immediately the woman was on her feet.

"You have been bought!" she screamed.

"Remove that woman!" thundered Justice Field. When United States Marshal J. C. Franke moved to obey, Sarah cracked him with her handbag. Then Terry went into action, knocking Marshal Franke down. Other officers dragged Terry outside where he broke free and pulled a bowie knife. He was finally subdued and disarmed. A loaded pistol was taken from his wife's handbag. Justice Field sent Terry to jail for six months and gave his wife thirty days. Both swore to newsmen that they would kill Field when they got out.

Terry filed an appeal, and the following year Justice Field returned to California. Because of the threats against Field's life, the United States attorney general had assigned Deputy Marshal Dave Neagle to act as his bodyguard. On August 14, 1889, Field's train had a short stopover at Lathrop. The jurist, with Neagle close at his side, went into the station dining room for a snack. The two were sitting at a table when Terry suddenly appeared and took a swing at Field. Dave Neagle drew and fired, hitting Terry squarely in the heart. Mrs. Terry ran into the room and fell, screaming, at her husband's side. Neagle grabbed her bag, which again contained a loaded pistol.

Three years later Sarah Althea Hill Sharon (?) Terry was committed to the state insane asylum where she spent the next forty-five years. She died in 1937.

Dave Neagle received much publicity after killing Terry, one paper saying that, "no braver man than Nagle [*sic*] ever walked this earth."[9] Neagle shunned the limelight, however, and did not trade on his notoriety. He lived out his years in obscurity in California, dying in 1926 at age seventy-nine, at his home in Oakland.

The gambler-gunmen of Tombstone—the Earps, Doc Holliday, Bat Masterson, Luke Short, Dave Neagle, et al.—left the Arizona mining town and passed on to their individual destinies, but Dick Clark stayed on. During the decade of the eighties he was the undisputed premier gambler of the town and his fame spread throughout Arizona and the entire Southwest.

After dissolving his partnership with Lou Rickabaugh, Bill Harris, and Wyatt Earp in the operation of the Oriental gaming rooms, he had purchased the Alhambra Saloon and Gambling Hall. The Alhambra, the Oriental, and Johnny Speck's Crystal Palace were the foremost establishments of their kind in Tombstone and rivaled the best in the West.

As a gambling house boss, Clark spent far fewer hours behind his faro box, turning the dealer's chores over to veterans like Napa Nick or Sleepy Tom Thomas and promising newcomers like Bones Brannan or Johnny Bauer. He paid these

salaried dealers, called "mechanics," twenty-five dollars for a
six-hour shift—high wages at a time when hard-rock miners
were making four dollars for ten hours of back-breaking labor.

The man known as Napa Nick in Tombstone was of such
august appearance and demeanor, with his snow-white hair,
Uncle Sam chin whiskers, and black broadcloth suit, that
many called him "Judge." They were amazed to learn, however, when two visitors from Napa City, California, chanced
to stop over in Tombstone, that the dignified-looking gambler
was in fact a former judge in that community, that he still
maintained one of the finest homes there, that his wife and two
lovely daughters were leaders of Napa City society, and that
the judge, despite his frequent and prolonged absences, was
universally considered to be one of the sturdiest pillars of the
town.

Sleepy Tom Thomas was also of dignified mien. His drooping eyelids, flowing tie, and silk topper made him look like a
somnolent banker. He kept a fine home on the outskirts of
Tombstone and employed a Chinese cook and a Mexican
gardener. His wife, a handsome woman of ample bosom and
roving eye, had her own horse and buggy and was often seen
at odd hours of the day or night in strange sectors of the town.
Finally she ran off with the district attorney, which gave the
ladies of Tombstone gossip fodder for weeks. Sleepy Tom
merely shrugged and returned to his faro table. To the dedicated frontier gambler, the human foibles that so excited ordinary folk—marriage and divorce, for instance—were of
little consequence; what really was important was the turn of
the next card.

Dick Clark nurtured the careers of a number of aspiring
young men who showed the aptitude for "the Life." Johnny
Bauer, known in Tombstone as "the Dutch Kid," came to the
mining camp from Tucson about 1880, studied under the tu-
telage of the master, and worked for Clark for more than ten
years. A clean-cut, handsome young man, Bauer had the
benefit of little formal education but could have passed for a
graduate of a prestigious eastern university with his fashionable dress and natural urbanity. At work, he was a wonder to
watch as his slim fingers manipulated chips, coins, or cards

"Dutch Kid" Johnny Bauer. He avoided liquor and drugs but had a weakness for the girls, and they for him. From Billy King's Tombstone, *courtesy C. L. Sonnichsen.*

with lightninglike dexterity. He never touched liquor or drugs, the opiates that destroyed many of his class, but he had a limitless sexual appetite and squandered his money on the Tombstone harlotry.

Bones Brannon, the son of a mule skinner, came to Tombstone as a boy, and after only a year or two of school, left to prepare himself for the life of a professional gambler. He begged jobs in saloons as a sweeper or errand runner in order to be near the great men—the Clarks, the Rickabaughs, and the Specks—and to study their moves. He dealt faro to boys his own age from an old cigar box in which he had fashioned a slot and spring to hold the deck. On a discarded piece of cloth he meticulously hand painted a "spread" of spades from ace to king in imitation of the faro layout he saw in the gambling halls. His cards were castoffs from these establishments, worn and limp. He constructed a casekeeper, the contrivance that looked like a Chinese abacus by which a record was kept of cards played in faro. He would open his game to his peers for anything of value and he learned to deal his dog-eared cards as adroitly as any seasoned mechanic.

Bones was a rosy-cheeked, cherubic young fellow, and when he was finally given the opportunity to deal faro in a house he found that his appearance worked to his advantage. Everyone wanted to tackle the game of the innocent-looking kid. Most left his table lighter in pocket. Perhaps it was his boyish appearance and his need to prove his manhood that drove Bones to the bottle. He was an alcoholic at a tender age and Demon Rum was the bane of his life.

Dick Clark trained Brannon, Bauer, and others, not only in the mechanics of the profession but in the philosophy of it as well. To the Dick Clarks of the frontier, gambling was an honorable calling, on a par with, if not a cut above, banking or the law. The real topflight high roller did in fact consider himself superior to the average man. Although most gamblers had received little formal education, all who were successful were graduates of a very hard school indeed, a school in which they had spent many thousands of solitary hours practicing and many additional thousands of hours at the tables where a mistake could be costly in money or in life itself. Complete self-control had to be mastered. Fear or indecision must never be shown because at a critical moment in a game the nervous flicker of an eyelid or the tremor of a hand might mean the difference in winning or losing a big pot.

The high roller had to learn every crooked trick in order to be on his guard against them, but if, like Dick Clark, he called himself a "square" gambler, he set for himself certain standards and scruples. He would not think of holding out an ace or hiding a cold deck under a bandanna in his lap *à la* Charlie Curran of Bodie. But if he had the ability to stack a deck while shuffling or to reverse a cut so smoothly that the other players could not detect the move, he saw nothing unethical in employing his hard earned talent. When professionals sat down to play "hard cards" for heavy stakes, the use of such skills was considered very proper and even necessary. A man making his living with cards could not long survive if he relied only on the whims of that fickle lady called Luck. Dick Clark was as straight a gambler as the West ever knew, and yet he wore a large diamond ring that he would turn into his palm when dealing in a big game and use as a mirror. The layman might find it difficult to comprehend the ethical difference between the use of Clark's ring and Charlie Curran's cold deck, but to Dick Clark and his peers the distinction was marked and fundamental. Anyone could stack a deck in private and hide it under a bandanna; it took a master and countless hours of practice to be able to read the faces of cards as they flashed across the tiny diamond mirror in the palm of a hand.

The perfidy of ostensibly righteous people appalled men like Clark. Billy King, a Clark protégé, used to tell a story illustrative of this feeling. A Reverend Mr. Benneck walked into King's saloon one day asking for help. He had come all the way from Maine, he said, to preach the gospel in wild, wild Tombstone, but his belongings were still at Fairbank, the nearest railroad station. The freighters would not move them on to Tombstone without payment in advance, and he was broke. King started a hat around for the clergyman, priming the collection with a generous donation of his own, and by the next day Reverend Benneck was moved, courtesy of Billy King and his customers. The following Sunday morning the preacher delivered his first sermon, denouncing the evils of John Barleycorn and closing with a demand that the saloons be shut down on the Sabbath.

There wasn't a gambler in the Territory who would stoop so low or display such ingratitude, Billy would say. Was it any wonder that the members of the fraternity felt their ethical standards were on a higher plane than those of the Reverend Benneck and his ilk?

One of the qualities that set the really topflight gamblers apart was their ability to lose as well as to win gracefully. This was something difficult to teach, but Dick Clark did most of his instruction by example. He could lose large sums with the same equanimity as that with which he won, and to him the payment of a debt was a matter of supreme importance. Clark was one of a group of Tombstone businessmen left holding the bag when the county treasurer defaulted. It is significant that the gambler was the only bondsman to pay over the five thousand dollars each had pledged. He simply accepted the fact that he had, as he put it, "made a bad bet" and considered payment of the money a matter of honor.

The legendary generosity of the frontier gambler was exemplified by Clark. He was always a soft touch for any tinhorn down on his luck. Whenever he heard of a miner who had lost his job or been injured in the mines, he would put fifty dollars in an envelope and send it to the unfortunate. Few knew of his philanthropy, for he did not advertise it. He sought no gratitude or praise; to him such acts were simply in keeping with the character of the big-time gambler as he envisioned it.

Clark was not a fighting man. During a thirty-year career spent in the toughest gambling places in some of the wildest camps of the West, he was never known to fire a gun in anger. Billy King, who was his lieutenant for more than ten years, could remember only one incident in which his boss handled a weapon. He and Clark were closing up the Alhambra gambling rooms about four o'clock one morning, and the proprietor was counting the money in the cash drawer of the faro table, when a Tombstone tough named Fred Kolan walked in, brandished a six-shooter, and demanded the money. Clark placed a stack of bills on the faro table and as Kolan reached for them, King seized his gun arm. Kolan fired and a bullet ripped through the faro layout into the floor at Clark's feet. The holdup man never got a second shot, for an instant later the barrel of a six-gun in Clark's hand smashed against his skull, knocking him senseless.

Dick Clark maintained his gambling interests in Tombstone for fourteen years, but frequently he would pack his bags and board a stage in search of opportunities in other towns. During the eighties and early nineties he confined most of his travels to the southwestern country—Arizona, New Mexico, and Texas.

He could find considerable action without leaving Arizona Territory. Nearby Bisbee experienced a boom in the late eighties, and Jim Letson's Turf Saloon and Tony Downs's Orient frequently provided interesting games. Chuck Rogers, who kept the Gold Coin in Globe, was a first-class gambling man and could be counted on for some high-stakes play. Prescott had a number of resorts, mostly skin-houses managed by tinhorns and sharpers, Cobweb Hall being the most infamous, but at the Palace and the Sazarac gambling men of Clark's class sometimes gathered for a game.

There was a "Palace" in Phoenix also, and it was for many years the best of the city's gambling houses. Gus Hirschfield had the longest tenure of the the Palace's many owners. When the place was torn down in 1911 many counterfeit coins were discovered in the debris. Hirschfield, who was still in town, explained to a reporter for the *Phoenix Republican* that employees in the old days had been instructed to get rid of bogus coins in order to keep them out of circulation and the practice had been to drop them in the crack between the wainscoting and the adobe wall.

Tucson had been a good sporting man's town for twenty years. One visitor to the town in 1870, when it was so raw and new that it lacked even one hotel, was amazed to find a number of gambling houses open around the clock seven days a week. An oft-repeated quip is credited to an anonymous bartender of early Tucson. When asked by a new arrival at four o'clock in the morning if it wasn't a little late for the saloons to be open, the barkeep is said to have responded that it was

Faro game in progress in the Orient Saloon, Bisbee, Arizona Territory. Owner Tony Downs stands at the left. Jack Ganzhorn keeps cases. To his left, with a tall stack of chips, is a concert-hall singer named Doyle. Behind Doyle in derbies are Jack Boston and the Dutch Kid. George Oakes is the lookout. The dealer has been variously identified as Johnny Murphy or Harry Emerson, and the silk-tiled player to his left as Smiley Lewis or Sleepy Tom Thomas. Courtesy Western History Collections, University of Oklahoma Library.

"a little late for the night before last, but just the shank of the evening for tonight."[10]

Bob Crandall, sometimes referred to by his contemporaries as "the handsomest man in the Southwest," was the best known of the early Tucson gamblers. The Legal Tender, the Fashion, and Congress Hall were popular gambling saloons for many years. The owner and boss gambler of the Legal Tender, Ezra C. Bartlett, was not averse to no-limit play when the opportunity arose. One of his exploits was talked about in Tucson saloons for years afterward.

Three New York sporting men, en route to California, had stopped for the night in Tucson and were amusing themselves by high-playing what they derisively called the "hick" town's penny-ante faro games. Bartlett heard of their tour of the Tucson houses and slid into the dealer's chair at the Legal Tender faro table. When the easterners arrived, followed by a gang of hangers-on, one of them threw five thousand dollars on the table and asked for a stack of chips. Bartlett tossed him five white chips, saying, "Whites are the cheapest I have and a stack will cost you twenty thousand."

It was either play faro against Ezra Bartlett at one thousand dollars a turn or be humiliated before the crowd. The New Yorkers played. They soon lost the five chips and pulled out their bankrolls. Within an hour they were plucked clean and Bartlett was $22,000 richer.

The Fashion was presided over by Eli B. Gifford, who in later years was a partner of Wyatt Earp in California racing. Gifford was a member of the Arizona House of Representatives in the early eighties and in 1886, together with Tucson sporting men Ben C. Parker and Billy Reid, donated the land upon which was built the University of Arizona.

A powder-flash photograph taken in Congress Hall in 1893 played a significant part in the history of Arizona Territory. Grover Cleveland had just been elected a second time as president and was expected to name a Democrat to replace the Republican governor of the territory. The choice was to be made between Louis C. Hughes and another politician who had the endorsement of the Democratic Central Committee. Fred G. Hughes, no relation to the candidate, was chairman of that committee and the leading booster for L. C. Hughes's opponent. He was also a faro dealer in Congress Hall. One day a photographer employed by the L. C. Hughes camp entered the gambling rooms and set up his equipment, ostensibly to take a picture of the interior of the establishment. What he captured on film was Fred Hughes dealing faro to a Chinese, a black, and two white freighters. The picture was sent to President Cleveland with the caption, "Here is Mr. Hughes' opponent's principal supporter at his daily work." Faro-dealing was still considered a respectable calling in the Arizona of 1893, but not so in Washington, D. C., and Louis C. Hughes soon afterward received the gubernatorial appointment.

During his swings through New Mexico, Dick Clark often crossed paths with John Dougherty, another high roller who had engaged in some memorable poker games over the years. A quiet, serious man who tended strictly to business and never courted trouble, Dougherty had two conceits: the smallness of his feet and the immensity of his poker bets. He would not sit down in a game without a personal bankroll of at least $100,000, and insisted that each of the other players show at least $10,000 before a card was dealt. He looked with disdain upon any coin or bill of less than five dollars and paid for a drink, a cigar, or a shave with a five-dollar bill, refusing change.

Legends are bound to grow around the memory of men such as this, and one Dougherty story, probably apocryphal, concerned a poker game held in Bowen's Saloon in Santa Fe in 1889. Dougherty and a wealthy Texas cattleman named Ike Jackson had locked horns in a no-limit game to determine the poker champion of the West. Came a hand when more than $100,000 was piled on the table and each player gave every indication of backing his hand all the way. Jackson, out of cash, wrote a deed to his ranch and 10,000 head of cattle, and, with Dougherty's agreement that this was worth $100,000, tossed it into the pile, raising the gambler that amount. Dougherty lacked sufficient cash to call or raise this bet, but he faltered not an instant. Turning to the throng of excited spectators who crowded around the table, he called for paper and pen. He scribbled a few lines and then stood up and faced L. Bradford Prince, the governor of New Mexico, who was one of the onlookers. Handing the paper to Prince, he drew a pistol and said: "Sign this, Governor, or, by God and by Jesus, I will kill you!"

The governor wasted no time in scrawling his signature, whereupon Dougherty threw the scrap of paper into the pot.

"I raise the Territory of New Mexico!" he announced triumphantly. "There is the deed!"

It was said that Ike Jackson slammed his cards on the table with a thunderous oath.

"Take the pot," he roared, "but it's a damned good thing for you that the governor of Texas isn't here!"

Silver City was a regular stop on Dick Clark's trips through

Johnny Speck, shown here with his son, ran the Crystal Palace in Tombstone and was for many years a friendly competitor of Dick Clark. From Billy King's Tombstone, *courtesy C. L. Sonnichsen.*

New Mexico. There the Bank Exchange Saloon enticed faro players with a local advertisement: "The belligerent portion of the community can find a particularly rampant specimen of the Feline species, usually denominated the 'Tiger' ready to engage them at all times."[11] Johnny Speck, whose Crystal Palace competed with Clark's Alhambra in Tombstone; kept a gambling saloon of high quality in Silver City for several years. Frank Thurmond, a San Antonio gambler of renown, was active there in the early eighties. Perhaps the best remembered and most successful of Silver City sporting men, however, was Ed Bradley.

Born in Johnstown, Pennsylvania, in 1859, Edward R. Bradley was out of school and working in a steel mill at the age of thirteen. Within a year he knew that the life of a mill hand was not for him and ran off to seek his fortune in the West. He traveled around the frontier as he passed through adolescence, taking short-term employment as a cowboy or miner, but he constantly studied the intricacies of gambling, which he had decided was his true calling. In his early twenties he was operating gambling rooms in Raton, Springer, and other rough New Mexico towns and, at Silver City, he opened the house that was to provide the basis for his fortune.

With his Silver City gambling profits he bought and stocked the Idle Hour Horse Farm near Lexington, Kentucky, and his horses won the Kentucky Derby four times. He owned and operated several gambling casinos in New York and New Jersey. By 1898 he was in Palm Beach, Florida, where he opened the Beach Club, a swank gambling house that became internationally famous and was operated continuously for forty-three years. With his security force of eighteen Pinkerton men at the Beach Club, his generous donations to both political parties and to churches of all faiths, and his virtual control of the local newspapers, Ed Bradley made his own law in Palm Beach. People believed he gave away practically all of the casino's profits and they were probably correct. "There are no pockets in shrouds," he was fond of saying. "I don't want to be the richest man in the cemetery."

When he died in 1941 at the age of eighty-one, the Beach Club was torn down, as stipulated in his will, the land donated

Ed Bradley, who made his first big stake in Silver City, New Mexico. Courtesy Keeneland Library, Lexington, Kentucky.

to the city for a public park, and all the gambling paraphernalia from the club was towed out to sea and sunk.

The state of Texas provided rich opportunity for high rollers of Dick Clark's caliber during the years of his excursions. El Paso, isolated at the extreme western end of the state, had been a gambling town for many years. Ben Dowell, an early Anglo settler, had established the first saloon and gambling hall in the town and was afterward elected El Paso's first mayor. When A. D. Richardson passed through in 1859 there were about four hundred inhabitants, mostly Mexicans, but "gambling was universal, with huge piles of silver dollars staked at the monte tables in the great saloons. $100,000 often changed hands in a single night. . . ."[12] By the 1880s the Coliseum Variety Theater and Gambling Saloon, owned and operated by the four Manning brothers, was the chief attraction for men of sporting inclination. Lou Rickabaugh, Clark's former partner in Tombstone, presided over an El Paso gambling club at this time.

Farther east, the Texas towns of Dallas, Fort Worth, Austin, and San Antonio were active gambling centers during this period.

Gamblers and gambling house proprietors played significant roles in the early history of Dallas. The town was originally incorporated in 1856 to establish order after the son of one of the first families was shot dead when caught cheating at cards. Twenty years later the gamblers had still not accepted domination by the civil authorities, and, in 1876, when Mayor Ben Long tried to impose control over them, the gamblers gathered in a saloon and defied the mayor and his police. After a three-day siege, a compromise was agreed upon that spelled out the prerogatives of the elected officials and the sporting brethren. The fraternity viewed the agreement as a contract between equals.

Julien Bogel and Billy Henser were leading sporting men of Dallas at this time, and Johnny Thompson's Variety Theater and Saloon was a headquarters for the estimated one hundred gamblers in the town. Free and open gambling was so important to the economy of frontier Dallas that when District Attorney Charles Clint tried to make a name for himself by closing the gaming rooms in 1883, a committee of prominent businessmen admonished him to cease and desist. They pointed out that to achieve business prosperity he would be better advised to emulate the enlightened policy of neighboring Fort Worth, which was enticing deposed Dallas gamblers to transfer to that city with offers of free rent and $3,500 in cash.

Luke Short was, of course, the premier Fort Worth gambling man after settling there in 1883, and his White Elephant Saloon was the scene of many memorable high-stake poker sessions featuring Dick Clark and other circuit veterans, one of whom was Fort Worth's own Nat Kramer.

A native of Texas, Kramer served his apprenticeship as a professional gambler in New Orleans and Shreveport and on the steamboats plying the Red River. He settled in Fort Worth after the Civil War and for forty years maintained his home there with frequent breaks for circuit excursions. To other frontier gamblers, Kramer was an enigma. During a career of more than fifty years he was never known to take a drink, to be involved in a quarrel, or to carry a weapon. "He is the most mysterious success I ever saw," Luke Short said in awe. "How he does it I would like to know, because I am tired of this business of packing a gun."[13]

Shortly before Kramer died in Fort Worth in October, 1905, he was asked how he would explain to Saint Peter a life spent as a gambler.

"Well," replied Nat Kramer, "I am just going to tell him that I have helped some and I have skinned some. Those I skinned could afford it, and those I helped needed it maybe."[14]

Austin's gifts to the sporting brotherhood were Phil Coe and Ben Thompson, but after Coe was shot to death in Abilene in 1871 and Thompson in San Antonio in 1884, no outstanding gambling man was dominant in the Texas capital. As late as 1890 three "honest" houses were in operation, two featuring faro and other banking games, and one a keno establishment. Dick Clark always made Austin a stop on his tours, timing his visit to coincide with a session of the Texas legislature, for it was an axiom among circuit followers that politicos were prime material for the professional gambler and, when herded together in one spot, were like sheep collected for shearing.

San Antonio boasted of a number of outstanding gambling emporiums beginning in the 1860s. Early establishments included the Comanche Club, the Jockey Club, the Buckhorn, the Black Elephant, and the University Club, the last named maintained by the Thurmond brothers for thirty-five years. Jack Harris took over the site of the old Bull's Head Saloon to open his famous Vaudeville Theater and Gambling Saloon in 1869. This location, at Commerce and Soledad streets, was known for years in San Antonio as Fatal Corner, because of its history of deadly encounters. Jack Harris, Ben Thompson, King Fisher, and Joe Foster, among others, received mortal wounds there. In addition to its notoriety as a region of sudden death, Harris's place was notable for being the first building in San Antonio to have electric lights installed. It was here, also, that the term "vaudeville" was said to have been first used in a theatrical sense.

Billy Simms, the only major figure to survive the Ben Thompson–Vaudeville Theater tragedy, later managed a gambling house called the Crystal, situated on the Main Plaza across from the courthouse. He was described in his more mature years as a gentleman-gambler of impeccable speech, dress, and manners, who was at home in the finest drawing rooms in the city. Other fine houses included Arthur Ware's Silver King; the Professor, named for one Professor Dieffenbaugh; the Globe, which featured classical musical concerts; the White Elephant, so ornate that a newspaper reported, "San Antonians are in ecstacy about its beauty"; and Scholtz's Palm Garden, a three-story building with several bars, billiard rooms, gaming rooms, and dining halls opening onto a tiered gallery overlooking a tropical garden.

Other, less pretentious establishments included the Gray Mule, the Washington, the Bella Union, the Revolving Light, and, at the opposite extreme from Billy Simms's Crystal and Scholtz's Palm Garden, the Clipper and the Green Front. Rowdy Joe Lowe, who had lost none of his propensity for violence and crooked dealing since fleeing a Wichita murder charge in 1873, presided over the Clipper—an appropriate name for a notorious skinning house. It was said that the proprietors of the Green Front could not keep a porter on the job because of the necessity of mopping up the blood and sweeping out the hair, pieces of ears, and eyeballs that littered the place after a night's frivolities. The Green Front featured "Girls! Girls! Girls!" with dances available at "two bits a spasm." *Tableaux vivant* with scantily clad females were presented nightly. One of these "livng pictures," featuring Georgia Drake as Miss Liberty bringing together a Union and a Confederate soldier, dissolved rather suddenly when an unreconstructed Civil War veteran shot Miss Liberty dead just as she lifted freedom's torch.

San Antonio gamblers of note included Henry Goldman, Kid Nash, Red McDonald, Sam Berliner, Will Ford, Harry Bennett, and Charlie Whitman.

Bennett was one of the gamblers expelled from Dodge City at the time of Luke Short's banishment. For several years he traveled the Southwest, dealing monte at army forts and cowboy camps. He was drummed out of Fort Reno when he took a month's pay from the officers there in a single evening. Bennett was as crooked as a rattlesnake, but he had plenty of nerve and was a slick operator. In Oklahoma Territory he passed from campground to campground, fleecing the cowpokes. He traveled alone, riding a mule, his only equipment a large box that contained some forty decks of monte cards. Upon arrival in a cow camp, he would open his game and in short order separate the cowboys from their cash. When they were broke or refused to buck his game any longer, he packed up and moved on, "accidentally" leaving one of his decks behind. In a month or so he would be back, invariably to find one of the cowboys banking a monte game with his deck. Bennett would then play against the bank, breaking it every time, for the cards were marked, of course, and he could read the backs as easily as the faces. In 1896 he came to the end of the trail when he was killed in San Antonio's Silver King Saloon by a man named Bob Marks. The gunshots were still reverberating through the hall when Arthur Ware, the owner, executed Marks on the spot.

Charlie Whitman, the son of a minister, could deal faro with the best and was an expert poker player. He knew how to ride a hot streak when luck was with him and was famous for having parlayed $100 into ownership of two Denver gambling houses in one night's play. He retired from gambling to marry the daughter of a Texas rancher and for a time lived quietly as a bookkeeper on his father-in-law's ranch, but the curious excitement of the gambling world drew him back. Again he was successful and in later years invested his winnings in a large ranch of his own where his remaining days were spent in baronial elegance.

Dick Clark varied his trips through the Southwest country with journeys to Denver, Kansas City, or Saint Louis if a political convention, cattlemen's meeting, or assembly of mine owners promised opportunity for high-grade poker with men of means. He even acquired a ranch in the San Pedro Valley near Tombstone so that he could attend cattlemen's conventions as a bona fide rancher. Many of the Southwest's most prominent and prosperous figures—men like John Chisum, Major Andrew Drumm, George W. Thompson, Thomas B. Catron, Colonel William C. Greene, and H. A. W. Tabor—prided themselves on their poker playing ability and welcomed the chance to pit their money and skills against a player of Clark's stature.

The famous John Chisum, whose cattle ranged both sides of the Pecos River from Fort Sumner to the Texas border and who was said to be the largest cattle operator of his time in the world, loved to tackle Clark's game.

Andy Drumm, who was worth over $2 million when he died at the age of ninety-one, was an excellent poker player and probably won more often than he lost, even when bucking professionals. He played one game in Kansas City in the early eighties against a Texas cattleman who was temporarily short of cash and agreed to wager cattle instead of dollars. Stakes were set at a steer to ante and two steers to "come in." When the game was over Drumm had won 750 steers, a large number of blooded bulls, a sizable herd of two-year-old heifers, ten mustangs, and a chunk of grazing land in the Texas Panhandle.

George Thompson as a penniless young man had banked a monte game on borrowed money in the Exchange Hotel in Las Vegas, New Mexico. One day he won $22,000, closed his game, boarded a stage bound for Trinidad, Colorado, and went into the cattle business. When he sold out to an eastern cattle company some fifteen years later, his holdings included

1 million acres of grazing land with seventeen miles of water frontage on the Arkansas River, 90 purebred breeding bulls, 44 cow ponies, and 15,700 head of cattle. The eastern company gave him $575,000 for his famous Chiquaque Ranch.

Bill Greene had tried to make it as a professional gambler but had been unsuccessful. He dealt faro for wages in Tombstone and other Arizona towns but promptly lost the few dollars he earned in an attempt to break other men's faro banks. He took to prospecting and finally struck it rich with holdings in the copper mines of Sonora, Mexico. He never lost his taste for gambling, however, and was a frequent participant in Dick Clark's big money games.

Another was Thomas B. Catron, wealthy lawyer and landowner, a power in the Republican party of New Mexico, a delegate to Congress from the Territory, and, after statehood, a United States senator.

Horace Tabor was a Colorado storekeeper who, before his dramatic rise to wealth and prominence, had limited his gambling to the grubstaking of prospectors. After his mine holdings at Leadville transformed him almost overnight into one of the richest men of the country and led to his election as lieutenant governor of Colorado and appointment to the United States Senate, he passed up few chances to play big money poker. Dick Clark fattened his wallet with Tabor money on many occasions. Once he cleaned Tabor of all his available cash and the silver magnate offered to wager a carload of ore on a nearby siding. Clark accepted and promptly won the ore, which he quickly sold to another party. He always said that was the closest he ever came to owning a mine.

Tabor was an easy mark for a topnotch professional of the Clark stripe, but if one story about him is to be credited, he picked up a trick or two from the pros that he used to advantage with others. He is said to have engaged a merchant in a game of draw poker on a train and to have steadily relieved the man of his cash. The tradesman was "close to the blanket" when he caught a powerful hand—four kings—and bet his remaining money and jewelry. He asked Tabor if, in addition, he could write a check for $2,000 to raise the pot. Tabor hes-

Horace Tabor, mining magnate. He learned a trick or two from the gambling professionals. Courtesy Denver Public Library, Western History Department.

itated, studied his hand carefully for several moments, and then agreed, provided the merchant would allow him to draw a queen.

A queen! The man glanced once again at his own kingly quartet and tried to hide his glee while accepting the proposal. When he wrote the check he inquired innocently if he might raise the amount to $3,000. Tabor, adding a queen from the deck to his hand, nodded and called the bet. The merchant spread his four kings on the table, and then watched with horror as Tabor placed beside them four aces and a queen.

The stunned trader stood up without a word and left the club car. An hour later he returned and bent over Tabor, who sat quietly smoking a cigar. "One question, Senator," said the merchant. "What the hell did you want with that queen?" Only then did Tabor laugh.

In 1888, Dick Clark was fifty years old. For thirty of those fifty years all his energies had been devoted to the science and art of gambling. He had been successful but he was not a wealthy man, for he had never learned to accumulate money. To Clark, the acquisition of money had just been a means of keeping score. Any excess beyond his basic needs for life and business had been frittered away, given away, squandered thoughtlessly. He was, however, at the pinnacle of his profession, liked and admired by his peers, a leading light of the sporting half-world he had chosen for his own.

But as he neared the half-century mark he began to feel that he had missed something important in life. He had never had a home, only a succession of lonely hotel rooms. He had never had a wife, only a series of faceless harlots. He had never had a child, only a continuum of youngsters eager to study at the feet of the master. His health was failing; the strain of innumerable thirty-six-hour poker sessions under almost constant stress was taking its toll. He had contracted tuberculosis, the nineteenth-century killer, and he managed to keep going only with the aid of alcohol, which he was consuming in ever greater amounts and, in the last few years, morphine. He felt life slipping away, and in 1888 he made a desperate effort to capture some of the things he had missed. He took a wife, a pretty, vivacious seventeen-year-old French Canadian named Louise d'Argentcourt, moved out of his room at the Cosmopolitan Hotel, bought a fine home in Tombstone, and adopted a little orphan girl. He filled the house with the best furnishings available and made every effort within the limits of his profession to perform the role of typical husband and father.

Disease and dissipation continued to drag him down. His body, once erect and powerful, became bent and frail. As his physique deteriorated, his personality changed as well. He became argumentative and easily provoked. Increasingly he relied on the morphine to relieve the pain in his body and still the devils that beset his mind.

By 1893 it was evident to Clark's wife and friends and even to the gambler himself that the drugs he was taking were harming him even more than his other ills. In October he determined to go to a doctor in Chicago who claimed to cure addicts. It was the year of the Chicago World's Fair and he took his wife and daughter along so they could enjoy the fair while he was undergoing treatment.

The doctor could do nothing for him, however, and the Clarks started back for Tombstone. During the journey Clark grew steadily worse, and by the time the train reached Albuquerque he had fallen into a coma. He was taken from the train and moved to a room in the European Hotel, where several doctors attended him to no avail. He never came out of the coma. At fifty-five years of age Dick Clark breathed his last in a hotel room of the sort that had been his only home for most of his life.

His body was taken to Tombstone and buried in the little cemetery outside the town. On the day of his funeral all the businesses in town and several of the surrounding mines closed down. The people of Tombstone honored Dick Clark because most of them genuinely liked the man. Perhaps, also, they mourned because they knew instinctively that with his passing another bond to the free Old West was broken and that when all the Dick Clarks were gone, a time, a mood, an epoch like none the world had ever seen, would be gone forever.

KINGS

Gambling is an art. You can't just say, Mister, I'm going to be a gambler any more than you can automatically sit down and paint. To be good at it, a man must study the science and human nature. . . .

Jed Jordan, *Fool's Gold*

5

*I always liked to set a lot of silver on the table in front of me all
the time. That's the main reason my table always got the biggest
play. It was like flies after molasses syrup.*

John Dunn
Max Evans, *Long John Dunn of Taos*

In the California of gold rush days no town could equal San
Francisco for gambling frenzy, but the once sleepy Mexican
pueblo lying to the south, Los Angeles, made an effort. An
1852 visitor swore that, although he "had seen the elephant
before" and had "been more than familiar with him under
many phases since," he had never been witness to such "perfect and full grown pandemonium."[1]

Most of the gambling was centered on one narrow street,
called "El Calle de los Negros" by the Mexicans and "Nigger
Alley" by the Americans.

Wrote the visitor, Horace Bell:

There were four or five gambling places, and the crowd . . . was so
dense that we could scarcely squeeze through. Americans, Span-
iards, Indians and foreigners, rushing and crowding from one gambling house to another, from table to table, all chinking the everlast-
ing eight square $50 pieces up and down in their palms. There were
several bands of music of the primitive Mexican-Indian kind, that
sent forth most discordant sound, by no means in harmony with the
eternal jingle of gold—while at the upper end of the street, in the
rear of one of the gambling houses was a Mexican maroma in up-
roarious confusion. They positively made night hideous with their
howlings. Every few minutes a rush would be heard, and maybe a
pistol shot would be heard, and when the confusion incident to the
rush would have subsided, and inquiry made, you would learn that
it was only a knife fight between two Mexicans, or a gambler had
caught somebody cheating and had perforated him with a bullet.
Such things were a matter of course, and no complaint or arrests
were ever made. An officer would not have had the temerity to attempt an arrest in Nigger Alley at that time.[2]

The largest and most lucrative gambling house in Los Angeles during these years was off the Calle de los Negros, on

the Plaza, and was managed by Aleck Gibson. Spanish monte was the popular game and Gibson's place contained some half a dozen tables, each heaped with the $50 gold ingots called slugs. "You would frequently see a ranchero with an immense pile of gold in front of him, quietly and unconcernedly smoking his cigarrito and betting 20 slugs on the turn."[3] A noted gambler from New Orleans, Damien Marchessault, dealt monte for Gibson and later became mayor of Los Angeles. "There was nothing strange in our having a gambler for mayor," said Horace Bell, "as in the good old times the gamblers were the cream of society and filled most of the offices of honor, trust and profit."[4]

The most famous gambler in southern California during the 1850s was undoubtedly an Irishman named Jack Powers who had come west in 1847 as a member of Colonel Jonathan D. Stevenson's regiment of New York Volunteers. As a sergeant in Company F, Powers had been stationed at Santa Barbara. The Mexican War had ended before the Volunteers arrived, and the men of F Company, a notoriously hard lot, debauched mightily in Santa Barbara while awaiting discharge. When they were finally mustered out, most headed for the goldfields of the northern counties, but Powers remained in the southern country, making his headquarters in Los Angeles.

He had interests in most of the gambling houses of the town and in a short time had acquired wealth estimated at a quarter of a million in gold. By all accounts he was a striking figure, handsome in appearance, graceful of carriage, and courtly in speech and manners.

There were some four hundred gamblers active in Los Angeles at this time and Jack Powers was their undisputed leader. As Horace Bell put it: "when he walked through a crowd of gamblers it was with the air of a lion walking among rats."[5] Powers was greatly admired by the Spanish population and had strong political connections that extended to San Francisco and Sacramento. Governors John McDougal and John Bigler were his close friends. Had he chosen to enter politics, Powers undoubtedly could have held high office. He preferred, however, to wield his considerable influence in the southern counties, bask in his popularity, spend money with élan, and enjoy his large ranch with its pack of hounds and stable of Thoroughbred horses.

He was a master of the flamboyant, attention-grabbing gesture. A magnificent horseman, he once wagered that he could ride 150 miles in eight hours. Using twenty-five horses and permitting himself only two breaks of seven minutes each, he covered the distance in six hours, 43 minutes and 31 seconds. He even rode an additional mile just to prove he wasn't tired.

On another occasion, after learning that a convicted murderer had expressed a wish to go to his death well attired, Powers ordered a tailor to outfit the man in whatever he liked, and the killer dropped through the gallows trapdoor in a fine new suit of navy blue broadcloth.

Powers intervened in another hanging, mounting the gallows steps as the noose was being fitted to the condemned man's neck, and making an emotional appeal to the assembled spectators to postpone the execution because a petition for clemency in the case had been presented to the governor and papers of commutation might well be arriving on the next day's steamship. Moved by Powers's oratory, the crowd demanded that the sheriff delay the hanging, and when the commutation did indeed arrive the following day, Powers's stock went up another notch.

He had his enemies, of course, including a group who brought suit against him, claiming he held his ranch property illegally. The Santa Barbara sheriff, W. W. Twist, another veteran of Stevenson's New York regiment, served him with eviction papers which Powers promptly tore up. An attempt was made to arrest him in Santa Barbara, but Powers, aided by an army of supporters, escaped to his ranch, taking the only cannon in the town with him. Sheriff Twist, at the head of a large posse, laid siege to the ranch for several days, but, daunted by the cannon and the fervor of the embattled Powers forces, finally withdrew ignominiously.

When the San Francisco Vigilante Committee of 1856 hanged James Casey and Charles Cora and began its scourge of those it deemed miscreant, a colorful former police judge and all-around reprobate named Edward ("Ned") McGowan fled the city with the committee's watchdogs snapping at his heels. McGowan's chief villainy, it appears, had been his friendship and loyalty to Casey, but in 1856 he was a wanted man with a reward on his head. He made his way to Santa Barbara where Jack Powers whisked him from under the noses of the pursuing vigilantes, at one point rolling him up in a carpet to prevent his capture, and helped him escape. The wrath of the San Francisco committee and its supporters centered on Powers after this incident and his popularity and influence diminished as rapidly as it had grown.

Increasingly isolated and embittered by his reversal of fortune, Powers turned to banditry. At the head of a gang of men who had remained loyal to him, he preyed on travelers through Santa Barbara County. In 1858 the Powers gang attacked some wealthy basque cattlemen who were driving a large herd north from Ventura County. There was a gunfight, two basques were killed, and Powers was shot in the leg. The gang hid out after this battle, but the doctor who had been summoned to treat the bandit chieftain's wound disclosed his hiding place and a vigilante posse of some fifty armed men from San Luis Obispo County closed in. Powers made his escape but knew that he was finished in California. He went to Sonora in Mexico, established a ranch, and tried to rebuild his shattered life. Fortune had completely deserted him, though, and his progress was ever downward. A few years later Californians learned that the once dashing and courtly cavalier had come to a particularly odious and gruesome end; he had been killed in a drunken melee and his body thrown into a barnyard where it was eaten by hogs.

At the same time Jack Powers's fortunes were rising and falling so dramatically in the southern regions of California, another Irish gambling man was acquiring a different sort of celebrity in San Francisco.

Tom Maguire, a former hack driver, bartender, and gambler from New York City, arrived in San Francisco in 1849. Unable to read or write, he was nevertheless proficient enough at cards to accumulate a sizable bankroll within a year. When Tom Bartell's Parker House went up in flames, Maguire purchased the property and spent $100,000 rebuilding the place. The

Tom Maguire, the illiterate gambler who first brought legitimate theater to the goldrush towns of California and Nevada. Courtesy The Bancroft Library, University of California.

lower floor contained the usual gambling hall equipment and ornamentation, but what distinguished the new Parker House Saloon was the second floor where was housed the city's first theater, called the Jenny Lind by its proprietor. This illiterate gambler had somehow developed a deep love for the theater, and he was to devote his life to bringing theatrical productions of the highest quality available to the rude miners of the gold-fields.

It was tough going, however. Maguire's early history of en-trepreneurship reads like an underwriter's nightmare. His original Parker House Saloon and Jenny Lind Theater opened in September, 1850. It burned down. He built another, even finer, place. Nine days after its grand opening it also burned to the ground. He rebuilt, was burned out, rebuilt again. He erected six buildings and lost them all in the space of two years. While they were open, however, the profits were so high in his houses that he continued to gain ground. Said the *San Francisco Herald* in 1851: "Mr. Thomas Maguire, so often burnt out and as often rising with energies unsubdued by misfortune, is now engaged in constructing a building which will be an ornament to the city."[6]

Maguire put up an imposing edifice, three stories high, con-structed of brick with a beautiful façade of white sandstone brought at great expense from Sydney in the Antipodes. More than two thousand miners packed the house on opening night, and all agreed it was the finest place of its kind in the West.

A year later he sold the building to the city for $200,000 to be used as a city hall and erected yet another place that he called Maguire's Opera House. By 1858 he had theaters in every major town of the mother lode and was bringing to Cali-fornia the greatest names of the American theater. Performing on Maguire's boards were Joseph Jefferson, John McCol-lough, Edwin Forrest, Madame Ristori, Lawrence Barrett, Madame Modjeska, Dion Boucicault, and Charles Kean. Adah Isaacs Menken wowed the miners with her scandalous rendition of "Mazeppa." Edwin Booth as a youth of twenty played Hamlet before Maguire's audiences, and James O'Neill, father of Eugene, played the role of Christ in *The Passion*

Play. All of Shakespeare's plays were produced in Maguire's theaters.

The illiterate gambling man loved fine music and was enthralled by grand opera. In later years he opened the Academy of Music in San Francisco and was the first to produce grand opera in the city. He made a trip to Italy expressly to meet his idol, Giuseppe Verdi.

Maguire maintained no office and drew up no contracts. He stood in front of his Opera House at eleven o'clock each morning and conducted business. A shake of the hand was all that he required to seal an agreement. A tall man with white hair and mustache and penetrating eyes, Maguire dressed in expensive high fashion and gloried in the self-styled title, "Napoleon of the Theater."

By 1862 western mining excitement was centered on the great new Comstock district of Nevada. While still maintaining his California interests, Maguire turned his attention to the new bonanza country. On July 2, 1863, he opened another opera house, even larger than his famous San Francisco place, at Virginia City, capital of the burgeoning mining district.

The Comstock had two great periods of frenzied activity, the middle years of the 1860s and the mid-1870s, and during those periods professional gamblers converged on the district. During the second boom period, a detailed study of Virginia City's recreational facilities was made by an official of the United States Geological Survey, who found that in the town of 18,000 there was available one gambling house for every 150 inhabitants.

Perhaps the most famous of these houses was the Gentry and Crittenden Saloon where a celebrated faro dealer named Hamilton Baker was the star attraction for several years. Baker would turn the cards for any amount, and bets of $5,000 were not uncommon at his table. The highest recorded wager was one of $30,000, placed on the turn of a single card. Baker became so well known that a number of gambling proprietors east and west vied for his services. He finally left Virginia City to take a job dealing for John Morrissey in a Saratoga casino for the incredible salary of $4,500 a month, but his career was

cut short by a railroad accident that left his right arm para-
lyzed.

Another popular dealer of faro in Virginia City was James
("K. B.") Brown, a rotund fellow who was chief of the fire
department and was welcomed in the city's best social, political, and financial circles. He was called K. B. by everyone,
including the press in numerous references. Nobody mentioned that the initials stood for "Kettle Belly."

A prosperous high roller named Matt Redding, "whose
smile could charm an ascetic," lorded it over the Virginia City
sporting crowd for a number of years. He wore a huge headlight diamond at his breast, and cuff links said to have cost
$6,000 each. He would make a grand tour of the gambling
halls nightly, a troop of admirers and hangers-on trailing behind. One night in 1874 a faro dealer named Barney Kenney
pulled a gun on him, and, although a Redding follower seized
Kenney's gun arm, Redding shot the dealer dead. He was acquitted of a charge of murder on a plea of self-defense, but the
incident changed his life. Kenney, known affectionately as
"Little Barney" by the sporting crowd, had been very popular,
and Redding's friends began deserting him. Somehow his luck
went with them and he finally drifted off to other camps, but
never again was he able to find the success and fame he once
had enjoyed.

Other prominent Virginia City gambling men included Tom
Diamond, Billy Dormer, Gus Botto, Miles Goodman, Jesse
Bright, Ramon Montenegro, Joe Dixon, Grant Isrial, and Joe
Stewart. Businessmen, both in and out of the sporting fraternity, held Stewart in specially high regard, and it was said that
either the Nevada Bank or the Bank of California would advance him sums on a moment's notice with no other collateral
than his word.

Tom Peasley was a well-known sporting man whose saloon
was named the Sazarac after a popular new cocktail introduced
into the town by Julia Bulette, a former New Orleans doxie
who was at the height of her reign as queen of the Virginia
City demimonde when she was murdered in 1867.

The Delta Saloon, jointly owned and managed by Jim Orndorff and Jack Magee, was unusual for its history of decorum;

in the many years the partners ran the Delta there was never a serious altercation in the place. The odds caught up, however, and on the same night Orndorff was killed by an obstreperous customer and Magee was murdered by his mistress.

Tom Buckner kept a place called the Sawdust Corner, noted for several unfortunate incidents. In 1874, Dick Carter, case-keeper at Buckner's faro table, killed a man in a fight over a woman named Katie Twist. Carter was nicknamed "Brigham" because of his reputation as a man of many women. In 1879 a mining engineer named Fosgard pulled a revolver and shot himself in the head while seated at Buckner's table. *The Territorial Enterprise* reported the tragedy, adding: "Mr. Fosgard seems to have been suffering from that fearful depression which sometimes seizes people in this section. It is particularly severe in persons of certain temperament and is very apt to increase with time."[7]

Pat Hogan also committed suicide. Well known in San Francisco sporting circles, Hogan operated in Virginia City for several years before returning to the Bay City where, after a long dry spell at the tables, he went to his room one night and put a bullet in his brain. Among his effects was found an ace of hearts upon which was written the following bit of doggerel:

> Life is only a game of poker, played well or ill;
> Some hold four aces, some draw or fill;
> Some make a bluff and oft get there,
> While others ante and never hold a pair.

William DeWitt Clinton Gibson was the impresario of a saloon and gambling hall at Gold Hill, another of the Comstock boomtowns. A gambler of great geniality, he was "Bill" to everyone, even after he was elected to the state senate. When, during his term of office, pressure was applied to make him change his stand on an important bill before the legislature, Gibson was reported as saying: "Gentlemen, I gave my word as a gambler that I would support this measure, and by the Eternal I'll keep my promise, if I am the only man to vote that way."

Among the Carson City gamblers of note were Tump Winston, Henry Decker and Adolph Shane. Vic Mueller ran the Headquarters, Gus Lewis owned the Old Sazarac, and Mark

Gaige kept two places in Carson, the Magnolia and the Occident. Dick Brown also divided his time between two enterprises, the Bank Exchange in Carson City and a place on the divide between Gold Hill and Virginia City, the Silver State Saloon.

A great rivalry existed for many years between Virginia City and Carson City concerning the relative abilities of the gamblers of the two camps. Virginia City boosters swore that their gamblers were more dexterous and proficient at their trade than any others, and Carson City adherents maintained as stoutly that their gamblers had no equal for skill and cunning in the manipulation of the pasteboards. Most unbiased observers gave the nod to Virginia City in the art of faro dealing, while acknowledging the superiority of Carsonites in the great American game of draw poker.

As chronicled in the pages of *The Argonaut* for March 23, 1878, however, there was one occasion when the men of Virginia City, in a showdown confrontation with the poker demons of Carson City, took the laurels—and the money—although resorting to the employment of outside reinforcement to achieve the victory.

Some of the Virginia City men on a visit to the opposing camp had been enticed into that game of draw at which the Carson City gentry so excelled. As usual, they were mauled pretty badly and, about eight o'clock in the evening, Billy Robinson of Virginia City wired the proprietors of that city's Delta Saloon: "Send down five hundred dollars by telegraph." Orndorff and Magee promptly dispatched the money but an hour later received another plea: "Send one thousand more and Joe Dixon."

Dixon was found and the situation explained. He removed a heavy sack of coins from his safe, rented a hack, and, with Jack Magee, made ready to ride to the rescue. Before leaving town, however, Dixon stopped at the Western Union office and sent off the following dispatch: "To Charles Huntley on board eastern-bound train at Reno—Get off and come to Carson by rapid conveyance. Meet me at Ormsby House before three o'clock. Business—Dixon." As he and Magee rode hard over the divide toward Carson City, Dixon said, "he is a lightning-striker, this Huntley. If our wire catches him, the game is ours."

It was just before midnight when Dixon and Magee, their horses foam-drenched and almost exhausted, pulled into Carson City and found the saloon where the Virginia City forces were struggling desperately to avoid annihilation. They took seats in the game, replacing two battered belligerents, and the eyes of the Carsonites lit up at the sight of Dixon's bag of golden specie.

Billy Robinson, furloughed from the game, sent off periodic telegraphic reports on its progress to an anxious gathering assembled back at Virginia City's Delta Saloon and the dispatches from the battlefront were posted for all to see. A cheer went up at one o'clock when Robinson reported: "Jack has just taken a pot of three hundred and sixty dollars." Then at 1:20 A.M. there was a great deal of backslapping and calls for drinks when word arrived: "Joe bluffed them out of seven hundred dollars. Set up the wine."

At 2:00 A.M., though, there came a bombshell: "We've just lost a pot of fifteen hundred dollars. Send down more coin— Joe."

The Virginia City gentry were undaunted by this setback. Within moments they had wired back: "We endorse your paper for ten thousand dollars—Orndorff and Magee, Grant Isrial, Dick Brown."

On the strength of this message, Joe Dixon secured the needed cash from John Pantlind, manager of the Ormsby House, left word where to send the anxiously awaited Charles Huntley, and hurried back to the field of battle.

It was shortly after three in the morning when Huntley appeared.

Joe and he had not met for years, and during the time had known each other only by correspondence; yet there was no gleam of recognition as Huntley slid into the game like a phantom. He showed the requisite amount of coin, and the Carsonites laughed inwardly because they had another victim. He looked like a divinity student. When he dealt, his thin hands played like lightning over the pack; his shuffle was the work of a magician, and the cards seemed alive.

Suddenly every player seemed extraordinarily proud of his hand and the raises mounted precipitously. When a Carson City player shoved a hugh stack of coins into the pot and murmured, "I'll go two thousand better," a hush fell on the table, but everyone saw the raise around to Huntley, who hesitated not for a second. "And five thousand more," he said, increasing the fortune piled in the middle of the table by that amount.

There was a long pause, and then, one by one, the players threw in their cards. The Carson City men stood up and wandered toward the door. The game was over and Virginia City had won. Dixon, Magee, and Huntley scooped the big pot into an oversized bag and, grinning, shook hands all around.

"Say, Charlie," Dixon asked, "what did you have?"

"Don't know," answered Huntley. "To tell the truth, I haven't yet looked at my hand. If a man looks at his hands, sometimes he gets confused and loses his nerve. I believe largely in the straight bluff."

Tom Maguire would on occasion take a hand in a game with the Virginia City boys, but his major interest continued to be his theaters and over the years he undoubtedly made a lot of money from these enterprises. By the 1870s he was recognized as being a millionaire and was hobnobbing socially with the mining magnates of the Comstock—the Fairs and Sharons, the Mackays, Floods, and Baldwins.

In his San Francisco past, though, he had once made a serious mistake, and it was ultimately to lead to his undoing. He had thrown the DeYoung brothers, publishers of *The Chronicle*, out of his theater, and they had never forgiven him for the affront. They carried on a vendetta against Maguire for twenty years, and the cumulative effect was to bring him and his theaters gradually into disrepute, resulting in his inability to engage the great names that had distinguished him in the beginning. As his theatrical business languished he turned to gambling again, but the old magic was gone and he met disastrous reverses.

In the early eighties he disposed of his properties for what he could get and returned to New York City. The *San Francisco Morning Call* published a brief item about him in 1886:

"Mr. Tom Maguire has just moved into a magnificently furnished house on Thirty-Third Street, New York. The California ex-manager is said to be the best-dressed man in the city."[8] But insiders knew that Maguire was broke in New York and that the proud old man had planted the item himself. He died, a pauper, in New York in 1896.

Ed Chase, overlord of "square" gambling in Denver. Courtesy Denver Public Library, Western History Department.

6

On June 6, 1860, a young man named Edward Chase arrived in Denver City, the provisioning center for the Pike's Peak or Busters. Little note was taken of the event at the time, for the twenty-one-year-old with the square jaw, prominent nose, icy blue eyes, and prematurely graying hair was to resident Denverites just another of the dozens of fortune seekers who were arriving daily. Denver would come to know Ed Chase and know him well, however, for as the town developed into one of the West's major gambling centers, he would become and remain for more than a half century the premier gambling kingpin.

Chase was born December 20, 1838, at Ballston Spa, New York, and raised at nearby Saratoga Springs, where his parents ran a fashionable hotel. He was introduced into the sporting life at an early age; his father owned a stable of Thoroughbreds and during the racing season the hotel was packed with the gaming brotherhood. Young Chase clerked at the hotel and came to know these men and prominent figures from other walks of life also—men like Daniel Webster and Henry Clay, each of whom took a shine to the youngster and corresponded with him in later years. He attended Zenobia Seminary, where he was a classmate of Leland Stanford.

There is little doubt that with these highly placed connections and his soon-to-be-demonstrated managerial ability, Ed Chase could have achieved early and great success in any field he chose. But he was an independent sort who wanted to do it all on his own, and the frontier beckoned. At the age of nineteen he headed west, in his pocket a stake of $1,500 won in an all-night poker session. He spent a year in Montana and then, with his brother John, who had joined him, moved on to the Pike's Peak country.

The Chase brothers prospected for a time along Clear Creek, but Ed soon tired of the pick and shovel routine and took a job as clerk in the Ford Brothers' store in the town of Golden. Finding a tough miner who could use his fists, Chase promoted a few prizefights, his battler taking on all comers. Soon he was offering games of chance in a small tent adjacent to the Ford store.

The furor in Denver over Charley Harrison and his Confederate sympathizers in the Criterion reached its peak in September, 1861, when Harrison went on trial. Spreading to the other camps, it caused a general reaction against gamblers. That month Ed Chase and three others were indicted on charges of larceny and conspiracy, accused of having taken $45 in gold dust from a man named Alfred Cushman "at a certain unlawful game of cards." The case was later dropped.

The departure of Harrison from Denver had its positive side for Chase; the town had no other resident gambler of Harrison's stature, and the twenty-two-year-old saw an opportunity and grabbed it. He still had little capital, but with the financial backing of the Ford brothers of Golden, he opened a tent gambling saloon on Blake Street in Denver. It was a rude affair indeed. Chase later recalled: "Furniture was scarce and the boys considered themselves lucky to have benches to sit on, while the card tables were covered with woolen blankets."[1]

No gambling enterprise ever had a more auspicious debut, however. Colonel John M. Chivington, presiding elder of the Methodist Episcopal Church for the Rocky Mountain District, and commander of the Third Colorado Cavalry, attended the grand opening ceremony with his military staff in full raiment. A huge man of stentorian voice, Chivington intoned the benediction, beseeching the aid of the Almighty for the success of the venture. A new gambling house proprietor could ask no more—house odds and God's help also.

In 1864, Ed Chase, one of a group of one hundred day volunteers, served under Chivington in the Third Colorado Cavalry. As captain of Company F he participated in the infamous Sand Creek Massacre in which some three hundred Cheyenne

Indians—men, women and children—were slaughtered. Before the attack on Chief Black Kettle's sleeping Cheyenne village, Chivington, the preacher-soldier, had exhorted his troops: "Kill and scalp every one, big and little! Nits make lice!" The colonel returned to Denver, proclaiming a great "victory," but a congressional committee later condemned his action and awarded the survivors of Black Kettle's band a large indemnity. General Nelson A. Miles called the attack "perhaps the foulest and most unjustifiable crime in the annals of America. . . ."[2]

Ed Chase could not have been proud of his part in the Indian wars but took heart in the success of his gambling business. He soon had accumulated enough profits to move across Blake Street to new and larger quarters in a two-story frame building. This was progress, and Chase and his new partner, Francis P. ("Hub") Heatley, called the place the Progressive Club. "There were seats for all comers," Chase recollected years later in a rare interview:

The tables were the best that had been known in Denver up to that time. The entire lower floor, 25 by 100, was devoted to gambling, with the exception of bar space. The second floor was also used by the sporting fraternity, but in a more quiet way. There were private rooms there which were rented to those who could afford to pay for them. The tables were run practically without limit. When one of the big games was on, I generally sat at the head of the table, so arranging it that a customer could place as high as $200 on double cards and $100 on singles. But they never broke any bank of mine. My profits were big at times.[3]

The recollection many Denver pioneers had of Ed Chase during this time was of a lean young man with gray hair seated on a high chair overlooking the first-floor gambling room of the Progressive Club, a rifle across his knees, eagle eyes taking in everything that went on in the place. Under those watchful eyes, proper decorum was observed at all times in the Progressive.

In the private rooms upstairs, the leading men of the city tried their luck. A group of them, including Jerome B. Chafee, later a United States senator, expressed a desire for a billiard room, and, as a result, the first billiard table in Denver was brought across the plains by ox team for installation in Chase's club.

One of the owners of a theatrical troupe playing Denver lost $300 at a Progressive Club faro table one night. The money had been the payroll for his performers and the theater man, in a desperate attempt to recoup, staked his half-interest in the troupe and lost that also. Chase suddenly found himself in the theatrical business. With his partner, Hub Heatley, he immediately began planning another place, one in which both the gambling and theatrical interests could be accommodated. They commissioned construction of a fine new brick building on Blake Street to house the Palace Variety Theater and Gambling Parlors, which was to be a Denver landmark for a quarter century.

The first floor of the Palace was devoted to gambling and was large enough to handle 200 players at once. Here 25 dealers presided over tables offering faro, wheel-of-fortune, hop-and-toss, corona, chuck-a-luck, roulette, over-and-under-seven, 21, and Spanish monte. A 60-foot-long bar was backed by a continuous mirror that reflected the magnificent gas chandelier with 500 faceted glass prisms which dominated the room. Upstairs was the 750-seat theater. Curtained boxes on either side were available for those who desired privacy and were attended by "pretty waiter girls." A string orchestra under the direction of Frank Holly played at the variety performances. On warm summer evenings Holly would deploy his musicians on the balcony over the front entrance to the Palace, causing traffic jams on Blake Street as passers-by in broughams, berlins, and phaetons stopped to hear the concert.

The Palace, unlike Tom Maguire's California and Nevada theaters, did not feature grand opera or Shakespearean drama. Its performers were strictly variety hall types, the singers and dancers, gymnasts and contortionists, jugglers and magicians, and blackface and ethnic comedians of the time. On the Palace boards appeared Eddie Foy and his partner, Jim Thompson; "The Leadville Nightingale," Lottie Rogers; Cora Vane; Miss Mayfield, "An Unrivaled Contortionist Pronounced by the Public As The Wonder of The Age"; Lou Spencer; Etta St.

Denver's Palace Theater. Three of the curvacious female performers who played here became wives of owners Ed Chase, Ed Gaylord and Bat Masterson. Courtesy Denver Public Library, Western History Department.

Clair; Donnelly and Drew; Ben Collins; Nellie McMahon; and a number of sister acts: the Hollands, the Barbours, the Duncans, the Wallaces, and the Emersons.

The Palace had its share of sensation over the years. In 1879 gambler Dave Stubblefield went to prison for killing a man in the game rooms, and in 1888 a man named Dan Burke was murdered there, but the tragedy of Effie Moore attracted national notoriety for the establishment. After winning $75,000 in the Louisiana lottery, the black sheep son of a prominent Canadian clergyman wooed the beautiful Effie, showering her with expensive gifts, including jewelry and an ermine cape. When she spurned his advances in one of the Palace boxes, he drew a pistol and shot her dead.

Ed Chase was now maintaining two successful Denver properties, the Progressive and the Palace, but he still looked farther afield for gambling house investment. In 1867 he went to Helena, Montana, which was enjoying flush times, and set up a gambling saloon with his brother John. Two years later, when the westward-building Union Pacific Railroad reached Cheyenne, the Chase brothers sold out in Helena and opened a gambling hall and variety theater in the end-of-the-track Wyoming boomtown.

The following year Ed and John opened still another place in Denver. A combination gambling house and theater like the Palace, this establishment was much smaller, and, because of its size, the brothers called it Cricket Hall. A *Denver Tribune* reporter, visiting the place in 1874, found that, in addition to the usual hall, stage area, and barroom, there was "an extensive room devoted to all games of chance that were ever invented. . . ." There was also, he said, "a sort of hypothetical 'Green Room' . . . " dedicated to purposes he said he would leave to his readers' imagination. The implication was that the Green Room was reserved for paying customers' amatory jousts with the "pretty waiter girls" employed by the house. "The 'Cricket' is a half-way 'standard' place of amusement. There is no ostensible price of admittance, but anyone who indulges in the so-called 'games of chance' is certain to pay very dearly for indulging in the experiment. The 'Cricket' is an 'all night' resort and is generally thronged with a strange mixture of people."[4]

In 1870, Hub Heatley died. Shortly thereafter Ed Chase disposed of the Progressive Club property and, still, later, elevated his head bartender at the Palace, Ed Gaylord, to full partnership in that enterprise.

In 1876, when gold was discovered in the Black Hills of South Dakota, Chase went to Cheyenne, jumping-off point for the Black Hills rush, and purchased the Inter-Ocean Hotel. Turning over management to his brother John, he went on to Deadwood and established a gambling house. For several years he maintained both these businesses in addition to his Denver properties.

The most degrading and humiliating episode of his life occurred in 1878. Acting in a manner completely atypical, the normally imperturbable and tightly controlled gambler in one brief spree resorted to firearms over a personal matter, drank himself into helpless intoxication, and allowed himself to be robbed. The sports of Denver were amazed, but they knew that it had to be a woman that turned Ed Chase inside out.

Women were his weakness. He loved them, many of them, and he paid dearly for his multiplicity of affections. He was married for the first time at the age of thirty-two. Within two years this marriage ended after a bizarre incident in which the wife, Margaret Jane Chase, disguised in male attire, burst into a back room of the Corn Exchange, a Denver resort, and tried to shoot a girl employee named Nellie Bellmont. Unsuccessful in this attempt, Margaret Jane sued for divorce, claiming that Chase was keeping the Bellmont woman in a "love-nest" at the Progressive Club. In her complaint she estimated Chase's worth at more than $200,000, including $75,000 in Denver property, $30,000 in Saratoga real estate, and $100,000 in cash and personal effects. She was granted the divorce but no alimony, since she held considerable Denver property in her own name. Of course, Chase had purchased this property and had put it into his wife's name to avoid loss by unfavorable judgment in possible civil suits.

Before the year was out, on December 21, 1873, Chase had married again, and it was this wife, Helen, who was the cause of his humiliating behavior in 1878. In early July of that year he was at his Deadwood City gambling hall when he was advised by a friend that Helen in his absence was carrying on with a man named George S. Brown of the Inter-Ocean Hotel in Cheyenne. Chase immediately returned to Denver. Helen was not to be found, but an examination of her mail confirmed his darkest suspicions. Chase caught the train to Cheyenne and hunted Brown down. Confronting him with a drawn pistol, the gambler shot point-blank at the other man's head, but Brown grasped Chase's arm at the instant of firing and the bullet just creased his face. The two men grappled and another shot was fired, striking Brown in the leg. Chase was over-powered by an officer who pistol-whipped him severely in the process. After a night in the Cheyenne calaboose the gambler was released on bail.

He headed back to Denver in search of his wife, but Helen learned of his coming and made herself very scarce. Chase then made a tour of the Denver gin mills, apparently trying to drink up all the booze in town. Police found him unconscious in a Larimer Street gutter at two in the morning. A bankroll of more than six hundred dollars was missing from his pocket; the great Ed Chase had been rolled like any ordinary Larimer Street drunk. He spent that night in the Denver cooler and was released in the morning upon his solemn promise "to take a bath, go to sleep and keep the peace."[5]

Chase straightened himself out after this deplorable episode, but his marriage was beyond repair. Four months later Helen filed suit for divorce, charging her husband with adultery and named as correspondent a saloon strumpet known as La Belle Stella.

In 1880, Chase married for the third time, taking as his wife Frances Minerva, one of the Barbour Sisters, a featured act at the Palace. This was to be a successful union lasting until the gambler's death more than forty years later. Chase's partner in the Palace, Ed Gaylord, impressed by Frances's ability to keep a man with the strong sexual drive of an Ed Chase at home in her bed, later married the other Barbour sister, Addie. Women performers playing the Palace apparently had a great appeal to the owners; Bat Masterson, who purchased the property from Chase and Gaylord in the late eighties, also found a wife on the Palace boards, a blond song-and-dance girl named Emma Walters.

Masterson was one of many celebrated gamblers in Denver during this period, some of whom would be associated with

Clifton Bell, whose private club rooms in Denver were patronized by the wealthiest men in the West. Courtesy Colorado Historical Society.

Ed Chase in various gambling house ventures over the next twenty years.

Clifton Bell, who dated back to the earliest days of the city, kept a succession of private clubrooms, catering to the gambling desires of wealthy mine owners, stockmen, and businessmen. Regular patrons included Horace Tabor, Edward

Walcott, and Thomas Bowen, all of whom later became United States senators.

Associated with Bell in several gambling enterprises were the Sampson brothers, James and Charles. During the nineties the Sampsons kept a popular gambling house called the Capitol, in which Ed Chase had an interest. A man named C. N. Scamehorn, who became addicted to faro and lost $12,000 in one year in Denver gambling houses, published a book in 1894 describing his misfortunes and castigating the men who had trimmed him.[6] Scamehorn considered James Sampson "the best adapted man for a successful gambler" he had ever met, being as "cold-hearted and determined as a bar of steel."

In addition to the Chases and Sampsons, there were several sets of brothers who maintained gambling establishments in Denver, including Jeff ("Soapy") Smith and his brother Bascomb, the Welsh brothers, Lou and Sam Blonger, and Pete and Charlie Persson.

A former Pony Express rider named Billy Cates for many years kept a place on Curtis Street called the Cates Club. He invested his gambling house profits in ranch property estimated in the mid-1890s to be worth more than $200,000. Scamehorn characterized him as "another coldblooded individual," but before he died in 1911, Billy Cates called Ed Chase to his bedside and asked him to distribute his estate among his former patrons who were experiencing hard times. "There are plenty of folks to help women and children," said Cates, "but nobody cares for broken-down old men." Chase administered the bequest, and when Cates's funds were exhausted, continued the philanthropic program with his own capital.

A legendary Mississippi River gambler finished out his days in Denver. Dick Hargraves had come to the United States from his native England as a youngster of sixteen and learned his trade while tending bar in a New Orleans gaming house. At the age of twenty in 1844 he turned professional after winning $30,000 in a poker game with a rich Louisiana planter. During his career on the river he was said to have won more than $2 million. Handsome and well-proportioned, the dashing Englishman fascinated women, and his amorous entanglements

Billy Cates. On his deathbed he asked Ed Chase to distribute his estate among down-and-out gamblers. Courtesy Colorado Historical Society.

led to several duels, the most famous of which was a meeting under The Oaks, the New Orleans dueling ground, with a prominent banker of the city. Hargraves killed the banker and later, in a knife fight at Natchez, also killed the banker's brother-in-law, who had sworn revenge on the gambler. To complete the tragedy, the banker's wife, her brother and husband dead, made an attempt on Hargrave's life and then committed suicide.

The adventurous Hargraves later joined a filibustering expedition to Cuba and served as a major in the Union army during the Civil War. He contracted tuberculosis during the war and went to Denver where he lived out his remaining days in relative obscurity, dying in the early eighties.

The most famous duel ever fought in Denver was between two women over the affections of a celebrated gambler and footracer named Corteze Thompson. Mattie Silks was for many years conceded to be Denver's leading madam and Cort Thompson was her "solid man." The athletic Thompson had done quite well touring the mining camps and challenging local sprinters to stake races. As a gambling man he was less successful, usually losing his fat purses at the faro tables. But he was "Mattie's man," and the prosperous madam kept him supplied with gambling funds.

In August, 1877, the sporting crowd of the city held an outing at Denver Park, just beyond the city limits. Late in the evening, after a great deal of alcoholic beverage had been imbibed—a circumstance undoubtedly influencing the later course of events—Madam Silks detected on the part of Katie Fulton, a business rival, an undue display of affection for Cort Thompson. Charges and countercharges were expressed in increasingly vituperative phraseology. Strident epithets were exchanged. Within seconds a duel had been suggested and agreed to, with Thompson acting as Mattie's second and Sam Thatcher seconding Katie. Some witnesses later claimed that a titillating feature was added to the drama when both ladies stripped to the waist before entering the arena, but this was never confirmed by any of the principals.

Bare-breasted or otherwise, Mattie and Katie stepped off the required paces, turned, and opened fire. A cry of anguish was heard and a body slumped to the turf. Onlookers surged forward, straining to see in the semidarkness made more obscure by clouds of gunsmoke. In the gloom they descried both madams standing erect and unharmed, while on the sod writhed Corteze Thompson, a bullet through his neck.

It was never disclosed whose bullet downed Thompson, or whether his wounding was deliberate or an accident caused by a combination of alcohol, poor light, and ineptitude with firearms. He recovered, Mattie Silks continued to dote on him, and he continued to lose her money in the gambling halls of Denver long after his racing days were over. He was banned from all of Ed Chase's resorts, however, because Chase had great regard for Mattie Silks and nothing but contempt for the man who would live at her expense.

During the eighties Ed Chase and a new partner, John J. Hughes, Jr., known in Denver as "Square-Shooter Johnny," acquired the Arcade, a Larimer Street resort of some notoriety. Former owners of this combination saloon, restaurant, and gambling house included Dick Clark's onetime partner, Jim Moon, who was killed in the place, and John Elitch, who would later open Elitch Gardens, a famous Denver amusement park. Chase and Hughes refurbished the entire building, installing in the second-floor saloon a beautiful mahogany bar brought from Saint Louis, expensive chandeliers, and a skylight uniquely fashioned with a faro tiger in stained glass.

Although several killings had taken place in the Arcade, accounting for its evil reputation, the first-floor dining room had always been known for its fine menu, and the new owners took pains to continue the tradition. Many considered the Arcade to be the best place to eat in Denver and, according to the *Denver Times*, "Sunday School teachers . . . often went there for Saturday night dinner even though it was a gambling house; they never felt that mattered in the face of superb food."

Bat Masterson and Wyatt Earp dealt faro for Chase in the Arcade. Other, less celebrated, dealers included Bob Stockton, G. S. Hunsicker, and Vaso ("Chuck") Chucovich. Stockton and Hunsicker quit Chase and went on their own, setting up gambling facilities in a four-story building on Tremont

Street, which had been opened originally in 1879 as Brinker's Collegiate Institute, a school for girls. It then became the Hotel Richelieu, and later still a house of prostitution. The former dealers ran this place only a short time, soon selling out to Ed Chase and Vaso Chucovich, the most improbable of Chase's many partners.

Chucovich was born in Dalmatia, then a part of Austria-Hungary. He left home and walked across Europe to take a job as a seaman aboard a ship bound for the United States. He jumped ship in San Francisco without a penny in his pockets. Although he was fluent in Italian, Greek, and Russian in addition to his native Dalmatian dialect, he could not speak a word of English. He spent some months in a monastery, where he learned the rudiments of the language, and then set forth to seek his fortune in the western mining camps.

At Carson City, Nevada, he worked in a stamp mill, separating gold from the ore by the use of mercury. He developed mercury poisoning and eventually lost all his teeth. He took a job as a bartender, but he was fascinated by the gamblers working the tables in the saloon and determined to study the art. A fast learner, he was soon gambling professionally and, in a year or so, had accumulated $46,000. A fast talker peddling mine stock got his $46,000, and Chucovich was left with a fistful of worthless stock. He went to Omaha and started over behind a faro table. By 1886, when he moved to Denver, he had built another stake of $74,000.

Ed Chase had ambitious plans for the former girls' school Stockton and Hunsicker were operating as a second-class gambling house, but the wily Chucovich had acquired first option to buy, and in order to get the place, Chase had to take the Slav on as a partner. The two were never friends and were as opposite a pair as could be imagined.

Chase was tall and spare, with white hair and chilly blue eyes. He dressed conservatively in suits of black or dark blue. His jewelry was never ostentatious. He spoke little but said what he meant and meant what he said. There was nothing frivolous about Ed Chase. His games were honest, his word was his bond, and he was extremely proud of his reputation as Denver's premier "square" gambler.

Vaso Chucovich was short and stocky with unruly red hair and bristling red mustachios. He had large, tender brown eyes and he smiled a great deal, displaying his brilliant white dentures. He was partial to corduroy suits of lavender, and usually wore a pink shirt embellished with a large headlight diamond. He was open, friendly, and loquacious but was prone to fly into violent rages when frustrated.

The partners' completely opposite manner of doing business is exemplified in an anecdote related by Mary Lathrop, a lawyer who handled both gamblers' real estate dealings for many years. She never sent Ed Chase a bill for her services, but he would pay her promptly and invariably in an amount about twice as high as she would normally have charged. She presented Chucovich a bill for twenty-five dollars on one occasion and he gave her ten, saying that another lawyer would have handled the job for that amount. Mary Lathrop marked his bill paid and handed it to him, together with the ten-dollar note, saying: "It would seem you need this more than I do, Mr. Chucovich. Get yourself another lawyer." In spite of his entreaties, she adamantly refused to represent him ever again.

Chase and Chucovich named their new property the Navarre, after Henry of Navarre, a historical figure remembered for his devotion to the gracious and elegant. There were public and private dining rooms on the first floor and saloon and gambling rooms on the second. Apartments on the third and fourth floors were available for customers' liaisons with the female employees of the Navarre. Patrons wishing to entertain their own female companions could enter through a special north entrance and retire to private dining rooms or secluded parlors, there to be served at the push of a button by discreet waiters.

In later years an even more covert access to the Navarre was provided by the owners. A tunnel was dug under Tremont Street from the Brown Palace Hotel to the Navarre and a railroad track installed. Special guests were thus able to travel back and forth between the establishments on miniature trolley cars pulled by Chinese coolies, entirely hidden from the view of the curious.

The owners outfitted all the rooms of the Navarre in the rich

The Navarre, a one-time girls' finishing school converted into a plush gambling house, was owned by Ed Chase and Vaso Chucovich, an unlikely pair. Courtesy Denver Public Library, Western History Department.

opulence that was the style of the 1890s. Red velvet carpeting and draperies were prominent throughout, and massive paintings of wide-hipped naked females hung from heavily paneled walls. Every saloonkeeper in Denver coveted the beautiful white and crystal bar that graced the main saloon. It was generally agreed that Chase and Chucovich had succeeded in their announced intent to make their establishment the finest place of its kind between Chicago and San Francisco.

The Navarre was undoubtedly unique in one respect: it was the only gambling saloon to contribute substantially to the treasury of a nation. During his lifetime Vaso Chucovich sent a large percentage of his share of the Navarre's profits to the region from which he derived, and upon his death most of his $1.25 million estate was bequeathed to Dalmatia. When this region became part of Yugoslavia, these funds accounted for a significant portion of the original treasury of the new country.

At the age of sixty, Ed Chase entered into his last gambling house venture. With the former owner of the Leadville Club, Bob Austin, he opened a new place in an old mansion on Curtis Street. Called the Inter-Ocean Club, this combination saloon, dance hall, and gambling house was handsomely appointed. There were a number of rooms, each devoted to a different game, and a staff of forty employees was required to run the place. Associated with Chase and Austin as dealers working on a percentage basis were many well-known Denver sporting men including Barney Boyce, W. S. Hunt, James Thornton, George Hunter, and "Three-Fingered" Jim Marshall. Thornton, one time member of the notorious Soapy Smith gang of skin-game artists, was given a chance to make it as a straight dealer in the Inter-ocean, but resorted to his old tricks and was shot dead in Chase's office in 1906 by Alton ("Big Al") Hoffses, who went to prison on a manslaughter conviction.

Over the years of his activity in Denver, Ed Chase had survived many reform movements, had frequently been arrested and fined, and on numerous occasions had closed his gambling operations until the "heat" cooled off, only to reopen on the same or different premises later. He was consistent in his philosophy of paying off the officials and charging the cost to business expense. Early in his career he had tried influencing civic officials by becoming one himself; he had served four years on the Denver Board of Aldermen in the late 1860s. Later he confined his efforts to the payment of periodic fines, donations of large sums to finance the campaigns of friendly political candidates, and the judicious bestowal of gifts and favors on incumbents. It was often charged in the Denver press that a majority of the city council "wore the Chase collar."

The payoffs were a constant drain on his resources, but his profits continued to mount. He invested heavily in Denver real estate and public utilities, which generated more wealth as the city grew.

In 1914 prohibition came to Colorado, bringing an end to the saloons and making even clandestine gambling unprofitable. At the age of seventy-six Ed Chase retired. He lived on in his fine house on Capitol Hill with his wife Frances until his death, after a short illness, on September 27, 1921.

Many in Denver were surprised that his estate amounted to only $650,000. He had made millions, but few knew that he had given most of it away. There had been no more generous contributor to every charitable drive in the city than the white-haired gambler. After his death, Mary Lathrop, his executor, revealed that much of his philanthropy had been performed anonymously at his instruction. He had carried on Billy Cates's dying request to render financial aid to broken-down gamblers and saloon bums long after Cates's resources were exhausted, and only Mary Lathrop knew that it was Chase money being used. Chase felt empathy for these derelicts, for he had not forgotten that he had once awakened, broken in spirit and pocket, in a Denver drunk tank.

Vituperation had been heaped upon him from pulpits for many years and he had borne the censure silently. He was a gambling man; he had always been a gambling man. He had not changed; Denver had changed. Condemnation had come, but Ed Chase survived it all, tight-lipped and taciturn as always. He had lived his life as he wanted—he had called the turn.

7

Spilling blood all over a gambling saloon never helped its business none.

E. S. "Kid" Highley
Charles Samuels, *The Magnificent Rube*

One day in the spring of 1895 the city marshal of Henrietta, Texas, read a letter from a former resident of the little town who had gone to Alaska several years before. The letter described a strange wilderness country where it got so cold that whiskey froze solid and men carried it in their pockets like a plug of tobacco and bit off a chunk when they wanted a shot of booze, where flour sold for a dollar a pound, and where some fellows had discovered gold and taken fifty thousand dollars' worth out of a mine within a week. While discounting for the tall tales, Marshal George Lewis Rickard was still intrigued with the idea of Alaska. Having recently buried both his wife of a year and their newborn baby, the familiar scenes of his hometown held nothing but sadness for him. He determined to head north to see for himself some of that remarkable land. He told friends he hoped to find enough gold to buy a cattle ranch upon his return to Texas.

Rickard, who predictably would be nicknamed "Tex" in the north country, was twenty-four years old in 1895. He was born January 2, 1871, in Clay County, Missouri. The Rickards were neighbors of the James family in Clay County, and Tex's mother always claimed that the instant he was born a posse was thundering past outside the house in pursuit of Frank and Jesse, the outlaw sons from the neighboring farm. The Rickard family's move to Texas in 1875 came about because of the James boys' troubles with the law; when Pinkerton detectives fire-bombed the James's farmhouse, the Rickards decided it was time to leave.

In 1882 when his father died, George Lewis Rickard was eleven years old and had completed only three years of schooling, but he was the oldest male in the family and was expected to provide the major financial support. In nineteenth-century

Texas, boys became men in a hurry. The youngster hired out as a cowpuncher and was paid a man's wages for a man's work. He spent his adolescence helping drive cattle to the Kansas railheads and beyond to new range country in Montana. After a dozen years of cowboying, he was trampled and almost drowned while moving a herd across the Big Washita River and decided it was time to try another line of work. That spring, also, he was married. The following year came the double shock of the loss of his baby boy after only a week of life, and the death a month later of his young wife.

Accompanied by a cowboy pal named Will Slack, Rickard set out on the long journey to Alaska. They went by rail to Seattle and embarked on a ship bound for Juneau, arriving in November. Travel into the interior was impossible until spring, and the two young Texans wintered in the port town which had an extensive saloon, dance hall, and gambling house district. Rickard, who had always been a better-than-average gambler with an inherent card sense, had sharpened his skills in the trail towns and range camps of the cattle country. He spent many hours that winter at the Juneau gaming tables and made expenses for himself and Slack.

In the spring they began the arduous and perilous journey into the interior, their destination Circle City, one thousand miles away. The trip, which was to be duplicated by tens of thousands of Klondike stampeders two years later, began with a ride on a harbor tugboat to the little Indian village of Dyea, a few miles from the foot of Chilkoot Pass. Here Rickard and Slack were faced with the laborious task of backpacking all their supplies to the summit of the steep and treacherous 3,500-foot pass. Each man had one thousand pounds of goods, and the 35- to 45-degree grade made the carrying of more than fifty pounds at a time impossible. This meant that some twenty trips would have to be made up that slope, each one a backbreaking effort. It was at Chilkoot that Will Slack began to lose enthusiasm for Alaska. He stuck with it, however, packed his supplies to the top, braved the hair-raising descent by sled down the opposite slope, and made the long trek, pulling the heavy sleds in temperatures that dropped to fifty below zero, to the headwaters of the Yukon River. Here

Tex Rickard, flanked by Klondike gamblers Coal Oil Johnny on his right and Swiftwater Bill Gates on his left, presides over a gambling table in Dawson. Courtesy Western History Collections, University of Oklahoma Library.

they were to build a boat for the final leg of the journey down the river to Circle City. But here Slack called it quits, shook hands with his friend, and started back for Juneau. He kept right on heading south, away from the numbing cold of the north country, and did not stop until he reached the Mexican border. Rickard never saw him again but learned years later that soon after his return his friend had been killed in a saloon gunfight.

Rickard joined another party, helped build the necessary boats, and rode the Yukon down to Circle City. The town, which was three years old in 1896, had been so named because someone had discovered that it lay within the Arctic Circle. It had a permanent population of five hundred catering to the needs of the sourdoughs working the mines along Birch Creek, sixty-five to eighty miles away. The major industry of Circle City was the purveyance of pleasure, as evidenced by the kinds of businesses in operation; there were only two general stores and three blacksmith shops, but no less than twenty-eight saloons, gambling houses, and dance halls.

Tex Rickard was dead broke when he arrived in Circle City, and he needed a stake to purchase the tools and provisions necessary to begin prospecting. He walked into one of the gambling saloons and asked for a job. He would do anything, he said—tend bar, deal cards, or sweep the floor. The owner of the place regarded the slim young Texan with the frank, open countenance for a moment, liked what he saw, and hired him on the spot.

In later years Tex Rickard's detractors would invariably say that he was the luckiest stiff they ever knew. They argued that it had to be dumb luck that brought fame and fortune to the hick from Texas with the third-grade education.

They were partially correct. Rickard *was* lucky. It was luck that put him in Alaska two full years before the great Klondike gold rush of 1898, time enough for him to have made and lost a fortune and acquired and lost ownership of two gambling houses. And it was luck that led him, seeking a job, into the gambling establishment of Sam Bonnifield.

The Yukon gold rush produced some colorful and memorable gambling men, but Sam Bonnifield was the greatest of them all. Originally from West Virginia, Bonnifield had gone west at an early age and practiced his trade in Kansas, Montana, and California before heading north. He had arrived in Alaska on the same boat with a high-rolling gambler named Louis ("Goldie") Golden, and the two maintained rival establishments first at Juneau, then at Circle City, and still later at Dawson. Bonnifield had two nicknames, equally apt. He was known as "Silent Sam" because of his taciturnity and "Square Sam" because of his undisputed honesty. A tall, slender man of about thirty, with startling electric-blue eyes, he was considered handsome by women and men alike.

Bonnifield could win or lose huge sums without a flicker of those remarkable eyes. The first week that Rickard worked for him, he saw Sam turn a card at the faro table on which $5,000 was riding. Goldie Golden had invaded the Bonnifield lair, as was his custom at least once a week, and tackled the tiger, placing five $1,000 chips on the queen to win. Sam turned and the queen showed second, winning for Golden. Without changing expression Bonnifield said, "Tex, if Goldie is quit-

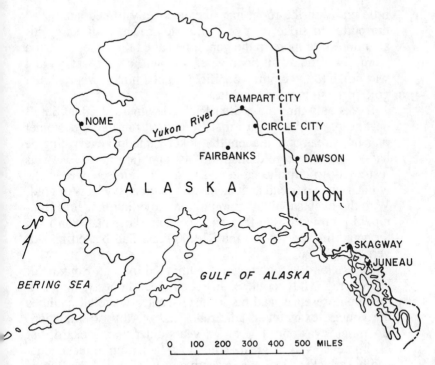

Towns of the Yukon–Alaska gold rush.

ting, pay him off. Five thousand dollars comes to a little over nineteen pounds and a half in dust. Oh, hell, give him an even twenty pounds!"

But Goldie was not quitting, and by four the next morning when he finally rose from the faro table, he had lost the $5,000 back to Bonnifield and $17,000 of his own dust as well.

Sam Bonnifield was a master at this sort of gamesmanship. On another occasion, a Montana gambler named Al Mitchell bragged in Dawson City that he could take Bonnifield at poker, tossed a $5,700 bag of dust on Sam's table, and challenged him to a game. After several inconsequential hands, Mitchell suddenly tried to throw his opponent off balance with a massive raise. Bonnifield murmured that it was getting a little chilly in the room and unconcernedly turned and asked the porter to stoke the fire in the stove. Then, directing his attention once more to the game, he called the raise without a word. Two and a half hours later Mitchell lost his last bet and was down to the cloth. Bonnifield flipped him a twenty-dollar gold piece to buy his breakfast.

It was only three days after Rickard witnessed Silent Sam's besting of Golden at faro that Bonnifield ran into a customer on a hot streak and in a lengthy poker game lost everything he had—$72,000 in gold dust and his gambling house. He was just about to quit the table and turn the premises over to the winner when a friend arrived carrying two heavy bags of gold. With the fresh supply of ammunition providing new life, Bonnifield returned to the fray and six hours later had won back the gambling house and the $72,000 and had busted his adversary.

Tex Rickard was completely enthralled by Sam Bonnifield. His courage, his coolness, his scrupulous honesty, his commanding presence, and his iron self-control were all qualities the young Texan found admirable and worthy of emulation. Bonnifield was only five or six years older than Rickard, but his influence was as great as that of a father, an influence that had been lacking in Tex's formative years. It was Sam Bonnifield who turned Rickard from a would-be gold prospector into a professional gambler and all-or-nothing plunger. As Charles Samuels, Rickard's biographer, so aptly put it, "for the rest of his life Tex Rickard gambled as though Sam Bonnifield were looking over his shoulder."[1]

Bonnifield held Rickard in high regard also, and he was convinced that Tex brought him luck. In less than a month after hiring Rickard, Bonnifield had won enough to move to new and larger quarters. He credited the Texan for his good fortune and, in a typical magnanimous gesture, turned over his old place and its complete set of gambling paraphernalia, furniture, and liquor stock to his protégé.

Rickard's first attempt at gambling saloon proprietorship lasted exactly two weeks. A high roller simply earthquaked his faro game one night, and Rickard, stripped of his dust, staked his house and lost. He wished the new owner luck and strolled down the street to Bonnifield's new place and asked for his old job back.

It was six months later, in January, 1897, that word reached Circle City of the great gold strike at Bonanza Creek in Canada's Yukon Territory and the camp's economy turned upside down. Cabins that had been in demand at Circle City for $500 suddenly could not be sold for $25, and the price of a good sled dog went from $50 to as much as $1,500. Circle City was virtually evacuated as the rush was on to the new diggings. Tex Rickard was one of the first to make the 300-mile run up the frozen Yukon River by dogsled. He staked a claim on Bonanza Creek and spent the rest of the winter burrowing into the frozen earth. He did hit pay dirt and sold his claim in the spring to a British investor for $60,000.

Rickard went back to Circle City, his original ambition of returning to Texas and buying a ranch still very much on his mind. Now he had the money to accomplish that goal, but somehow the feverish excitement of the Klondike held him. When a pal named Tom Turner showed up in Circle City with news of a new boomtown called Dawson City fast springing up at the junction of the Klondike and Yukon rivers, Tex forgot about the Texas ranch.

Rickard went to Dawson City and, with Turner as partner, opened a tent saloon called the Northern. The place was an instant success and in four months the partners had a combined net worth of more than $400,000. Then in one night the bankroll and the saloon were gone. A group of sourdoughs from Circle City came in that night and began laying heavy bets at the roulette table. They gave the middle numbers, 13 to 24, a big play, concentrating especially on the numbers 17 and 23. They won bet after bet and Rickard made repeated visits to his safe for more dust.

"Whenever they lost they just piled on more dust and told me to roll the ball," he later recalled. "We rolled ourselves right out of house and home that night. At the same time other customers were taking us good at faro. I'd put the fifty-seven thousand dollars I had left over from my Bonanza-strike money into that place, along with plenty of Turner's dough. That night we lost the whole joint, and every nickel we had in the world."[2]

For more than a year after losing his business, Tex Rickard worked for twenty dollars a day as a house dealer and bartender in Dawson City gambling saloons. His goal now was to raise enough stake to start another saloon. As soon as his shift was finished he would sit down at a table and play against the house. Many nights he went to bed hungry. There were winning nights, of course, but the streaks never were long enough to build the capital he needed.

Sam Bonnifield was on hand at Dawson City and his Bank Saloon and Gambling House at the corner of Front and King streets was considered the finest place in town. He and his old competitor, Goldie Golden, tangled one night in the biggest poker game on record in the high-rolling Klondike. There was already $50,000 in the pot when Goldie kicked it by $25,000. Bonnifield saw the raise and elevated it another $25,000. When Golden called there was a cool $150,000 on the table. Goldie spread four stately queens on the green felt but watched with horror as Silent Sam laid down four perfectly healthy kings.

Goldie Golden made $60,000 at Dawson City in 1897 and the following year he was broke. He staged a comeback a couple of years later and owned a piece of a gambling saloon at Nome. One winter's night he got the itch to buck the faro tiger, but it was so cold outside that he refused to go down the street to another house. He sat down at the faro table in his own saloon and told the dealer to turn the cards. For seventy-two hours he wrestled that tiger, never stopping to sleep, taking his meals at the table, wearing out a parade of dealers. When the marathon session was over, he had lost $180,000, which was everything he owned, including his share of the establishment. After the dealer raked in his last bet, Goldie reached across the table, grabbed the faro box and hurled it to the floor. "What the hell kind of faro bank is this," he roared, "when not even an owner of the joint can make expenses bucking it?"

The other owners commiserated with him. They proposed that he buy his share back, paying in installments from his percentage of the house profits, but Goldie shook his head. He had his fill of Alaska, he said, he would accept $1,000 to pay his way home to the States. He made it clear that the money was not a loan, but a gift. "Getaway money" he called it, and assured them all that no one in Alaska would ever hear of him again. And no one ever did.

Sam Bonnifield participated in some extended gambling sessions, although none on the order of Golden's three-day endurance test. One memorable game at his Bank Saloon in Dawson City began at seven in the evening and finally broke up at seven the following night. Playing with him were two of the most famous of Yukon gambling men, Dan Egan, better known in the Klondike as the Montana Kid, and Harry Woolrich.

The Montana Kid had made his original stake running whiskey into Dawson City by dogsled. He claimed to have the fastest dog team in the world, a team the Canadian Mounties could not catch. When in the chips, he fed each of his dogs a five-dollar steak daily. He was quick to seize any opportunity to make a fast buck. It was the Montana Kid who brought into Dawson City a copy of a Seattle newspaper that carried the story of the sinking of the *Maine* in Havana Harbor. He went into partnership with one Judge Maguire, who hired a hall and gave readings of the paper each evening at seven, nine, and eleven o'clock. Listeners were charged $2.50 apiece to hear the news.

Harry Woolrich arrived in Dawson City in November, 1898. A dark, saturnine man in his mid-fifties, he was well known in the Pacific Northwest as a clever and daring high-stakes operator. It was said that he had once won and lost $50,000 at a sitting in a Butte, Montana, gambling hall. Besides his skill, Woolrich had the reputation of being fantastically lucky, and he never lacked for financial backers in a big game. When he sat in, his dark hat shading his eyes and his omnipresent cigar jutting from his expressionless mouth, there would always be a crowd around him. Generally the Woolrich gallery had more than mere spectator interest in the game; he was usually playing with their money.

Woolrich was a principal in a story that illustrates the peculiar gallantry of many of the sporting gentry. Myrtle Brocee, a performer at the Tivoli Theater in Dawson, was Woolrich's mistress. After a bitter quarrel with the gambler, she shot herself to death in his room. At an inquest Woolrich and five other gamblers swore under oath that they had slept with Myrtle, but each insisted that the girl retained her chastity. Woolrich declared flatly that she had died a virgin. The people of Dawson City were moved by this display of chivalry and on the day of her funeral, business houses closed and respectable citizens and sporting folk alike followed Myrtle Brocee to the cemetery where she was buried in a beautiful silk-lined casket with silver handles purchased by Harry Woolrich.

One night Woolrich won $60,000 and announced that he was forsaking the world of cards. He would, he said, return to the States and live out the remainder of his years in quiet luxury. A crowd of backslapping cronies escorted him to the docks and cheered as he purchased a ticket on a departing steamer. It seemed the boat was delayed. Woolrich shrugged and, together with his coterie of well-wishers, walked back uptown to buy his pals a drink. In the Monte Carlo he stepped over to the faro table and fished a half-dollar from a vest pocket. "Here's my final bet, boys," he laughed, tossing the coin on the faro spread. The coin was lost and he threw down another fifty-cent piece.

Twenty-four hours later Woolrich was still at the faro table. The steamship was gone and so was his $60,000. He reached into a pocket, drew out his ticket and placed it on the layout. The cards were turned and the ticket followed his money into the dealer's bank.

Following the play of the big-time plungers was the chief amusement in Dawson City. At the height of the gold rush era, hundreds and sometimes thousands of miners would throng Front Street hoping to be witness to one of the high-stakes games. When a gambler hit a streak of luck many of the onlookers would try to ride with him, placing bets on the same faro cards, roulette numbers, or points at the craps table.

One unforgettable night a small-time faro fiend named One-Eyed Riley went on a winning spree that was phenomenal. It began at midnight in Bonnifield's Bank Saloon. Riley, starting with picayune bets, couldn't seem to lose, and was soon betting the limit and winning. The word spread down Front Street and by morning, when he left Bonnifield's to get breakfast, hundreds were following in his wake. After eating, he began a tour of the Front Street resorts, betting the limit in each, and continuing to win. He broke the faro bank in Bill Jenkins's Sour Dough Saloon and closed down Joe Cooper's faro game in the Dominion. At the Monte Carlo a succession of dealers was thrown against him, but he bested them all until a celebrated faro dealer named Shepherd was roused out of bed to come and stop One-Eyed's onslaught. Finally, as it always does, the luck changed, and, after losing several bets in a row, Riley called it quits. Counting up his winnings, he found that he was ahead $28,000. In great haste to get out of the north country, Riley paid a dog-driver $1,000 to take him over the winter trail to Skagway where he could get a boat home. Hundreds cheered his departure, but several months later they learned that at Skagway he had encountered some of the minions of the crooked gambler Soapy Smith and had lost his entire fortune in a dice game.

There are many ways to lose money. A noted Klondike gambler named Sam Wallace had come north with a $50,000 stake provided by a syndicate of West Coast gamblers. By means of careful and judicious play he managed to turn a clear profit of $100,000 for his time in the Klondike. Returning to the States, he divided the money evenly with his backers, retired from the profession, and went into the steel business with his $50,000. A short time later he was broke and working as a laborer in a steel mill at ten cents an hour.

One of the most cautious of the Dawson City gamblers was a faro player known only as "the Oregon Jew." Flashily dressed in cutaway coat, spats, and hard hat, he would appear in one of Dawson City's gambling emporiums every afternoon at four, jauntily twirling a gold-headed walking stick. His system was unvarying. After purchasing a small stack of chips, he would begin placing small bets at the faro table. If he lost

Swiftwater Bill Gates and friend in the Klondike. Gates is the shorter man wearing the necktie. Courtesy Alaska Historical Library.

the stack, he would rise and immediately leave, convinced that his luck was bad for that day. On the other hand, if he won he would gradually increase the size of his bets, testing the strength of his run of luck. Should the signs continue favorable, out would come the bankroll and every wager would be for the limit of the table.

The most flamboyant of Klondike gamblers was William F. Gates, a small man with shoulder-length hair and a luxuriant handlebar mustache. In 1896, Gates was working as a hashslinger in a Circle City roadhouse. He joined the wild rush to Bonanza Creek in the winter of 1897, where he met a man named Jack Smith who had recently sold his claim on the creek for $155,000 and had taken a lease on a tent saloon outside the new town of Dawson City. Gates talked Smith into bankrolling him and letting him operate the gambling concession for the remaining three weeks of the lease. During those three weeks Gates was almost unbeatable in the Bonanza, as the saloon was called, and picked up most of the loose money in Dawson City. With their winnings the partners purchased a lot in the center of the booming town and opened the Monte Carlo Dance Hall and Saloon, which was to become one of the most famous pleasure palaces north of Seattle.

Somewhere Gates had been tagged with the nickname "Swiftwater Bill," reportedly because of the dexterity with which he piloted a canoe over the treacherous White Horse Rapids. Gates confided to his friend Jed Jordan that he was deathly afraid of fast water, and when his prospecting partners proposed to challenge the fearsome rapids in a raft, he had chosen to walk around, and the name had been given to him in derision.

In Dawson City, Swiftwater Bill reveled in his sudden affluence. He strutted Front Street in a Prince Albert coat, opera hat, and spatted shoes. A huge diamond sparkled on his bosom and he was never seen without a starched collar, said to be the only one in Dawson. When the collar was being cleaned he would stay in bed so that no one could see him without his trademark. In his rounds of the town he would stop in every saloon and buy drinks for the house. When overseeing the games in his own Monte Carlo, he welcomed high rollers.

"The sky's the limit, boys," he would cry. "If the roof gets in your way, why, tear it off!"

In most accounts of the Klondike gold rush, Swiftwater Bill is depicted as a profligate clown, mainly because of his well-publicized marital adventures later in the States and a vitriolic book on his life penned by one of his irate mothers-in-law. Jed Jordan, who kept a successful gambling saloon at Nome and was himself no slouch at a poker table, regarded Gates as "just about perfect" as a player.

Jordan once saw Gates win $30,000 in a poker game at Nome. "Swiftwater Bill was good," he insisted:

He knew when to be daring, which wasn't often. . . . He was never ashamed to drop out. One time I saw him fold his cards in a game in which there wasn't more than $10 in the pot, and he had four jacks and a thousand dollars in front of him that he could have bet. But he thought he was beat and would not throw a few dollars away to find out if he was right. He was also uncanny in spotting a man who was bluffing. . . .[3]

In a poker game he was ruthless. If his grandmother was holding a pair of tens and he had four aces he would sandbag her. . . .

In a game in Jed Jordan's Ophir Saloon in Nome, Gates pulled off a coup that Jordan felt was a demonstration of pure poker genius. "He was sitting in a seven-handed draw game with two strangers, one on his left, the other on his right," Jordan recalled:

The stranger on his right was dealing when Bill got four aces on the draw. This miracle would have made most people suspicious, but old Bill was as happy as a Cheechako. There was considerable betting around the table and the pot mounted to around $1,000. Bill had shoved his entire stack into the game.

Just at this moment, right before the draw, one of the strangers upset his drink. I happened to be looking straight at the dealer at the time and I saw him milk the cards. Everybody in the game had turned to help mop up the spilled drink.

Swiftwater Bill put down his hand, covered it with his pipe and came over to the bar. He was in danger of being frozen out and he wanted me to lend him some money. . . .

"That fellow is milking," I whispered to him.

"Jed, you are a cynical man," Swiftwater Bill said blithely. "I have a good hand and that fellow would not hustle. Is my credit good for $500?"

I let him have the $500 and shrugged. It was his business, not mine. I began to wonder if I had misjudged Bill as a poker player.

He went back to the table and threw the entire $500 into the pot as a raise. Each of the two strangers met the bet. Everybody else was out of the game.

Then came the draw. Bill was holding four aces. He could either draw one card or stand pat. The choice was up to him. What did he do? He threw away two of his aces and a third card, held on to his remaining pair, and asked for three cards.

In the showdown, he won the pot. On a pair of aces. It amounted to about $2,500.

Bill had figured out what I couldn't see.

If the game was fixed, the only hand that could beat him was a straight flush, and that would have to be held by the player on his left. Bill could not improve his hand, but the man on his left could. Therefore, Bill reasoned, the fellow on the left was holding say, the six, seven, eight and nine of spades, because the dealer could not have dared hand him a pat straight flush, not with four aces already being dealt out. When the dealer milked the cards he transferred the five and ten of spades from the bottom to the top of the deck. If Bill took one card, the opponent on his left would get the five of spades. If Bill stood pat, the man would get the ten.

The cheats could not lose. Either way, the fellow filled his straight flush. Except that Bill broke up his fours and took three cards and ruined the deal[4]

Swiftwater Bill was, as Jordan testified, "a great gambler and a thoroughly honest one," but it was his penchant for the dramatic gesture and well-publicized libidinous escapades that forever enshrined him among the legendary characters of the Klondike gold rush. In Dawson City he lusted for a curvaceous entertainer named Gussie Lamore. For the hand of the busty Gussie in marriage he was willing, he said, to present her with her weight in gold dust, which he adjudged to be about $30,000, or two coffee cans' worth. Miss Lamore coquettishly kept her suitor dangling while she played the field, perhaps in search of a better offer. Gates learned that she had an inordinate fondness for eggs, a commodity that was rare in the Arctic interior. When two cases of the precious eggs arrived by boat, he purchased them both for $2,280, thus cornering the market in Dawson City. Gussie resisted his ovular blandishments and, in a fit of pique, he had the entire shipment of eggs fried, ate two or three, and fed the remainder to a pack of stray dogs off the Dawson City streets.

Gussie finally agreed to marry Gates, took his two coffee cans of dust, and left for San Francisco to prepare for the wedding. Bill remained behind to dispose of his interest in the Monte Carlo and wind up some other affairs. When he finally arrived in California, he learned that Gussie had departed for parts unknown, taking the coffee cans to remember him by. In retaliation for this perfidy Gates a month later married Grace Lamore, Gussie's sister, and set her up in a fine new home in Oakland. Grace proved to be as treacherous as her sister, however, and left him after only three weeks to file for divorce. Between them the Lamore sisters took the wily gambler for over $100,000.

Bill returned to Alaska, financially scarred by his amatory adventures but with libido undamaged. He decamped from Skagway with fifteen-year-old Bera Beebe and headed for Dawson City. Bera's mother, who had come north with her two daughters, hoping to open a hotel, took after the elopers in pursuit as hot as could be managed in that icy country. When she caught Gates in Dawson City he assured her that he "had done the right thing" and married Bera, and so charmed his new mother-in-law that she loaned him the $35,000 she had brought to start her hotel business.

Gates fathered two children by Bera, but several years later he took her back to the States and deserted her to run off with seventeen-year-old Kitty Bardon, the daughter of his own sister. Now two enraged mothers-in-law dogged his erratic trail to Alaska and back. In Seattle, Bera's mother had him arrested for bigamy, but Gates talked Bera into divorcing him and the charges were dropped. Subsequently he and his niece were legally married, but this union also ended in divorce.

Hounded by creditors, he declared bankruptcy in 1906. At Coeur d'Alene, Idaho, he was married once again, this time to eighteen-year-old Sadelle Mercier. He put in a brief appearance at Rawhide, Nevada, during that camp's boom, and then, in 1909, he sailed to Peru, professedly to search for the lost gold mines of Pizarro, but perhaps to escape the tangled connubial web he had woven. For twenty-eight years he chased legends of hidden wealth in Latin America, until he was killed accidentally in 1937 by a rifle bullet fired by a Peruvian Indian.

Of all the boomtowns in the frontier West where gamblers congregated, Dawson City probably had the lowest percentage of crooked practitioners. Most of the famous Dawson City gamblers—Square Sam Bonnifield, Tex Rickard, Harry Woolrich, Goldie Golden, and Swiftwater Bill Gates—were celebrated for their honesty. Credit for this condition has been given by some to the presence in Dawson City of a contingent of Northwest Mounted Police who took a dim view of cardsharps and skin-game operators. The standard punishment for such malefactors was an extended session chopping logs on the enormous woodpile behind the Mounties' barracks. To the gentry whose livelihood was dependent upon the softness of their hands and the nimbleness of their fingers, such a sentence was greatly to be dreaded. The Mounties undoubtedly contributed to the high standard of honesty prevailing in the Dawson City saloons, but the very inaccessibility of the camp also played a large part. Crooked gamblers, if their duplicity was revealed, could not skip out of town easily; they were trapped and at the mercy of their angry victims. Each year with the spring thaws, a few were found frozen to death along the trails leading out of town. Some may have died in an effort to escape the town, but many had been taken out and left to die by enraged miners.

The port towns of Alaska—Juneau, Skagway, and Nome—where there were no Mountie woodpiles and where ships were available for hasty departure, if necessary, harbored most of the sharpers. One of the slickest of gambling cheats operated in Dawson City for a time before his notoriety spread to the point that he was barred from most houses and was forced to move elsewhere for his action. "Eat-Em-Up Jack" Blackburn had enormous hands, "the size of two big Bibles," according to one gambler who knew him. "He could (and often did) take a deck, extract five cards while he was shuffling and conceal them in the palm of one hand, then deal around the board, pick up his own cards and transfer cards back and forth from his palm, and see to it that all the cards were returned to the deck after the hand had been played. You had to admire him, artistically speaking."[5]

Blackburn was famous in the fraternity for outcheating other cheats. He was an innocent appearing fellow with a guileless face and the manner of a raw greenhorn. This front was useful in trapping suckers into his crooked games, but it also often made him the target for other sharpers new to the north country. Once he sat in a poker game with two strangers who, he soon realized, were out to fleece him. One of them dealt a hand and Blackburn was given four kings before the draw. The betting was opened by the dealer's confederate for the minimum amount. Blackburn, glancing at his cards, sighed and threw in his hand. "I fold," he said.

The hand was played out without comment, but after the game was over one of the sharps cornered Blackburn at the bar. "What in thunder made you lay down those four kings you had before the draw?" he demanded.

Blackburn answered: "If you will tell me how in thunder you knew I had four kings, I will tell you why in thunder I laid them down."

Eat-Em-Up Jack gained his nickname in another game with hustlers out to skin him. One of them dealt him six cards and Blackburn picked them up. According to the universal rules of poker, such a hand is dead and the holder relinquishes all claim to the pot. But Blackburn saw that three of his six cards were aces.

"It's time we had a drink," he said. "I'm buying. And, bartender, bring each of us a sandwich from the lunch counter, please." The game was held up briefly while the players enjoyed their drinks and sandwiches, and then continued. There was some spirited betting and finally Blackburn showed his three aces and won the hand. He was reaching for the pot when one of the sharpers yelled, "Hold on there. You've got six cards!"

Blackburn carefully separated the cards in his hand. There

were three aces and two others. The deck was counted. Fifty-one. The floor and the chairs were scrutinized and at last Blackburn was searched, but nowhere was the missing card to be found.

Weeks later one of the skin-artists, unable to contain his curiosity, hunted up Blackburn. "Come on, Jack," he pleaded. "I dealt that hand and I know I gave you six cards. I lost my money and I will die game, but what the hell did you do with that extra card?"

Blackburn winked. "I just slipped it in my sandwich and et it," he said.

Thus was born the cognomen "Eat-Em-Up Jack."

Tex Rickard, after fifteen months of twenty-dollar-a-day bartending, wheel spinning, and card dealing, concluded that if he was ever to make his fortune in the north country, it would not be at Dawson City. He had managed to accumulate a little capital from his many bouts with the faro tiger, but property prices were sky-high in Dawson. He decided that his best bet was to go to a new camp and get established before a big boom blew prices out of sight. There was talk in the fall of 1898 of rich strikes in the creeks near the little town of Rampart, downriver from Circle City. Rickard went to Rampart and put up a small gambling saloon. His opening festivities included a grand ball and prizefight. Music for the ball was provided by a harmonica-playing miner, and the "ladies" were a few Siwash Indian women he had hired for the occasion. The prizefight was a slugging match between two local brawlers that ended when one butted the other on the chin, knocking him cold.

The self-appointed mayor of Rampart City was Al Mayo, an Alaskan pioneer who had spent almost forty years in the Arctic. Mayo was the proprietor of the Florence Hotel in which the following sign was prominently displayed:

HOUSE RULES—MAYO'S HOTEL

Craps, Chuckluck, Stud Horse Poker.
Black Jack games run by the management.
Dogs bought and sold.
Insect Powder for sale at the bar.

Always notify the bartender the size of your poke.
Spike boots must be removed at night.
Dogs not allowed in bunks.
Every known fluid except water for sale at the bar.
Fire escapes through the chimney.
Special rates to ministers and to the gambling "profesh."

Rampart, Alaska, 1898.

Rickard met two men in Rampart who were to remain his close friends for many years. Rex Beach, whose writings, together with those of Jack London and Robert Service, did much to popularize the Klondike for American readers, recalled meeting Rickard, whom he described as a "slim, dark, likeable fellow with a warm, flashing smile and a pleasing Southern accent. He could be friendly and animated, or as grim as an Apache. Tex had been raised in the cow country, and showed it."

The other new acquaintance was Wyatt Earp, who had been on his way to Dawson City but was forced to winter at Rampart City when the river iced up.

The boom at Rampart never did develop to the degree expected and it was slim pickings for Rickard that winter of 1898–99. In the spring, however, he heard of a big new strike at a place called Nome on the Seward Peninsula. After disposing of his gambling shack and settling up his debts, Rickard was off again.

At Nome, Tex and a partner named Jim White put up a tent saloon on a $100 lot in the center of the budding town. Rickard had only twenty-one dollars in his pocket when he got off the boat at Nome, and his partner had very little more in the way of cash, but White did own the invaluable tent and the partners bought their lot and stocked their saloon on borrowed money.

Rickard called the place the Northern and had a gala opening on the Fourth of July, 1899. All drinks sold for fifty cents and the bar receipts alone amounted to $935 on opening day. The single roulette wheel and faro table in operation contributed considerably more. The place was a success from the start and from that day until the end of his life Tex Rickard was never broke. He would back a few losing hands and invest in

Left to right, *Ed Engelstadt, Wyatt Earp, and John Clum on the beach at Nome. Courtesy Arizona Historical Society.*

a few sour projects, but invariably he would bounce back by reliance on his legendary luck, resourcefulness, imagination, and willingness to take the big risk.

Ten days after the Northern opened, Jim White sold out his interest for $10,000. With a new partner named George Murphy, Rickard stayed on to turn profits the first year that netted him $100,000 as his share. In May, 1900, he replaced the tent with a frame building that was elegant by Alaskan standards, with crystal chandeliers, an ornate back-mirrored bar, and a piano. The Northern never closed and six bartenders were on duty day and night.

Stashed under the mirror behind the bar were rows of miners' pokes, bags of gold dust left in Rickard's trust by sourdoughs returning to their diggings. There were no banks in Nome and Tex Rickard was the most trustworthy man in town. His Northern Saloon became the Bank of Nome. In 1901 he was asked to run for the office of mayor but declined. Having a professional gambler as mayor might hurt Nome's development, he said, as this would not be understood or approved of by the world outside Alaska. He did agree, however, to serve on the city council.

Major competition for the Northern was the Dexter Saloon, owned and operated by Wyatt Earp and Charlie Hoxie. The Dexter was the first two-story building in Nome. Downstairs was an extensive barroom, and upstairs were twelve rooms devoted to gambling. Earp and Hoxie advertised the place as "the Only Second-Class Saloon in Alaska." Other gambling saloons of note were Boozer Brown's, Gus Seifert's, Jed Jordan's Ophir, the Nevada, run by Jim Wilson, and Wilson Mizner's combination saloon, gambling hall, and flophouse called the McQuestion Hotel.

Mizner, whose piebald career included con game activity, transatlantic liner cardsharping, Broadway playwriting, and Florida land speculation, was, by all accounts, a peerless raconteur, and many of the stories concerning Tex Rickard's Nome activities are attributable to him.

One of the best of such stories concerned a gambler named Frank McLeod who, according to Mizner, traveled with Rickard to Hot Springs, Arkansas, one winter, and while there got into a heated argument with the Texan over the loan of some money. When Rickard returned, alone, he told Mizner that if McLeod showed up in Nome there would be trouble because the town was not big enough for both of them. McLeod did show up and Mizner relayed the message. "But McLeod was tough too," Mizner said. "He asked me to go to The Northern and give Rickard a message from him. It was, 'I say he can meet me now, in the middle of the street, and tell him to come out of his place with his gun smoking.'"

Mizner raced to Rickard's place and repeated McLeod's challenge. "He was there, weighing gold dust," said Mizner:

His hand did not tremble over the scale. He grinned in his funny way, and said, without raising his voice, "I heard that bum McLeod was back here without a quarter to his name. Now, I'm worth nearly half a million. Tell him it ain't an even gamble. I ain't laying no half million bucks against nothing for anyone. But tell McLeod that the minute he gets himself a load of dough, I'll gunfight him any-where."[6]

Rickard always prided himself on running the squarest joint in Nome, but Mizner used to chide him that, despite the owner's vigilance, many less-than-pure sports infiltrated the Northern, and to prove his point, gathered a "larceny-haunted set of faces" around a Northern poker table one night and dealt out a hand from a deck containing fifty-two aces. Not one of the sharpers, staring at a hand containing five aces, questioned the reliability of the deck, but each discarded his duplicate ace and asked for one card on the draw. When every player received yet another ace there was a moment of utter stillness. Then it dawned on the sharpers what Mizner had done. "We laughed for an hour," he said.

Rickard was an honest gambling man, but he considered it only good sense to push any advantage that came his way for all he was worth. A case in point was a draw poker game Rickard liked to tell about in later years. "Another feller opened under the gun and I was the only one that stayed," he recalled:

I wasn't fixin' to stay, but this feller was nervous. He kept pullin' the top card off his hand and shoving it under the bottom. I could just catch a look at the corner of each card as he pulled them off the top, over and over again, sayin' nothin' and waitin' for me to move. I stalled quite a while. I wanted to read his hand two or three times to make sure I had it right. Finally I was sure my hand could lick him. So I gave the bet a small hoist and he gave it a big boost. I kicked it a little more and he kicked it again. Then I gave it a hell of a kick, right through the ceiling. He called. I never told him how I licked him.[7]

Like most gamblers, Rickard was ever alert for an omen or sign which would give him some insight into the vagaries of the Goddess Fortune. When a crooked faro player and dope addict named Policy Bob lay dying in an opium delirium, Rickard visited his cabin to pay his respects. Rickard had little use for the swindling hophead but did not believe that anyone, even a bum like Policy Bob, should pass on completely alone.

He sent for one of his employees to sit with Policy Bob during his last hours and, as he waited for the man to arrive, became aware that the dying man was mumbling something. Putting his ear to Bob's lips, he heard, "Copper the deuce! Copper the deuce!"

When his man showed up, Rickard said: "You stay with him. I've got to run. Never had a better tip! Tip from a dying man! What more could a guy ask?" He hurried to the Dexter where he coppered the deuce, that is, he placed a copper check or coin on the faro layout deuce to indicate he was betting that the card would appear first rather than second on a "turn" from the dealer's box.

He was $11,000 out at four o'clock the next morning when his employee brought the news that Policy Bob was dead.

"What a son-of-a-bitch that guy was!" Rickard thundered. "Policy Bob never turned an honest card in his life and the bastard even doublecrossed me on his deathbed!"

During the four years that Tex Rickard had an interest in the Northern Saloon in Nome, his share of the profits amounted to more than half a million dollars. But when he decided in 1902 to return to the States, only $15,000 in cash remained. Much of his fortune had been dissipated in handouts to unfortunates and grubstakes to prospectors. Jafet Lindeberg, one of the three "Lucky Swedes" who founded Nome, left a strong testimonial to the generosity of the Alaskan gamblers:

Say what you will, the gamblers are the best developers of a mining country. In my long frontier life I have never seen a time when a gambler refused a man or woman who asked him for money. And I have seen men in actual need refused by plenty of other people. . . . There have been . . . more rich strikes brought in by men who were grub-staked by gamblers than by any other class of people. Everybody jumps on them and criticizes them, but, after all, most of them are damn nice and if I was broke I'd rather ask a gambler for a lift than anybody else.[8]

It might be added that of the Alaskan gambling men none was more noted for his generosity, or was an easier touch, than Tex Rickard. So it was that his half million in profits had dwindled to only $15,000 when Tex chose to leave Alaska. He sold his interest in the Northern to George Murphy for $50,000 and, with a total of $65,000 and seven years' experience of incalculable value, sailed for the States.

In Seattle he got wind of a secret diamond mine in South Africa and went off on a wild goose chase that netted him nothing but a pleasant cruise. He returned to the West Coast and in San Francisco met a young girl, Edith Mae Myers, whom he had known briefly in Nome. A few weeks later the two were married in Sacramento. Rickard still talked of going back to Texas and establishing a cattle ranch, but the sporting life now held him in a strong grip. He went to Seattle and opened a saloon in the heart of the city's tenderloin district. Called the Totem, the place was fitted out on the order of an Alaskan gambling saloon. The day before his grand opening he received a visit from an emissary of the city's racketeering clique who advised him that he would be expected to fork over twenty percent of his gambling profits. Rickard threw the man out of his place. When the doors opened the next night, two uniformed policemen took up stations on either side of the entrance. When Rickard remonstrated, arguing that he could keep order in his own establishment, the officers replied that they would stay that night and every night, on orders from city hall. Rickard knew that a brace of blue uniforms as permanent fixtures outside his doorway would drive away business quicker than a quarantine notice and threw in the sponge. After only one day he sold the Totem and, disgusted with the way business was conducted in an established society, caught the next ship for Nome.

E. S. ("Kid") Highley, a gambler who had cleaned up with a place in Skagway, was on his way north to try his luck in Nome, and he and Rickard formed a friendship on this trip. George Murphy was still running the Northern in Nome and dealt Rickard and his pal Highley in as partners. The Northern still prospered, but Rickard's bride detested the Alaskan climate and late in 1904 Rickard left the north country for the last time. He sold his interest to a man named Frank Hall, who was short of cash but agreed to pay off in installments. Rickard received the last payment in 1906, just before a storm struck Nome, destroying almost everything including the Northern. Rickard's reputation among sporting men for having fantastic luck went up another notch; that big blow held off until he cashed his last payment check, they said, and proved that now even the weather was favoring him.

Whiskey has pushed more gambling money across the table to sober men than all the dumb players on earth.

John Dunn

Max Evans, *Long John Dunn of Taos*

For several years Tex Rickard had been hearing glowing reports of a boom district in southwest Nevada where new strikes of gold and silver had been made and wide-open mining towns were flourishing that rivaled Virginia City and Carson City of an earlier time. After they left Alaska, he and Kid Highley headed for this new bonanza country.

Tonopah, the first of the latter-day Nevada mining camps, had been founded in 1900 after the discovery of high-grade ore in the vicinity by Jim Butler, a rancher and part-time prospector. Sporting men from all over the West converged on the fledgling town and thirty-two saloons were operating before a single private dwelling, other than a tent, had been erected.

Jim Butler sold his claims and opened a saloon that featured behind the bar a large picture of himself and his burro, captioned "We started Tonopah." During the town's heyday some high-stakes play took place in the Butler Saloon with $16,000 once being wagered on a single roll of the dice and, on another occasion, $22,000 on a turn of the roulette wheel. Among the early arrivals who maintained gambling saloons were Jim Reilly, W. S. ("Ole") Elliott, Charles ("Rusty") Coe, Wyatt Earp (back from Alaska), and Tom Kendall and George Wingfield, proprietors of the Tonopah Club, the largest and best of the whiskey and wagering emporiums.

George Wingfield's spectacular story of success was improbable enough to raise a dubious eyebrow on a Horatio Alger. Wingfield was a penniless young man of twenty-three when he arrived in Tonopah from Winnemucca, Nevada, in 1902. Before turning to the tables for a career, he had been a jockey, a cowhand in Oregon, and a prospector. In every endeavor he had been eminently unsuccessful. Taking a job as dealer in Kendall's place for an hourly wage, he risked his

Jim Butler. He and his burro started Tonopah. Courtesy Nevada Historical Society.

George Wingfield, who parlayed a twenty-five-dollar-a-day wage as house dealer in the Tonopah Club into the greatest fortune in Nevada. Courtesy Nevada Historical Society.

earnings every night at the tables of rival establishments. One night he hit a streak of luck and ran his few dollars into a $2,200 stake. With this thin bankroll he leased a room in the Tonopah Club and opened a roulette game in partnership with Jack Hennessy. The profits from the wheel mounted and he soon had enough to buy half-interest in the club from Kendall. Over the next three years his share of the proceeds amounted to $150,000. He continued to gamble independently during this period and later estimated that his total take for the three years was in excess of $600,000.

When rich ore strikes were made about twenty-four miles south of Tonopah in Esmeralda County, Wingfield invested heavily in the new mines. The town of Goldfield sprang up near the diggings, and Wingfield transferred to the new town and brought in as a partner George S. Nixon, president of the First National Bank of Winnemucca. Together the Winnemucca banker and Tonopah faro banker, by means of stock acquisitions and judicious use of options, gained control of the most productive mines of the district. With the aid of Bernard Baruch, later an advisor to Presidents Franklin Roosevelt and Harry Truman, they combined their holdings in 1906 into the Goldfield Consolidated Mines Company. Over the next thirteen years, Consolidated paid out more than $29 million in dividends to its stockholders.

In 1906, at the age of twenty-seven, George Wingfield was personally worth more than $2 million. "You cannot bluff him," wrote a mining journalist of the time. "He is a man of his word, generous to a fault, possessed of the mingled restlessness and honesty that mark a few of the best professional gamblers. He is the Jack Hamlin of a later day, and had he lived in the golden age of Bret Harte, he would have been as famous as the sportsman whose memory is enshrined forever in the story of Poverty Flat."[1]

Bernard Baruch reminisced about Wingfield in an interview forty years later:

The first time I saw Wingfield was when I went out to Goldfield. . . . He was carrying five revolvers—two here, two here and one here.

He also had four Pinkerton detectives with him. . . . Wingfield was the best shot I ever saw. Out at the mines, someone would throw a bottle up, end over end, behind him, and he'd wheel around and get one of his guns up in a single motion and break the bottle. Now, that's shooting. . . .[2]

Labor trouble at the mines had prompted Wingfield to arm himself so extensively. A miners' strike had been instigated in Goldfield by the Industrial Workers of the World union (IWW), the feared "Wobblies" of the period. It was a time of great unrest in the western mining towns, with violent acts perpetrated by both the mine owners and the men they employed. Only a few months before, the former governor of Idaho, a bitter foe of the unions, had been murdered by a bomb blast in his front yard. The IWW agitators in Goldfield threatened mine shaft bombings and attacks on owners and "company men." Wingfield loaded himself with guns, brought in Pinkerton detectives, and hired "Diamondfield Jack" Davis, a tough gambler and gunman, as a personal bodyguard, before a settlement was reached with the strikers early in 1908.

Diamondfield Jack was festooned with even more weaponry than his boss. According to Goldfield legend, when Davis went looking for trouble he wore three overcoats, with a revolver in each coat's two pockets, a bowie knife in a scabbard at his belt, and a sawed-off shotgun slung across his back. It was said that he had been sentenced to hang five times but had escaped each time. Actually, he had once been given the death sentence for a dual murder in Idaho. Because of postponements, several dates had been set for his execution, but he had finally been pardoned after another man confessed to the double killing.

Davis acquired his nickname because of his oft-stated claim that he held title to a field of diamonds near Florence, Colorado. He carried a fistful of loose, uncut diamonds in his pocket and showed them off at the least provocation. His inamorata in Goldfield was Evelyn Hildegard, better known in the western camps as "Diamond-Tooth Lil." Fresh from the 1904 World's Fair in Saint Louis, where she had been a fea-

Diamondfield Jack Davis, reaching in his pocket for a handful of diamonds or a gun. He carried both. Courtesy Nevada Historical Society.

tured singer, Lil sported a half-carat stone set in one of her gold front teeth.

In appreciation of Davis's help during the strike, George Wingfield provided him with expert counseling on mining stock investments and when Diamondfield Jack left Goldfield he was in good financial shape. He later invested in successful mining ventures in Idaho, Utah, Montana, and California and became a very wealthy man.

His wealth never approached that of his former employer, however. George Wingfield's Nevada financial empire continued to expand. After a few years he bought out George Nixon, paying his associate $3 million for his mining interests. From there he went on to acquire controlling interest in virtually all of the major gold and silver mining companies in Nevada. Nixon, for his part, gained control of banks in Reno, Carson City, Winnemucca, and Tonopah, building a fortune that was estimated at the time of his death in 1912 at $35 million. With Nixon's passing, George Wingfield became the most powerful man in Nevada. He controlled a dozen banks in the state and a great deal of property, including some of the leading hotels and largest cattle ranches. Nixon had been a United States senator and Wingfield was offered appointment as his successor, but he declined. In Nevada he was known as "King George," but in Washington he would be, he said, using an expression from his gambling house days, "just another white chip."

Tex Rickard had struck southwest Nevada in the waning days of 1904, too late to get in on the fun and profit at Tonopah but just right to share in the prosperity at Goldfield. On February 15, 1905, in partnership with Kid Highley and Jim Morrison, he opened the famous Goldfield "Northern," at the corner of Crook Avenue and Main Street, in the heart of the mushrooming town. At the other three corners were the Palace, the Mohawk, and the Hermitage, all first-class saloons and gambling houses. In Goldfield these, together with the Northern, were known as "the Big Four." There were forty gambling saloons in town, including the Montezuma Club, the Glad Hand, the Three Wheels, the Grotto, the Alamo, the

Monte Carlo, the Phoenix, the Oriental, the Mint, the Combination, the Silver Dollar, and the Last Chance.

The doors never closed at the Northern Saloon, which offered three tables for craps, three for roulette, three for faro, and five for blackjack, fourteen in all. Eighty-five housemen were employed to run the games. Behind the Northern's two bars, each thirty-two feet long, three shifts of bartenders, twelve to a shift, worked around the clock. Six barrels of whiskey a day disappeared over the mahogany bars, as well as many gallons of wine, gin, and beer. In two years the Northern grossed over $7 million. On an initial investment of $100,000, the owners pocketed profits of $50,000 a month.

Goldfield attracted gambling men from all over the West. Johnny Nolon and Grant Crumley, late of Cripple Creek, Colorado, were on hand. Nolon, a former Pony Express rider, had run the toniest gambling house at Cripple Creek during the boom period of the nineties. A small, quiet, devout Catholic, always impeccably dressed, Nolon was an easy touch for moochers of all castes. Back in Cripple Creek he had nightly covered his pool tables with blankets and allowed the town's bums to bed down there. His place in Cripple Creek had suffered two major disasters, a fire in 1896 and an onslaught by the ax-wielding fanatic, Carrie Nation, who, on a saloon-busting visit to the mining town, singled out Nolon's place and destroyed much of his property and raised several lumps on Nolon's cranium when he attempted to restrain her.

Grant Crumley was one of three brothers, sons of a Presbyterian minister, who were prominent in Cripple Creek's sporting and criminal circles. The other brothers, Newt and Sherman, headed a gang of train robbers, but Grant confined his activities to gambling and ran the Newport Saloon until Cripple Creek's blossom faded in 1902.

Wyatt Earp worked as a floor boss in the Northern. "Bones" Brannon, onetime protégé of Dick Clark in Tombstone, dealt for Rickard in Goldfield, as did "Long John" Dunn, a lean, leathery veteran of many gambling wars who opened a place called the Alamo next to the Northern and lost it in one night's play. Dunn walked next door and asked Rickard for a job behind a table.

"I'm paying twenty-five dollars a shift," Rickard said. This was about triple what dealers were making in most Goldfield houses.

Dunn snorted. "Hell, you don't think a man of my ability would risk his life at your gaming table for that sum, do you?" he said.

Rickard laughed and told him to work all the hours he wanted and take out what he thought he was worth. Dunn worked through two straight shifts, sixteen hours, and pocketed a hundred dollars a day of Rickard's money. He figured in that time he made two or three thousand for the house. The proprietors agreed and made no objection.

Like Rickard, John Dunn was a former Texas cowboy who had driven longhorns to the Kansas railheads before turning to gambling as a profession. Born in Victoria in 1857, he had gotten into serious trouble at an early age, killing his brother-in-law and being sentenced to life imprisonment. He had escaped from prison and for a time operated as a smuggler at Matamoros on the Rio Grande. It was at Matamoros that he began gambling professionally, opening a monte game. One night he got into a dispute with a Louisiana Cajun who jerked a knife and slashed Dunn's hand. Dunn pulled a shotgun from under the table and blew the Cajun's head off.

This act mandated an immediate change of locale and he departed hastily for New Mexico. At Elizabethtown, or E-Town as it was called, he was backed in a poker game by the town marshal, who was also a wanted fugitive from Texas. The marshal staked Dunn to $300 and told him to win enough to set them both up in business.

"I did just that," Dunn said later. "I really played my best. I had cards in my sleeves, my hat, coat and anywhere else I could stash 'em. So did everybody else that knew how. When the game broke up next morning, me and my partner bought the very saloon the poker game was held in."[3]

Dunn ran gambling halls in Taos, Rapid City, and Cheyenne and later joined a troupe of gamblers traveling with a carnival in California. Long John was six-feet-four-inches tall, with a loose and gangling body. "Hell, you couldn't miss old John," a gambling pal once said. "He stood out among humans like a whore in church. When he stood behind a big stack of silver at one of his gambling places he made you feel like it was almost a privilege to lose your money to him, and he'd always make you laugh, even if you didn't want to."[4]

Dunn dealt an honest game in the Northern because that was the only kind of game Tex Rickard would have, but the tall Texan loved to turn a dishonest dollar and enjoyed even more bragging about it afterward. He often told the story of the tin-horn who piked his monte game and detected Dunn short-pay-ing him.[5] The tinhorn had won a $30 bet and as Dunn pushed the stack of coins across the table, $20 stuck to his long fingers as if covered with glue. The bettor caught him, but while he turned to crow to an observer about his sharpness of eye, Dunn lifted $40 off the tinhorn's stack. Amazingly, this daring reprobate lived to advanced years, dying in 1953 at the age of ninety-six.

It might seem odd that Tex Rickard would trust a slicker like John Dunn to deal for him. But all gambling house owners had to rely on the honesty of their employees and, according to one of the gentry, they were seldom cheated by their help. "I have known the worst crooks on the outside, who, when placed behind a house bankroll, would play square with the proprietor and fight like a fiend to protect his money. It was a code of honor among the fraternity that the care of a money layout was a sacred trust."[6]

Goldfield had many gamblers of the Dunn stripe. Almost legendary was Charles ("Rusty") Coe who, in his sixty years had turned up in boomtowns from the Mississippi to the Pa-cific. Born in New Orleans in 1844, Coe had worked as a deckhand on steamboats plying the Mississippi to Saint Louis. At the age of eighteen he was gambling professionally on the river. During the Civil War he served under General Robert E. Lee and received a leg wound that left him with a slight limp for the rest of his life. He returned to gambling after the war and was a familiar figure in gambling houses in Saint Louis, Kansas City, Abilene, Albuquerque, Taos, Denver, Tomb-stone, Tucson, Reno, and finally Tonopah and Goldfield. He was an accomplished manipulator of cards but had been forced to shoot his way out of several tight places when his deck-stacking had been detected. He was banned from the Northern and most places in Goldfield but maintained a place of his own, the Esmeralda, in Tonopah. In later years he lived in Los Angeles and established a gun store that supplied many of the weapons used in the early western motion pictures.

Tex Rickard's fame as a square gambler and a man to be trusted preceded him from Alaska, carried by veterans of Circle City, Dawson City, and Nome. As in the north, many miners considered the gambler more trustworthy than a bank. The story of the one-day run on the John S. McCook Bank in Goldfield and how Rickard saved the bank was told years later by Billy Murray, who tended the cashier's cage in the Northern.[7]

"I didn't know anything about bookkeeping," said Murray:

I didn't know anything about cashiering. But Tex told me to go in there and take care of the cash, and I did. I had a little grocery order blank book and an indelible pencil. When they made up the cash from the games and the bar and brought it to the safe, I counted it and made a note in the book. If one of the games needed more money I gave it to the dealer and deducted it from the record. As long as I could add and subtract I was all right.

When the run began on the McCook Bank, the miners drew out their deposits and headed for the Northern to put their savings in Rickard's safekeeping. Soon the safe was full and Billy Murray in his little cage was up to his knees in sacks of gold and silver coin. Rickard handled that problem. He called over two of his floor bosses, loaded them with cashbags, and slipped them out the back door. They scooted up the alley and delivered the money right back to the bank. Murray swore that some of those bags went in and out of his cage at least ten times that day. When the McCook Bank closed that night it had as much cash on hand as when it had opened its doors.

The stunt pulled off by Rickard that first brought his name into national prominence was his promotion of the Joe Gans–Battling Nelson lightweight title fight held in Goldfield on Labor Day, September 2, 1906. The bout was conceived by a group of Goldfield mining stock salesmen and saloonmen headed by Rickard as a publicity gimmick to advertise Goldfield and attract investment capital. Expenses were underwritten by the group and the fight itself was not expected to be a money-making project.

Through Rickard's shrewd promotion and genius for ballyhoo that generated reams of interesting newspaper copy, the fight accomplished its objective, bringing the mining town hidden away in the remote Nevada desert a million dollars' worth of publicity. In achieving this, Rickard also managed to award combined purses of $33,500 to the fighters—an unheard-of payday for lightweight boxers in 1906, cleared more than $13,000 in profits for the financial backers, and, only incidentally, of course, made his name known in sports circles from coast to coast. Years later, after many had forgotten that Joe Gans, the champion, won the fight on a foul in the forty-second round, they would remember vividly that this was the first of Tex Rickard's great fight promotions.

A nationwide depression and the IWW strike against Consolidated Mines combined to put a damper on Goldfield in 1907, and early the following year Rickard decided to move on to a promising new camp called Rawhide, one hundred fifty miles away. Even as he pulled out in a big open touring car for the drive across the desert, Rickard began to promote his new base of operations. Seeing an abandoned wooden church on the outskirts of Goldfield, he pulled over and tacked a sign on the door: "This Church Closed. God Has Gone to Rawhide!"

That very evening he paid $8,000 for a lot in the center of the new town, and ten days later held a grand opening celebration for his latest—and last—Northern Saloon. George Graham Rice, a notorious swindler and con artist, was present at that opening and later called it

an orgy that cut a new notch for functions of this kind in southern Nevada. The games were reported to have won for the house $25,000 on this first night. Champagne was a common beverage. Day was merged into night, night into day. Rouged courtesans of Stingaree Gulch provided a dash of femininity . . . to the grand *bal masque* that concluded the festivities.[8]

Profits from the Rawhide Northern averaged one thousand

dollars a day over the next three months, according to Kid Highley, who once again was in partnership with Rickard. The Rawhide boom was to be short-lived, however, petering out within six months. In April, Rickard attempted to generate new interest in the town by whipping up national publicity for a Rawhide event—the death of a gambler.

Riley Grannan had been a well-known figure in the sporting world for many years, principally around the racetracks. He was said to have won $150,000 his first year at the tracks and was famous for having placed the largest single bet on a horse-race up to that time—$275,000. He helped to design the first form charts in America and held a reputation as a first-class bookmaker, one who stood by the odds he quoted and did not "lay off" to shorten them. From Saratoga to Santa Anita he was known as "the Napoleon of the betting ring." Grannan reveled in his fame as an all-out plunger and would bet on anything from the outcome of a European war to the direction a flea would jump. He was forty-four years old and dead broke, having experienced an unfortunate session at the Tanforan Track near San Francisco, when he showed up in Rawhide early in 1908. Tex Rickard gave him a job dealing faro in the Northern while the great plunger looked around for better prospects.

He talked George Graham Rice into advancing him $20,000 to start a gambling house and put part of it down on a $40,000 lot at Rawhide's main intersection, a chunk of real estate that had been free for the taking only months before. With the balance of Rice's loan he began a tour of the town's faro banks. He hit a hot streak in one saloon, breaking the bank at $52,000, then bet the entire amount against the saloon on one turn from the box and lost. He was still dealing in Rickard's place and trying to raise the capital for his own saloon when he contracted pneumonia. His friends brought in a doctor from Reno at a cost of $500, but within a few days Riley Grannan was dead.

The sports of Rawhide kittied up for a $2,000 satin-lined, silver-handled casket in which Grannan was displayed in state at the Variety Show House, a gambling saloon and theater on Nevada Street near Stingaree Gulch, the camp's red-light dis-

Riley Grannan, famous in his time as "the Napoleon of the betting ring," but today best remembered for the words read over his grave. Courtesy Keeneland Library, Lexington, Kentucky.

trict. The gambler's last wish had been that he be buried in his hometown of Paris, Kentucky, and the $1,800 cost of transporting his body across the country was borne by the Rawhide sporting fraternity.

Tex Rickard and Rice, who had been the leaders in raising the funds to pay for this expensive sendoff, made certain that all the news services were informed of the great gambler's passing and the elaborate funeral arrangements being made in the fabulous new mining town in Nevada. The story appeared on front pages in newspapers from coast to coast.

For delivery of the funeral eulogy, Rickard enlisted a defrocked Methodist minister named Herman W. Knickerbocker. Some say Knickerbocker delivered his address extemporaneously; others claim it was written for him by Sam Davis, a Carson City newspaperman. Laden with Edwardian floridity, the address praised Riley Grannan as a "dead game sport" who had reached the apex of human philosophy. He had accepted the tragedy of the world and taken both victory and defeat with studied composure.

Neither his life nor his money had been wasted, for in his calling he had contributed generously to the greatest task of mankind, that of "scattering sunbeams in a world ever shadowed by gloomy clouds." As a gambler he was a public benefactor who "smoothed the wrinkle from the brow of care, changed the moan to a song, wiped away the tear, and replaced it with the jewel of joy."

The 2,000-word eulogy was taken down in shorthand by a booster in Rickard's saloon called "Rattlesnake Shorty," who had once worked as a court reporter. Later published in pamphlet form, it was hawked in railroad stations, carnival lots, and saloons across the country and tens of thousands of copies were sold. It has been reprinted in many languages and is today considered one of the most famous funeral eulogies ever given in the United States.

Knickerbocker's overblown and grandiloquent extolment met with such success partly because of a national sense that the day of the "dead game sports" like Riley Grannan was rapidly passing. Rawhide was one of the last bastions of the free-wheeling frontier gambler and its moment in the sun was brief. Five months after the first stampede to Rawhide, a fire swept the camp, destroying most of the buildings, including Tex Rickard's Northern Saloon. The mines were unfulfilling of their first great promise and the boomers scattered rather than rebuild.

Rickard went to Ely, Nevada, and took a job fronting for a hotel in return for a share of the profits. He was clearly marking time, watching for a break.

In 1910 he made his move, securing the promotion rights to a world heavyweight title fight between the reigning champion, Jack Johnson, and the former champion, Jim Jeffries, who had retired undefeated some years before. It was a promotional plum that the western gambling house operator snatched from the eastern big city and wise-money crowd. Johnson, the first black heavyweight champion, was intensely disliked by the almost universally white sporting establishment because of his brash and flamboyant behavior in general and his open dalliances with white women in particular. After a succession of "white hopes" had failed in attempts to dethrone the black king, the immensely popular Jeffries was finally cajoled into returning to the ring to restore the heavyweight crown to the white race. In addition to the emotional racial overtones of the bout, it was a matchmaker's dream, pitting two champions who are, even today, included high on every list of the greatest heavyweights of all time.

When it became known that Jeffries would fight, promoters from coast to coast competed for the promotion rights. Rickard got them because he could not be bluffed or intimidated and was willing to think in bigger figures and take greater financial risks than his competitors. Silent Sam Bonnifield's protege had learned his lessons well.

The fight was held on July 4, 1910, at Reno, Nevada. It was evident from the start that time and inactivity had reduced Jim Jeffries to something less than the remarkable fighting machine he once had been. He lasted almost fifteen rounds but finally collapsed from the brutal pounding administered by the grinning black champion.

More than fifteen thousand people paid a total of $270,000 to see this fight, both figures record-smashers. The magnitude of that $270,000 gross can best be appreciated in the perspective of the times by comparing it to the gate receipts of the five-game World Series that year which totaled a little over $174,000. Rickard made a tidy profit of $60,000. More valuable than money, his fame as a fight promoter was firmly established.

The goal he had carried with him when he went to Alaska fifteen years earlier—that of owning a ranch in Texas—still tugged at his brain. He finally went back to Texas and looked over the prospects but found property values too high for the kind of spread he envisioned. He took a ship to Paraguay and leased 325,000 acres on which he stocked 50,000 head of cattle. In 1915, however, he returned to America and began promoting prizefights once more.

Beginning with the Jess Willard–Jack Dempsey heavyweight title fight held in Toledo, Ohio, on July 4, 1919, Rickard sailed through the decade of the twenties, which has been called the Golden Age of American Sport, setting previously unimagined records for fight attendance and gate receipts. With each major promotion, he somehow managed to exceed his previous successes. An audience of twenty thousand was on hand in Toledo and paid a record $450,000 to see Dempsey destroy Willard and take the title.

Two years later at Boyle's Thirty Acres in Jersey City, New Jersey, Dempsey defended his title against Georges Carpentier, the French champion, and Rickard induced 77,000 to pay $1.55 million to see the fight. It was the first million-dollar promotion.

In 1923 the Jack Dempsey–Luis Firpo fight at New York's Polo Grounds drew 82,000 and another million-dollar gate. Three years later, when Gene Tunney took the title from Dempsey at Philadelphia more than 120,000 paid nearly $2 million to watch the bout. In 1927 Rickard rematched Tunney and Dempsey at Soldiers Field, Chicago, and Tunney again won in the controversial "Battle of the Long Count." Gate receipts amounted to an amazing $2,658,000.

By 1928, Tex Rickard's name was as familiar to Americans as those of the sports giants of the era: Dempsey and Tunney, Ruth and Gehrig, Red Grange, Bill Tilden. Late that year he went to Miami in company with Jack Dempsey to promote a Jack Sharkey–Young Stribling bout. Intrigued with the southern Florida area and its commercial promise, Rickard began to lay plans for an American Monte Carlo complete with luxury hotel, gambling casino, horseracing track, and sports arena.

On his fifty-eighth birthday, January 2, 1929, he began to experience abdominal pain. A doctor diagnosed the problem as indigestion, but when the pain worsened Rickard checked into a hospital, where he learned his appendix was gangrenous. Four days later he was dead.

His body was to be taken to New York for a funeral at Madison Square Garden, the huge arena that he had built, and interment would be at Woodlawn Cemetery. Even in death Tex Rickard traveled first class. His remains were taken north by private railroad car in a solid bronze casket that weighed 2,200 pounds and cost $15,000. Crowds turned out at every stop on the line to catch a glimpse of the car bearing the famous promoter. In New York City people stood silently along the entire sixteen blocks that the casket was transported from Pennsylvania Terminal to the Garden. The following day 15,000 New Yorkers stood in line in bitter cold temperatures to file past Rickard's body as it lay in state. It was a remarkable tribute to the memory of the uneducated cowboy, marshal, and professional gambling man from Henrietta, Texas.

"For an out-and-out gambler, he probably was the greatest success of his age," wrote W. O. McGeehan, a popular sportswriter who had been Rickard's severest critic. "There probably never will be one like him, for luck gave him the cards and he knew how to play them."[9]

If the man who taught Tex Rickard how to play those cards read McGeehan's words, he must have nodded in agreement. But the cards dealt Silent Sam Bonnifield by Fortune had not been the best.

Soon after Rickard left Alaska for the last time, to go to Nevada, Bonnifield had moved from Dawson City to Fairbanks. There he opened a bank handling the gold dust of the district's miners. When the financial panic of 1907 hit, the seemingly emotionless gambler, who had made and lost fortunes without a change of expression, completely collapsed, terror-stricken that his depositors might lose their savings. He was found one day, on his knees in the snow, his face streaked with tears, praying to God for guidance. None of his depositors lost money, but Sam Bonnifield bankrupted himself covering the losses.

In 1943 he was killed in an automobile accident in Seattle. His body lay unclaimed in the city morgue for a week before some old-time sporting men realized that the great gambler was dead and arranged for burial. Penniless and forgotten, he had been living in a Seattle flophouse. Among his few effects were stacks of IOU's dating back to the Klondike gold rush, forty-five years before.

QUEENS

I've never seen anyone grow humpbacked carrying away the money they won from me.

"Poker Alice" Ivers
Nolie Numey, *Poker Alice*

9

*The Mexicans are inveterate monte players and perhaps the
shrewdest in the world. . . . When they think they have the advantage they bet very high and will risk not only their money but their
clothing and their very liberty. I have known more than ten instances
where men have bet their liberty and losing, become peons.*

Ben Thompson
William M. Walton, *Life and Adventures of Ben Thompson*

In contrast to eastern America, where during the nineteenth
century public gambling was an exclusively male activity, the
western frontier did produce a few professional women gamblers. That there were not more was explained in blunt fashion
by Dan Spencer, veteran boom camp bartender: "Gambling
was a man's job, like prize fighting or steer roping. . . . Most
of the girls knocking around the towns in those days was too
dumb to make professional gamblers and those that was smart
enough would generally rather get the boys excited about *them*
than about cards."[1]

But the very paucity of females in the early West undoubtedly contributed to their acceptance by the sporting fraternity.
In the new camps a woman—any woman—was an attraction,
and gambling hall entrepreneurs were quick to exploit feminine allure to draw customers to their tables. Crooked owners
found that distaff dealers, by playing to the chivalrous natures
of their tough patrons, gained a certain advantage; the same
trapper, cowhand, or miner who would unsheath a weapon at
the first suspicion of cheating on the part of a male dealer
would laugh and josh a dainty female caught in an identical
offense.

The influence of Mexican culture in the Southwest played a
part in the development as well. When the first Anglo trappers
struck the isolated Mexican settlements they found gambling
a long-established custom. Men and women of all classes
regularly patronized the *salas*, or gambling halls, and women
were frequently employed as dealers. A banking game similar
to short faro was most popular, and the Americans called it

Doña Maria Gertrudis Barcelo, known throughout old Santa Fe as La Tules. From Harper's New Monthly Magazine, *April 1854.*

"Spanish monte" to differentiate it from the notorious skinning game, three-card monte. The American players were soon dubbed "Los God Damnes" by the women dealers who heard the expletive so frequently.

Most famous of these Mexican gambling women was a Santa Fe monte dealer and gambling hall proprietress named Doña Gertrudis Barcelo, known throughout the city as La Tules. For a century the origins of this woman were shrouded in mystery. She was born about 1805 in Barcelona, Spain, in Sonora in Old Mexico, or in Taos, New Mexico, depending on which of her stories was accepted, for she told them all at various times. In one account she was brought from Spain by her mother, who died in New York, and the young girl made her way alone across the continent to Taos and, eventually, Santa Fe. In another, she came to Taos with her father, Joaquin Barcelo, a soldier, who was killed by Indians. In yet another, she came to the New World from Spain at the age of fourteen with her lover, a Spanish lieutenant. Gossip had it that she had been an adolescent street prostitute in Taos, where she caught the roving eye of a Spanish officer named Luis Corzo Velazquez, who brought her to Santa Fe as his consort. Later she was said to have taken up with a gambler named Gonsalvez who ran a *sala* on El Calle de San Francisco. Gonsalvez died or departed, so the story went, and his mistress was left with a sizable stake and the gambling house which she parlayed into a fortune.

In an effort to learn the true history of the mysterious La Tules, Fray Angelico Chavez in the late 1940s researched the old Catholic church records and discovered that Gertrudis was the daughter of Juan Ignacio and Dolores Barcelo, a respected family of Valencia, a small village south of Santa Fe.[2] On June 20, 1823, she married Manuel Antonio Sisneros at the nearby town of Tome, and subsequently gave birth to two sons. Sisneros established his family at Santa Fe, and being a hunter by trade and adventurous by nature, disappeared for long periods.

Gertrudis had an innate bent for cards and soon was dealing monte in a public gambling hall. Capitalizing on her charm and beauty, she built up a sizable and loyal clientele and in a few years had accumulated sufficient winnings to purchase her

The old Santa Fe gambling house of La Tules. From Harper's New Monthly Magazine, *April 1854.*

own *sala*. A long, low adobe building, situated at San Francisco Street and Burro Alley, this gambling house, which was to become one of the best-known in the West, extended the width of an entire block to Palace Avenue. The owner, called by her patrons Tules, an affectionate diminutive of Gertrudis, was always the center of attention as she presided over her monte table, but through most of the length of the building a variety of games, staffed by male employees, was offered. At the far end, space was reserved for the *bailes* or balls the proprietress often presented.

By the time the bearded, buckskinned traders and trappers from America began arriving in increasing numbers in the 1840s, La Tules was a Santa Fe institution, renowned for her gambling skills as well as the beauty of her olive skin, dark auburn hair, and flashing black eyes.

The *sala* of La Tules originally had catered to the Mexican common soldiers garrisoned at Santa Fe, but the woman gambler soon began to attract the major politicos and leading merchants of the city to her place of business. As her profits mounted, she completely renovated the building and installed finely carved furniture from Spain, Turkish carpets, and elegant glass mirrors and crystal chandeliers hauled by bull train from the United States. Private quarters were provided her important guests, where they dined on sumptuous meals prepared by celebrated chefs brought from Mexico City. In attendance for the patrons' pleasure were the most beautiful courtesans of the city. Influential men of the province and visiting dignitaries from the distant capital of Mexico City were guests at the *bailes*. During his infrequent appearances in Santa Fe, Manuel Sisneros, La Tules' husband, often entertained the customers with guitar music and improvised comic songs for which he was noted.

But it was Gertrudis who was undisputed monarch of her realm. A female servant followed her everywhere and, in the ancient custom, fell to the floor and allowed her body to be used as a footstool at the bidding of her mistress. La Tules owned jewelry, fine gowns, and houses in various parts of the city. She had a remuda of mules and an elegant upholstered carriage that conveyed her in state to fiestas in nearby villages.

She rode with one of her leather-bound gold chests at her feet and an armed escort of uniformed guards, superbly mounted.

Don Manuel Armijo, governor of New Mexico, was smitten by the beautiful and exciting gambling lady. It was generally believed in Santa Fe that he had taken her for his mistress and had provided a suite of private rooms in the governmental palace to pursue this liaison. Certainly, Armijo spent much time with La Tules, and she became privy to the secrets of government, information she was to use later in a manner that may have changed the course of history for the United States.

One of the first Anglos to leave a description of early Santa Fe's most famous gambling personality was Josiah Gregg, who made several trips to the provincial capital during the years between 1831 and 1840 as a trader on the Santa Fe Trail. In 1843 he wrote of "a certain female of very loose habits, known as La Tules," and, as an illustration of the "purifying effects of wealth and character," sketched the rise to riches and social standing of the woman. "She still continues her favorite 'amusement,' being considered the most expert 'monte dealer' in all Santa Fe. She is openly received in the first circles of society: I doubt, in truth, whether there is to be found in the city a lady of more fashionable reputation than this same Tules, now known as Señora Dona Gertrudis Barcelo."[3]

Matt Field, who arrived in April, 1840, later wrote:

Our introduction to fashionable society took place at the house of Señora Toulous, the supreme queen of refinement and fashion in the republican city of Santa Fe. . . . Señora Toulous was not handsome, her only pleasant feature being an eye of shrewd intelligence, lit up during our interview with that expression of mischievous brightness which can make any countenance agreeable. Her figure was neat, her manners free and not ungraceful, and, on an after occasion, when she moved through the waltz with one of the young American visitors, the really elegant ease which she displayed would have made her an object of attraction in a soiree dansante at Washington. This fine lady had become wealthy by dealing monte . . . and her bank was open almost every evening. . . .[4]

G. Douglass Brewerton met La Tules in 1844. "When I saw her," he recalled, "she was richly but tastelessly dressed—her fingers being literally covered with rings, while her neck was adorned with three heavy chains of gold, to the longest of which was attached a massive crucifix of the same precious material."[5] In another written account Brewerton was even harsher in his assessment of La Tules, describing a woman "whose face . . . bore most unmistakenly the impress of her fearful calling, being scarred and seamed, and rendered un-womanly by those painful lines which unbridled passions and midnight watching never fail to stamp upon the countenance of their votary."[6]

Susan Magoffin, who became in 1846 the first American woman to cross the Santa Fe Trail, found "a stately dame of a certain age, the possessor of a portion of shrewd sense and fascinating manner necessary to allure the wayward, inexperienced youth to the hall of final ruin." Mrs. Magoffin added with a contemptuous sniff that the celebrated gambling lady wore false hair and teeth and that, as a final mark of her degradation, she smoked cigarettes.[7]

Undismayed by these less-than-flattering American opinions, La Tules continued to prosper. She had amassed a great deal of gold over the years and, since there were no banks in Santa Fe or Taos, made several shipments to banks in the United States. The story goes that freighters escorting one of these shipments, packed in twenty buckskin bags loaded on ten mules, were ambushed by bandits and buried the treasure in the desert. They were killed by the bandits without divulging the location of the cache, and treasure seekers ever since have been searching for the hidden La Tules gold.

Señora Barcelo set no limit at her table and many men tried to break her without success. Matt Field described one onslaught by a Kentuckian who vowed to break the bank of La Tules or break himself in the attempt. The game continued all night as the tide of fortune moved back and forth between dealer and player.

The cards fell from her fingers as steadily as though she were handling only a knitting needle. But the man opposite to her exhibited the full reverse of this. His fingers trembled, as, with an affectation of unconcern, he drummed upon the table; and his eye watched each card as it fell with searching and intense scrutiny. . . . The slip, slip of the cards, and now and then the jingling of coin, as the stakes were removed or replaced, alone broke the midnight stillness.

Once La Tules paused and called to an attendant to bring a new pack of cards, but the trader objected:

"No, Señora, we have played so far with this pack, and they are good enough for the rest of the game."

Toulous smiled as courteously as though she had received a compliment, although the abrupt objection and the tone of the delivery evidently betrayed a suspicion of foul play. . . . Without speaking she waved back the attendant who presented the new cards and went on dealing the former pack as composedly as one might lounge upon the ottoman reading the latest novel.

Luck now ran with the Kentuckian and he began to double his bets. La Tules was obliged to call for a new bag of gold and a pile of glittering coins was poured onto the table before her. " 'Yes, pour them out, old lady,' said the trader, in a loud voice, as he lifted his newly filled tumbler of Pass Whiskey to his lips. 'Pour the yellow rascals out; we may as well make one job of it before morning!' "

Dawn was approaching when the flow of fortune reversed and ran steadily in the dealer's favor. The trader refused to slack off on his wagers,

swearing that he would make or break before he left his seat; concluding with an imitation of the cock that was crowing outside, and drinking the health of the Spanish lady in the again refilled glass which was at the moment handed to him. . . . When daylight was peeping through the door cracks, Senora Toulous once more swept the table, and the reckless trader was left without a dollar.

"Wake snakes!" shouted the sturdy Kentuckian, as he jumped up from the table and commenced dancing about the apartment. "Wake snakes! Hail Columbia! I'm off for California to-morrow! and, I say, old lady, I'll see you again in the fall!"

The Señora curtsied and disappeared through a side door with the dignity of an Empress and the same skillfully modeled smile, followed by her attendant with the heavy bags of gold and Mexican dollars. That man is now fighting under the Mexican Government against the dreaded Comanches, and this was the third time he had hazarded the earnings of years, and sacrificed them at the monte bank![8]

In 1846 came the war between Mexico and the United States. As General Stephen W. Kearny at the head of a column of seventeen hundred Americans approached Santa Fe, Governor Manuel Armijo assembled a force of four thousand to protect the city. At the critical juncture the governor's confidant, Dona Gertrudis Barcelo, prevailed upon him to withdraw his army without a fight. The city could be destroyed, she argued, and to what purpose? Don Manuel should lead his men into Old Mexico. She would remain behind to gather information from the Americans which she would report to him. At the propitious moment he would return, surprise the Americans, and win a great victory.

Don Manuel was not hard to convince. In the golden coach his subjects called "the wheeled tarantula," surrounded by his ninety-man bodyguard, and leading a personal caravan loaded with $50,000 worth of American manufactured goods, he quickly withdrew from Santa Fe. On August 19, 1846, General Kearny marched into the city without a shot being fired.

During the American occupation, the gambling *sala* of La Tules prospered as before. Now her patrons were American officers and civil authorities. General Kearny, before turning over the city to the newly appointed governor, Charles Bent, and Colonel Sterling Price, who was to command a small garrison of occupation troops, planned a grand ball that was intended to cement relations between the Americans and the Mexicans. Señora Barcelo was greatly perturbed to learn that she had not been invited, but General Kearny was even more chagrined when he was told that the military treasury contained insufficient funds to pay for the event. La Tules contacted the general and suggested a solution: she would loan the United States Army the necessary money if she were taken to the ball on the arm of an American officer. The grand ball was held and in attendance was Dona Gertrudis Barcelo, escorted by Colonel David P. Mitchell.

On yet another occasion, La Tules and her treasury came to the aid of the United States military. Colonel Alexander Doni-

phan received urgent orders to take a detachment to Chihua-
hua but lacked funds for the necessary provisioning. Again the
señora came forward with the capital, one thousand dollars,
which was loaned to the United States Government at two percent per month interest. Properly provisioned, Doniphan led
his Missouri Volunteers into Mexico and won a major victory
at the Rio Sacramento.

In the Mexican-American struggle La Tules was playing
both ends against the middle. She had promised Don Manuel
Armijo that she would provide him with information concerning the American military strength. Now, as the days of occupation lengthened, Armijo infiltrated agents into the city with
orders to lead a revolt against the occupation forces. In Mora
and Taos rebellions had already erupted, and the time was
ripe, Don Manuel believed, to take over the capital from the
few hundred American soldiers garrisoned there.

In the secluded chambers of Dona Barcelo's *sala* the conspirators held secret meetings to prepare for their uprising.
They included Colonel Don Diego Archuleta, Don Tomas Ortiz, Miguel Armijo, Padre Juan Felipe Ortiz, Nicolas Pino,
Manuel Chavez, Domingo Baca, Pablo Dominguez, and Juan
Lopez. The surprise attack was planned for Christmas Eve,
1846. At the sounding of the church bells, Charles Bent was
to be seized in the governor's palace, and Colonel Price was
to be taken in his quarters. A special squad was assigned the
task of spiking the American guns. Without leadership or cannon, the Americans would fall easy prey to Don Manuel's
army, which would launch a synchronal attack on the city.

A week before Christmas, La Tules requested a meeting
with Charles Bent and told him of the scheme. On Christmas
Eve the Americans were ready. Secret orders were issued to
arrest the ringleaders moments before the ringing of the bells.
La Tules, perhaps suffering remorse at her betrayal, warned
Diego Archuleta and Tomas Ortiz two hours before the appointed time that the coup should be called off because the
Americans now knew about it. Archuleta and Ortiz fled the
city and escaped the general roundup of conspirators a short
time later. Don Manuel and his army never returned to Santa Fe.

La Tules had been instrumental in preserving American control of Santa Fe, but war has its ironies. Governor Charles Bent, believing the danger was over, repaired to his home in Taos, where, on January 19, 1847, he was slain in an uprising of Indians and Mexicans. Among those killed in an effort to protect him was Manuel Sisneros, husband of the woman who had saved the governor less than a month before.

During the American occupation, Santa Fe became what one soldier called a "great gambling mart," with more than a hundred monte tables in operation.[9] Finally, in September, 1847, the American officers suppressed gambling and banned the sale of liquor to soldiers. The *sala* of La Tules was excluded from his edict, of course, since she did not cater to common enlisted men but entertained only wealthy and powerful mercantile chiefs and the highest military and government American officials. The profits mounted.

In 1850, Doña Gertrudis Barcelo employed an American attorney to draw her last will and testament. Less than two years later she died quite suddenly and was buried on January 17, 1852. In accordance with her instructions, the funeral was very elaborate. Carrying out the directions in precise detail was the Right Reverend Juan Felipe Ortiz, once denounced as a conspirator by La Tules. Named as heirs in Gertrudis's will were a sister, a brother, and two stepdaughters. No mention was made of her sons, Jose Pedro and Miguel Antonio, whose fate remains one of the mysteries surrounding this unusual woman.

In the 1940s writer Ruth Laughlin researched the life of La Tules for her novel *The Wind Leaves No Shadow* and acquired an oxhide money chest and a monte table that had once belonged to Santa Fe's most famous gambler. These two items are the only tangible remaining legacy of La Tules—except, of course, for that treasure buried in the desert.

Eleanore Dumont, better known in the mining camps as Madame Mustache. From Billy King's Tombstone, *courtesy C. L. Sonnichsen.*

10

There were few women gamblers in those days, for women have too many nerves; there are too many temptations which make them display their emotions—feminine instinct prohibits the usual poker face. One must have a countenance that can remain immovable hour after hour.

"Poker Alice" Ivers
Nolie Numey, *Poker Alice*

Miners entering San Francisco's Bella Union Saloon and Gambling Hall one day in the spring of 1850 were pleasantly surprised; presiding over the roulette wheel was a beautiful young Frenchwoman with creamy white skin, large, luminous, black eyes, and dark tresses falling to her shoulders. This was Madame Simone Jules, the first female of record to be employed professionally in an American gambling house. The new croupier created a sensation in San Francisco, and soon women-starved forty-niners were standing in line to lose their dust to the sweetly smiling mademoiselle.

The Alta California, one of the town's newspapers, took a dim view of this development, grumbling editorially: "A woman's place is in the home and indeed not at the gambling tables. There is no clearer proof of this than the example of twenty-year-old Mme. Jules as roulette croupier in the Bella Union."[1] No better advertisement could have been purchased by the house; the Bella Union was packed night and day. To bolster their slipping business, other gambling halls followed suit and in a few days women dealers were to be seen throughout Portsmouth Square. Most, like Mme. Jules, were French nationals, lately arrived in California as wives or paramours of agents sent from France by the wealthy gambling syndicates that provided much of the investment capital used to build and furnish the original Portsmouth Square gambling saloons.

A petite Parisian named Marie Ferrand came to California with her husband in 1849. Following the success of Simone Jules in the Bella Union, Marie was given a quick course in the dealing of *vingt-et-un*, or 21, by M. Ferrand and went to work behind a table. Later the couple moved to Sacramento where Ferrand was striken with cholera and died. Marie then joined a group of her countrymen who were setting out for the northern mining district. She bought a one-eighth interest in a mining claim the men were working while she dealt a 21 game in a rough Nevada City saloon named the Bella Union after the famous San Francisco house. Here she met a young forty-niner named Alfred T. Jackson, who fell victim to her Gallic charm. In 1851, Marie sold her share of the gold claim for $7,000 and with a $40,000 bankroll she had accumulated at the tables, bade adieu to Jackson and California and booked passage back to France. She and Jackson carried on a correspondence, however, and a year later she returned to California, married her American lover in San Francisco, and went with him back to the eastern states.

Simone Jules and Marie Ferrand disappeared from the pages of western history as suddenly as they appeared, but one of the gambling Frenchwomen of gold rush California stayed on to create, in a twenty-five-year career, one of the enduring legends of the frontier.

One morning in 1854 the northbound stagecoach wheeled into Nevada City, the same mining town from which Marie Ferrand had recently departed. Stepping down at the station was a young woman who stopped traffic on busy Broad Street. In her middle twenties, she was expensively attired in chic Parisian fashion that accented the trimness of her figure. She was small and delicate of feature, with dainty, dimpled hands, a mane of curly black hair, and doelike eyes. Soft down on her upper lip somehow enhanced the voluptuous curve of her mouth. Ignoring the stares of the men on all sides, she checked into the National Hotel. Within a few days she took over a vacant Broad Street storefront, moved in furniture, and began dealing a 21 game in the place she called the Vingt-Et-Un. She said her name was Madame Eleanore Dumont, but that was all that she would say; her previous life was a closed book that she would not open.

There were a dozen gambling halls in Nevada City, but the Vingt-Et-Un was an immediate success. The charm of the pretty little Frenchwoman brought the miners into her place in droves. No spree on the town was complete without a session at the Madame's game. The Vingt-Et-Un was unique not only for the comeliness of its dealer but also for the high level of decorum demanded by the owner. Disporting miners could guzzle their red-eye and tanglefoot in the other resorts, they could roar and curse, blow clouds of smoke from their cheroots, and spray tobacco juice all over the floor, but at the Madame's place they were required to put out their butts and get rid of the cuds. Cussing and loud, boisterous talk were not permitted. A momentary lapse on the part of a miner brought admonition in the form of a reproving waggle of a delicate finger and a pursing of the Madame's pretty lips. The other customers did the rest, threatening bodily harm to the offender if he did not obey the rules imposed by the little lady. Hats in hand, like so many schoolboys, the miners waited quietly in line for their turns at the table and the opportunity to joust with Mme. Dumont. She paid her losses with a smile and collected her winnings with a rueful murmur and a sympathetic pat on the hand. Since 21 odds heavily favored the dealer, she won much more than she lost. After closing her game, she would uncork bottles of champagne and treat the losers. More than one miner averred that he would rather lose to the Madame than win from somebody else.

It soon was evident to Eleanore Dumont that she was not capitalizing completely on the success of her establishment, because only a limited number could play at her table at a time. She needed to expand and take in a partner. Nevada City gambler Dave Tobin filled the bill. For a daily wage and a percentage of the house take, he agreed to move into new and larger quarters with the lady, to bring in faro, chuck-a-luck, and roulette tables, and to provide the mechanics to man them. The new place, called the Dumont Palace, thus provided opportunity for the miners to drop some of their dust while they waited for the big thrill of the evening, a confrontation with the Madame.

For two years the Dumont Palace reaped a golden harvest. Meanwhile, the relationship between Eleanore and Tobin developed into more than a business partnership. The petite Frenchwoman and the tall, dark-haired gambler, described by a contemporary as "handsome as a twenty-dollar goldpiece," were soon sharing, in addition to the profits, the same bed in the National Hotel.

This consummate arrangement was shattered, however, when Tobin showed signs of wanting to take over complete control of the gambling house. The Madame flew into a rage. In the boudoir she submitted to him, she said, but in the gambling rooms, *par Dieu*, he would submit to her. Tobin shrugged, announced that he had had enough of that game, and demanded a final settlement. He left Nevada City and returned east where he was later reported to have amassed a fortune with a gambling house of his own.

Nevada City turned sour for Eleanore Dumont after the falling-out with her partner-lover. She closed her place and began to tour the other camps of the northern California goldfields. She became a familiar figure at Rough and Ready, Timbuctoo, and French Corral; she opened her game in the Yuba River towns of Bullard's Bar, Downieville, and Sierra City; she visited Oroville and Forbestown on the Feather River; and she worked Happy Camp, Orleans Bar, Yreka, and Humbug City on the Klamath. It was in these camps that the legend began to grow, the legend of a "sporting" woman whose favors could not be purchased, a woman of beauty and refinement who just happened to gamble for a living.

She later moved to the southern mining districts, remaining for more than a year at Columbia, dealing her game in George Foster's City Hotel. When the excitement broke at Washoe, she transferred to Virginia City, Nevada, where she managed perhaps the most elegant of her many gambling establishments. The furnishings in this place were said to have cost $30,000. Providing soft counterpoint to the slip-slip of the cards, dry rattle of the dice, and clatter of the wheels was a string orchestra. Losers were served French champagne in cut-glass goblets, courtesy of the Madame.

Boom camp excitement was now in her blood, however, and no town held her interest for long. When gold strikes were made in Idaho and Montana in the early 1860s, she was off on the heels of the first boomers. We hear of her in Salmon City, Orofino, Lewiston, Idaho City, and Boise in Idaho, and at Bannack, Virginia City, Helena, Florence, and Butte in Montana. Always she was alone, a solitary feminine figure in the rough, masculine world of the coarse gold rush miner and the hard-eyed boom camp gambling man. She resisted the blandishments of all, making her own way on her own terms. She was an enigma to the boomers, which only added to her mysterious allure. Tales of her coolness and courage were carried by word of mouth from camp to camp. On several occasions when tempers flared, she was reported to have averted bloodshed by means of her quick thinking and a gentle admonition for the boys to behave themselves. It was said that at Boise even the homicidal Boone Helm, most vicious member of the cutthroat crew headed by gambler-turned-outlaw Henry Plummer, was subdued by her charm.

For some women, the approach of the thirtieth birthday signals an apprehensive study of the mirror in search of tiny lines, telltale signs of decaying youth and beauty. Eleanore Dumont, when she gazed into the mirror at age thirty, had greater reason than most women for concern. The years of concentration on the cards under poor light, the irregular hours, regular drinking, and constant stress had combined to etch furrows into her forehead and paint dark circles under her eyes. Her figure, once pleasantly buxom, now tended to corpulence. Most dismaying was her short upper lip. There the fine fuzz had gradually coarsened and darkened into a hirsute adornment that would have been the pride of a sixteen-year-old boy but which horrified Eleanore. It was about this time that a grinning miner told a friend that he was going to buck the game of "Madame Mustache," and Eleanore Dumont was tagged forever with the sobriquet that was to become one of the most famous in the West.

Perhaps not coincidentally, the Madame's decline began at this time. No longer was she the self-sufficient gambling lady who set the highest standards of deportment in her establishments, turned away the amorous, and held herself aloof from the other "sporting women" of the camps.

At Bannack she entered into partnership with a fellow named McHarney in the operation of a seven-room, two-story log house featuring multifaceted vice. On the lower level a long bar, a dance floor, and a variety of gambling tables were available, while upstairs bedrooms were provided for the dance hall girls to entertain their patrons. McHarney was the Madame's first partner since Dave Tobin, and he did not last long. One night a disgruntled gambler named MacFarlane kicked up a fuss and McHarney reached for a gun. But MacFarlane was too quick and in seconds the Madame's partner lay dead on the floor. Madame Mustache took care of the necessary arrangements with such dispatch that hardly a bet was missed at the tables. She had the corpse removed and fresh sawdust scattered on the floor. She posted one thousand dollars bond to bail out MacFarlane and, less than an hour after the killing, took him on as a partner, replacing the departed McHarney. To the Madame, it would appear, one Mac was as good as another.

Thereafter it was the Madame's policy to handle malcontents personally, and, so goes the story, this led to her abrupt departure from Bannack. When a drunken miner known only as Idaho Jack went on a rampage in her establishment, Mme. Dumont attempted to subdue him by herself. Her feminine wiles failing, the little woman tangled with the hulking rowdy. She was doing quite well, manhandling Idaho Jack by his beard, until he clamped his jaws on her delicate hand. Screaming with rage and pain, the Madame broke off the fight and sent for the law. Idaho Jack was arrested and Eleanore brought charges of grievous assault with deadly weapons—a set of powerful molars.

At the trial Jack's smirking lawyer put his client on the stand and asked him if he would please open his mouth. The bearded miner yawned wide and the jury gasped. Idaho Jack was as toothless as a chicken!

The Madame knew that she had been trapped by a set of dentures but carried the argument no further. Now she was the laughingstock of the town, and she never could stand to be laughed at. When the next stage left Bannack, she was on it.

She next appeared at Fort Benton, a burgeoning supply point for the new Montana goldfields. Here she maintained a whiskey, women, and wagering emporium similar to her former place at Bannack. A very disparaging description of this

place has been left by Louis Rosche, who captained steamboats up the Missouri to Fort Benton in the 1860s.

The inside of the gambling house was worse looking even than
the outside. The bar and the gaming rooms were housed in one big
downstairs room. A rickety set of stairs led up to a second-floor
balcony where I saw doors leading to about a dozen smaller rooms.
The place was foggy with smoke and smelled of sweating, unwashed
bodies and cheap whiskey. The floor was filthy. The male customers,
nearly all of whom chewed, were remarkably bad marksmen, the
spittoons, placed at strategic locations, all going unscathed. . . .
Faintly from one of the upstairs rooms I could hear the gibberish
of a drunken man and the high, shrill laughter of a woman who was
quite sober.

Obviously, after a dozen years of chasing gold rush rain-
bows, Eleanore Dumont had lowered her standards consider-
ably. Captain Rosche was as uncomplimentary in his word
portrait of the saloon's proprietress:

I would not have known that this was the famous Madame Mustache. She was fat, showing unmistakably the signs of age. Rouge
and powder, apparently applied only half-heartedly, failed to hide
the sagging lines of her face, the pouches under her eyes, the general
marks of dissipation. Her one badge of respectability was a black
silk dress, worn high around her neck.[2]

Despite her decline, Madame Mustache was very popular at
Fort Benton, primarily because of an incident that transpired
shortly after her arrival. When it was learned that the steamboat *W. B. Dance* was approaching town with passengers
aboard stricken with smallpox, the Madame strapped a pistol
belt around her waist and marched to the riverbank, a panicky
crowd in her wake. With drawn guns she ordered the riverboat
captain away. After a few tense moments of indecision, he
swung the vessel around and and steamed back downriver.
Madame Mustache returned through cheering crowds to a jam-
packed gambling saloon. Everyone in Fort Benton seemed to
be there, talking about the plucky lady and congratulating
themselves on having avoided an epidemic. Especially happy
was the Madame who was raking in the cash. Nobody seemed

to care what happened to the poor devils on board the river-boat.

In the late sixties the Union Pacific Railroad was stretching steel across the plains of Nebraska and Wyoming, and the work crews provided lush pickings for members of the sporting fraternity willing to endure the rigors of continual movement from tent town to tent town. Madame Mustache joined the cavalcade with a wagonload of gaming equipment and a troupe of girls who doubled as dealers when not more intimately occupied. One of these camp followers was a raw-boned, mannish-looking fifteen-year-old named Martha Jane Canary. Despite the tutoring of the Madame, this girl never could get the hang of a faro-box, nor was she much better at the other service she was supposed to provide. She could talk a lot, however, and could spin outlandish yarns, mostly concerning mythical adventures she claimed to have had. There would come a day when all that talk would earn for her a kind of fame—as Calamity Jane.

In 1869, Eleanore Dumont had traveled the gamblers' circuit for fifteen years. During that time she had been in on every boom camp commotion of consequence in California, Oregon, Washington, Idaho, Montana and Nevada. She had traveled tens of thousands of miles by means of the most primitive conveyances, crossing and recrossing deserts and mountains in pursuit of that extraordinary excitement that lured boomers from one camp to the next. She had survived saloon gun battles, drought, blizzard, fire, flood, and epidemic. She was tough. But she was tired and needed a rest.

The polestar of civilization, comfort, and modernity in the West of 1869 was San Francisco, and that was where she headed. The city had experienced great growth, she found, and had undergone drastic changes. It was now so civilized that gambling was no longer looked upon as an honorable profession, and most of the big-time sporting men were gone.

But if the day of the high roller was past in San Francisco, another, older, profession was in its ascendancy; the city by the Golden Gate was becoming as noted for the quantity and quality of its parlor houses as it had been during the gold rush days for the wide-open gambling. Eleanore, who had acquired some experience in this line of work, chose to drop the "e" from her title and became "Madam" Dumont. She opened a house on Waverly Place, devoid of the gambling equipment that might bring down the wrath of the municipal authorities, but featuring a covey of voluptuous girls, exclusively French. As the operator of this tony assignation house, called the Parisian Mansion, Eleanore displayed characteristic energy and ambition. Each day she took her girls on a tour of the streets in a handsome carriage drawn by a fine team of high-stepping chargers. Decked out in elegant finery, feather boas flying and imitation jewelry flashing, the French girls would wave and smile enticingly at the men on the streets, a constant reminder that erotic bliss was available nightly at the Parisian Mansion. When trade grew slack, the madam would take several of her courtesans out on the town just before daylight, when bleary-eyed celebrants were calling for a last round before hitting the hay. Like a mother hen she would lead her little brood to the bars where the girls would sip drinks and pose prettily. This gentle sales promotion usually generated business. It pays to advertise.

The Parisian Mansion lasted less than a year. On October 8, 1869, Eleanore closed her place and moved on. The date has been established by an entry in the diary of an unemployed magician named John Henry Anderson, who evidently was not an admirer of the madam but was well enough acquainted with her and her house to take note of her retirement:

October 8. . . . Mlle Dumont has apparently gone out of business. S [told] me early this morning carriages took the ladies and their baggage, and shortly after dinner she saw the proprietress depart, without a word to anyone, as perhaps fitting. A man came later this afternoon and took two loads of chairs, but not the beds. Is Parisian Mansion no more? . . . The Dumont woman was vanity itself. Vain, mustachaoed, always making airs. Some say she was a gambler here in the early days but I opine she was an engot [?]. It is no surprise she succumed [sic]. Customers complained that they came to see the ladies and not her. . . .[3]

It is not likely that Eleanore "succumed," but rather that she grew restless running a bagnio in tame San Francisco and yearned once more for the peculiar ebullience of a gambling house in a frontier town. She turned up again in Nevada, dealing her game in Virginia City and Carson. The fevered excitement at Pioche drew her like a magnet, a local paper heralding her arrival: "The noted lady gambler has engaged space in Handsome Jack McKnight's popular emporium and will be found there nightly from now on. If you enjoy a fast game of twenty-one, pay the little lady a visit."[4]

At Pioche she was credited with averting bloodshed by heading off a gang of unemployed miners marching to attack Mexican workers who had been hired in their place. With good humor and gentle joshing she managed to convince the angry miners that their quarrel was with the mine owners and not the Mexicans and, according to the *Pioche Record*, was mainly responsible for preventing a serious riot.

Shortly after this episode Eleanore Dumont disappeared from the mining towns and was absent from her usual haunts for several years. The details of this hiatus are incomplete, but she seems to have married and settled on a ranch in eastern Nevada. According to one version of this story, her husband was handsome Jack McKnight of Pioche.[5] In another, a cattle buyer calling himself "Colonel" Kai Carruthers captured the Madame's heart.[6] But all accounts agree that the husband got control of Eleanore's savings and decamped, leaving her broke and embittered.

And so it was back to the mining camps and the *vingt-et-un* table for Madame Mustache. We hear of her at Panamint, the "Suburb of Hell," in 1874, and later at Eureka and Aurora in Nevada. News of the rush to the Black Hills in South Dakota drew her to Cheyenne, the Hell-on-Wheels jumping-off place for the Hills, where she remained several months before going on by wagon train to Deadwood City. The principal town of the new mining district was lively and the gamblers were thriving, but here the Madame faced an unfamiliar situation: she was not the only celebrated woman gambler in town. There were, in fact, two others, and one of these, a fair charmer going under the mellifluous name of Lurline Monte Verde, had a history every bit as remarkable as that of Madame Mustache.

The dark-eyed brunet known in Deadwood as Monte Verde used several names during her eventful life. Born into the prominent Siddons family of Missouri, niece of Claiborne Fox Jackson, last elected governor before the Civil War, she had been christened "Belle," and as Belle Siddons had been graduated from the Missouri Female Seminary at Lexington. In the years immediately before the war the pretty and vivacious belle had been the toast of Saint Louis society. Suddenly, with the bombardment of Fort Sumter, she was caught up in the maelstrom of sectional strife. Missouri, perhaps more than any other state, was deeply divided on the issue of secession. Governor Jackson and the Siddons family were strong supporters of the cause of the South. Jackson's policies resulted in his removal from office, and Belle's Confederate sympathies led to her becoming a spy for the South.

Saint Louis was headquarters for the Union's Department of the Mississippi. Junior officers under Major General H. W. Halleck were most attentive to the charming southern belle. They escorted her to the opera house and to balls and, disarmed by her ingenuous smile and manner, let fall secret military information. In December, 1862, General Newton M. Curtis ordered the arrest of Belle Siddons as a suspected Confederate agent. Confronted with incriminating evidence found among her belongings, she boasted to General John M. Schofield that she had supplied much valuable information to Confederate Generals Nathan B. Forrest and Sterling Price.

Schofield ordered her detention in the Grant Street Prison for Rebels, but after several months of incarceration she was released on her promise to leave the state for the war's duration. She went to Texas where she remained until Lee's surrender. She returned to Missouri and operated for a time as a lobbyist at the state capitol. In 1868 she married Dr. Newt Hallett, an army surgeon, and accompanied him to Fort Brown, Texas. Dr. Hallett instructed his bride in the basics of medicine and dissection. Belle also proved to be an apt pupil in the study of gambling, for which the doctor had a fondness.

The marriage was to last less than a year; Dr. Hallett died of yellow fever in 1869. That year the big news in Texas was the success of the great longhorn cattle drives to the Kansas railheads. Belle, taking a new name, set out on a new life. She went to Kansas and, calling herself Madame Vestal, dealt 21 in a succession of cow towns. By 1875 she had settled in Denver and opened her own place, a huge tent on Blake Street.

With the rush to the Black Hills, many of the sports deserted Denver and Madame Vestal decided to move with the action. She purchased several large freight wagons and told her dealers, stickmen, and bartenders to load furniture and fixtures, fold up the tent, and climb aboard, for they were off for the Hills. She herself led the little caravan northward, riding in a four-horse omnibus that she had outfitted as a rolling boudoir, with carpeting on the floor, a four-poster bed, and fancy curtains on the windows. She paused at Cheyenne before undertaking the long haul northward and, for a lark, took an entertainer's job at the Bella Union Theater, where she was billed as a "serio-comic singer."

Perhaps to enhance the aura of mystery that always surrounded her, she arrived in Deadwood with a new name, Lurline Monte Verde, but the gambling hall habitués of Abilene, Wichita, Dodge City, Cheyenne, and Denver knew her well and gave her an effusive greeting. According to a correspondent from the *New York Tribune*, upon her arrival she "stood upon a board and was borne through the town on the shoulders of four strapping miners."

She set up her tent on a lot on Main Street, in the heart of Deadwood's "bad lands" district, and the place soon became one of the town's most popular resorts and its proprietress a Deadwood attraction to be pointed out to visitors. "Monte Verde, with her dark eyes and tresses," wrote the *Tribune* reporter "deals 'twenty-one' and dances a jig with a far-off look in her left eye."[7] Another writer described her as a "flawlessly groomed beauty, artfully jeweled and gowned," and noted that she was that rare bird in the sporting world, an abstainer who spurned alcohol in any form.[8]

Following the death of her husband, the little gambling lady during her years on the frontier had managed to hold her male admirers at a distance. One night in 1878, however, a cocky young fellow with an arrogant grin and a reckless, devil-may-care glint in his eye swaggered into her place. His name was

Archie McLaughlin and even one much less experienced in the reading of human nature than Lurline Monte Verde would have known instantly that his middle name had to be "trouble." The gambling lady, however, had never avoided danger, had even courted it, and perhaps that was the very thing that drew her to McLaughlin. At any rate, she fell hopelessly in love.

McLaughlin was a road agent. He had a gang that preyed on shipments of bullion out of the goldfields. On the night of July 2, 1878, the gang attempted to rob a treasure-bearing stagecoach at Whoop-Up Canyon on the road between Deadwood and Rapid City. Guards within the coach opened fire, killing one bandit and severely wounding another. The gang fled to a hideout in the hills where John Brown, the wounded gang member, lay in agony for nearly a week. Finally, McLaughlin, who knew of his lover's medical experience, sent to Deadwood for her.

Monte Verde came to the mountain cabin and dug out the slug from Brown's body. Her patient recovered, but Monte Verde would always regret her act of mercy, for Brown, captured shortly thereafter, confessed and named his accomplices. Officers arrested McLaughlin and two others near Cheyenne, placed them in chains, and started for Deadwood with their prisoners. On November 3, 1878, at little Cottonwood Creek near Fort Laramie, masked vigilantes held up the officers and hanged McLaughlin and his companions.

When she heard the news, Lurline Monte Verde, completely distraught, attempted suicide by swallowing poison. She recovered, but something within her had died. The coquettish smile was gone from her face. She began to drink heavily and became addicted to opium. Closing her Deadwood gambling operation, she set out on an aimless circuit of the border towns. She showed up briefly in Cheyenne, Leadville, Las Vegas, New Mexico, and Tombstone, but no camp held her for more than a few months.

During a routine raid on a Chinese opium den, San Francisco police in October, 1881, picked up a woman whose body and mind were ravaged by drugs and alcohol. It was determined at the jail that she was near death, and she was transferred to a hospital ward. There her mind cleared for a time and she related her story, the strange tale of Belle Siddons–Mrs. Hallett–Madame Vestal–Lurline Monte Verde. She was forty years old when she died.

As celebrated as Lurline Monte Verde and Madame Mustache were in Deadwood, for a time in the camp's heyday the veterans were outshone by a young Texas firebrand named Kitty LeRoy. "Kitty the Schemer," as she was soon dubbed in Deadwood, arrived in July, 1876, on the same wagon train that brought in Wild Bill Hickok, Colorado Charle Utter, and Calamity Jane. As a dissembler Kitty eclipsed even her companion, the inveterate braggart, Martha Jane Canary.

Opening a Main Street gambling dive called the Mint, Kitty loudly announced that she was queen of gamblers of San Francisco's Barbary Coast. She owned the most sumptuous gambling halls in Yokohama, Hong Kong, and other parts of the Orient, she said, and at the moment was on her way to the South African diamond fields and had condescended to drop into this backwoods camp on a playful impulse.

When she plunked down $4,000 in cash for a quarter interest in a local mine, the *Black Hills Pioneer* suggested that thereafter the "Gambling Queen of the Barbary Coast" should be called the "Quartz Queen of the Black Hills."

Madame Mustache, the grand dame of western gambling, asked to comment on Kitty's claims, snorted contemptuously and called her a bare-faced liar. She was in fact a liar, but for a time Kitty the Schemer had great success at the Mint, primarily because of the fascination she held for men. Since the age of ten, when she started her career as a jig dancer in Johnnie Thompson's Variety Theater in Dallas, Kitty had known that men and money could be easily parted by something with which she had been abundantly supplied by nature, an attribute later to be called "sex appeal." Whether she possessed beauty is open to doubt. A newspaperman who obviously had been victimized by her charms described her in glowing terms: "Kitty LeRoy was what a real man would call a starry beauty. Her brow was low, and her brown hair thick and curling. . . . The magnetism about her marvelous beauty was such as to drive her lovers crazy. . . . " She wore in her ears "immense diamonds, which shone almost like her glorious eyes," and her teeth "were like pearls set in coral."[9]

A Deadwood resident, far less admiring, described her as having "a large Roman nose, cold grey eyes, a low cunning forehead," but even this detractor had to admit that "there was something peculiarly magnetic about Kitty."[10]

Her physical appearance aside, it was generally agreed that Kitty was a clever gambler. "A good player . . . inordinately fond of money," conceded the Deadwood townsman; "a terrific gambler," gushed the bemused newsman. "Kitty was sometimes rich and sometimes poor, but always lavish as a prince when she had money," said the reporter. "She dealt vantoon and faro, and played all games and cards with a dexterity that amounted to genius."

To say that Kitty LeRoy was flamboyant would be an understatement. According to the hyperbolic journalist, she dressed like a gypsy, "had five husbands, seven revolvers, a dozen bowie-knives, and always went armed to the teeth. . . . She could throw a bowie-knife straighter than any pistol bullet, except her own." It was said that more men had been killed in fights over Kitty than over all the other women in the town combined.

She could do her own fighting when the occasion demanded. Once she donned masculine clothing to challenge a fellow who refused to fight a woman. She gunned him down, and then, suddenly contrite, called for a preacher and married her victim before he died. She claimed to have chosen her first husband from an assortment of suitors because he was the only one with nerve enough to let her shoot an apple off his head as she rode her horse past at a full gallop.

Another husband was a German prospector who had made a modestly successful strike in the Black Hills. She got $8,000 in gold from the German, but when his claim played out, broke a bottle over his head and kicked him out the door.

Kitty the Schemer was twenty-eight when her remarkable career came to an abrupt, violent end in Deadwood. Her fifth husband, a man named Sam Curley, balked when she tired of him and showed him the door. He pulled a .45, blew a large hole in Kitty, and then turned the gun on himself.

Madame Mustache, meanwhile, quietly dealt her 21 game. The years had taken a heavy toll on the little Frenchwoman. John F. Finerty, correspondent for the *Chicago Times*, observed her at work in the fall of 1876, and described her in scathing language: "She had a once-handsome face, which crime had hardened into an expression of cruelty. Her eye glittered like that of a rattlesnake and she raked in the gold dust or chips with hands whose long white fingers, sharp at the ends, reminded me of a harpy's talons."[11]

But young Doctor Henry Hoyt, who was in Deadwood at the time, remembered the Madame rather differently in his memoirs written fifty years later. She had, he recalled, "quite a shadow on her upper lip," but was "one of the most popular women of her class in Deadwood." She was "always polite and well-gowned and her table was always the center of a crowd. Rarely without a smile, her voice low and musical, she presented a very attractive picture as she would call out her game, with a very charming accent: 'Gentlemans, I haf twenty-one, vat haf you?' a phrase that was heard so often it almost became a byword in Deadwood."[12]

Each man's description was no doubt distorted by his personal view of the practice of gambling. Doctor Hoyt enjoyed gambling and the company of the sporting brethren. A year or two later at Las Vegas, New Mexico, he took a stab at backing a faro game himself, suffering a rather severe financial setback as a result. Finerty saw gambling as a "social evil, of the very lowest type . . . offensively visible wherever the eye might turn." In Deadwood he observed the "thimble-rigging devilment" in a half dozen "hells," and thought the female dealers all "resembled incarnate fiends" even more than the male gamblers, who were "vulture-like." He contended that the miners "would prefer playing faro or monte with men, for the women were generally old and unscrupulous hands, whose female subtlety made them paramount in all the devices of cheating and theft."

The restlessness that had characterized the career of Eleanore Dumont drove her out of Deadwood as it had driven her from one camp after another for almost thirty years. She showed up briefly in Eureka and Reno in Nevada, and then in 1879 appeared in Bodie, California.

"Shooting Town, U.S.A." they were calling the boom camp of fifteen thousand in the mountains of eastern California. The phrase "bad man from Bodie" was coming into fashion when Madame Mustache hit town. A newspaper in a rival town reported that a little girl, informed that her family was moving to the notorious hellhole, dropped to her knees and, rolling her eyes heavenward, murmured: "Goodbye, God, we're going to Bodie." Boomers of Bodie objected, claiming that what the girl really said was "Good! By God, we're going to Bodie!"

Madame Mustache was there, just as she had been to every major boomtown in three decades. She still smiled engagingly as the miners crowded around her table, and her fingers still flew nimbly over a deck of cards, but inside she was empty— empty and very tired. There came a night when a couple of sharp professionals faced her over the green baize and her luck ran badly. Relentlessly the pair of gamblers cut into her bank. She lost hand after hand but would not close her game. Finally, one of the men tapped her for all she had.

When she flipped the card that broke her, she knew that she was through, finished for good. At forty-nine she had neither the ambition nor energy left to start again. But, professional to the end, she could still flash her famous smile and say matter-of-factly as she stood up, "Gentlemen, the game is yours."

She left the gambling house and walked to her cabin. In life, as in gambling, there must be losers. She had thought of herself as a winner, but that night she knew that she was a loser.

The next morning, September 8, 1879, they found her in the cabin, an empty poison bottle in her hand. The *Sacramento Union* noted her passing with these lines: "Bodie: September 8. A woman named Eleanore Dumont was found dead today about one mile out of town, having committed suicide. She was well-known throughout the mining camps."

Lottie Deno, the mystery woman of Fort Griffin. From The Story of Lottie Deno, *courtesy John Warren Hunter.*

*I gamble only to make money. I don't think I have any of the so-
called gambling instinct. I'm like the guy that plays the big bass viol
in the orchestra, who comes home at three or four o'clock in the
morning and his wife asks him to play a little tune, and he says, "Go
to hell." I feel that way about cards. They're my business, not my
pleasure.*

Frank Tarbeaux
Donald Henderson Clarke, *The Autobiography of Frank Tarbeaux*

Since a woman who gambled professionally was considered
by conventional nineteenth-century American society to be
unfeminine, perhaps even unnatural, most such women chose
to conceal their identities or to disseminate contradictory stories regarding their origins and prior lives. Many used assumed names. Some, like Belle Siddons, to confound the curious even more, adopted different names in different towns.
Many were known only by nicknames they had chosen or that
had been chosen for them. Thus, dimly remembered by posterity, are "Madame Varnish," who dealt faro for a number of
years in White Oaks, New Mexico; "Buckskin Alice" of Leadville; "Minnie the Gambler," consort of Charlie Utter, who
followed him from Colorado to Texas and dealt stud poker in
an El Paso resort as late as 1904; "Creede Lily" and "Kilarney
Kate," popular distaff gamblers of Colorado's San Juan mining
district; and "Poker Nell," who had a dentist in Casper, Wyoming, embed matched diamonds in her front teeth, not neces-
sarily to improve her looks but in the hope that a poker opponent might be momentarily disconcerted at a crucial point in a
game when she flashed her brilliant smile.

   Mystery surrounds the secretive, of course, and an aura of
mystery is apparent in the careers of almost all the women
gamblers of the West. Perhaps the greatest enigma to westerners for years was a young woman who emerged from a stagecoach one day in 1876 at the remote Texas settlement of Fort
Griffin. In her early thirties, she was of medium stature, with
a full-busted, small-waisted figure. She was tastefully dressed
in a high-necked, wide-skirted dress with fashionable mutton-

chop sleeves. A wide, feathered hat was pinned to her dark auburn hair. Clear gray eyes calmly met the stares of stage station loungers. By the end of the day she had moved into a tiny cabin on the edge of town, and by evening of the following day had made her headquarters behind a gambling table in the rear of the Bee Hive Saloon. Lottie Deno had come to Fort Griffin.

A lady, a loner, a figure of wonder and speculation, she would remain for more than two years in one of the wildest and wooliest hellholes ever spawned on the frontier, and then one day she would vanish as suddenly as she had arrived, leaving only a terse note and a legend.

Fort Griffin was established in 1867, one of a chain of military outposts set up on the Texas frontier to provide protection from the savage Plains Indians for the westbound settlers. A reservation for the local Tonkawa Indians, a friendly tribe, was nearby. A town, also named Fort Griffin, sprang up some five hundred yards from the post, and, although it probably never had more than four hundred permanent residents, for fourteen years this little settlement was considered by many to be the toughest community in all of Texas. Here came hide hunters from the buffalo ranges, bullwhackers and mule skinners, bluebelly soldiers and Tonk Indians, wolf hunters and cowpunchers, outlaws on the dodge and bounty hunters on their trails, pimps and prostitutes, gamblers and gold-brick salesmen, snake oil medicine men and peddlers.

Life was cheap in "The Flat," as the town was commonly called to distinguish it from the fort. One twelve-year resident estimated that during his stay thirty-five men were "publicly killed," eight or ten others were found dead in or just outside town, and "about a dozen" were executed by lawmen or vigilante groups.[1] Among the famous and infamous who spent time at The Flat were Pat Garrett and John Poe, buffalo hunters, who a few years later as New Mexico lawmen would run Billy the Kid to ground; Wyatt Earp; "Hurricane Bill" Martin, horse thief and all-around hardcase; his paramour, "Hurricane Minnie"; John Selman, gunman, whose long string of victims would include John Wesley Hardin; Doc Holliday and his consort, "Big Nose Kate" Elder; and John Larn, who, after serving as sheriff, was shot to death by vigilantes in his own jail cell.

Vice and violence swirled around Lottie Deno at Fort Griffin, but she lived and worked amid the debauchery and bloodletting with a cool detachment that amazed the frontiersmen. She was dealing faro one night in the crowded gambling room above Wilson and Matthews' saloon, while at another table two gamblers known in Fort Griffin as "Monte Bill" and "Smoky Joe" were locked in a high-stakes poker game. Suddenly one of the two accused the other of cheating, guns were drawn, and the roar of gunfire filled the room. There was a general stampede for the exits. When Sheriff Bill Cruger came running, he found the room empty except for Monte Bill and Smoky Joe, both of whom lay dead on the floor, and Lottie Deno, who sat calmly counting her chips at the faro table. The startled sheriff allowed as how he would have cleared out of there with all the rest when the shooting started. "Perhaps," said Lottie with a small smile, "but then you are not a desperate woman."

Bill Cruger had succeeded John Larn as Shackelford County sheriff. Larn was elected in February, 1876, replacing a former buffalo hunter named John C. Jacobs, who had been appointed to the office when the county was organized in 1874. Jacobs probably knew Lottie Deno better than anyone at Fort Griffin. In an interview fifty years later he described her as

a wonderful woman, . . . on the portly side, a fine looker, and in manners a typical Southern lady. . . . She was so unapproachable that very few people, other than those of the gambling fraternity, became intimately acquainted with her. She had nothing to do with the common prostitutes that infested such dens as the Flat under the hill from Fort Griffin. I have had many interviews with her as an officer in regard to the doings and whereabouts of outlaws who frequented the Flat. She could be relied upon to tell the truth. She was pretty much a "lone wolf operator," and sometimes held "gentlemen games" at her adobe hut, for men who never played in public at the gambling dens. She always had one or two admirers on her staff of the best men in the country, but never played them for all they were worth. In other words, she was not a "gold digger." Lottie was truly a diplomat and stood apart from the rabble.[2]

Lottie Deno was respected as a clever and fearless gambler by the men of her profession. Some of the Fort Griffin sports, mentally adding up the gold and greenbacks they had seen her stash away in her carpetbag, began to call her "Lotta Dinero."[3] Jacobs was on hand the night Doc Holliday got on a hot streak in the Bee Hive and broke Mike Fogarty's faro bank. Fogarty was out three thousand dollars when he turned his faro box over, indicating that he was busted. Lottie Deno then sat down in Fogarty's chair and announced that she would take Holliday's game with a fifty-dollar limit. The consumptive dentist placed his bets on the painted oilcloth and told her to turn. Within a short time Lottie had won back Fogarty's three thousand dollars and stripped Doc of his roll also.

Mike Fogarty and Owen Donley dealt in the Bee Hive and each managed the place at times, but the owner was veteran sporting man "Hair Lip John" Shannsey. During the building of the Union Pacific Railroad, Shannsey had gambled and sold whiskey in construction camps across Nebraska and Wyoming and had acquired a reputation as a top rough-and-tumble brawler. The big event of the 1868 Fourth of July celebration in Cheyenne had been a prize-fight between Shannsey and a professional pugilist named Mike Donovan. After absorbing a severe beating on this occasion, Shannsey gave up thoughts of a prize ring career and concentrated on the green baize and pasteboards. He dealt faro in the Kansas cow towns before moving to Fort Griffin and opening the Bee Hive, a deadfall one frontiersman called "the most famous saloon that ever graced or 'disgraced' a town." Over the door of his place Shannsey painted a picture of a large bee hive with the following invitation:

> Within the Hive, we are alive;
> Good Whiskey makes us funny.
> Get your horse tied, come inside,
> And taste the flavor of our honey.[4]

When the military post at Fort Griffin was closed in 1881 and the town died, Shannsey went to Colorado City, Texas, where he operated another gambling saloon. In later years he settled in Yuma, Arizona, and served as mayor of the town.

Two early residents of Shackelford County have left written

impressions of the mystery woman known as Lottie Deno. Sallie Reynolds Matthews was raised at Fort Griffin and nearby Albany, the county seat. She remembers Lottie as being "fairly good looking" and "very intelligent." She particularly recalled Lottie's beautiful red hair.

She was not at all afraid of doing the unconventional or unusual, and she illustrated this characteristic when she gave a masked ball one night at the same time another dance was on at the hotel. I have never heard of any reproach against her character other than her gambling, though she was shunned by the better class. However, she did not try to mix with them, but kept entirely to herself.[5]

Edgar Rye, a lawyer who came to the Texas frontier from Kentucky in 1876, was intrigued by the female gambler who was "prominent among the wild, dare-devil, reckless characters who frequented the resorts of the Flat," but yet "exhibited all the traits of a refined, educated woman, who had been nurtured in high society, and was a gentlewoman by birth."[6]

Some who came to Fort Griffin recalled seeing Lottie Deno in other Texas towns. She had dealt her game, they said, at Jacksboro, at San Angelo, and at Fort Concho, where someone had tagged her "Mystic Maud." A few old-timers remembered that as early as ten years before she had maintained tables in San Antonio's finest gambling emporiums. Nobody seemed to know anything of her background, though, from whence she came, or why she had chosen the precarious life of a professional gambler on the raw frontier.

Nobody knew, that is, but John Jacobs. The young woman took Jacobs into her confidence, saying that she was troubled and just had to talk to someone. She told him her history and asked him never to divulge her true identity. Fifty years later he related her story, but still did not reveal her name; that secret he took with him to the grave.

She was born April 21, 1844, at Warsaw, Kentucky, daughter of a wealthy and prominent plantation owner and member of the state legislature. She was christened Charlotte, but from infancy the family called her Lottie. Her father owned a stable of fine racehorses, operated his own race course, and had a decided taste for the sporting life. One of the girl's earliest recollections was sitting on her father's knee and receiving detailed instructions on the mathematical science of the poker hand draw. She attended a convent school where she was taught the social graces which so distinguished her at Fort Griffin.

In 1861, when she was seventeen, she was the quintessential southern belle, pretty and vivacious, heiress to the sweet life that was the birthright of a daughter of the rich and powerful in the antebellum South. Then came the Civil War. The young gallants who had courted her went off to fight and be slaughtered at Shiloh and Gettysburg. Her family lost all its holdings. The shock of events would kill her father and paralyze her mother with a stroke.

Her world turned upside down, Charlotte impetuously ran off with Johnny Golden, a jockey who had ridden many of her father's Thoroughbreds to victories during the glory days. By marrying young Golden, Charlotte cut herself off completely from her family, for he was considered beneath her in social caste and had a reputation for wild and reckless behavior. The fact that he was Jewish did not help.

Golden served for a time in the Confederate Army but soon deserted. His young wife at his side, he spent the remainder of the war years traveling through the South, scratching out a living as a small-time gambler. It was during this period that Charlotte acquired advanced education in the mysteries of the pasteboards. After the war the couple went to Texas where Golden knifed a man to death in a fight over a card game and skipped out, leaving his wife penniless.

Charlotte then turned to gambling, the only profession she knew. She remained about three years at San Antonio where she adopted the name "Lottie Deno." She dealt her game at the Comanche Club, the Jockey Club and Jack Harris's Vaudeville Saloon before finally settling in permanently at the University Club, a high-toned gambling house catering to San Antonio's bankers, businessmen, and cattlemen. This place was owned and operated by the Thurmond brothers, Frank, Bob, and Harrison.

Frank Thurmond, a tall, slender Georgian a few years older than Lottie, fell for the buxom redhead. Lottie was strongly attracted to the handsome gambler, but she was already married, albeit to a callous and improvident tinhorn. Her response to the dilemma was to disappear. She vanished from San Antonio, stopping briefly at several Texas frontier settlements before emerging finally as the mysterious woman gambler of Fort Griffin.

This, then, was Lottie's story as she related it to John Jacobs. "When Lottie told me all this, she broke down and began to cry," Jacobs recalled. "Then she said: 'Mr. Jacobs, I have just received a letter from my husband. He has located me here, and says for me to join him in San Angelo and go west with him, to Arizona or California, where we will make a new start. I am afraid to go to him. Please advise me what to do.'"[7]

Jacobs did not disclose how he counseled the woman, but in the events that transpired in the following days, the hand of the former lawman can be clearly discerned. Lottie did not go to San Angelo. A few days later Johnny Golden, described contemptuously by Jacobs as "a go-between for outlaws and crooks . . . not in Lottie Deno's class," showed up in Fort Griffin. Jacobs held an earnest discussion with two of his pals, City Marshal Bill Gilson and Deputy Sheriff Jim Draper. That night the officers took Golden into custody, saying that they had a fugitive warrant for his arrest in the knife murder.

Bystanders were surprised when Gilson and Draper did not lodge Golden in the town hoosegow but instead started for the fort. Explaining that they wanted to keep him in the post guardhouse for safekeeping, the officers marched their prisoner into the darkness. A few minutes later, shots were heard. Marshal Gilson and Deputy Draper returned and reported that Golden had attempted an escape and they had been forced to shoot him. Johnny Golden thus became another statistic in Fort Griffin's violent history, and the woman known as Lottie Deno was free.

"When Lottie Deno heard of the killing of Johnny Golden she was greatly distressed," said Jacobs. "She seemed in a way to blame herself with his death and was inconsolable. She gave me the money to pay all of his funeral expenses, which amounted to about sixty-five dollars, for a coffin and trimmings and a new suit of clothes at E. Frankel's store. Lottie remained in her room as the hack carrying the remains was driven out to the cemetery. . . ."[8]

Soon after the death of Golden, Lottie Deno vanished from Fort Griffin. No one saw her go, for she had the Fort Concho stage driver pick her up along the road about a mile south of town. When she did not appear at her regular stand behind a table at the Bee Hive, Sheriff Cruger led a delegation to her little adobe house. There they found the furnishings neatly in place and a note pinned to the bedspread: "Sell this outfit and give the money to someone in need of assistance."

When the auburn-haired lady gambler departed the toughest town in Texas, Lottie Deno disappeared from the frontier, for she was never to use that name again. She went to San Antonio and married Frank Thurmond, and it was as Charlotte Thurmond that we trace her later history.

The Thurmonds went to Silver City, New Mexico, that year of 1878. There, in a resort called the Gem, a combination saloon, dance hall and theater, Thurmond dealt faro and his wife served as lookout, occasionally taking a turn at the box. Alfred Henry Lewis, a popular turn-of-the-century novelist and author of many short stores of western color, knew the Thurmonds in New Mexico and based several of his fictional tales on the real-life experiences of the gambling couple. In his *Wolfville* tales, published between 1897 and 1908, Lewis featured gambling man "Cherokee Hall" and a woman he called "Faro Nell," characters based upon his friends Frank and Charlotte Thurmond. Some of the stories were drawn from the couple's experiences in New Mexico and others from earlier adventures. All were embellished and reshaped by the imagination of the writer. A story in *Wolfville Nights*, published in 1902, for example, concerned Cherokee Hall's loss of $40,000 at faro to Doc Holliday and how the money was won back by Faro Nell. This was obviously suggested by the episode at Fort Griffin when Lottie Deno recovered Mike Fogarty's $3,000 loss to Holliday.

The Thurmonds spent two years at Silver City and a season at Kingston, another New Mexico mining town, where, on one memorable occasion, Charlotte won $9,000 in an evening

Frank Thurmond. He married a pretty redhead and Lottie Deno disappeared. From The Story of Lottie Deno, *courtesy John Warren Hunter.*

from a wealthy easterner. Frank had mining and cattle investments in the country around Deming, New Mexico, and in 1881 he and Charlotte relocated there. Charlotte retired from the gambling profession at this time and Frank returned to the old life only sporadically, making gambling forays into the

Charlotte Thurmond. The children of Deming called her "Aunt Lottie." From The Story of Lottie Deno, *courtesy John Warren Hunter.*

Indian Territory on occasion and joining the rush to the Yukon in 1898. The Thurmonds were considered solid citizens of Deming and Frank eventually became vice-president of a local bank. They had no children of their own, but neighborhood kids were always welcome at the home of the matronly woman they all called "Aunt Lottie." In 1908, Frank Thurmond developed cancer of the throat and died at the age of sixty-eight. Charlotte lived on alone until 1934 when she died just a few months before her ninetieth birthday.

Alice Ivers, about the time she took to the tables and became the celebrated Poker Alice. Courtesy Denver Public Library, Western History Department.

12

At my age I suppose I should be knitting. I would rather play poker with five or six experts than to eat.

"Poker Alice" Ivers
Nolie Numey, *Poker Alice*

America's centennial year of 1876 was the high noon of the romantic and violent Wild West era. In that memorable year George Armstrong Custer made his celebrated last stand; the outlaw gang of Frank and Jesse James was shot to pieces while attempting a bank holdup in Northfield, Minnesota; and Wild Bill Hickok was assassinated as he sat in a poker game in Deadwood, Dakota Territory.

It was a significant year also for the women gamblers of the frontier. That was the year that Madame Mustache, Lurline Monte Verde, and Kitty LeRoy met and competed in Deadwood, and it was the year that the mysterious Lottie Deno appeared in Fort Griffin. It was also the year that a young Englishwoman first took a dealer's seat at a gambling table in Lake City, Colorado, and began a career that would extend into the next century and to the very end of the frontier gamblers' era.

Alice Ivers was born in Sudbury, England, February 17, 1851. The only daughter of a schoolmaster, she received a proper middle-class upbringing and was educated at a female seminary. She was in late adolescence when her family emigrated to America, stopping briefly in Virginia before moving on west to Colorado. There the petite English blonde met and married Frank Duffield, a mining engineer. In 1875, Duffield took his bride to a remote mining district on the western slope of the Rockies. They went over Slumgullion Pass to a newly established town called Lake City in honor of nearby Lake Cristobal. In the spring of 1875, Lake City was composed of three log cabins and half a dozen tents, but by late summer when the Duffields arrived, the population had mushroomed to five hundred and the number of wooden buildings had grown to sixty-seven. By 1877 when it reached its peak, Lake

269

City had grown to a population of 2,500 housed in five hundred permanent dwellings.

As in all isolated mining communities of the West, gambling was the major recreational activity, engaged in by all classes. Before his church was constructed, Presbyterian minister George M. Darley, founder of the first church on the western slope, held services in gambling saloons, using a faro table for an altar. A district judge, in town for a session of court, spent an evening at the gaming tables and the next day was upset to find one of the witnesses, a participant in the game of the previous night, in a state of intoxication. The judge imposed a ten dollar fine on the witness, who peeled off a bill from a large wad and, grinning, said, "That all you need? It's your money, you know."

There were few women in camp and there was little for Alice to do in the way of amusement. She was not the sewing circle and tea-crumpet-and-gossip kind of woman anyhow, always preferring the company of men. She insisted that her husband allow her to accompany him to the gambling saloons where she stood behind him as he played. She was fascinated by gambling, and when Frank Duffield was killed in a mine accident, it seemed only natural to her that she should turn to the table to support herself.

Alice was an intelligent and skillful gambler and soon earned the respect of her miner patrons and the male members of the sporting fraternity. Someone dubbed her "Poker Alice" and the name stuck with her for the remainder of her life.

Lake City became a quieter place after 1877 and Alice moved on. She dealt her game in Alamosa, Central City, and Georgetown and was on hand at fabulous Leadville during its heyday, when it grew incredibly from a few hundred to a city of 18,000 in a year. There were in Leadville at the height of the excitement, according to a business census taken in June, 1879, ten dry-goods stores, four banks, thirty-one restaurants, and four churches. Listed also were no less than 120 saloons, 19 beer halls, and 118 gambling houses and private club-rooms.

In the early eighties Poker Alice turned up in Silver City, New Mexico, then enjoying a boom. Bucking the tiger at a

The Reaves brothers' casino in Guthrie, O. T. The large sign over the archway reads: "This is a SQUARE HOUSE. *Please report any unfairness to the Proprietor." Courtesy Western History Collections, University of Oklahoma Library.*

Silver City faro table, she broke the bank, cleaning up several thousand dollars. She immediately packed up and headed for New York City, where she lived lavishly until the money ran out.

Returning to the West, she played the Kansas cattle towns and in 1889 joined the run into the Unassigned Lands of Oklahoma. She was at Guthrie, capital of the new territory, for some two years, conducting a game in the Blue Bell Saloon, Bill Tilghman's Turf Exchange, and the Reaves brothers' casino, a large establishment that opened on April 23, 1889, the day after the land opening. First in a tent, then in a frame building, and finally in a large brick structure, the Reaves brothers operated their casino, never closing the doors for fifteen years. Over the bar a prominent sign gave fair warning to potential troublemakers: "We, the citizens of Guthrie are lawabiding people. But to anyone coming here looking for trouble, we always keep it in stock with a written guarantee that we will give you a decent burial. We will wash your face, comb your hair and polish your boots. Place your sombrero on your grave and erect a memento as a warning to others saying he tried and failed."[1]

In 1891, Poker Alice was in Arizona, spending several months at Clifton, dealing at the Midway, the El Moro, and the Blue Goose. She soon departed Arizona, perhaps resentful of the kind of thinking that produced an editorial in a local paper inveighing against the presence of women in saloons:

There is a law in Arizona which prohibits women from visiting saloons. It is a wise law and should be strictly enforced. The women who visit saloons in Morenci, Clifton and other towns in Arizona where they are permitted, are of the lowest character and regular crime-breeders. . . . In Clifton and Morenci a respectable woman can hardly go on the street without coming in contact with these brazen-faced, blear-eyed, degenerate creatures. How long will this continue? . . . The fallen women should be driven from the saloons and public view. . . ."[2]

Alice did not consider herself a "fallen woman." She was not a prostitute selling her body, but a professional, a woman engaged in what was considered a man's work. She met men on an equal basis, asking no quarter and granting none. She took her booze straight, smoked cigars, packed a .38 on a .45 frame, and could cuss like a mule skinner. She prided herself on dealing an honest game but could admire crooked work if performed adroitly. Only the clumsy cheat drew her contempt. She had a single idiosyncrasy that other members of the fraternity thought strange: she refused to gamble on Sunday. The miners in the camps she frequented worked a six-day week and Sunday brought the biggest play in the gambling saloons, but Alice stubbornly refused to work on the Sabbath. This quirk was the only visible repressive remnant of her straitlaced upbringing.

From Arizona, Poker Alice joined the rush to Creede, a new camp high in Colorado's San Juan Mountains. Here she took a job dealing in Ford's Exchange, owned and operated by Bob

A faro game in Morenci, Arizona Territory, 1895. Courtesy Arizona Historical Society Library.

Ford, infamous in song and story as "the dirty little coward who shot Mr. Howard and laid Jesse James in his grave." Ten years earlier, when he was twenty-two, Ford had acquired instant notoriety by gunning down from behind the most celebrated bandit in American history. He and his brother Charlie, both minor members of the James gang, had killed their leader for reward money totaling ten thousand dollars and a promise of amnesty from prosecution for the murder and participation in the gang's crimes. They had received their amnesty and the reward, and had further enriched themselves on a theatrical tour of the eastern states in which they lectured audiences on how they finished off the great outlaw.

When the reward money had been dissipated and theater patrons tired of the tale of the James killing, Charlie Ford committed suicide and Bob Ford returned to the West, taking

up the precarious life of the professional gambler. He continued to trade on his notoriety, always wearing a sombrero with
the broadest brim in town so that he could be instantly spotted
and pointed out as the man who killed Jesse James. He operated in a number of camps, finally ending up in Creede, which
was to be his last stop.

Creede, like Deadwood fifteen years before, seemed to attract women gamblers. Calamity Jane was there, still dealing
her clumsy game, still taking on all comers in either drinking
or sexual bouts, still spinning her tall tales. Kilarney Kate was
on hand, as was Creede Lily, who attained a kind of fame by
dying on the same day as Bob Ford. None of these competitors
was in Poker Alice's gambling class, and all resorted to the
most ancient profession during periods of adversity. Alice
stuck to gambling, working her eight-hour shift in Ford's Exchange every day but Sunday, drawing her wages, and backing
other games as the notion struck her. She was never rich, but
neither was she ever broke. Gamblers down on their luck
knew she was always good for a touch.

Creede cooled as did all red-hot mining camps, and Alice
drifted on. She went to Deadwood, which no longer was the
feverish boomtown it had been back in the seventies, but the
mines were still producing and the miners still wanted to
gamble. Romeo Dwyer and Jack O'Dell kept the most elaborate gambling saloon in town, featuring a popular faro dealer
named Frank DuBelois. Another well-patronized establishment was operated by Mike Russell. Poker Alice went to work
in the saloon of a gambler known as "Bedrock Tom."

Her table was next to that of a dealer named W. G. Tubbs.
When play slowed, Alice and Tubbs vied for the sparse business and became friendly rivals. One night a drunken miner,
after dropping his dust at Tubbs's table, charged the dealer
with cheating and, brandishing a knife, advanced on the
gambler. He had backed Tubbs against the wall when Poker
Alice calmly drew her pistol and sent him sprawling, a bullet
through his arm.

Shortly thereafter, Tubbs proposed marriage. Alice accepted
and the couple vowed to abandon the sporting life forever.
They bought some land north of Deadwood and settled down

Poker Alice in retirement. Courtesy Denver Public Library, Western History Department.

to a life of bucolic domesticity. They were happy in their little cabin hidden away in the mountains until the winter of 1910, when Tubbs came down with penumonia and died one night during a howling blizzard. Alice, with the frozen corpse of her husband at her side, drove a team and wagon forty-eight miles through icy winds and heavy snowdrifts to Sturgis, the nearest town. There she pawned her wedding ring for twenty-five dollars to pay for the burial.

Later that day she walked into a Sturgis gambling hall and asked for a job. The first twenty-five dollars she earned went to reclaim her ring.

Alice married once more. While working at the gambling house in town, she had hired a man named George Huckert to stay on her place and tend some stock that she owned. Several times Huckert asked her to marry him, but Alice always turned him down until one day she sat down and figured up the back wages she owed. "You know, I owed him about $1,008.00 and all I had was about fifty dollars on hand," she explained later, "so I got to figuring it would be cheaper to marry him than pay him off."[3] A few years later Huckert died and Alice was widowed for the third time.

During prohibition she ran a roadhouse near Bare Butte Creek between Sturgis and Fort Meade. There her patrons, principally soldiers from the military post, were provided liquor, gambling, and girls six days a week; Alice still would not work on Sunday. One night there was a ruckus. Some drunken cavalrymen who had been banned from the place tried to force their way in. Poker Alice was a small white-haired woman in her seventies by this time, but she still knew how to handle a shooting iron. She blasted through the door and a Fourth Cavalry trooper was killed.

Alice was arrested, stood trial, and was acquitted by a jury. The case drew attention to her illegal roadhouse operation, however, and the reformers closed her down. She spent her last years in a little house in Sturgis, puttering around a garden or rocking on her front porch, a black cigar clenched in her toothless mouth.

In 1930 she became seriously ill and doctors told her she should have major surgery, but at age seventy-nine her chances of pulling through were slim. "Cut away," she said. "I've faced big odds before."

Poker Alice died February 27, 1930, and was buried in the Catholic Cemetery at Sturgis, South Dakota.

KNAVES

A gambler is the only person who in the exercise of his profession learns to smile in defeat, and yet is fearful to exult in success. The first leads to poverty, the other to jail. If he loses he is a pauper; if he wins he is a robber.

Jefferson Randolph ("Soapy") Smith
Frank C. Robertson and Beth Kay Harris,
Soapy Smith, King of the Frontier Con Men

13

I am conducting a fair legitimate business. My mission is to trim suckers.

Charles ("Doc") Baggs
Forbes Parkhill, *The Wildest of the West*

Wherever there is gambling, there will be found the crooked gambler; wherever a game of chance is played with money to be wagered, there will appear those who would eliminate the element of chance. In the history of gambling on the western frontier some of the most fascinating characters were those who set out deliberately to fleece their fellows by sundry and devious methods. Theirs was a hazardous undertaking indeed. In a land where little or no law existed, where most men went about fully armed, and where the killing of an exposed cheat was generally considered an honorable and necessary act, a great deal of raw courage was required to practice systematic robbery, committed in full view of a crowd, aided only by the tools of the craft—a deck of cards, a wheel, or three shells and a pea.

To be successful and to survive, these sharpers had to develop a high degree of proficiency with both gambling paraphernalia and with weapons. Some of the more sanguinary episodes in frontier history involved the sure-thing gentry. Many came to sudden and violent ends, but a surprising number lived to advanced age.

Most of the crooks were inveterate plungers themselves, who, after fleecing working-stiff miners or cowboys to accumulate a bankroll, would tackle another man's game, a game sometimes as crooked as their own.

Cardsharping in the Far West had an ambitious beginning. When the gamblers who had followed the United States Army during the war with Mexico entered Mexico City late in 1847 in the wake of American troops, they found that the principal game played below the border was Spanish monte. To the surprise of the sharpers, the game was being dealt by the Mexican professionals with honest cards. Veteran skin-game dealer Bill

Clemmens saw an opportunity to turn enormous profits. With several confederates he hurried to New York City and commissioned a playing card manufacturer named Bartlett to produce thousands of decks of marked monte cards. Soon Clemmens and his cohorts were back in Mexico introducing the decks into games throughout the occupied area.

A hitch soon developed, however. The Mexican monte cards were produced by a single, government-appointed manufacturer and were of high quality. Gamblers on both sides of the table refused to use the inferior Bartlett cards. Clemmens then called on the Mexican manufacturer and placed an order for one hundred gross of the marked cards, sweetening his purchase order with an advance of $5,000. The manufacturer agreed to produce the cards if Clemmens would furnish the plates. Clemmens sent to New York for the plates and production was commenced. Before the new packs could be introduced, however, the American troops began to leave Mexico.

Clemmens and his partners were faced with a problem. They were the owners of almost 15,000 packs of crooked monte cards in which they had a capital investment of several thousand dollars. The Mexican company, which had no qualms about the use of the marked decks to cheat American occupation soldiers, would not allow the cards to be used in fleecing the natives. Spanish monte was practically unknown in the United States and there was no market there for the cards. It seemed as if their Yankee initiative and imagination had led the boys astray.

Then came the discovery of gold in California and the great rush of 1849. The native Californians were inveterate monte players and the game caught on quickly with the newly arrived argonauts. The Clemmens syndicate transferred to the goldfields and reaped a rich harvest. Several members of the group were able to retire with comfortable fortunes. Others returned to Mexico City with an order for an additional two hundred gross of the cards, but by the time they got back to San Francisco, monte players and dealers alike were looking on Mexican cards with deep suspicion and refusing to use them.

Perhaps the most notorious skin-game operator during the

California gold rush was William B. Thornton, known throughout the camps as "Lucky Bill" and the man upon whom Bret Harte is said to have based his fictional gambler, Jack Hamlin.

Born in Chenango County, New York, Thornton in the 1840s had ventured as far west as Michigan. In 1849 he joined a California-bound wagon train, arriving on the Pacific Slope, it is said, with most of the money of the other travelers. Although he was called Lucky Bill, the factor of luck was missing from Thornton's game. He was a thimble-rigger, a wizard of the pea and three shells swindle. He would entice greenhorns with the ancient come-on: "The hand is quicker than the eye. Bet you ten you can't tell which shell hides the little pea." Of course the suckers had no chance because as he shuffled the shells Thornton would palm the pea. He kept his fingernails long for this purpose, and could snatch the little cork ball, or "pea," from under a dozen pairs of intent eyes with a dexterity unmatched by his light-fingered peers, who generally relied on the less difficult French "finger-palm" pickup.

A tall, broad-shouldered man with curly black hair and large gray eyes, Thornton cut a handsome figure among the rude forty-niners. In addition to his deft hands and imposing figure, he had the other necessary attributes of the first-rate skin-game artist—supreme self-confidence, a glib line of gab, and an innate knowledge of human nature.

Thornton headquartered at Sacramento where the original gambling facility was Jimmie Lee's Stinking Tent. Other gambling houses in town were the Mansion House, the Humboldt, the Diana, the New Orleans, the Woodcock, and the Empire, the last-named managed by Andrew J. Butler, brother of General B. F. Butler who ten years later would be the captor and military governor of New Orleans.

The operators of most of the places barred thieving games. Horace Bell, writing in 1881, attested:

I hereby bear witness that these games were played at the Humboldt with a greater degree of fairness, integrity and honor than could have been found in any other country on the face of the earth, because if a man were caught cheating he was killed on the spot—that such contemptible thieving as three-card monte, chuck-a-luck, and such kindred games, were no more tolerated at the Humboldt at that time than they would be in the grand reception room of the Palace Hotel today; and I will say as much for the New Orleans, Woodcock and the Empire . . . and all other first-class gambling houses at the time.[1]

There were other houses, however, whose owners were not so fastidious. When Jimmie Lee erected a more substantial place called Lee's Exchange, a group of sharpers took over his old Stinking Tent, changing the name to the Round Tent. Dirt-floored, with a plank bar, the Round Tent was only about fifty feet in diameter, but it was brightly adorned with bunting and hanging lanterns. A band on a small platform produced a constant racket that passed for music. The place was jammed with tables.

Near the doorway Thornton opened his game with no more elaborate accouterments than a small platform suspended from a strap around his neck, three tiny cups shaped like half walnut shells, and the tantalizing cork pea. As his nimble fingers manipulated the shells and the pea, his resonant voice inveigled the suckers. There was always a crowd around him. In his first two months in Sacramento he pocketed $24,000.

In 1851, Thornton and a sharper known as Sidney Charles teamed up to tour the outlying camps. At Hangtown the pair made $2,000 but just managed to slip out of camp ahead of an angry mob. Fearful that lynch-minded miners would be watching the roads, the partners hid out in the woods for some time. Finally, filthy and half-starved, they stopped a stage-coach on the Sacramento road and climbed aboard.

One of the passengers eyed Thornton suspiciously, finally demanding, "Ain't you the gambler they call Lucky Bill?"

Bone-weary and weak from hunger, Thornton sighed, "Why do you ask?"

"Because you took a brother of mine for all he had," growled the man, drawing a wicked-looking bowie knife, "and I'm going to cut your heart out."

Thornton clawed for his pistol, but the other passengers interfered, saying that if a battle was to be fought it should be taken outside the confines of the coach. The driver halted the six-horse team and there was a rush to get out.

Lucky Bill was just stepping to the ground when his opponent threw the knife. The heavy blade entered Thornton's side between two of his ribs. As he sank to the ground, Bill raised his revolver and shot the other man in the shoulder. Both were taken to Sacramento where they received treatment and recovered.

For another year Thornton worked the gold camps of California. He made many enemies, but there were those who defended him, citing numerous instances of his kindness and generosity. It was said that he would not let a day pass without refunding some of the money he took from his victims. "I once saw Bill rope in a teamster for two yoke of cattle on the corner of Fourth and J Streets in Sacramento, and sell the loser one yoke for sixty dollars, which was all the money the man had," recalled one old pioneer. "Then Bill loaned him the other yoke to pull his wagon into the mountains, and told him to forget the incident."[2]

Thornton was also renowned as a lady-killer. Many claimed that his dark good looks and seductive voice could enchant any woman. In 1852 there were very few of the female sex for Bill to enchant in California, however, which perhaps led to his decision to make the long trip back to the States. He returned to Michigan where he remained a short time. When he headed west again, he had three young girls in tow. He and his harem were overtaken at Peoria by the girls' fathers who wrested two of their daughters from the gambler's clutches. The third, a starry-eyed adolescent named Martha Lamb, clung to her paramour and refused to return home.

Despite the loss of $20,000 in a faro game shortly before leaving California, Thornton had taken a small fortune with him back to Michigan. So profligate had been his spending, however, that by the time he reached Saint Joseph on the return trip he was broke. Out came the three shells and the little pea, and by the time he reached his destination, the Carson Valley of Nevada, he was again a wealthy man. He established a ranch near the little town of Genoa and stocked it with several thousand head of cattle and horses. He built a sawmill and operated the Carson County Toll Road. After turning several profitable land deals, he was recognized as one of the most prosperous and respected settlers in the area.

But Lucky Bill still maintained contact with some of the unsavory characters of the district, including a suspected cattle thief named Bill Edwards. When, in the spring of 1858, a man named Henry Gordier was murdered and his herd of prize Durhams stolen in the Truckee Valley, Thornton and Edwards were suspected of complicity in the crime. It was reported that some of Gordier's Durhams were seen among Thornton's herds. A vigilante committee arrested Thornton and presented the charges before a jury of eighteen. There was testimony that while under the influence of alcohol Thornton had bragged of being involved in the Gordier murder and in robbery and other crimes in the district. The jury convicted him of planning the murder of Gordier and of "harboring thieves, desperadoes and murderers." The sentence of death by hanging was to be carried out that very day, June 18, 1858.

A noose was placed around Lucky Bill Thornton's neck as he stood in the bed of a wagon under an improvised gallows. When asked if he had a last request, he replied that he would like to sing his favorite song, "The Last Rose of Summer," which he boomed forth in his rich baritone until the vigilantes started up the team and the wagon slid out from under him, choking off the last chorus.

And thus, finally, did luck run out for the notorious Lucky Bill.

In August of 1862 three men rode into the little mining camp of Gold Creek in Montana Territory. The Stuart brothers, James and Granville, who had helped found the camp, eyed the newcomers with suspicion. Although poorly provisioned, each of the three sat a splendid mount and each trailed another fine horse. James Stuart noted in his journal:

One of them, B. F. Jermagin, had no saddle on the horse he rode, but only some folded blankets strapped on the horse's back in lieu of a saddle. The other two men showed they were on the gamble and one of them, William Arnett, kept his belt and revolver on and rather posed as a "bad man." The third, C. W. Spillman, was a rather quiet, reserved, pleasant young man, of about twenty-five years, he being the youngest of the three.[3]

The new arrivals were definitely "on the gamble" and wasted no time in setting up a monte game in a tent saloon. "Our monte sharps are about to take the town. Getting decidedly obstreperous in their conduct," James Stuart wrote a few days later. James had a professional interest in the newcomers; an earlier journal entry indicated that he had taken a crack at backing a monte game himself: "I have lost three hundred dollars staking a man to deal monte for me in the past three days. Think I will take Granville's advice and quit gambling." But quit he did not, and several days later he found his luck on the outside of the game better than it had been on the inside: "Our stranger monte sharps opened a two hundred dollar monte bank and I broke it in about twenty minutes."[4]

Early Montana historian N. P. Langford credits Arnett, Spillman, and Jermagin (spelled "Jernigan" by Langford) with opening the first gambling establishment in Montana.[5] However, the enterprise was to be short-lived. Riding into camp on August 25 came two heavily armed and determined-looking men. John Bull, the leader of the two, said that he and his partner, a man named Fox, had come from Elk City, Idaho, in search of thieves who had stolen six fine horses at that place. When told that men answering the descriptions of the horse thieves were in the camp, Bull asked for the cooperation of the miners in making arrests. Spillman was found in the Worden and Company Store and was taken without a struggle when Bull braced him with a shotgun. Several miners guarded the prisoner while Bull and Fox went after the other two. Arnett was dealing his monte game in a saloon with Jermagin acting as lookout when Bull and Fox came through the doorway. Bull ordered the two to throw up their hands, but Arnett, who kept a Colt revolver on his lap while dealing, made a grab for the weapon. Bull blew him backward off his chair with a full charge of buckshot in the chest, killing him instantly. Jermagin sprang to his feet, hands held high, and pleaded with the man hunters not to shoot him.

When preparations were made the following day for the burial of William Arnett, it was found that the monte cards in his left hand and the revolver in his right were clutched so tightly that they could not be taken from his dead fingers. He was lowered into the ground still holding the tools of his profession and went off to his next life, presumably, well prepared.

At a trial of the remaining two gamblers before a miners' court, Jermagin managed to convince his accusers that he was innocent of the crime of horse stealing. He had been picked up afoot on the trail from Elk City by Arnett and Spillman, he said, and permitted to ride into Gold Creek with them. His story was confirmed by Spillman. Jermagin was released and given six hours to leave the country. He was gone in much less time.

Spillman, who put forward no defense and seemed to accept his fate stoically, was convicted and sentenced to hang, with the execution to take place in one-half hour. He wrote a short letter to his father in a firm hand, and, although there remained a few minutes of life for him, asked his executioners to get on with the job. James Stuart wrote that he "walked to his death with a step as firm and countenance as unchanged as if he had been the nearest spectator instead of the principal actor in the tragedy. It was evident that he was not a hardened criminal and there was no reckless bravado in his calmness. It was the firmness of a brave man, who saw that death was inevitable, and nerved himself to meet it."[6]

Spillman was hanged and his body buried beside Arnett's. Bull and Fox, their job accomplished, started back for Elk City, trailing the six horses. "Everything quiet in town," noted Granville Stuart in his journal.[7]

Spillman's hanging was the first execution in Montana. Because of the incident the little mining camp at Gold Creek came to be called "Hangtown" and was so designated on many western maps for years.

The incident at Gold Creek set a pattern for crime, violence, and stretched hemp retribution that characterized the history of Idaho and Montana mining towns throughout the decade of the sixties. From the first discovery of gold on Orofino Creek in 1860 and the resulting rush, the Northwest goldfields attracted a criminal class that often used the semirespectable profession of gambling as a front for the more nefarious activities of dry-gulching, road-agentry, and murder. Many tinhorns and clumsy crooked dealers left for the Northwest a jump and a half ahead of California and Nevada vigilante committees. With the outbreak of the Civil War in 1861, draft dodgers and deserters from both the Union and Confederate armies escaped to the Northwest territories and swelled the ranks of the Bummers.

Most famous of the period's badman gamblers was Henry Plummer, the handsome, ne'er-do-well son of a prosperous Connecticut family. Plummer ran away from home at the age of fifteen and joined the rush to the California goldfields. Endowed with great charm, easy eloquence, and sleek good looks, he was elected to the job of city marshal at Nevada City. This was in 1853 when he was only nineteen years old. At about the same time he took up gambling as a profession.

A man named John Vedder came home one night and discovered Plummer in bed with Mrs. Vedder. Plummer pulled a pistol from under a pillow and shot Vedder dead. He was tried and convicted of this killing and sentenced to ten years in prison, but his many friends gained his release after a few months on a petition that he was dying of consumption.

Plummer returned to Nevada City and was soon in trouble again, almost killing a man in a bawdy house brawl. Hardly had that difficulty blown over than he got into another fight in a brothel and this time killed a man, one Jim Ryder. While awaiting trial for this killing, Plummer bribed a jailor and escaped to Carson City, Nevada, where he was hidden by Billy Mayfield, another gambler. When Sheriff Jack Blackburn demanded that Mayfield turn Plummer over to him, a fight ensued during which Blackburn was stabbed to death by Mayfield. Captured soon afterward, Mayfield was placed in the custody of Abe Curry, who kept prisoners under contract at the Carson City Warm Springs.

One night, while Curry and some friends were engrossed in

a poker game, Mayfield, with Plummer's help, slipped his chains and escaped. "It was a king full against a queen full. I decided that if I couldn't go on that hand, I couldn't go at all," Mayfield explained in a letter to *The Territorial Enterprise*. The paper printed the gambler's letter, to the great enjoyment of the sports of Washoe.[8]

Now wanted in California and Nevada, Plummer and Mayfield headed north. In an effort to confuse the authorities, they wrote letters under assumed names to several California newspapers giving detailed accounts of the hanging of Henry Plummer and Billy Mayfield in Washington. Somewhere in Washington the pair split up and shortly afterward Mayfield was killed in a quarrel over a card game.

Plummer dealt cards at Walla Walla and at Orofino murdered the owner of a gambling house. He escaped to Lewiston, Idaho, where he took a dealer's job in a gambling house and posed as a respectable citizen. Secretly he organized the motley crowd of hoodlums and desperadoes that had converged on the town. When a vigilance committee was formed, Plummer was a charter member. He made vigorous speeches denouncing the criminal element and demanding a return to law and order, while at the same time he was directing the activities of the miscreants who preyed on the miners.

With the discovery of gold in Montana, the miners moved on to the new fields, and Plummer and his cohorts followed. He got himself elected sheriff at both Bannack and Virginia City. The cutthroats in his gang became so numerous that it was said in some localities they outnumbered the honest miners. The law-abiding citizens finally organized and turned on their tormenters. In a series of lynchings in January and February, 1864, the Plummer gang was wiped out. Plummer was hanged January 10, 1864, ironically enough, from a scaffold which he, as sheriff, had ordered built only shortly before.

Another renegade gambler of the Idaho mining towns in the sixties was J. Ferdinand Patterson, a tall, blond man with icy blue eyes. Patterson was a native of Tennessee who had lived in Texas and was a veteran of the California gold rush. At Yreka, California, he had been a participant in a three-way shooting match with gambler Hough Tate and Captain William

Renegade gambler Ferd Patterson in 1863 shortly after he scalped his paramour, Blonde Venus. Courtesy Idaho Historical Society.

Terry, who had commanded a company of volunteers during the Indian troubles in 1854–55. At the outset of the fracas, someone shot out the lights, enveloping the room in darkness, and the three combatants began firing with only the flash of their opponents' pistols as targets. No one was killed in this strange skirmish, but Patterson and Terry were slightly wounded.

Shortly thereafter, Terry got the drop on Patterson, stuck his revolver in the gambler's face and pulled the trigger. Patterson collapsed and Terry mounted up and rode hard until his horse gave out after one hundred twenty miles. Stopping the first stage from Yreka, Terry asked if the authorities were looking for the murderer of Ferd Patterson. He was astonished to learn that the gambler was still walking the streets of Yreka. The pistol ball had deflected upon striking Patterson's forehead and had burrowed between skull and scalp, stunning but not killing.

In 1858 at Waldo, Oregon, Patterson got into another gunfight with a gambler called Fraser River George. He managed to break George's arm, but he himself received several bullets in the leg and body. Herman Reinhart, who was there, later recalled: "It was supposed to be impossible for him to live; three or four of his ribs came out in places, and his side was all shot to pieces, but to the surprise of all, he got over it."[9]

Patterson arrived in Portland in 1861, accompanied by a woman known as "Blonde Venus." The Civil War was being fought a long way from Portland, but the secession issue was an emotional one in the Oregon town. Patterson was a staunch supporter of the cause of the South and hesitated not at all in expressing his opinions. Captain Staples, master of the steamship *Columbia* that plied between Portland and San Francisco, was a Union sympathizer. He demanded that Patterson join him in a toast to Lincoln and the Union armies. Patterson cursed Staples and guns were drawn. When the smoke lifted, Captain Staples lay dead on the floor.

Patterson was released on a plea of self-defense, but his popularity was greatly diminished among the citizens of Portland, who were predominantly northerners and loyal to the Union. When, in a drunken rage, he scalped his paramour, Blonde Venus, public opinion was aroused and he was arrested. "It was all a mistake," he claimed when he had sobered somewhat. "I was only trying to cut off a lock of her hair and the knife slipped." A witness named Tom Donahue, however, swore that the act was deliberate. Patterson was fined heavily and placed under a peace bond. After promising Donahue he would some day even the score, he skipped out, leaving his bondsman holding an empty sack.

He drifted to Idaho City where he was welcomed by the tinhorn and hoodlum crowd. His ego, never puny, was further inflated as they proclaimed him "chief" of the sporting gentry. Only one man stood between Ferd Patterson and complete domination of the ruffian element at Idaho City and that man was Sumner Pinkham.

"Old Pink," as he was called, was a formidable adversary indeed. A big man, with iron gray hair and full beard, Pinkham was "bold, outspoken, truthful, self-reliant, . . . without a particle of braggadocio or bluster, careful always to say what

Sumner Pinkham. Everyone in Idaho City knew that he and Ferd Patterson must tangle. Courtesy Idaho Historical Society.

he meant, and to do what he said. Fear was a stranger to him, and desperate chances never found him without desperate means."[10] A native of Maine, he was one of the first to cross overland to the California diggings in 1849. As a professional gambler he had worked the California gold camps and had managed a gambling house in Marysville for a time. In 1862 he joined the rush north to Washington and on into Idaho. At Florence he gained the grudging respect of the roughs, and when elections were held at Idaho City, Pinkham was the popular choice for sheriff. Soon afterward he was appointed deputy United States marshal. Old Pink was generally given credit for the comparative peace and quiet of Idaho City, where no organized outlaw gang of the Plummer ilk threatened the citizenry. With his Yankee background, Pinkham was as solidly Union in his political beliefs as Patterson was secessionist. That the two would tangle was never doubted; the remarkable fact was that almost two years passed before the first serious clash came.

On the Fourth of July, 1864, trouble developed over the flying of the Stars and Stripes. When Patterson objected to the raising of the flag, in language Pinkham found offensive, a bare-knuckle, eye-gouging, groin-kneeing battle ensued. Both men were adept in back-alley fighting techniques and the scrap was said to have been a classic of its kind. Pinkham, though bloody and bruised, eventually defeated the other gambler.

Everyone in Idaho City knew that this was just a round in a fight that could end only with the death of one of the two men. The showdown came on June 13, 1865, at Warm Springs, a spa near Idaho City. The enemies met on the porch of the resort hotel. For a moment both hesitated. Then Patterson, unable to stand the tension any longer, snarled: "Draw, will you?"

With almost a sigh of relief that the long wait was over, Pinkham answered, "I will!" He swept back his coattails and dragged out his immense dragoon Colt revolver. He was earing back the hammer when Patterson fired a shot from the little double-barreled derringer he had pulled from a coat pocket. A bullet hit the sheriff in the shoulder, causing his answering shot to go wild. A second bullet plowed into Pinkham's heart and the fight was over.

Later that day Patterson was arrested and placed in the jail at Idaho City. The town was in a state of great excitement. Pinkham's friends were advocating an immediate lynching, while the supporters of Patterson vowed to protect the prisoner and see that he had a fair trial. Finally, a rope-carrying mob numbering a hundred marched on the jail. The angry group was met by a determined corps of thirty heavily armed Patterson partisans who had barricaded the doors and windows. A bloody battle seemed imminent, but the Pinkham men, after some discussion, decided Patterson's life was not worth the loss of any of their own, and they dispersed.

At his trial Patterson was acquitted. Realizing, however, that Pinkham's friends were not mollified and that his life was in extreme jeopardy in Idaho City, Patterson left town under the protection of an armed body of his friends who escorted him as far as Boise. He continued on to Walla Walla where he became even more bullying and obnoxious.

"He drank so much he became reckless and overbearing to his best friends," wrote Herman Reinhart, who was in Walla Walla at this time.

I have seen Patterson go into a saloon and go up to a game where a lot of men were playing faro and take some of his friend's bet off a card and go away and if the man would make any remarks [Patterson] would abuse him or throw part of it back to him and threaten to act so and so to him. Most of his friends through fear would say nothing, and Ferd would go to some other game or go out to spend the money.[11]

In Walla Walla, Patterson found Captain William Terry, his old enemy from Yreka, keeping a saloon. Before a large crowd he made Terry get down on his knees at the point of a gun and humbly apologize for trying to kill him back in California.

Tom Donahue, who had testified against and been threatened by Patterson years before, was also in Walla Walla. On the morning of February 15, 1866, Donahue saw Patterson

come out of the Bank Exchange Saloon and go into Dick Bo-
gle's barber shop. Neither the gambler nor his barber looked
up when Donahue sidled into the shop and approached Patterson's chair.

"Ferd," said Donahue in a quaking voice, "you must kill me
or I will kill you."

With a disdainful laugh Patterson answered, "Certainly,
Donahue, I'll be glad to oblige you, but at present I am unarmed. My guns are over at the Idle Hour."

Donahue nodded. He had heard what he wanted to hear. He
then pulled a revolver from beneath his overcoat, stuck the
barrel in Patterson's whiskers, and pulled the trigger. With a
roar that drowned out the reverberation of the gunshot, Patterson leaped from the barber's chair. Donahue was streaking
through the doorway. Patterson lurched after him, mouthing
curses and spitting blood. On the sidewalk Donahue turned
and fired again as Patterson came through the doorway. The
gambler crumpled, dead when he hit the ground.

Donahue's trial resulted in a hung jury. He managed to escape before a second trial, and disappeared from the region.

After recounting the story of Ferd Patterson in 1890, Nathaniel P. Langford added:

To certain of my readers, some explanation for detailing at such
length the life of a ruffian and murderer may be necessary. Not so,
however, to those familiar with mountain history. They would understand that both Patterson and Pinkham were noted and important
members of frontier society, representative men, so to speak, of the
classes to which they belonged. Their followers regarded them with
a hero-worship which magnified their faults into virtues, and their
deeds of more than chivalric daring. Their pursuits, low, criminal,
and degrading as are esteemed in old settled communities, were
among the leading occupations of life among the miners. Said one
who had been for many years a resident of the Pacific Slope, after
spending a few weeks in the Atlantic states: "I can't stand this society. It is too strict. I must return to the land where every gambler is
a gentleman."[12]

14

All our games were not with saps. Men who would accumulate money playing with saps would get together and play hard cards. The chances of making money were slimmer, but you might be a little luckier than the rest, or a better player. Those were tough games among the experts.

Frank Tarbeaux
Donald Henderson Clarke, The Autobiography of Frank Tarbeaux

One of the gentleman gamblers who trod the dusty streets of Idaho City and Florence and worked the gambling saloons of Bannack and Virginia City with the Pattersons, the Pinkhams, and the Plummers was young Johnny Bull, who was destined to survive the internecine killings and vigilante lynch mobs of the violent sixties and whose career was to span more than forty years on the Northwest frontier.

After the shooting of Arnett and the hanging of Spillman at Gold Creek in 1862, Bull had returned to Elk City. He was later at Bannack, where he reportedly killed a character known as Bad Jim Kelly. During these years he was one of an army of skin-game sports who moved from one camp to another scratching a living from the pockets of the miners with a deck of monte cards and a come-on line. Although he was a sure-thing gambler and a con man of promise, there is no evidence that John Bull ever degenerated into banditry as did Bill Buntin, George Ives, and other gamblers of the Plummer ilk.

John Edwin Bull was born in England in 1836. Small and dark, with a full beard and piercing black eyes, he would in time become as celebrated a card sharp as the West ever produced, but he first came to the attention of the fraternity through his association with a gambler named Langford Peel, who was the young man's teacher and idol.

By the time Bull teamed up with him in the mid-1860s, Langford ("Farmer") Peel had been one of the frontier sporting world's most famous personalities for almost a decade. Like Bull, he was a native of England. Somewhere he acquired a vocabulary and fund of knowledge that led some to believe he was a graduate of Harvard College. Others scoffed at this notion, saying that his education had been obtained in the gambling dens of Mississippi River towns and there alone. It was agreed, however, that he was a fellow of striking appearance, tall and slender, wide of shoulder, with a catlike grace to his walk. His hair and beard were blond, his eyes large and blue. He spoke in a low, clear voice, with a tone of authority that commanded attention. Kind and gentle on most occasions, Peel, when aroused by an insult, real or imagined, could be a vicious killer. Those who had seen him in action declared that his skill with a revolver was as remarkable as his quickness to use it.

At the age of seventeen Peel was a bugler in a cavalry regiment during the Mexican War. After his discharge he settled for a time in Saint Louis, where he married a woman from a prominent family. He served another army hitch before turning to gambling as a full time occupation at Leavenworth, Kansas, in 1856.

He turned up in Salt Lake City in 1858, broke and desperate to break a long streak of bad luck at the tables. Inquiring around town for friends who might help him out with a fresh stake, he learned that two former Leavenworth gamblers named Conley and Rucker were in the city and prospering. Peel had helped both these men back in Kansas when the cards were running the other way and he was in the chips. He hunted up Conley first and found him acting as lookout at a faro table. Conley refused his request for a loan of twenty-five dollars. The faro dealer, a man named Robinson, motioned to the cash drawer. "Your credit is good with me," he said. "Help yourself."

Peel reached over and took five half-eagles from the bank. His eyes, as cold and hard as the gold pieces in his hand, never left Conley's face. Suddenly, he seized the casekeeper and flung it at the lookout's head. Conley dove for the door as Peel unsheathed his revolver. Robinson grabbed his arm before he could bring the weapon into action. Cursing Conley bitterly, Peel explained how he had helped the Leavenworth gambler previously and denounced him for his ingratitude.

He then left and went directly to Commercial Street and the

faro game of Oliver Rucker, the other former acquaintance. Placing his stack of coins on a layout card, he told Rucker to deal. Rucker pushed the money away, saying he wanted none of Peel's game. With an oath, Peel grabbed a chair and flung it across the table. Rucker ducked out the back of the room and ran into a store next door. Peel stalked relentlessly after him and found his quarry crouching in the store with a pistol in his hand. The gamblers' guns roared almost simultaneously and both men were hit. They continued firing as they fell to the floor.

In one account of this battle it is said that Peel, with three bullets through his body and his own weapon empty, crawled to Rucker's side and plunged a bowie knife into his adversary's heart.[1] Another version, told some years later to a reporter for the *Helena Independent* by a man named W. D. Wier, who claimed to have been an eyewitness to the fight, had the two gamblers lying about eight feet apart in a large pool of blood. A doctor arrived, took one look at the two wounded men, and told them to make their wills as they had less than fifteen minutes to live. Rucker, still grasping in his bloody left fist the bankroll from his faro game, whispered weakly that the money should be sent to his mother in Tennessee. "Tell her I'm dead, but for God's sake don't break her heart telling her I went like this," he pleaded.

"I've got a wife in Leavenworth City," said Peel. "Write and tell her I fit till the last minute; aye, and I fit to the last minute."[2]

Rucker died, but Peel, with a ball in his shoulder, another through his thigh, and a bullet wound in his cheek, somehow survived. He was carried to the Salt Lake House where his wounds were treated. Conley had disappeared, but Rucker had other friends who demanded the arrest of the wounded man. Peel's friends, with the aid of certain Mormon officials, spirited the gambler to a hiding place twelve miles from town. When he had recovered sufficiently, he made his way on horseback to California. He spent some months in San Bernardino, Los Angeles, and San Francisco before moving on to Virginia City, Nevada.

Shortly before Farmer Peel's arrival in the Comstock country, a notorious bully named Sam Brown had been shot to death by tough hotelkeeper Henry Van Sickle. For months Brown had lorded it over the sporting crowd at Washoe, declaring himself chief and shooting an occasional victim to prove it. When Peel, with his reputation for a hair-trigger temper and gun-wielding ability, turned up in Virginia City, wise heads nodded and got down their bets on Peel for the new chief.

Peel made no claims, but when a sport named Dick Paddock challenged him, saying, "You don't look like a chief to me" and invited him into the street, he found himself defending the title. Peel and Paddock squared off in the street, as innumerable Hollywood actors would do a century later, and began to burn powder. Paddock went down, seriously wounded; Peel was unscathed. Dick Paddock survived this encounter, but, according to a contemporary newspaper,[3] he was a man "who would rather look down the barrel of a gun than waste wind," and a few years later he was shot to death in the Delta Saloon by a police officer.

From the day he accepted Paddock's challenge, Langford Peel was considered chief at Washoe. There can be little doubt that he enjoyed the title and the deference he received from the sporting gentry. There were, of course, upstarts who disputed his right to the title.

John Dennis, known in Virginia City as "El Dorado Johnny," felt a strong urge himself to be chief. One day, decked out in his finest, he stopped at a barber shop and ordered the works—shave, haircut, whisker trim, and shine. Pomaded and powdered, he took on alcoholic fortification in Pat Lannon's saloon.

"What sort of corpse do you think I'll make?" he asked the saloonkeeper.

"You don't look much like a corpse now," replied Lannon.

"Well, I'll be a corpse or a gentleman in less than five minutes," said Johnny, downing his drink and heading for the door.

He found Langford Peel presiding over his monte table in Pat Lynch's saloon, and invited him into C Street. Within moments, El Dorado Johnny was back in Pat Lynch's, laid out in state on a billiard table. Langford Peel paid for a fine coffin and all the funeral expenses, and everyone agreed that Johnny made a fine-looking corpse.

Peel reportedly killed six men at Virginia City, but compared to the brutal Sam Brown who had preceded him, he was thought to be mild-mannered and of a genial disposition. When angered, however, he could be a tiger. On one occasion he was arrested on a disorderly conduct charge and brought before a justice of the peace named Davenport, who sported a long, flowing beard. Judge Davenport found Peel guilty and gave him his choice of a $100 fine or twenty days in jail. Peel, apparently contrite, asked permission to go out and get the money. Soon he was back, guns buckled on and breathing fire.

"I've come to settle with you," he said. Grabbing Davenport's whiskers in both hands, he slammed the magistrate's head repeatedly against the wall. Several peace officers were present, but no one moved to stop him. When he felt that the judge had been sufficiently chastised, Peel released him and strode from the room. The matter had been settled to his satisfaction and evidently to the satisfaction of Judge Davenport, for there were no further repercussions.

Dan de Quille, editor of Virginia City's *Territorial Enterprise*, castigated Peel in his paper and demanded the arrest of the chief. Several of the printers decided to have some fun at the expense of their boss, a nonviolent Quaker. After the appearance of the editorial they told him that a very angry, tough-looking hombre with six-guns prominently displayed had been in the office looking for him.

De Quille picked up an ornamental stiletto from his desk and headed for Peel's C Street hangout. He found the gambler lounging at the bar. De Quille positioned himself at Peel's right side, and, reaching around his back, suddenly pinned him against his side with his own left arm. The editor's right hand came up and held the point of the stiletto at Peel's throat.

"I am de Quille of the *Enterprise*," he said to the surprised Peel. "You have been looking for me?"

"I have not!" Peel cried. "Whoever says so is a lair. I wish you no harm. I respect a man who has the guts to say what he thinks."

De Quille put down his blade and began an apology.

"No need to apologize," said Peel. "You got the drop on me, and no one ever managed that trick before. Here, let me buy you a drink."

Some time during Peel's reign in Virginia City, John Bull arrived in the Nevada camp. The chief took a liking to the clever young sharper and enlisted him as a partner in his monte game. When table play slowed somewhat in early 1867, the two left Virginia City together. They spent several months at Belmont and then went on to Salt Lake City. Nine years had passed since Peel's hasty departure from the Mormon capital.

During their Salt Lake City stopover, the partners had a serious argument but managed to patch up their differences before heading north to Helena, Montana. Accompanying them now were two women. John Bull's mistress has not left her name to posterity, but the woman with Peel was Belle C. Neil, an accomplished faro dealer. Upon arrival at Helena, Belle had no difficulty landing a job as dealer in John Chase's gambling hall. Helena pioneers remembered Belle Neil as the handsomest woman to hit the town up to that time.

In Helena, as in the other towns he had graced, Langford Peel made staunch friends and bitter enemies. He delighted in interfering in the business of others, and, in so doing, charmed some and infuriated many.

One evening he watched a faro game in which six miners were systematically being relieved of their dust by a crooked dealer. Placing a hand on the shoulder of one of the players, Peel asked how much he had lost and was told seventy dollars. Peel then asked each of the miners the extent of his losses. Turning to the dealer, he ordered him to return the money. When the sharper hesitated, Peel pushed back his coat and rested his hand on the butt of his revolver. The dealer started counting.

Peel then reached across the table, flipped over the crooked box, and explained to the awestruck miners how they had been fleeced. "Go across the street," he said. "You likely won't win there either, but at least the game is on the square."

On the night of July 22, 1867, Langford Peel and John Bull were seated in a game at the Exchange, the Main Street gambling house run by Sam and Charles Greer. It is not known whether the smoothed-over Salt Lake City disagreement flared anew or some new discord erupted, but suddenly hot words were being spoken and the two partners were on their feet. Peel's notoriously low flash point was soon reached and he slapped Bull's face, at the same time reaching for his gun.

"I am not heeled," Bull said quickly. "But you cannot make a mark I will not come to."

"Go then, damn you, and heel yourself," growled Peel.

"I will be back," Bull promised.

"Come fighting."

Bull went to his rooms and wrote letters to his family and friends. He gave directions for the disposition of his property in the event of his death, carefully loaded and oiled his six-shooter, and walked back toward the Greer brothers' Exchange.

He had been gone about an hour. For most of that time Langford Peel had kept a sharp eye on the doorway, warily awaiting the return of his friend-turned-foe. About midnight he stood up, walked to the door, and stepped out into the July night. Bull was nowhere in sight. Smiling, Peel decided that the little gambler wanted none of his game. He sauntered down the street to Chase's, three doors away, and went in to get Belle.

A man named John R. Drew later claimed to have seen all that then transpired.

When they came out together on Main Street, the woman was holding Peel's right arm. They started toward the restaurant and had gone only a little way when, from behind a pile of dry goods boxes, a shot was fired which struck Peel in the side. He reached for his hip pocket to get his own pistol, but the badly frightened woman held to his arm with an iron grip. Before he could jerk his arm loose, a second shot was fired and Peel fell to the ground. Then Bull stepped from behind the boxes, and standing directly over Peel, fired a bullet into his head. So close was the weapon held that Peel's face was all powder stained.[4]

Others would testify that when Peel and Belle stepped from the garish light of the gambling house into Helena's Main

Street, they almost collided with John Bull. In this version, both men were momentarily startled by the sudden confrontation. Then, as they recognized each other, both went for their guns. Peel, encumbered by the woman holding his arm, was too slow. John Bull pumped three shots into him before he could get into action.

Any one of Peel's three wounds would have been fatal. He had been hit in the throat, in the face, and in the chest above the heart.

Bull was placed under arrest by John Xavier ("X") Beidler, Montana's legendary vigilante leader and early-day lawman, who described the events of that night some years later. Beidler and a group of friends had been to a circus, playing in Helena:

After we had taken in the circus, we all went down town and naturally fell into the John Ming Saloon, and Len Robinson, who was the concoctor . . . asked me if we had seen Johnny Bull yet. . . .

He said: "Johnny Bull has killed Farmer Peale."

I asked him if he was in earnest as Peale was such a rattler that I didn't think he would be killed.

I immediately went up town and found Farmer Peale dead. The officers, Howie, Featherstone, and Bob Hereford were all anxiously looking for Bull. . . . I learned from a friend that Bull kept his horse in Monte's stable at the end of Main Street. . . .

Beidler recognized Bull's horse in the stable and told stableman Monte that he was looking for the gambler. A few minutes later Monte left the stable and Beidler, suspicious, followed close behind. Monte entered a house and Beidler burst through the door behind him, to find Bull and Monte talking.

I stepped up to Bull and told him to come with me. He wanted to know if I was going to hang him. I said: "No, sir. I will put you in gaol and give you a hearing."

I held my pistol on him during this time and asked him to take off his belt, pistol and knife which he had on, and lay it on the table. I then ordered Monte to put on the belt and pistol and told Bull not to be alarmed as I was going to take him to the Marshal's by the back road, because if I had taken him down Main St. his friends would have rescued him—or his enemies would have hung him.

John Xavier "X" Beidler, who arrested John Bull for the killing of Langford Peel. Courtesy Montana Historical Society.

The words on Langford Peel's grave marker hastened the departure of John Bull from Helena. Courtesy Montana Historical Society.

We reached the office and Bull was happy, being afraid of the vigilantes. I told Monte to . . . go up town and tell Neil Howie to come at once to the Marshal's office . . . and not let anyone know about the capture. . . .

Howie was much surprised to see the murderer captured and I told Howie that I had promised Mr. Bull that he should be tried by the court and that we must protect him. Howie took Bull by the hand and said: "What I said goes and we will protect you."

That took another load off of Bull's heart.

[We] went and put him in the County Jail and afterwards we strolled up town and great crowds of men were congregated at street crossings and corners discussing the situation. We were asked several times by Peale's friends why we didn't go and rustle to get . . . Bull and not let him escape—while Bull's friends said that if we found him we couldn't arrest him. Their imprecations were heaped upon us by both sides so thick and fast and almost beyond human endurance, and I finally got tired and told them to go down to the County Jail and talk to him if they wanted to through the bars. There was a rush to the jail . . . and Featherstone, who was jailor, seeing a big crowd coming, thought it must be either the Viglantes to hang Bull or his friends to release him, and got his buck-shot gun. . . .

The crowd demanded to see Bull, but Featherstone held them off with the shotgun. Finally he permitted two of the mob, "one of them . . . a Peale man and the other a Bull man," to approach and talk to Bull and satisfy themselves that he was indeed incarcerated. The crowd then dispersed and the excitement died down.[5]

Defended by a battery of lawyers headed by W. T. Pemberton, John Bull stood trial for the killing of Langford Peel. The jury split, nine for acquittal on his plea of self-defense, and three for a verdict of guilty of murder. He was released and immediately left the region.

Perhaps his departure was hastened by the words engraved on the marker erected over Peel's ashes:

SACRED

TO THE

MEMORY OF

LANGFORD PEEL

BORN IN

LIVERPOOL

DIED
JULY 23, 1867
AGED
36 YEARS
IN LIFE, BELOVED BY HIS FRIENDS, AND RESPECTED BY
HIS ENEMIES.
VENGEANCE IS MINE, SAYETH THE LORD.
I KNOW THAT MY REDEEMER LIVETH.
ERECTED BY A FRIEND.

L. P. Langford, curious about the lines from Scripture, asked the "friend" their meaning.

The friend had the idea that, as Peel did not have fair play, the Lord would avenge his death in some signal manner. The other sentence was thought to properly express the idea that the man was living who would redeem Peel's name from whatever obloquy might attach to it, because of his having "died with his boots on." Could there be a more strange interpretation of the scriptures?[6]

15

Gyps and cons are all cases of the biter being bitten. I got into my three-card monte gyp that way because I loved to kid, and because I loved to trim suckers.

Frank Tarbeaux
Donald Henderson Clarke, *The Autobiography of Frank Tarbeaux*

Whether in flight from the vengeance of Peel's "redeemer," or simply in search of the latest frontier excitement, John Bull shook the dust of Helena from his boots and next turned up more than five hundred miles away in Cheyenne, Wyoming, then experiencing its wildest period as the terminus of the Union Pacific Railroad. Here the sporting crowd of the phenomenon known as "Hell-on-Wheels" was encamped for the winter.

During the construction of the Union Pacific west from Omaha, Nebraska, a series of local headquarters was established that served as supply points for the engineers and temporary campgrounds for the laborers. At each terminus there blossomed a jerry-built town of tents, shacks, and lean-tos accomodating a population of ten thousand. At least half of this number were honky-tonkers—sure-thing gamblers, accompanied by their ropers, cappers and steerers; saloon and dance hall operators; con men; boosters; madams, whores, and pimps; dips; yeggs—the complete roster of the quick buck clan. As the rails stretched westward and the railroad officials moved the base of operations to a new, advanced site, the clan followed. Whiskey barrels, gambling equipment, tents, cots, the whole array of the paraphernalia of vice would be loaded on flatcars and the crew was off to the next shebang. This rolling city of sin was appropriately dubbed "Hell-on-Wheels."

The first of the terminus towns was the Siding, just west of Fort Kearney. Then came North Platte, Indian Prairie, Devil's Acres, and Julesburg. At each succeeding stop the sporting crowd became increasingly obstreperous. At Julesburg a group of gamblers defied the railroad bosses and jumped the land set aside for shops by General Grenville M. Dodge. Gen-

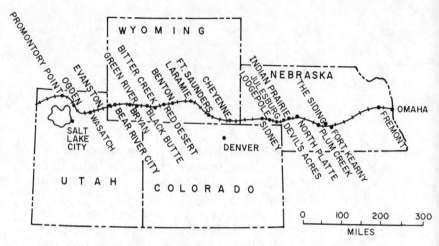

The Union Pacific railroad, Omaha to Promontory Point, and the Hell-On-Wheels Towns.

eral Jack Casement was sent by Dodge to Julesburg with orders to clean out the troublemakers. Casement rolled into town with a hundred veteran soldiers and, in a sharp engagement, scattered the renegades.

Hell-on-Wheels next ground to a halt at Cheyenne, and here it was that John Bull joined the party. He was greeted like a hero returned from the wars. Women clung to him and men rushed up to pump the hand of the man who had gunned down the famous Langford Peel. No matter how crowded the saloon he entered, he found there was always room for him at the bar. Invariably there was one unclaimed bed at the hotel, one open seat at the gambling table, room for one more at the jam-packed restaurant. It was fine for a young man's ego and, he soon learned, excellent for his business. The suckers fought for a chance to get at his game.

He prospered in the face of fierce competition, for gamblers and gambling games were everywhere. Sam and Charlie Greer had come down from Helena and opened the Gold Rooms in Cheyenne with a celebrated dealer named "Fat Jack" overseeing one of the tables. Other well-known sporting figures in town included Eleanore Dumont, dealing her 21 game and taking a cut from a covey of girls she had working; "Corn-Hole Johnny" Gallagher; veteran riverboat gambler George Devol; Charlie Storms, teamed in the operation of a brace faro game with Colonel A. B. Miller, onetime owner of the great racehorse, Border Ruffian; W. J. ("Billy") Martin; Ed Chase, up from Denver for the excitement; Jeff Standifer, a former partner of Ferd Patterson; and Ben Marks, who was to be associated with John Bull at Omaha, Council Bluffs, and other cities in later years.

Ben Marks, like Doc Baggs, Canada Bill Jones, Frank Tarbeaux, and others with whom John Bull teamed, called himself a gambler but was in fact a confidence man. His object always was to steer his victim into a trap, lead him to believe he was on the inside of a sure thing, and then milk him dry. Marks had worked his way westward from his home in Council Bluffs, Iowa, relying on his wits and the easy spiel of the gifted grifter. His only tools were his deft fingers and three greasy monte cards. Since he dealt his three-card monte game on a board suspended from his shoulders, he could set up anywhere there were suckers, and, with his ropers and shills, turn a moderate profit.

But in Cheyenne, overrun as it was with the Hell-on-Wheels horde, he found the competition tough. Ben bent his sharp wits to the problem of bringing suckers to him. There were numerous gambling houses competing for the sucker's buck, of course, but what Ben wanted was something different, a place into which the mark could be enticed by his own greed and properly swindled.

"Then Ben had an idea which was eventually to revolutionize the grift, an idea which was to become the backbone of all big-time confidence games," records David W. Maurer, historian of the con racket in America.

On the front of a Cheyenne building Marks posted a sign reading, "The Dollar Store." Exhibited in the store's window were items of all kinds: decorative, utilitarian, simple, gaudy. The articles had but one thing in common—all were worth more than a dollar. Bargain hunters and something-for-nothing chumps were not long in making an appearance. Inside, like spiders, Ben and his cohorts waited. Once he entered the store, the sucker's interest was "switched" from the dollar bargains to one of several three-card monte games being dealt on barrelheads. The merchandise gathered dust in the window, for nothing was ever sold in the Dollar Store, but Ben's customers usually left his establishment lighter in pocket than when they entered.

"Thus, in a very crude form, developed what we know today as the 'big store'—the swanky gambling club or fake brokerage establishment in which the modern payoff or rag is played," writes Professor Maurer.

It became the device which enables competent modern operators to take, say, $75,000 from a victim and at the same time conceal from him the fact that he has been swindled. Although today there are several types of stores used, they all operate on the same principle and appear as legitimate places doing a large volume of business. So realistically are they manned and furnished that the victim does not suspect that everything about them—including the patronage—is fake. In short, the modern big store is a carefully set up and skillfully managed theater where the victim acts out an unwilling role in the most exciting of all underworld dramas. It is a triumph of the ingenuity of the criminal mind.[1]

In the spring of 1868 the rails pushed on and Hell-on-Wheels rolled deeper into Wyoming. Laramie was the next town upon which the gang descended like a swarm of locusts. Then came Benton, Green River, Bryan, Bear River City—town after town as the steel snaked on toward Utah and the historic linkup with the Central Pacific at Promontory Summit.

Typical of the tent towns was Benton City, which for three months in the summer of 1868 squatted on the parched plain near the marker that indicated the road had stretched seven hundred miles from Omaha. At Benton City there was no grass, no trees, no water. The North Platte River was two miles away and water hauled to Benton City brought one dollar a barrel and ten cents a bucket. In July lots were selling for $800 to $1,000, and within a month twenty-three saloons and five dance halls were going full blast around the clock. The

North Star offered gambling in a variety of forms, while a house called the Buffalo Hump Corral specialized in a game called rondo coolo, played with a stick and ivory balls on a table similar to a pocket billiard table. The biggest house in town was the Empire Tent, a building measuring forty by one hundred feet, with wooden sidewalls and a canvas roof. Reflector-backed lamps mounted high on the walls provided brilliant lighting.

A. B. Miller was elected mayor of Benton City, but he did not allow his civic duties to take him too far or too long from his faro table. Miller and his partner, Charlie Storms, hired a young man fresh from the States as casekeeper for their game. It was the first regular employment as a gambler for John Philip Quinn, who was to spend many years as a professional "gam" before publishing a book of his experiences, *Fools of Fortune*, one of the earliest exposés of gambling in America. Quinn reported that in Benton City he slept in a tent that was barricaded on all sides by three-feet-high stone slabs, protection against the bullets that whined and ricocheted through the camp at night.

In the three months of Benton City's existence, more than one hundred people died, most of them violently. Then, as suddenly as it had mushroomed on the plains, Benton City wilted and died. Down came the tents and cracker box buildings, and Hell-on-Wheels rolled on. By October the $1,000 lots had been given back to the prairie dogs and Benton City was no more.

At Bear River City a vigilance committee was organized in an effort to control the rampant lawlessness. On the night of November 11, 1868, three prisoners were taken from the makeshift calaboose and lynched. The action was applauded by the editors of *The Frontier Index*, a newspaper that had been moving with the railroad. "We have never been connected with the vigilantes at any time though we heartily endorse their actions in ridding the community of a set of creatures who are not worthy of the name of men," stated the paper editorially two days after the hanging.[2]

A few nights later a gang of gamblers led by Tom Smith stormed the jail, released the remaining inmates, and burned the building. Smith then set fire to the office of *The Frontier Index*. When storekeepers grabbed rifles and opened up on the gamblers, a raging gun battle ensued. Tom Smith stood in the middle of the street and emptied two revolvers into a log store in which were barricaded a number of townsmen. Bullets from the building cut his coat and hat and winged him in one arm. Somehow he survived to gain acclaim two years later as the heroic city marshal of Abilene, Kansas. A detachment of soldiers from Fort Bridger, dispatched to Bear River City to bring order, counted forty dead and wounded as a result of the battle.

A *Chicago Tribune* correspondent named Jim Chisholm, after following the line of Hell-on-Wheels for some months, wrote a story from the comparative quiet of the gold camp at Wyoming's South Pass:

What a contrast is there between the quiet life of this mountain camp, and the roaring hells of railroad towns which I have but recently quitted. Cheyenne, Laramie, Benton, Green River . . . the very mention of the names calls up a crowd of reminiscences which on the whole are anything but refreshing.

The sight of a gambler from Green River who came up here on a brief visit recalled vividly to my mind a succession of old familiar horrors—the flaring gambling tents—the dance houses—the eternal strumming of old banjoes—the miserable females who have to dance all night till the broad day light, with about as much hilarity as so many prisoners in the treadmill—the game of Faro—the game of three card Monte—the game of Roulette, Black and White—the hundred and one games too numerous to mention—the perpetual tumult and uproar and din of mingling cries—"all down, all set, make your game—seven of diamonds and the red wins"—"Come now boys, I only want one more couple for the next set"—quarrels, cursing, drinking and the flash and bang of pistols—shameless pimps, shameless women, broken gamblers, thieves—depravity that flaunts its banner in the broad daylight—such are a few of the memories that haunt the vacant chambers of the brain.

I often speculate on what will finally become of all that rolling scum which the locomotive seems to blow onward as it presses westward. Will they get blown clean off the continent at last into the Pacific Ocean? One is gradually surrounded by the same faces in

Bear River Tom Smith, whose first notoriety resulted from his role in a riot in the Hell-On-Wheels town. Courtesy Kansas State Historical Society.

each successive town, the same gamblers, the same musicians, playing the same old tunes to the same old dance, the same females
getting always a little more dilapidated. As the excitement died out
of one town, and the railroad leaves it behind in a kind of exhausted
repose, these old familiar faces die out to reappear in a new state of
existence. Up go the old tents in a new location and round it come
all the old bummers. Here is the Empire Tent which got busted down
at Benton. There goes Billy Martin who kept the big gambling house
at Cheyenne. There is Fat Jack who used to have a table at Charlie
Greer's, now running a game of his own. In they come creeping day
by day to the new town. Here comes John, who plays the earphone,
and Al who plays the fiddle and Brad who sings comic songs. Here
comes Mag and Moll, and gantle Annie, and Moss Agate, and the
Schoolmarm, and Mormom Ann, and Crazy Jane, and all the pioneers of vice, to keep the dance agoing till the town is danced away
again to another point. I happened to be in Green River before the
high tide had quite begun to ebb from Benton, so for a time we
enjoyed compartively speaking a sort of immunity from these float-
ing wrecks. But they had commenced to gather in when I departed
and I suppose are now in full blast. The gamblers are, to give the
devil his due, of a friendly, generous disposition and helpful to one
another in a manner which could do honor to a Christian. But for
this, how many would be "busted" beyond all remedy and left behind in the cold. There are always a crowd of hangers on around the
tables who watch when one of the lucky number "makes a raise" and
asks him for a "stake." Nor do they often ask in vain. It is their only
hope for a meal. . . .[3]

The denizens of Hell-on-Wheels were not blown into the
Pacific Ocean when the transcontinental railroad was completed, as Chisholm suggested, but they were blown to the
four corners of the frontier. For John Bull the next attraction
was the White Pine mining district of eastern Nevada and its
cluster of camps, then in first bloom.

Somewhere he had acquired a wife, whom he took to Chicago and set up in a boarding house at 771 West Van Buren
Street. She bore him two children. To the other boarders she
explained that her husband was seen so infrequently because
he was a "traveling man." About 1880 this woman died and
Bull placed his children in foster homes.

A "traveling man" John Bull certainly was. By train, by

riverboat, and by stagecoach he journeyed back and forth across the great Northwest for many years, extracting green-backs from greenhorns. For short periods he would light in a likely-looking town, but as soon as play slowed or there were signs of local vexation at the presence of sharpers, he was back on the move.

Omaha was his roosting place for a time during the early seventies. Ten years later Bull told a Helena newspaperman that he had engaged in the "transfer business" at Omaha, but, of course, the only "transfers" he arranged were those of cash from the pockets of the unwary into his own.

Omaha's leading resident gamblers at this time were Dan B. Allen, Tom Dozier, Frank Shaw, Tom Ratliff, and Dick Wilde. Shaw and Ratliff kept gambling rooms over Hornberger's sa-loon at 1321 Douglas. In later years Frank Shaw returned to his native Minneapolis and was a power in a syndicate con-trolling gambling in that city. Wilde maintained a well-ap-pointed hall above his saloon at the corner of 12th and Farn-ham, and Dozier and Allen presided over elaborate facilities down the street at 211 South 12th.

Queen of Hell's Half Acre, the Omaha tenderloin district, was Dan Allen's woman, Anna Wilson, who ran the finest parlor house in town. Once, when some overambitious police raided her place, Anna calmly handed them a letter. "Anna Wilson and her girls have paid their fine. Lay off," it read, and was signed by the police judge. The title of "Queen of Hell's Half Acre" was not assumed by Anna imprudently. She had been formally crowned by the district's sports at a grand ball in a hall next door to Clayton's Crystal Saloon. For her coro-nation Anna was decked out in diamonds said to be worth $10,000. Some time during the night's festivities a gang from the Crystal Saloon swiped Anna's stones. Dan Allen ordered the thieves to return the gems and threatened dire conse-quences if they did not comply. He was promptly told where they were hidden and Anna soon had her diamonds back.

Some time later Anna had an opportunity to repay her lover. A group of southern gamblers, working in concert, made a determined attack on Allen's games. When play started, Allen had $22,000 in his bank, but after several hours he was almost

broke and the combine was preparing to tap him for everything he had. Allen dispatched employee George Crawford to
Anna's bordello with the terse message: "Send money." Crawford later said that Anna spoke not a word but opened a canvas
telescopic grip and began to toss in stacks of large denomination bank notes, making no effort to count the money. When
the bag was full she snapped it shut and handed it over to
Crawford, who hurried back to Allen's gambling hall. With
the additional capital the gambler broke the streak of the
southerners, recouped his losses, and cleaned them out.

Another noted gambling man in Omaha at this time was
Bob Louden, described as "a king among his class, . . . handsome, magnificently proportioned, reckless and vain, . . . the
sort of man for whom some foolish girl would sacrifice her
honor and endure abuse in order that she might enjoy his ca-
pricious and temporary favor."[4] To Omaha with Louden came
a woman known as Carrie Baxter, tall and statuesque, with
exquisitely carved features and a body both stately and voluptuous. Once the star attraction at a Cincinnati parlor house,
Carrie, after joining Louden, withdrew from the frail sister-
hood. In Omaha she was said to have practiced the profession
of shoplifting, which was considered a step upward on the
underworld scale.

The handsome couple quarreled and went separate ways, he
to the table of another frontier town, she to Denver where she
broke completely with the underworld life and became a sales-
woman in a dry goods store. Later she became a post office
employee. From Denver she went to Hays City, Kansas,
where she was accepted as a lady and admitted into the finest
homes. Carrie had created an entirely new life for herself, a
life of respectability.

When a Hays hotel owner threw a lavish society ball, Carrie, with her beauty and natural queenly demeanor, was the
unchallenged belle. But appearing at the ball also was a ghost
from her past, the gambler Bob Louden. The former lovers
eyed each other covertly but gave no outward sign to indicate
their past association. As the evening wore on, however,
Louden became increasingly drunk. Perhaps he was jealous of
Carrie's newly won standing in the community, or perhaps he

could not resist boasting that the ravishing woman had once been his bed companion, but he blurted out her scandalous history and mocked her before the crowd. Suddenly a derringer appeared in Carrie's hand, there was a shot, and Bob Louden fell dead.

A trial of sorts was held and a jury wasted little time in bringing in a "not guilty" verdict. It was the consensus of opinion in frontier Hays City that there had never been a more justifiable homicide.

A frequent Omaha visitor in the early 1870s was veteran circuit gambler John Jackson Cozad. Born in Virginia in 1830, Cozad ran away from home at the age of twelve, studied the pasteboards, and for thirty years was a familiar figure in river towns and mining camps throughout the frontier. He had been to South America and had sailed around the Horn to San Francisco in 1849. His game was faro and so adept was he at the game that he had been banned from many plush clubs in both the East and the West and had been forced to use other names and disguises to gain admittance.

John J. Cozad had a dream. It was his ambition to found a community that would be the cleanest city in the United States, a city with no saloons, no vice—and no gambling. He had made one unsuccessful attempt, the town of Cozaddale in Ohio, but the site had been too close to sinful Cincinnati, and he had pulled out, although the town remained and still bore his name.

Then, in the summer of 1872, Cozad simply earthquaked the Omaha faro tables and came away with winnings of more than fifty thousand dollars. He purchased forty thousand acres of prairie land along the Union Pacific Railroad in central Nebraska and built a home for his wife and two small sons, John Jr. and Robert Henry. He platted a townsite and gradually a small town, named Cozad, developed.

In 1882 he shot and killed a man named Alf Pearson in a dispute over Pearson cattle on Cozad land. The county offices were controlled by cattlemen, notably I. P. ("Print") Olive, who could be counted on to favor the Pearson side of the argument. Although Cozad had shot in self-defense when Pearson pulled a knife, he felt that he could not get a fair trial in

John Jackson Cozad, so feared by faro dealers that he was barred from many establishments, dreamed of a city free of vice. Courtesy Nebraska State Historical Society.

the district. He fled to Colorado and, with a murder warrant open for him in Nebraska, took the name Richard H. Lee. A newspaper estimated his worth at this time at about $300,000. His son, John Jr., was also a fugitive, having jumped bail on an arson charge and left the state. Cozad's wife quietly sold the Nebraska property, sewed the money into the lining of her clothes, and, with her younger son Robert, slipped away to meet her husband in Denver.

John Jackson Cozad never saw his dream of a sin-free city become a reality. But he did see his two sons grow to manhood and become eminently respected and successful citizens. The older boy took the name Frank Southern and became a prominent physician in Philadelphia; Robert studied art and became the internationally acclaimed painter, Robert Henri.

A sure-thing gambler named George Mehaffy was associated with John Bull during the early 1870s in Omaha, and on at least two occasions Bull found himself in serious trouble with the Omaha authorities because of that association. In July, 1873, he was arrested with Mehaffy, charged with the stabbing of Samuel Atwood, an employee of the Omaha & Southwestern Railroad, but managed to beat what he always claimed was a "bum rap." The two were then arrested by Captain J. J. McNeligh, general superintendent of the Western Detective Agency, and accused of having robbed Missourian James Wilkinson in a crooked card game. Indicted with Bull and Mehaffy were Charles ("Doc") Baggs, Ben Marks, and a couple of shills named Cuming and Connor. The *Omaha Bee* reported that "Bull 'staked' the others, but was perhaps not concerned in the robbery, although he confessed that he was around to see that things were done according to Hoyle."[5] All were acquitted and freed with the exception of Mehaffy, who was convicted, but he later escaped and left the country.

Ben Marks, after leaving Cheyenne where he had scored with his Dollar Store, returned to his hometown, Council Bluffs, just across the Missouri River from Omaha. There he opened a large clubhouse featuring a faro game dexterously dealt with one hand by Charlie Stebbins, who had blown off an arm while practicing his other vocation of safecracking. In his clubhouse Marks also had a prize ring and a circular track that he used in setting up suckers for fixed fights and footraces.

Another Council Bluffs gambler named Charley White came across the river to Omaha, and, in partnership with Charles D. Bibbins, H. B. Kennedy, and Jack Morrison, opened a large resort on Douglas Street that was the finest in the city during the 1880s. Called the Diamond, it offered an ornately furnished barroom on the first floor with pool tables and horse parlor facilities in the rear. Amid sumptuous surroundings upstairs were tables for faro, hazard, poker, and roulette.

During the years that John Bull headquartered in Omaha he patronized the town's gambling halls, but his income was derived from working the trains. In the years following completion of the transcontinental railroad, some of the most expert sharpers in the annals of American skullduggery rode the cars out of Omaha, preying on travelers. Former Mississippi riverboat gamblers like George Devol and Canada Bill Jones came north to skin marks and either teamed up with, or competed against, veteran eastern cardslicks like Pat Sheedy and westerners such as John Bull and Frank Tarbeaux.

Some train gamblers were utterly lacking in finesse and robbed their victims by any method, including strong-arm holdup. George Jean Nathan interviewed one of these gamblers for a *Harper's Magazine* article in 1910. Described by Nathan as "a gray-haired, pleasant-faced man of about forty-eight . . . , one of the most famous gamblers of his day in the Western states," this fellow had worked the Nebraska trains with two confederates. "Poker was our game, not three-card monte as you might suppose," he told Nathan. The sharpers would start a game, lure a well-fixed sucker in, accuse him of cheating, and "find" a hold-out card on him. They would then take his money under threat of exposing him as a cheat. "On one of the Denver trains, worked by another gambler and myself, we cleaned up $30,000 in six months," the crook confided. "$5,000 of this amount we got by luring two men into a big stake game and holding them up with revolvers."[6]

Sometimes more than one team of hustlers would be working the same train, which resulted in some interesting confron-

tations. One such meeting of skinning gamblers involved Pat
Sheedy, who recognized another crooked gambler on a train,
but this fellow did not recognize Sheedy. The sharper had enticed a group of men around his seat and was loudly announc-
ing his willingness to bet $500 against $250 that he could shuffle the deck and cut the queen of spades with one try. Sheedy
elbowed his way to the front of the crowd and said that he
would take that bet if the gambler would let him shuffle. It
was agreed and the stakes were put up. Sheedy riffled the cards
and placed the deck face down on a table. The crooked gambler grinned, pulled a knife from beneath his coat, and drove
the blade through the deck, saying, "I guess I have cut the
queen."

"Show us the queen," Sheedy said. The gambler pulled out
the knife and sorted through the deck. The queen was not
there. Sheedy had palmed it.

When the railroad officials finally cracked down on the gamblers, Pat Sheedy went back to his former haunts. He operated
in and around Chicago for several years and then went to New
York, where he was associated with the famous eastern gambling house proprietor, Richard Canfield. About the turn of
the century Sheedy achieved some notoriety as the go-between
in the negotiations for the return of Gainsborough's painting
of the Duchess of Devonshire, stolen by the highly successful
international thief, Adam Worth.

George Devol, with whom John Bull teamed for a time in
1876, had been trimming suckers for thirty-five years. Born in
Ohio, he ran away from home at the age of ten to become a
cabin boy on a riverboat. On the Mississippi and Ohio rivers
he looked with wonder on the elegantly dressed, soft-handed
gamblers with their perfumed, handsome women and seemingly endless rolls of high-denomination currency. By the time
Devol entered his teens he could palm cards, false cut, and
deal bottoms and seconds with ease, and was fleecing youngsters in river towns from Cincinnati to New Orleans. He was
seventeen at the time of the Mexican War and made his first
big money trimming soldiers on the Rio Grande.

Working mostly in the southern states, he made and spent
many hundreds of thousands of dollars in the years preceding

George Devol, who estimated that he won over two million dollars during his gambling career. From Forty Years a Gambler on the Mississippi.

and during the Civil War. After the war he ventured west, joining the army of con men, sharpers, and skin-game artists riding Hell-on-Wheels. He dealt faro for a time in the Gold Rooms at Cheyenne, and in the early '70s worked the trains running between Cheyenne and Omaha, and between Omaha and Kansas City.

He was a big man, weighing over two hundred pounds, with a large head and huge hands. "I could hold one deck in the palm of my hand and shuffle up another," he claimed. But his most unusual physical characteristic was a remarkably thick skull which he used to great advantage in numerous brawls. Devol would grasp an adversary by the coat, shoulders, arms, or anything else he could enclose in his great paws, lower his head, and ram it into the poor fellow's face, usually smashing the victim's nose flat, closing both of his eyes, and sometimes breaking his jaw.

"I don't know (and I guess I never will while I'm alive) just how thick my old skull is," wrote Devol in 1887,

but I do know it must be pretty thick, or it would have been cracked many years ago, for I have been struck some terrible blows on my head with iron dray-pins, pokers, clubs, stone-coal, and bowlders [sic], which would have split any man's skull wide open unless it was pretty thick. Doctors have often told me that my skull was nearly an inch in thickness over my forehead. . . .

I am now nearly sixty years of age, and have quit fighting, but I can to-day batter down any ordinary door or stave in a liquor barrel with "that old head of mine;" and I don't believe there is a man living (of near my own age) who can whip me in a rough-and-tumble fight. I never have my hair clipped short, for if I did I would be ashamed to take my hat off, as the lines on my old scalp look about like the railroad map of the State in which I was born.

Devol's most famous butting feat took place in New Orleans in 1867. The Robinson Circus, featuring William Carroll, "The Man With the Thick Skull, or The Great Butter," was playing the town and some sporting men arranged a butting match between Carroll and Devol. The Robinson brothers claimed their star could out-butt any man or beast with the possible exception of their elephant. "Dutch Jake," and other

New Orleans gamblers who had seen Devol in action, were willing to bet $10,000 that Carroll had met his match.

"I was at least fifty pounds heavier than Carroll," Devol recalled, "and I knew that was a great advantage, even if his head was as hard as my own. . . . I did not strike my very best, for I was a little afraid of hurting the little fellow. . . ."

They came together and Carroll went sprawling. When he got up, shaking his famous head in pain, surprise, and wonder, he put his hand atop Devol's head and said: "Gentlemen, I have found my papa at last!"

"He had the hardest head I ever ran against," Devol admitted,

and if he had been as heavy as I was, I can't say what the result would have been. . . . My old head is hard and thick, and maybe that is the reason I never had sense enough to save my money. It is said of me that I have won more money than any sporting man in this country. I will say that I hadn't sense enough to keep it; but if I had never seen a faro bank, I would be a wealthy man to-day.[7]

Like Devol, Canada Bill Jones made several fortunes at three-card monte, but as fast as he won it he lost his money at the games of other gamblers. Devol was a faro fiend, but Bill's downfall was the short-card game. He could not resist a game of poker, euchre, or seven-up, and at the peak of his career it was said that short-card artists followed him around the country, relieving him systematically of his monte winnings. It was Canada Bill who gave rise to one of the most famous of gambling anecdotes.

After losing his pile in a backwoods village gambling shack, Jones was admonished by his partner: "Didn't you know that game was crooked?"

"Sure," said Canada Bill, "but it was the only game in town!"

Born in a gypsy tent in Yorkshire, England, Bill Jones emigrated to Canada, where he learned the three-card monte game from Dick Cady, a veteran Canadian monte thrower. No slouch at the game himself, Cady realized that in young Jones he had a budding genius. By the time Jones left Canada for the rich pickings to be found in the antebellum southland, he

Canada Bill Jones, acknowledged by his peers as the greatest three-card monte sharp. Courtesy Western History Research Center, University of Wyoming.

was a polished manipulator of the pasteboards. Two decades of experience on the southern rivers honed his native ability to a fine edge. Many believed Canada Bill Jones to be the greatest monte sharp to ever "pitch a broad."

"Canada Bill was a character one might travel the length and breadth of the land and never see his match, or run across his equal," wrote his longtime partner, George Devol:

Imagine a medium-sized, chicken-headed, tow-haired sort of a man with mild blue eyes, and a mouth nearly from ear to ear, who walked with a shuffling, half-apologetic sort of a gait, and who, when his countenance was in repose, resembled an idiot. . . . His clothes

"He got out his wallet and put up $1,700," etc.   [Page 193.]

George Devol and Canada Bill skinning a sucker. Canada Bill flashes the cards; Devol, the bearded man, points to the table where the "mark," reaching for his wallet, should place his bet. From Forty Years a Gambler on the Mississippi.

were always several sizes too large, and his face was as smooth as a woman's and never had a particle of hair on it. . . . He had a squeaking, boyish voice, and awkward, gawky manners, and a way of asking fool questions and putting on a good natured sort of a grin, that led everybody to believe that he was the rankest kind of sucker—the greenest sort of country jake.[8]

Canada Bill's displays of charity were legendary even among the gamblers, who as a class were noted for generosity. As Devol said of him:

There never lived a better hearted man. He was liberal to a fault. I have known him to turn back when we were on the street and give to some poor object we had passed. Many a time I have seen him walk up to a Sister of Charity and make her a present of as much as $50. . . .

Once I saw him win $200 from a man, and shortly after his little boy came running down from the cabin, Bill called the boy up and handed him the $200 and told him to give it to his mother.[9]

Returning one day from one of his "business trips," Canada Bill noticed in the Omaha depot an agitated young woman with a badly frightened little girl clinging to her skirts. When Bill asked what troubled her, the woman said that a friendly stranger had volunteered to transfer her baggage for her as she changed trains. Without thinking, she had given the man her purse containing the baggage checks and all her money. Now he had disappeared.

Instantly, Bill grasped the woman's hand and pulled her quickly to the baggage room. He was just in time to head off the stranger who was in the act of departing with purse and baggage.

"Hand it over," Bill demanded.

Checking the bags through to Butte, the woman's destination, Bill purchased tickets for mother and daughter, and returned the purse with the balance of money intact. As he helped her onto the train, he slipped the woman another ten-dollar bill. She repeatedly thanked him and asked for his name and address, saying that her husband, a Butte miner, would want to write and return the money.

Canada Bill shook his head. "Bill's luck," was his only comment. The woman did not know what he meant, but to Canada Bill such an opportunity to render service to someone in trouble was a fortuitous circumstance. He was convinced that helping others brought him luck at the tables.

Canada Bill was the originator of a gambling con game known as the "rube act," which was later copied by Frank Tarbeaux and others. With his naturally ungainly, retarded appearance and ill-fitting, rough clothing, Bill easily assumed the role of the backwoods bumpkin who was the central character in the charade. For the ultimate detail of realism in the completion of his costume, he would, just before boarding a train, walk through a pile of fresh horse manure, leaving an aromatic residue on his boots. He usually teamed with two or more well-dressed, prosperious-looking accomplices who steered the suckers to him and set them up for the old bent-card monte trick. Devol, Doc Baggs, and John Bull capped for Canada Bill on the trains out of Omaha. Baggs and Bull also acted as steerers for Frank Tarbeaux, who has left a vivid description of the rube act as he performed it.

"It's the funniest act in the world to look at and I nearly died laughing when I first saw it," Tarbeaux said:

This gyp should be seen and heard to appreciate its artistry. It loses a deal of its color in cold type. . . .

We worked generally on railroad trains. I worked in it mostly out of Omaha. . . . The steerers got on the train, and each of them selected a sucker. Conversation was easily opened, and when a steerer decided his sucker had enough money to make him worth while, he'd raise his hat as a signal to me.

I had gotten on the train in a linen duster and a hard hat. I had folded up the hard hat in the duster and tossed it up on a hat rack. From my pocket I took a soft hat, and put it on. I had a dickey, with a rubber band around the neck, which when pulled up, dressed me so far as the eye was concerned in a hickory shirt. The duster had concealed a homespun suit, dyed with butternut, a popular form of dress with rubes. We used to call them "humspuns." With tobacco juice leaking from the corner of my mouth, my make-up was complete. . . .

Signaled by his confederate, Tarbeaux would approach the steerer and mark and strike up a conversation, speaking in a barnyard dialect matching his appearance. He had been to the "big city" to sell a herd of horses, he confided, and was on his way home with the proceeds. Here he flashed a large roll of greenbacks. When the accomplice warned him that it was not wise to display such large sums in public, Tarbeaux scoffed, saying that he had been to some "fast" places in the big city and knew what he was about. He had gone to one place where a fellow had three cards:

"One of the cyards had an ole man on it; another had a' ole

woman on it, and the other had a little boy with the hoop. and he could sneak 'em around so fast you couldn't tell. You had to find the little boy with the hoop.

"He tole me Ah couldn't find it, and Ah thought Ah could tell wha' it were. Then we just got to bettin'. He axed me if Ah would bet three hundred dollars Ah could find it. Ah said Ah would, and Ah jus' pulled the cyard right out and put it up. But when Ah went to pick it up it weren't there; it were another cyard.

"An' then he slicked 'em over again, an' Ah bet him three hundred dollars more, and gosh durned if Ah could tell it. Ah lost six hundred dollars, but Ah didn't keer. Ah tole him if he'd show how to do it Ah'd give him three hundred dollars for the cyards. . . . Ah been practicin' it. Ah c'n do it so fast Ah can't tell wha' it is mahself. Ah got the ole cyards right here."

Tarbeaux would throw the cards clumsily and the steerer would offer to bet five dollars he could pick out the little boy. Tarbeaux would take the bet and pay off when his accomplice chose correctly. At this point Tarbeaux would drop a bill or a card on the floor and, as he stooped to pick it up, the steerer would quickly mark the "boy with a hoop" card by bending a corner slightly, at the same time winking at the sucker. He would then propose a wager of one hundred dollars that he could pick the card again. Tarbeaux would accept, lose the bet, and, apparently angry, pick up his cards, ready to leave.

The confederate would then give the mark a slight conspiratorial nudge with the elbow and urge the rube to throw the cards once more for his friend.

"Ah won't play for no chicken feed," the rube would retort testily. "Ah'll bet yo' all yo' got. That's what Ah'll do."

The steerer would put up his roll and the sucker, convinced that he was in on a sure killing, would add the contents of his wallet. The mark would turn the wrong one and lose, of course, as Tarbeaux, before throwing, had straightened the corner on the "little boy" card and bent one of the others.

The rube would then leave, perhaps for another car where a second partner had roped a new mark, perhaps to drop off at the next stop to await his companions' return trip.

A train conductor once told a Tarbeaux confederate that he understood the workings of the rube act and that the rube was supposed to look like a dolt. "But that Tarbeaux is the real thing. He *is* a damned fool, isn't he?" the conductor wanted to know.

"And that tickled me pink" said Tarbeaux, "because I was proud of my make-up, and proud of my acting in the Three-Card Monte Gyp."[10]

Frank Tarbeaux was born August 24, 1852, at the present site of Boulder, Colorado. He always claimed he was the first white child born in Colorado. His father, Herbert Tarbeaux, of Huguenot ancestry, was a horse dealer and trader. His mother, Mary, came from the Schofield family of famous military men. She had four brothers, all West Point graduates, one of whom, John Schofield, became commanding general of the United States Army. Tarbeaux's parents married in New York and moved west in the late 1840s, finally establishing a ranch twenty-five miles from Denver. Young Frank fought Indians before his voice changed, killed his first man at the age of fourteen, and was making his way as a professional gambler before he reached eighteen. He was still in his early twenties, but already an accomplished sharper, when he worked the rube act on the trains running out of Omaha.

The golden age of the railroad gamblers came to a close in the mid-1870s as rail officials received hundreds of complaints from swindled victims. It was George Devol who provided the last straw. He and a partner named Jew Mose were working the Cheyenne to Omaha run. "One evening I picked up a man on the sleeper and beat him out of $1200," Devol recalled sadly. "That game settled our hash, for he proved to be one of the directors of the road, and as soon as he reached Omaha he had a lot of handbills printed and hung up in the cars, not only prohibiting gambling, but that conductors permitting the game in their cars would be at once discharged."[11]

Canada Bill Jones wrote the general superintendent of the Union Pacific Railroad, offering to pay $10,000 a year for the exclusive rights to run a three-card monte game on the Union Pacific trains, and promising to limit his victims to commercial travelers from Chicago and Methodist preachers. The railroad official politely declined Bill's generous offer.

Bill had only a few more years to live. He was completely

destitute when he died at Reading, Pennsylvania, in 1880, and was buried at public expense. A group of western gamblers heard of his passing, reimbursed the mayor of Reading for the burial costs, and arranged for the erection of a monument over the grave of the slickest monte sharp of them all.

George Devol, who estimated that he won more than $2 million during his forty years as a gambler, retired from the profession about 1886 at the insistence of his wife. When he died at Hot Springs, Arkansas, in 1903, he was virtually penniless, having eked a bare subsistence in his last years by peddling copies of the book that recounted his adventures during his prime.

Young Frank Tarbeaux moved on to other pastures when the railroads cracked down. As a member of various gambling mobs, he toured the West during the seventies, playing in mining towns and cow camps throughout the frontier. As he explained the mobs' operations:

When a band of cowboys came in and sold their cattle, or a group of miners came in with dust, we would sit up all night and day spelling each other until we cleaned them out. If we hadn't done it some one else would. They were bound to lose their money. . . .

We used to play cards with our guns on the table. A man would have been killed as quick as a monkey if there was anything wrong. . . .

They used to tell me I was crazy to go into these cow and mining camps as I did, and take the money away, and I guess I was crazy. As I look back on it I know I was. But I didn't know any different.

Tarbeaux claimed that he did not have to resort to cheating to make money in these games, that his skill was sufficient:

When I was fifteen years old I was a pretty good card player. My wife doesn't believe it now when I tell her that it was a rare man who could win from me at cards when I was a mere boy. But it is true. There is no need to cheat at cards when a man is a master of them. Most men don't play cards; they play at them. A master does not have to deal from the bottom of the deck or resort to other devices which have more place in fiction than in fact. I was born with what is called card sense, just as some persons are born with ability at music, or at writing, or painting.

My custom was to get with the people who had the money. That is where the con game came in. And, since not one player in 10,000 really knows anything about cards, where was the necessity for cheating during the play?[12]

Later on, Tarbeaux toured the Southwest with the Cooper-Jackson Wagon Show, operating skin games with a group of gamblers. Later still he traveled extensively outside of the United States, forming acquaintance with many celebrated people, including King Kalakaua of Hawaii, Oscar Wilde, Hadden Chambers, Marie Corelli, Sir Gilbert Parker, and Frank Harris. Parker and Harris were both so impressed by Tarbeaux that they wrote fictional works based on his exploits.

Harris, in a novelette entitled *A Gambler's Luck*, described Tarbeaux as he remembered seeing him at their first meeting in a Leadville saloon in 1877:

He had on a white ruffled silk shirt that set off his mahogany skin. The glance he flashed at me as I entered the room startled me; it had the wild challenge of a hawk's. I couldn't at first explain the imperiousness of it. The upper part of his face was very fine indeed; the nose regular, the forehead good, broad and well shaped; the eyes magnificent, a clear hazel with red-gold specks in them—a mixture of heat and light.

Parker first met Tarbeaux at Fort Leavenworth, Kansas, in 1886, and in his *Tarboe, The Story of a Life*, he recorded his impression of the gambler, saying that he was

a striking, clean-shaven, good-looking man whose years it would be impossible to say, for he had no gray hair, and yet there was a look, not of age, but of long experience, in his face. . . . It was a figure and face not to be forgotten. There was a touch of the foreigner in his looks and yet he did not speak with an accent. . . . It was a face that never wrinkled with emotion. Its only life was in the eyes and at the mouth and they were most expressive. He had the impassive look of a Jap and was vigilant in a curious, quiet way. . . . It was to be said that he had not had complete social training, and yet he was well dressed and had dignity. I can say truthfully I never met a man with greater social gifts, although it was clear he had limited education. . . . His charm lay in keen intelligence, a rare natural philosophy, and in humour of an original kind.

Tarbeaux was seventy-seven in 1930 when Donald Henderson Clarke set down the gambler's recollections. Tarbeaux still had every tooth, said Clarke, and there had never been a point of decay in any of them. "His once dark eyes have faded a trifle, but they still sparkle eagle-like in a proudly handsome countenance. This amazing man still dresses like a beau, rides like a hero, and shoots like a demon. Doctors have told him that his physical condition is perfect."[13]

At about the time the railroad officials banished the train gamblers operating out of Omaha, gold was discovered in the Blacks Hills and John Bull joined a gamblers' rush to Deadwood and the new boom camps of Dakota Territory. Within a few months there were thirty gambling saloons open around the clock in Deadwood.

A gang of thieving sharpers under the leadership of a swaggering bully named "Ten Die" Brown preyed on the Deadwood miners from the camp's earliest days. Brown's pack of sure-thing tinhorns and thugs included members known only as "Pancake Bill," "Kentuck," "Nutshell Bill," and "The Miner." This motley crew drew the line at nothing, including the use of knockout drops, slung shots, and garrots, in their lust for gold.

Gamblers of a somewhat higher order drawn to the new camp included Tom Dosier, Frank Tarbeaux, Wild Bill Hickok, Colorado Charlie Utter, Bill Hillman, Johnny Oyster, Lurline Monte Verde, Charlie Rich, Billy Allen, Johnny Varnes, Tim Brady, Wyatt and Morgan Earp, Charlie Clifton, Madame Mustache, Turkey Creek Jack Johnson, Jim Levy, Charlie Storms, Tom Hardwick, Lew Shoenfield, Tom Mulqueen, and Johnny Owens.

Wild Bill Hickok was already a western legend when he reached Deadwood in July, 1876, having been immortalized nine years before in an article by George Ward Nichols in *Harper's Magazine*. Although Hickok had never experienced half the adventures with which he was credited by Nichols and later lurid writers, he had lived an eventful and exciting life for most of his thirty-nine years. Before turning to the gambling tables, he had been a Union spy in the Civil War, a scout

Wild Bill Hickok was already a Western legend when he struck Deadwood. Courtesy Kansas State Historical Society.

for the Indian-fighting army on the Plains, a detective, and a frontier peace officer in several wild and woolly border towns. He had toured with Buffalo Bill Cody, titillating eastern audiences with melodramas purporting to represent the heroic derring-do of the famous Plains scouts. As a gunfighter he was said to have no equal, and it was probably true that Hickok had sent more men over the hill than any of the gunmen of Deadwood, of whom there were many.

"Hickok . . . was a gambler by profession," wrote one Black Hills old-timer, "and, while no one would say that he was a man to violate the peculiar code of ethics governing the gambling fraternity, it is not improbable that his reputation as a gunfighter won for him many a stake over the poker table which his cards could not win."[14]

Bill Cody once witnessed a poker game in which Hickok was matched against a player who, from time to time, would drop cards into a hat resting on his lap. When finally the player had built the hand he wanted, he bet two hundred dollars. The other player pushed the money into the pot and Wild Bill, drawing a pistol, placed the muzzle under the other fellow's nose. "I'm calling the hand in your hat," he said. Raking the pot with his left hand, Hickok asked the other players if there were any objections. There were none.

On another occasion, when Hickok was in danger of being cleaned out by a pair of crooked poker sharks, he called the largest raise of the evening with his last greenbacks. At the showdown one of his opponents displayed the winning hand and Bill tossed in his cards. "Hold it!" he said, as the sharper reached for the pot. Drawing two revolvers, he leveled them at the swindlers. "I have a pair of sixes and they beat anything." The slicks watched glumly as Hickok cleared the table.

In Cheyenne in 1874, Hickok sat down at Bowlby's faro table, wearing blue-tinted spectacles and with his shoulder-length hair tucked up in his hat. No one in the Gold Rooms recognized the famous gunman. Wild Bill bet $50 on a card, lost, and Bowlby raked the money. Hickok came back with another $50 on the same card and this time Bowlby turned it a winner. He pushed $25 across the oilcloth.

"I bet fifty," said Bill.

"The limit's twenty-five," said Bowlby.

"But you took fifty when I lost."

Bowlby shrugged. "Fifty goes when you lose."

Hickok was carrying a weighted billiard cue he used for a walking stick. With a roar he cracked the dealer and his lookout over the head. Dropping the stick, he plunged into the money drawer with both hands and stuffed his pockets with greenbacks. Swinging around, he drew two guns and bellowed, "Let everybody fill his hand!" His glasses and hat had fallen off and his long hair tumbled to his shoulders.

"It's Wild Bill!" someone yelled, and the room was emptied in seconds.

The next day Hickok was visited by Bowlby and the Cheyenne city marshal. Bowlby estimated that Hickok had taken about $700. "I'd feel better if you would split the money with me," Wild Bill offered. Bowlby accepted this generous proposal and all three adjourned to the Gold Rooms bar to seal the deal with a friendly drink.

The murder of Hickok on August 2, 1876, in Deadwood by a nondescript saloon bum named Jack McCall capped the Wild Bill legend and has become one of the most publicized events in the history of the American West. McCall shot Hickok through the back of the head as he sat in a poker game in the Number Ten Saloon. Legend has it that at the moment he was killed, Bill was holding two pairs, aces and eights, a hand known ever since that episode as the "dead man's hand." Motive for the killing was never established, but it was generally accepted among the sporting men that McCall's act had been at the instigation of gambler Johnny Varnes.

Only a short time, before, Hickok and Varnes had confronted each other over drawn guns. They had been playing in a game in the Senate Saloon when a dispute developed involving Varnes, Tim Brady, and another player. Varnes pulled a pistol and attempted to rake the pot, but Hickok also drew and demanded that Varnes hand over the money to Brady. Varnes, awed by the Hickok reputation, meekly submitted, but the story went that later he plied the barfly McCall with booze and paid him to murder Wild Bill.

A month after the Hickok assassination, Varnes and Charlie

Colorado Charlie Utter sits by the grave of his friend Wild Bill. Courtesy Western History Collections, University of Oklahoma Library.

Storms threw lead at each other but only managed to hit a bystander in the leg. It is not known if this altercation had any connection with the Hickok affair.

Gamblers of gunslinging notoriety were thick in Deadwood. James H. Levy, an Irish Jew, arrived in the Black Hills with a fearsome reputation earned in the mining camps of Nevada. He had first come to the attention of the sporting fraternity at Pioche in early 1871. There Mike Casey and Tom Gossan had a dispute and shot it out in the street. Casey was faster and mortally wounded Gossan. Before he died, Gossan bequeathed $5,000 to the man who would avenge his death and kill Casey. Jim Levy was not long in applying for the bequest. He goaded Casey into a fight and shot him at close range. It was unclear whether Casey died as a result of the bullet wound or the fearful beating about the head administered by Levy. During this melee a bullet from Dave Neagle's pistol broke Levy's jaw, disfiguring him and leaving him with a sinister visage to match his growing reputation.

It was the practice of mining companies in the district to hire armed guards to protect their interests from encroachment by neighboring concerns, and Levy, with his new reputation for toughness, was so employed by the Raymond & Eli Mining Company. In January, 1873, in a battle in a mine tunnel with gunmen hired by the adjacent Pioche Phoenix Mine, he shot and killed one Tom Ryan. Arrested by lawmen on the road to Hamilton, he was returned to Pioche. His feet had been badly frostbitten in his effort to escape. As in the Casey killing, murder charges against him were dropped.

Levy transferred from Pioche to Virginia City, Nevada, where he spent some time at the gambling tables before moving on to Deadwood in 1876. In March, 1877 he was in Cheyenne and got into an argument with another gambler named Charlie Harrison in the Shingle & Locke Saloon. (This, of course, was not the Charley Harrison of Denver fame who had been killed fourteen years before by Osage Indians.) Harrison stated that he hated Irishmen, and especially Jewish Irishmen, whereupon Levy jerked his revolver. Harrison announced that he was unarmed, but that if Levy would wait until he got a gun, he would give him "a turn." Obtaining a weapon at the

Senate Saloon, Harrison emerged into the street and, seeing Levy standing near the corner of 16th and Eddy streets, emptied his pistol at his enemy. Levy, unscathed, fired once, dropped Harrison with a minor wound in the chest, then ran across the street and shot him again as he lay on the ground.

Harrison was taken to his rooms in the Dyer Hotel; Levy went around the corner to the Oyster Bar Restaurant and ordered dinner. He was arrested there by City Marshal Bat Carr. Harrison lingered two weeks but died on March 22.

Levy was at Leadville and Tombstone and then turned up in Tucson in early 1882. Here he had trouble with John Murphy, who ran a faro game in Eli Gifford's gambling saloon, the Fashion. The two exchanged hot words in late May and when Levy sat down at Murphy's table on June 5 the stage was set for fireworks. Levy had told friends he would "waltz on Murphy's faro layout and shoot the checks from the table." During the course of play, Levy claimed he had been cheated and the dealer called him a liar. Others interceded and the two gamblers agreed to settle their differences later, "across the border."

Levy left and attempted to borrow a revolver from George Duncan, a gambler who had known Levy for some eight years. Duncan tried to calm his pal and get him back to his hotel. Meanwhile, Murphy, joined by two others, Boll Moyer and Dave Gibson, was on the streets looking for Levy. They found him as he was entering his hotel and, without warning, gunned him down. Of the five bullets in his body, four would have been fatal. Held on murder charges, the three killers overpowered their guard and escaped. They were never brought to trial.

Another hardcase gambler in Deadwood during the boom years was Tom Hardwick. A Confederate veteran from Missouri, Hardwick had drifted west after the Civil War. About 1870 he organized a gang of two dozen whiskey peddlers and wolf hunters operating out of Fort Benton, Montana. Twice he was taken captive by Arapahoes and he later claimed that he hated Indians even more than he hated Yankees. In 1872, the "Green River Renegade," as Hardwick was then known, murdered some forty friendly Assiniboine Indians in Alberta,

Canada. The formation of the famous Northwest Mounted Police was a direct result of this atrocity. Hardwick avoided the Mounties by staying out of Canada. He turned to gambling and roamed the western states, taking short-term jobs as private detective, sheriff's deputy, and hired gunman. He died in his native Missouri in 1901 at the age of fifty-seven.

John Owens, although celebrated as a gunman of quick and deadly accuracy, was an entirely different kind of man from either Levy or Hardwick. A Texan by birth, Owens fought for the Confederacy under Quantrill, moved west after the war, and saw service as a civilian scout with the United States Army at Fort Laramie, Wyoming. One night he sat in a poker game at Chug Springs, a stage station and roadhouse on the Fort Laramie–Cheyenne road. The owner of the station, a man named Patton, was in the game. As the night wore on and the stakes rose, the other players dropped out and Owens and Patton went at it, head to head. By morning Patton was cleaned out—money, station and all—and John Owens found himself in business.

It was the first of many saloons, dance halls, and gambling houses he was to operate in Wyoming and Nebraska. For a time he kept a resort near Fort Laramie called the Hog Ranch. He opened a place in Lusk as soon as the railroad reached that point. Later, at Newcastle, he operated the Castle Theater and a large gambling establishment called the House of Blazes because of the guns that so frequently blazed behind the battle-scarred doors. At times he had interests at Sydney and Crawford, Nebraska.

In addition to his gambling and business ventures, Owens served in several law enforcement jobs, most notably the position of sheriff of Weston County, Wyoming, a post he held for sixteen years. He was a skillful gunfighter, and some old-timers compared him favorably with Hickok. He neither smoked nor drank. Slender of build and handsome of feature, he was quiet and unassuming. He treated women with a courtly deference much marveled at in the rough camps in which he operated. He was admired for his generosity and was considered to be scrupulously honest in his gambling and business affairs. He died on his eighty-fourth birthday in 1927.

John Bull spent much time in Deadwood during that camp's big years of 1876 and 1877, but he left often, either to visit his family in Chicago, or simply to work the suckers on the railroads and stagecoaches of the Northwest.

Gambling activities on stagecoach runs could be extremely dangerous because of the close proximity of the passengers and the lack of space to maneuver if trouble developed. One violent eruption occurred on a stage bound from Salt Lake City to Virginia City, Nevada, during the seventies. Bill Graves was at the reins of the Concord coach; his passengers were professional gamblers Joe Goddard, Mike Conoley, Bill Ayers, and Gaspard LeCoeur. The four were involved in a game of "hard cards," and the coach was almost into Virginia City when all hell broke loose. One of the players accused another of holding out cards. In an instant accused and accuser had their irons out and smoking. The other two gamblers instinctively joined the action. When the roar of gunfire subsided, Bill Graves halted his double team, climbed down, and peered into the coach. The four gamblers were sprawled grotesquely in a blood-spattered confusion of scattered cards and money. Goddard, Ayers, and Conoley were dead. Only LeCoeur, although well-ventilated and bleeding profusely, managed to survive.

One of John Bull's stagecoach trips has been recorded by Henry Hoyt, a young doctor making his first trip into the Wild West in May, 1877. Anxious to get in on some of the excitement at Deadwood, Hoyt had taken the Northern Pacific Railroad to its terminus at Bismarck, Dakota Territory. There he secured a seat on the first stage of a new line running from Bismarck to Deadwood. Coincidentally, another passenger on the stage was John Bull, whom Hoyt had met previously in Chicago where Hoyt had boarded in the same house with Bull's family. The gambler took his young friend aside and told him in confidence that he had a partner also making the journey, but that he did not want it generally known that he and the other were in cahoots. He pointed the man out to Hoyt, saying that his name was "Fish." Hoyt described this partner as "a small man with features of Jewish type, dark eyes, hair and skin [who] sat wrapped up in a heavy overcoat with collar turned up, and was silent as the Sphinx." The man called Fish was undoubtedly Frank Tarbeaux, playing his favorite role.

"The Concord coaches used at this period had three seats, each seating three passengers, the rear and middle seats facing the boot, the front facing the rear," wrote Dr. Hoyt. "Fish, myself and Bull occupied the front seat facing the other six. In front of Fish sat a man whom I will call Prentice, a capitalist from Minneapolis. In the middle of the back seat was a young man from Minnesota who had sold out his business and was to try his luck at gold-digging."

The first day out from Bismarck the travelers got acquainted, and all were voluble with the exception of Fish who kept his own counsel. The second day he suddenly opened up with what Hoyt called "a line of Rube talk that would fool almost any one." Running on with his bucolic patter, Fish spread a bandanna on his knees and produced three monte cards he claimed he had gotten from sharps who had skinned him in Chicago. Two of the cards were spots, the third a queen. He challenged anyone to pick out the queen, made several awkward feints and passes and threw them on the bandanna. John Bull quickly hauled out a roll, bet one hundred dollars, and turned the queen. The rube threw again and again Bull won. Now quite angry, Fish refused to play with Bull any more, saying that he would take the bet of any other man.

Bull and his partner had been setting up the Minneapolis capitalist for shearing and the mark was reaching for his wallet, but before he could get down his wager, the young gold seeker in the rear pushed forward, threw down a roll of bills, and turned a card—a two-spot.

Prentice and the other passengers were now suspicious and none would bet. But midway in the journey they met a coach traveling in the opposite direction, and the victim of the gamblers, now broke, changed coaches to return home, leaving an empty seat on the Deadwood-bound stage. Shortly thereafter the coach overtook a covered wagon carrying three men on their way to open a business at the Black Hills diggings. Eager to get to his destination, one of the men took the empty seat on the coach, telling his companions he would meet them in Deadwood.

The gamblers now had new blood. Said Hoyt:

We had jogged along for a short time when Fish began to spin his
yarn again, but this time he told an entirely new story, and instead of
three cards he worked with only two. Bull won as before several
times, and was barred. While talking and idly shuffling the two
cards, Fish, apparently without knowing that he did so, tore a tiny
bit from the corner of the picture card. This bait proved too much
for the new victim. His roll came out as rapidly as that of number
one. . . .
     It was the old story. He was sure Fish had blundered and he was
quick enough to bet on what he thought was a *sure thing*. He appeared afterward "a sadder and a wiser man."

It might be wondered why the other passengers did not warn
their new companion against the sharpers' tricks. Perhaps a
demonstration of six-shooter prowess given earlier in the day
by John Bull had something to do with that. Wrote Dr. Hoyt:

We pulled into a prairie-dog town, the driver pulled up for a few
minutes, and everybody jumped out. Prairie-dogs were in every direction, barking an invitation to try our markmanship. Out came
revolvers and several volleys were fired without result, as Mr. Prairie-Dog is wary and very hard to hit.
     Bull watched the scene for a time. Suddenly his hand flew to his
hip; a big six-shooter of the dragoon type with a short barrel was
drawn. The gun barked, and a dead dog was the result. He apparently took no aim at all.

At Deadwood, Bull helped Dr. Hoyt get established with a
room and an office in the I.X.L. Hotel. One day Bull stopped
in at the doctor's office to boast that he had at last bested the
Minneapolis capitalist who had eluded his trap on the trip in.
"I finally landed him in my game and cleaned him for five
hundred dollars. I have lain for him for days and have got him
at last," he gloated.
     Shortly after Bull left, his supposed victim appeared at the
office, and to the doctor's surprise, seemed no less joyful than
the gambler. He had taken Bull to the tune of five hundred
dollars, he announced. Completely baffled now, Hoyt asked
how that could be. Prentice explained that he needed cash for
his business and asked him to take a draft. "He bit," chortled

the man from Minneapolis. "Took the draft and counted out five hundred dollars in change. The draft was for one thousand dollars and it was *no good!*"

"Such was life in the Far West fifty years ago," wrote Dr. Hoyt in 1929. "John Bull was a character in his way, one of the best in his line, and withal a kind-hearted man and a mighty good friend."[15]

When the excitement at Deadwood subsided somewhat, John Bull moved on. Denver became his major base of operations for several years and his name ornamented the police blotters of the Colorado capital frequently.

In 1877 he was arrested and fined twelve dollars for public drunkenness. In January, 1879 he engaged in a little scrimmage with a man named C. C. Joy at the corner of Sixteenth and Larimer streets, in the heart of the sporting district. Joy, described by the *Rocky Mountain News*[16] as a "very large, powerful man," had a previous disagreement with Bull, who went and "heated himself" for an attack. When the two met on the corner Bull stepped up to the larger man and "made a motion as if to strike him." Joy then "jumped to one side and knocked his opponent down before he could draw a revolver which he had his hand on. After knocking him down, Joy kicked the prostrate man several times. . . ." Bull would have received "rather a severe pummeling," said the *News*, had not a bystander pulled off the joyless Joy. Both combatants were charged with disturbance of the peace and were fined.

About this time Bull entered into partnership with circuit veteran Jim Moon, who had opened a combination restaurant, saloon, and gambling house in Denver called the Oyster Ocean. Moon, whose real name was John E. Wilcoxon, ran away from his Philadelphia home at the age of fifteen. Heading west, he got as far as Iowa when the Civil War broke out and he enlisted in the 44th Iowa Infantry. A broad-shouldered, deep-chested man of great strength, Moon was often in difficulty because of his uncontrollable temper, and his army career was cut short when he almost killed another soldier in a fistfight. Taken in chains to Memphis, he somehow avoided a court-martial and received an honorable discharge.

John E. Wilcoxon, known to the frontier gambling world as Jim Moon. Courtesy Denver Public Library, Western History Department.

Back in Iowa after the war, he opened a saloon in Dubuque. Before long he got into trouble again and had to leave town hurriedly. He became an itinerant professional gambler, traveling extensively throughout the southern states during the Reconstruction period, and making stops as far removed as west Texas and Cuba. In the early seventies he worked the cattle towns of Kansas, teaming for a time with Dick Clark. A reporter for the *Topeka Daily Commonwealth* described Moon at this time as "a well proportioned, athletic man, with brown hair and mustache." He was the owner of a "tout ensemble that is decidedly prepossessing," and had, said the reporter, "more of the style of the New York gambler than anyone in town."[17] It was during this period that he adopted the name "Jim Moon." The reason for the name change is not known, but given the man's history of violence, it is a good bet that some serious altercation had prompted the adoption of an alias.

At Ellsworth, Moon met a young German girl named Emma DeMarr who had left her home in Leipzig at the age of fifteen to come to the United States. When Moon departed the Kansas cow towns for Colorado, the girl went with him. The two were together at Cheyenne and then, at Salt Lake City, they had a falling-out. Moon headed for the gambling towns of Nevada, Emma for the warm shores of southern California. After several months at the tables of Reno, Carson City, and Virginia City, Moon followed Emma to Los Angeles and married her, she later claimed, "at the point of a pistol."

The newlyweds traveled through Arizona. At Prescott, Moon hit a hot streak at the tables and stayed on for three months. Returning to Los Angeles with a sizable bankroll, he bought a saloon called the Woodbine. Soon he was in another fight, singlehandedly taking on a gang of laborers and injuring some of them badly. He disposed of his saloon and went first to San Francisco and then back to Salt Lake City. Here Emma decided to go to Europe to take in the Paris Exposition, then in progress, and to visit her parents who had moved to Sweden. Shortly after her departure, Moon, who could not stand to be separated from Emma for any length of time, followed

and remained in Europe for several months. On his return in
1878 he told friends that he had blown $7,000 of a $12,000
bankroll on the trip.

Settling in Denver, Jim and Emma Moon opened the Oyster
Ocean. John Bull held a financial interest and also ran a gambling concession in the establishment. Bull was living with a
woman at this time whom he called his wife, and the Bulls
and Moons were involved as a foursome in the operation of
the combination restaurant-saloon-gambling house.

On the night of October 14, 1880, all four were involved in
a fracas that, if filmed, would have made an excellent Mack
Sennett one-reeler. A Denver police officer named Johnny
Holland had hasseled Moon on previous occasions, and when
he entered the Oyster Ocean that night with a partner named
Merrill, the short-fused Jim Moon watched him with a jaun-
diced eye.

"I was in the far bar-room . . . and Bull was standing by
me counting some money," Moon testified at a hearing into the
affair.

Our wives were sitting at a table eating. Nothing was said to the
officers until they started to go out. . . . I heard Holland say to my
wife: "It will make you sick." I stepped out and said I did not want
my wife insulted. Holland replied: "I don't know as she is your
wife." I then told him to get out of the house. After some words he
pulled a gun and I jumped on him and grabbed the gun. We had a
scuffle and fell upon the floor.

Merrill then got into the fray and John Bull came storming
out of the bar to leap upon Merrill. Meanwhile the women
started throwing chinaware. Presumably the officers were their
targets, but, according to Moon's testimony, their accuracy
was imperfect. "The women fired plates, cups and saucers,
some of which hit me," he said ruefully.

John Bull testified that he "had a long tussle" with Officer
Merrill. "I had been drinking a good deal but I knew what I
vas doing." The quick and deadly pistoleer, slayer of Lang-
ord Peel and survivor of dozens of tense border town con-
rontations, vehemently denied having engaged in crockery-

pitching during the melee. "I did not throw any dishes, but a table fell over and dumped a good many dishes on Merrill and me," he said.

Officers Holland and Merrill finally made an undignified departure. Reinforcements were summoned, but they were met at the Oyster Ocean door by a thoroughly aroused Jim Moon who, with leveled revolver, refused arrest. Later Moon and Bull were apprehended separately, placed under arrest, released on bond, and subsequently fined.[18]

This incident, with all its farcical aspects, did not diminish the reputation of either Moon or Bull in the Denver sporting world. The gamblers' deportment assumed heroic proportions in the retelling, and a little over a year later a Colorado paper would refer to John Bull as "the man, who, in company with notorious Jim Moon . . . revolutionized the government of Denver by whipping the entire police force and taking the city at the point of their revolvers."[19]

Less than three weeks after the Oyster Ocean orgy, Jim Moon demonstrated the unflinching raw courage that was his most admirable attribute. On October 31, drunken mobs stormed through the Chinese section of Denver, beating and lynching Chinese in a senseless demonstration against cheap Oriental labor. After a day and night of terror, General David J. Cook rode into the quarter at the head of a hastily assembled militia company to restore order.

In the doorway of a Chinese laundry, a six-gun in either hand, stood a glowering Jim Moon.

"So you are in this too!" Cook shouted.

"Hell, no!" bellowed the enraged gambler. "These chinks do my laundry and I'm here to see that nobody bothers them."

Moon was said to be the only white man to stand and defy the mob. It was later reported that he had saved sixteen Chinese by hiding them in the basement of the Arcade gambling hall.

A week after the riots Moon was again in the news. During an argument he struck a man named Sam Hall a terrible blow on the head with the barrel of his six-gun, fracturing the man's skull and killing him. Self-defense was claimed; a jury agreed, and Moon was quickly freed.

One of General Cook's volunteer militiamen during the Chinese riots had been a handsome young gambler and con artist named Clay Wilson. Moon had known Wilson for several years. The two had gambled together at Reno and Leadville, and for a time Wilson was a house dealer at the Arcade, a Larimer Street establishment in which Moon had an interest. They were friends of sorts, but Wilson was a puzzle to Moon and to most of the fraternity.

A native of Ohio, Wilson had come to the frontier at the age of sixteen and taken at once to the sporting life. His dark good looks, quick intelligence, and extensive vocabulary set him apart from the general run of short-card men and grifters working the camps. But it was Wilson's notebook that really distinguished the young gambler and aroused the curiosity of his fellows. Wilson seemed to be constantly pulling out the little book and making mysterious notations in it. Once Jim Moon caught a glimpse of a page over Wilson's shoulder and was asked what he had seen. "Chicken scratches, that's all," grunted the big man, dismissing what he could not understand with an impatient wave of his hand.

In June, 1881, Moon's wife Emma left him again after a series of violent arguments. Moon decided that she had taken up with Clay Wilson. On the night of June 15 he burst into Wilson's bedroom, blood in his eye and six-gun in his hand. Emma was not there, but Moon told Wilson that he was sure they were seeing each other. He would not shoot an unarmed man in his bed, Moon said, but warned that when next he saw Wilson on the street he was going to burn powder, and Wilson had better be heeled.

The following day Wilson walked to the Arcade about noon, accompanied by a friend named Charlie Lundin. At the doorway sat Jim Moon getting a shoeshine. Wilson walked past without a word. At the bar he ordered drinks for himself and Lundin. A few minutes later Moon approached, his shoes gleaming and his coat pushed back over the butt of his pistol.

Moon's fist shot out and Lundin went down, flattened by the single blow. Wheeling on Wilson, Moon dared him to reach for his gun. Clay's face paled slightly, but with stolid self-control he turned and slowly walked toward the door.

Moon followed, roaring insults. His fingers curled near his gun butt.

Wilson knew that Jim Moon was no back-shooter, and continued walking. Confounded by this enemy who would not fight, Moon almost choked with rage and frustration. For one instant his voice hinted of indecision.

Wilson's moment had come. He whirled, drew, and fired in one motion. Two bullets ripped into Moon's massive chest. Roaring like a wounded bear, Moon forgot his own weapon and lunged at the smaller gambler. Even as the blood drained from his mortal wounds, he crushed Wilson with his powerful arms. Wilson managed to jab the muzzle of his pistol into Moon's body and pull the trigger. The bullet ranged downward through the big man's pelvis. Moon's legs crumpled under him and he sagged to the floor. Wilson took dead aim and planted a slug under Moon's right ear. Then it was over.

A grand jury refused to indict Clay Wilson for murder and he was released. It was many years later that his mysterious little journal fell into the hands of the police when he was convicted on a con game rap. Unable to decipher what they felt was a clever code, the police turned the notebook over to cryptograph experts. They were astounded to learn that for years Clay Wilson had recorded his criminal history—in Sanskrit.

A month before the sudden demise of his former partner, John Bull had acquired his own place, the Turf Exchange, at 449 Larimer Street. Described as a "combination gambling hall and gamblers' hotel," the Turf Exchange had been a popular hangout for the sporting gentry some years before but had fallen on evil days. The fraternity was notified of the reopening in the pages of the *Rocky Mountain Daily News*.[20] The place had been refurbished throughout and the new owner gave assurance that henceforth business would be conducted in a thoroughly first-class manner. At the May 7 opening the public was invited to a "grand free banquet" by John E. Bull, manager.

In January, 1882, Bull was shot through the foot in an upstairs room of the Turf Exchange. This incident was put down officially as an accident, but it was common knowledge in the Denver underworld that Bull had been shot by gambler Jim Bush, and that the only accident was that the bullet had lodged in Bull's foot and not his heart.

Jim Bush was the blacksheep brother of William H. ("Billy") Bush, business agent for H. A. W. Tabor and proprietor of the Windsor Hotel, a Denver showplace. Billy Bush had managed a succession of fine hotels, including the Teller House in Central City and the Clarendon in Leadville. In 1882 the newly opened 300-room Windsor was considered the finest hotel in the West. Ten years later Bush would open the Brown Palace in Denver to surpass in elegance his earlier houses, but at the time there was nothing to compare with the Windsor for Victorian opulence.

Bad-news brother Jim, meanwhile, had courted trouble in border towns for years. He had been arrested with Rowdy Joe Lowe for drugging and robbing a man in Ellsworth, Kansas. At Leadville he had killed a man named Arbuckle. His trial had ended in a hung jury, and at the time of the Bull shooting he was awaiting a second trial. "All those who know him have prophesied that he will yet "die with his boots on'," noted a Denver newspaperman in 1882.[21] Against all the odds, Jim Bush consternated the soothsayers, and lived to be seventy-eight. He died in 1920 of a stroke.

Charles ("Doc") Baggs, John Bull's former Omaha colleague, was trimming suckers in Denver at this time. Listed in the Denver City Directory as a "traveling agent," Baggs had converted almost completely from skin-game steerer to out-and-out bunco operator. He is credited with the invention of the gold brick confidence scheme with which he fleeced a number of prominent men, including Tom Fitch and L. B. Howard, officers of the Cedros Island Mining Company of San Diego, and Leadville banker H. M. Smith. Fitch and Howard handed over $15,000 for one of Doc's bogus bricks, and Smith contributed $20,000 to the Baggs "bag." Miguel A. Otero, later governor of New Mexico, was taken for $2,400 by Baggs in April, 1882. Otero went to Dave Cook of the Rocky Mountain Detective Association and asked him to try to get the

*Charles "Doc" Baggs, one of the sharpest of the sharp.
Courtesy Denver Public Library, Western History Department.*

check back. No chance of that, Baggs told Cook. He had already disposed of the check, getting seventy-five cents on the dollar for it.

John Bull may have worked with Baggs in some of his confidence games. In May, 1882, two men named Dilts and Flowers were milked dry by a quartet of con men who gave their names as Frank Pine, J. H. Park, J. A. Rearden, and Dr. James. Pine and Park were arrested and charged, but the two called Rearden and James vanished. The *Rocky Mountain Daily News* identified Rearden as John Bull and Dr. James as "none other than the ubiquitous 'Doc' Baggs."[22]

Interviewed about this time by a Denver reporter, Doc admitted that he had been arrested "about a thousand times," but said that he had never been convicted of a crime. The epitome of dignity in his cutaway coat, striped trousers, and stovepipe hat, a silk umbrella tucked under his arm, Baggs claimed to have made several fortunes but to have lost them all bucking the faro tiger. "I defy the newspapers to put their hands on a single man I ever beat that was not financially able to stand it," Baggs declared indignantly. "I am emotionally insane. When I see anyone looking in a jewelry store window thinking how they would like to get away with the diamonds, an irresistible desire comes over me to skin them. I don't drink, smoke, chew, or cheat poor people, I pay my debts."[23]

Oscar Wilde visited Denver in 1882 and created a stir with his favorite expression, "too, too divine." The *Denver News* published a long, anonymous "Ode to Oscar" which included the lines:

> If thou dost boast of being too, we will
> Produce Charles Baggs, M. D., who is as too
> As thou art, and a durned sight tooer.[24]

After leaving Denver, Doc Baggs traveled throughout the country for many years, working his cons. As late as 1930, according to Frank Tarbeaux, Baggs was in good health at the age of ninety-three, living quite comfortably under another name on an estate located near New York City.

In August, 1883, John Bull had his last run-in with the Denver constabulary. Next door to the Arcade was Murphy's Exchange, a gamblers' hangout known affectionately as "the Slaughterhouse," because of a number of killings that occurred there. Here Bull was involved in a "little row" and successfully resisted the efforts of an officer named Schultz to arrest him. The next evening the two met on the street and when the officer made a move to draw his pistol, Bull struck Schultz on the arm with his cane. The gambler was arrested and taken before a magistrate, charged with felonious assault. At the hearing, debate revolved around the question of which end of his heavily loaded walking stick Bull had used. Since it was shown to the satisfaction of the court that the gambler had struck out with the small, light end of the cane, the magistrate ruled that there apparently had been no intent on Bull's part to kill or maim. He was fined one dollar and costs.

By this time John Bull had disposed of his interest in the Turf Exchange and soon departed Denver, again on the prowl, stalking "greenies" wherever he could find them.

Nearby Cheyenne was an early stop, but competition for the dishonest buck was still as keen as it had been when he operated there back in the days of Hell-on-Wheels. Cheyenne had been a jumping-off place for the rush to the Black Hills in 1876 and sharpers had converged on the Wyoming town again. The *Cheyenne Weekly Leader* had noted in February of that year: "A fresh invoice of Denver gamblers and sneaks arrived yesterday. That dying town seems to be 'taking a puke' as it were, of this class of citizen."[25] Many of these thimbleriggers, con artists, and bunco men stayed on in Cheyenne after the Black Hills boom was over, remaining like the dirty ring in the bathtub after the water has run out. Working the unwary of Cheyenne were gentlemen of colorful cognomen: California Jack, Bedrock Tom, Squirrel Tooth, Poker Dan, Wiffletree Jim, the Preacher, the Coon Can Kid, and Timberline.

Bull traveled east into Nebraska, stopping briefly at his old stomping grounds in Omaha, and at the gambling resorts of Gus Saunders and Tom Quick in Lincoln. Quick was a city councilman and fire chief at Lincoln, but his main interest was his saloon and gambling house, the finest in town.

As the Northern Pacific Railroad was completed across Montana, Bull returned to the country he had frequented twenty years before. The boom at Virginia City was a decade in the past and that once flourishing mining camp was almost a ghost town. Long gone was Allen Hankins who had operated the fanciest gambling hall in town.

Hankins had returned to his hometown of Chicago, where, with his brother George, he prospered under the aegis of Chicago gambling kingpin Mike McDonald. John Bull remembered the superstitious antics of Al Hankins, notorious in a profession where the use of hexes, signs, charms, and relics was not unknown. Hankins would burn an old shoe every morning to bring good luck to his house. The chairs of the players were periodically sprinkled with salt and pepper, and, if a gambler showed signs of breaking one of the Hankins's banks, the proprietor would dash up with a shaker in each hand and give him another dose in an effort to hoodoo him.

Although there was no action in old Virginia City, the new camp at nearby Butte had much to offer. There was the Combination, a famous gambling hall that ran for two years, twenty-four hours a day, before closing its doors for a brief period because the star dealer was ill. There, too, was the hugh Morehouse and Dutch Henry gambling house, big enough to accommodate two thousand players at once; King and Lowrie's Saloon and Gambling Hall; the White Elephant Saloon; and the Atlantic Bar, where fifteen bartenders were on duty and as many as twelve thousand glasses of beer slid across the mahogany bar on a Saturday night. There was a solid block of saloons on North Main Street known as the Dardenelles. J. W. Kenney and Pete Hanson ran the popular Clipper Shades Saloon in the heart of the parlor house district where Molly Demurska kept the finest house and the prettiest girls in town. One of Butte's most memorable occasions was the celebration held the day Town Marshal Jack Jolly and Molly were married.

Some high-stake games were played in Butte when the mines were paying big. In one notable poker game Swede Sam Wallin held a hand containing three aces, and it was good enough to claim a pot worth $25,000. For years Butte old-timers talked of the night that mining magnate Freddie Heinze plunged at roulette. At one time that evening he was almost $200,000 ahead. Distracted by a girl who rubbed sensuously against him as he played, Heinze grabbed $5,000 worth of chips and thrust the stack into her hands. "Go buy yourself a fur coat," he said. The girl gone, Heinze's luck changed, and before the night was over he was out $60,000.

Bert Bell broke the faro bank in a Butte house one night and sat with a mountain of gold coins and stacks of currency before him and a crowd of admirers behind him. The owners ordered the faro box turned over, indicating that their funds were exhausted and the game was over. But Bell, feeling invincible, insisted on buying the house's stock, fixtures, and lease on condition that the proprietors reopen the game with the proceeds. This they did, and in the morning they staked Bell to breakfast money.

Bell was a slick cardsharp who made his money cheating at short-card games, principally poker and euchre, and lost it at faro to which he was addicted. He practiced second dealing two hours daily to maintain his skill. A veteran gambling contemporary called him the most perfect dealer of seconds he ever saw. "He was also an excellent bottom dealer and quick run-up artist. He was expert at the false shuffle and location work. Every dollar he made above bare living expenses he placed in the bank—faro bank." A slim blonde with hard blue eyes, Bell had completely devoted his life to gambling. He never drank or took drugs and "did not dally with the skirts." After twenty years of firsthand observation of frontier cardsharps, the old gambler called Bert Bell "the most cold-blooded, the most abstemious and careful in his habits, and the slickest worker in several forms of graft" that he had ever known.[26]

Following the line of the railroads through Montana, John Bull stopped at Helena, another town with much to offer the professional gambler. Here was the combination theater and gambling house of "Black Hawk Jack" Hensley and his wife, Josephine, known throughout the sporting world as "Chicago

Joe." One popular gambling house in town displayed the ad-
monitory sign: "Don't forget to write home to your dear old
mother; she is thinking of you. We furnish paper and envel-
opes free, and have the best whiskey in town." Dan Floweree,
owner of the Exchange Saloon and Gambling House, was considered to be an honest gambler, and some storied high-stakes
poker games were held in his place. In 1878, Floweree
brought one thousand head of cattle from Oregon and ranged
them along the Sun River. The cattle prospered and so did
Floweree, who in later years became one of the state's foremost ranchers.

John Bull was interviewed by the editor of the *Helena Independent*, who retold the story of the killing of Langford Peel
many years before. "Mr. Bull finds a strange fascination in
Helena and its surroundings," wrote the newsman. "Possibly
this is due to his tragic memories connected with the
place. . . . He thinks he will pitch his tent once more in this
city, and end his eventful career among those scenes which
have been indelibly stamped upon his memory."[27]

Bull did not remain long in Helena, however, probably because the Montana Territorial Legislature, while not outlawing
gambling entirely, had by statute specifically banned certain
games, including three-card monte, Bull's bread-and-butter
provider. Others declared illegal were thimble-rig, the patent
safe game, black and red, two-card box at the fair, and the
strap game.

The fast-growing city of Portland next drew Bull. The best-
known saloon in town was that of August Erickson, who
claimed to offer the biggest scuttle of beer in the United States
for a nickel. The tremendous bar in Erickson's place measured
674 feet in length. Another unusual saloon was the Museum,
which featured an orchestra of ladies, pink-gowned and pro-
tectively ensconced within an enclosure charged with electric-
ity. Other popular resorts were Bob Smith's Monte Carlo, the
Boss Saloon, the Warwick Club, Emil Weber's, and Fritz Blazier's.

Dealers in the Portland houses were paid four dollars a shift.
Most places employed boosters who were paid the same and

given twenty dollars a day stake money, more if circumstances warranted. Following the pattern of gambling hall
hired help, most of the employees plowed their wages back
into the games as soon as they completed their shifts. One of
Blazier's boosters, off-shift and trying to stretch his meager
earnings into a bankroll of consequence, got lucky one night.
Sitting in a stud horse poker game across from a shrewd old-
timer, he noticed that all the queens, kings, and aces were
slightly crimped. Came a hand in which the booster had some
powerful cards up and a deuce in the hole. He covertly
crimped the deuce and bluffed out the other man. "As fast as
he would crimp a high card I would crimp a small one just like
it," he later said. He won a bundle that night, quit his job, and
left Portland with three hundred dollars in his kick.[28]

The underworld of Portland was controlled by a combine of
crooked gamblers and criminals headed by burly Jim Turk, an
Englishmen who had made his first stake on the Pacific Coast
selling liquor to Indians. The "Bad Lands," as Portland's
North End was called, was a district of disreputable saloons,
low-class gambling dens, brothels, and sailors' boarding
houses. Turk was undisputed lord of this domain for several
years and took the lead in the lucrative practice of shanghaiing
sailors. According to one report, Turk drugged his own son
and delivered him to a ship's captain, justifying his action with
the remark that the boy had been associating with bad companions and a few months at sea would do him good.

Other important figures in the Portland tenderloin district
were "Shanghai Larry" Sullivan, Joseph ("Bunco") Kelly, the
White brothers, Mysterious Billy Smith, and Jack and Pete
Grant. Sullivan was a former fighter who once won a 75-round
bare-knuckle battle in Portland. After the turn of the century
he went to the Nevada boom camps and was associated with
Tex Rickard in the promotion of the Nelson-Gans fight at
Goldfield.

Although Sullivan kidnapped enough sailors to earn the
nickname "Shanghai Larry," it was Bunco Kelly who really
worked the shanghai racket hard. At one time, it was said, he
was netting close to two thousand dollars a month with his
activities. The Maritime Union of London offered a reward of

£100 to anyone who would kill him and deliver his ears. Kelly was so crooked that he could not even operate his nefarious traffic in human bodies honestly. He once shanghaied a woman known as Tacoma Kate and collected for delivery of an able-bodied seaman, and on another occasion he sold a wooden Indian wrapped in canvas. According to one gruesome report, he delivered to an unsuspecting captain the bodies of thirty-nine drunks who had stumbled into the basement of an undertaking parlor and killed themselves by drinking formaldehyde. Kelly finally ended up in the Oregon State Penitentiary on a murder conviction.

From Portland, Bull went to Spokane, Washington, which was known in the 1890s as "the Road to Hell" because of the low moral tone. "Dutch Jake" Goetz and his partner Harry Baer, who had amassed $200,000 in the Coeur d'Alene mining camps, were the town's leading gamblers during this period. They erected an elaborate four-story saloon, theater, dance hall, and gambling resort, which burned to the ground in the great fire of 1889. Undaunted, the partners put up a huge tent and maintained business as usual. Five years later they constructed another building that was a Spokane landmark for years. The entire third floor of the establishment was a vast clubroom where a thousand men could play keno simultaneously.

One night in 1898, John Bull walked out of the People's Theater onto Spokane's Howard Street. He was accompanied by Fiskey Barnett, manager of the theater. It was obvious both had been drinking, but they were laughing, seemingly the best of friends. Either in a thoughtlessly playful or suddenly vicious mood, Barnett without warning jabbed his glowing cigar into Bull's face. The fiery end hit the gambler squarely in the eye and he bellowed in rage and pain. He clapped one hand to his eye and reached for his gun with the other. Barnett dodged behind a large woman who happened to be in front of the theater and pulled a gun of his own. Bull, half-blinded, advanced upon the crouching Barnett, his six-gun bucking in his hand. Barnett emptied his pistol at the enraged gambler.

When the firing stopped and the smoke lifted, the woman lay on the sidewalk, one of Bull's bullets through her lungs.

She would totter on the verge of death for many weeks before finally recovering. Barnett was holding up a bloody hand from which a slug had neatly clipped a finger; he was unhurt otherwise. John Bull lay face down, four bullets in his body. His left arm was shattered, and blood ran from wounds in his groin, chin, and neck.

A doctor amputated Bull's mangled arm at the shoulder and removed the bullets from his chin and groin. He would not touch the slug in the neck because of its critical location. Fisky Barnett was fined ten dollars for firing a pistol within the city limits, but the fine was waived in the case of Bull, who was not expected to live.

The tough old gambler recovered and, amazingly, lived on for more than thirty years. In 1921 the bullet in his neck, which he had carried for twenty-three years, began to bother him. A surgeon in Excelsior Springs, Missouri, removed the slug and found that a sharp projection had punctured Bull's windpipe. The gambler, at eighty-five years of age, underwent the operation aided only by a local anesthetic. Still he was not ready to call it quits; it was not until September 9, 1929, that old John Bull finally cashed in his chips at the age of ninety-three in Vancouver, British Columbia.

16

Money has no value except to back a good hand.

Jefferson Randolph ("Soapy") Smith
Frank C. Robertson and Beth Kay Harris,
Soapy Smith, King of the Frontier Con Men

On May 9, 1898, Ice Box Murphy penned the following letter
on the stationery of the Horse Shoe Saloon, Seattle, Washington:

Friend Jeff:
    I understand Bowers has gone to Skagway. I wrote him to Victoria
and Vancouver, but have rec'd no answer. I was in good shape here
to get on my feet but old Bull had me pinched on a deal that Bowers
and I was in, and because I didn't turn the proceeds over to him, he
had Durff swear his life against me, &c., which caused me some
trouble. Bull has lost many friends and is not in it. I will have things
all right in a few days. Jeff, it makes no difference what people say
for or against you, I am always your friend and I hope you are doing
well. I will make some money here, but it won't be through the Bull
click. Write me soon as you get this. I have two letters for Bowers.
One from Skagway and I think it is from you. As soon as I know
where Bowers is I will forward them on to him.
    Write by return mail. Ever your friend,

Jno. W. Murphy.[1]

This letter was written at the time of the Klondike excitement when gamblers and con artists from all sections of the
country were moving into Seattle on their way to the new
boom camps of the Far North. Murphy was a skin-game
booster and small-time safecracker from Denver. Those
named in his letter were all prominent members of the Denver
underworld who had gravitated northwestward with the rush
to the Klondike.
    "Old Bull," of course, was circuit veteran John Bull, who
had organized a "click" in Seattle and was attempting to overlord crooked work in that town. "Durff" was undoubtedly
Adolph W. Duff, alias Kid Duffy, a twenty-four-year-old gambler, pickpocket, and drug addict from Colorado Springs who

was in later years a leading member of the Lou Blonger bunco gang in Denver. "Bowers" was the "Reverend" Charles Bowers, gambler, bunco steerer, and chief lieutenant of the man to whom the letter was addressed, the notorious Jefferson Randolph ("Soapy") Smith, Jr.

The career of Soapy Smith, perhaps more than any other individual's, capsulized the transition from the era of the nineteenth-century sharper to that of the twentieth-century racketeer. Among his other accomplishments, Smith is credited with adding the phrase, "sure-thing game," to the lexicon of the American gambling world. "I am no ordinary gambler," Soapy once proudly proclaimed. "The ordinary gambler hazards his own money in an attempt to win another's. When I stake money, it's a sure thing that I win."[2] He was brash and arrogant, treacherous and avaricious, but he undeniably possessed considerable leadership ability, great personal charm, and a distinctive, wry sense of humor. It was said that no one who knew the man really disliked him.

Once in Denver he was brought into court, charged with fleecing two visitors to the city out of $1,500. He offered an ingenious defense. His gambling hall, he argued, was an institution of public education, quite similar to the Keeley Institute, famous for the cure of inebriation. Those afflicted with the gambling urge could be permanently cured in his house, for they had no chance of winning and were so informed by a sign over the doorway: "Let the buyer beware." (Soapy neglected to mention that the admonition was in Latin, a language unfamiliar to all but a tiny minority of his clientele.) As the clincher to his case, Smith advised the court that the two victims had sworn never to gamble again. "I should be recognized as a public benefactor," he said. "Praise, instead of censure, should be our portion."[3] This man who had talked many a mark out of his hard-earned bankroll talked his way right out of the courtroom; he was acquitted.

Smith's cynical philosophy and convoluted logic were evident later at Skagway where he ruled the underworld of that Alaskan seaport and systematically victimized gold seekers headed inland. When honest businessmen of the town protested, Smith retorted that his cohorts were providing a public

Jefferson Randolph "Soapy" Smith, a kind of genius in his field. Courtesy Denver Public Library, Western History Department.

service. Not only were they stimulating local business by keeping in circulation money that would have left the town, but they were performing the charitable act of preventing innocent greenhorns from plunging farther into the Arctic wastes. "Infinitely better that any man who is such an infant as to try to beat a man at his own game should lose money here at the seaport," quoth Soapy, "than he should get into the inhospitable Arctic, where such an idiot would lose it anyway or be a burden on the community."[4]

Soapy Smith was born into an old and respected family of Noonan, Georgia, in 1860. Three of his father's brothers were doctors, one was a minister, one a farmer, and two others, like Jefferson Randolph, Sr., were lawyers. About 1876 the elder Jeff Smith moved with his family to Round Rock, Texas, where he practiced law. These were the days of the great cattle drives, and young Jeff became a cowboy and went up the trail to Kansas.

After three months of eating the dust of a herd of ornery Texas longhorns, he struck a Kansas cow town. He had always been interested in gambling and in every saloon the games beckoned. Soon the back pay of the teenaged cowboy was gone, but instead of being angry or morose, he was elated. He had watched a man, by the deft manipulation of a deck of cards, make as much money in a few minutes as it had taken himself three months of drudgery to accumulate. His goal in life was set.

Broke, but a great deal wiser, Jeff Smith returned to Texas. He took back with him a deck of cards and at every opportunity practiced the tricks he had seen in Kansas. He became skilled in the dealing of seconds and bottoms; he learned locations, the false shuffle, and the phony cut. He taught himself to build run-up hands and the delicate art of the hand-crimp. Soon he was taking the pay from his fellow cowhands with regularity and they finally refused to play with him.

At a circus in San Antonio he watched an old gambler named Clubfoot Hall work the thimble-rig game. Fascinated by the venerable shell and pea swindle, Smith offered to shill for the game in return for Hall's instruction in its techniques.

When the circus left town, Jeff Smith left with it. From that day on he never soiled his hands with honest toil.

He worked towns throughout the West with his shell game. Then one day in 1885 he saw a swindle in Leadville that he was to be identified with for life. At the corner of Third and Harrison streets a middle-aged, well-dressed man was selling small bars of soap, and, to Smith's astonishment and instant admiration, he was getting five dollars a bar.

Smith saw at once that the soap salesman was working a variation of the old thimble-rig, but that in place of a pea and shells, he was using large denomination bank notes and paper-wrapped soap bars. He would unwrap a bar and wave a twenty- or fifty-dollar bill under the noses of the onlookers. Then, as he ran on with a polished spiel, he would apparently wrap the bill around the soap, replace the wrapper, and toss the bar into a pile of paper-wrapped bars in front of him. When he had repeated this action several times, he would invite those watching to dip into the pile and pick out soap bars of their choice, which they could purchase for the paltry sum of five dollars each. The suckers pushed and shoved in their eagerness to buy up the money bars. Of course, when they opened the wrappers, there were no bank notes. The sharper had proven once again that the hand is quicker than the eye and had palmed each bill as he seemingly wrapped it around the soap.

Jeff Smith lost no time in making the acquaintance of this skin artist, a man named Taylor, and temporarily put aside his own "tripe" and "keister" to shill for the soap grifter.

"Taylor was quite a character himself," recalled Willis A. Loomis, Leadville city marshal.

He never drank, smoked, or went into saloons. Every afternoon he opened his game at the principal street corner, ran it for about an hour, and closed up. He paid his license and obeyed the law. . . .

Among his boosters was a green-looking kid—they called him Smith—who would walk up and pick out a lucky soap cube. The kid would whoop with joy on finding the soap was wrapped in a twenty or a fifty, and this would encourage the crowd to buy. . . .

Taylor was a heavy-set, genteel sort of man and looked more like

a prosperous business man than a sharper. Whether Taylor was his
real name I never knew. There was a rumor that he was an abscond-
ing bank cashier, but I never received any inquiries about him at my
office. . . .[5]

One day Taylor did not appear at his usual street corner; he
had departed Leadville as unobtrusively as he had arrived.
Shortly afterward, Jeff Smith also left town, headed for
greener pastures and greener suckers.

His next stop was Denver, where he quietly began operation
of the soap grift on Seventeenth Street, the artery leading from
the Union Station to the heart of the city. Passing daily were
scores of wide-eyed pilgrims, fresh off trains from the East;
cowboys from the ranges of Colorado, Kansas, and Wyoming, in the big city for a spree; miners, down from the hills,
back pay bulging their pockets. All were fresh fodder for
young Jeff Smith, whose supple fingers had quickly mastered
the soap trick, and who had developed a fine spiel of his own
that he delivered in a deep, booming voice, softened by the
mellifluous accents of his native Georgia.

During one of the lackadaisical clean-up campaigns that the
Denver city officials periodically mounted with such fanfare
as an appeasement to the constantly grumbling reform element, a policeman arrested Smith. Filing his report, he could
remember little about the offender other than the fact that he
had been engaged in selling soap. Beside the name, "Smith,"
he wrote "Soapy," and unconsciously dubbed the young
sharper with the nickname he was to make famous.

Although he could make a good living selling nickel bars of
soap at five dollars a crack, Soapy Smith had visions of greater
things, and, since his genius was organization, he was soon
bringing together as colorful a group of con men and gyp artists as ever roped a mark, threw a broad, or cut up a score.

For a period in the early days of the loose-knit organization
that came to be known as the Soapy Smith Gang, the well-
traveled Doc Baggs lent his experience and prestige to the
group. The "Reverend" Charles Bowers, piety personified,
followed Baggs as chief steerer for the gang and held that post
for many years. Bowers was a "grip" man. By devious meth-

ods he had learned the closely guarded handshakes of practically all fraternal orders and secret societies. In the hotel lobbies and railroad stations that he haunted, he kept a sharp eye out for a pin or emblem that would identify a likely mark as a member of such an organization. Once he had spotted his quarry, he would move in to give the appropriate secret sign and in a few moments he and the mark would be sauntering in the direction of one of Soapy's games.

Syd Dixon and "Judge" Van Horn were disbarred attorneys who worked as steerers and doubled as Soapy's legal brain trust. Dixon was the playboy son of a wealthy eastern family. He had traveled worldwide and squandered a fortune before becoming addicted to opium and settling into a life on the fringes of the underworld. His speech, dress, and bearing, smacking of gentility, were invaluable assets in his assignment as roper of well-fixed eastern businessmen. Van Horne's weakness was alcohol, which he consumed in vast quantities. The bulbous red nose that adorned his face was a monument to his epic bouts with the bottle.

"Ice Box" Murphy had been a road companion of the famous hobo, "A No. 1," before becoming first a safecracker and then a booster for Soapy Smith. He had gotten his nickname after an unfortunate safe blowing experience. Confederates had hoisted the diminutive Murphy, armed with explosives, through the transom of a butcher shop. In the darkened shop he prepared and set off his charge. His cohorts rushed in to find the abashed Murphy standing in a pile of powder-blackened steaks and chops. Instead of the safe, he had blown the icebox!

Clay Wilson, killer of Jim Moon and the man who kept his private journal in Sanskrit, was a member of the gang for a time and helped Soapy pull off a number of lucrative cons.

There were several gang members who were not too bright but were handy to have around in the event a victim took umbrage and threatened violence. "Banjo" Parker, "Fatty" Gray, Big Ed Burns, and "Frisco Red" Harris, a former prizefighter, supplied the muscle for the gang.

To maintain his delicate touch at thimble-rig, Soapy at times would open his shell game in Denver. Always waiting in the wings to relieve the master was "Sure-shot" Tom Cady, also known as "Troublesome Tom," who was ranked second only to Smith in dexterity at thimble-rig. Cady was considered an expert gunman who seldom missed—hence his nickname, "Sure-shot." In addition to a revolver, he always carried a sword cane. He was an extremely dangerous man and most Denver underworld figures gave him a wide berth.

It was a toss-up whether Jimmy Thornton or "Dolly" Brooks (known also as "the Duke of Halsted Street") took the gang's sartorial prizes. Thornton was tall and handsome with a full mustache, waxed and twisted to fine points. He constantly strove to enhance his wide reputation as a lady-killer. Dolly Brooks dressed, according to Soapy's biographers, "in garments of broadcloth, an immense puff tie, high collar, barrel cuffs, top hat, polka-dot silk vest, diamond stud, and 'toothpick' shoes, while from his watch chain dangled a gold nugget and a solid-gold toothpick—the last gasp in frontier elegance."[6]

In stark contrast to the splendidly attired Brooks and Thornton was Henry Edwards, better known in Denver as "Yankee Hank Fewclothes." Even in the bitterest of Colorado winters, Yank Fewclothes was never seen in a coat, vest, or topcoat. In the summer he often discarded his shirt. He was a genial sort and proved to be a productive steerer for the gang.

Operating on the fringes of the gang was a loan shark named Jimmy Bruce, nicknamed "the Great Gobblefish." Bruce preyed on gamblers suffering long losing streaks, advancing them money at an interest rate of ten percent per week. He would never spend money for anything that he could cadge. It was said that when he felt the need of a drink he would intentionally walk into a horse on the street, fall to the ground, and cry for whiskey. When someone in the gathering crowd produced a bottle, he would seize it and pour liquor down his throat until the bottle was empty or it was wrested from him.

Headquarters for the Soap Gang during the early years was the Arcade, at 1613 Larimer Street. Since all visitors to Denver who possessed a drop of sporting blood had to stop in at this renowned resort, Soapy's steerers spent a great deal of time there, ready to entice prospects to one of the boss's street corner skin games. Soapy himself was a habitué of the place. Like so many of his ilk, he was bitten with the faro bug, and most of his ill-gotten gains eventually found their way into the tiger's bottomless maw. When seized with a faro fit, Smith could not leave the game until he had broken the bank or himself.

When frustrated or threatened, Soapy's natural inclination was to resort to his wits rather than weapons. Although he customarily carried a gun and a knife for defensive purposes, he rarely employed either. One such occurrence in August, 1889, when he was caught up in a faro frenzy was recorded, however. After losing his roll bucking the tiger, he had put up his watch for a one hundred dollar stake to continue playing. His luck changed and he won back most of his losses. He then pushed one hundred dollars across the table to reclaim his watch. When the dealer refused, Soapy's temper flared. He jerked his blade, slashed the layout, and, leaning across the table, held the knife to the throat of the dealer, who reconsidered quickly and produced the watch.

Smith's uncharacteristic behavior was probably due to the strain of problems he was having at the time. For several weeks he had been under attack in the pages of the *Rocky Mountain News*, which referred to him as an "astute scoundrel" and a "distinguished blackleg." His soap swindle had been described in detail and it was charged that he "owned" the town:

Soapy, in the language of the fly-by-night fraternity, "has" Denver. . . . He has it to do with what he will in so far as all professional swindling and stealing is concerned. . . . The city is absolutely under the control of this prince of knaves, and there is not a confidence man, a sneak thief, or any other parasite upon the public who does not pursue his avocation under license from [this] man. . . .[7]

Smith might have laughed off this article as he had similar castigating editorials in the past, but for the inclusion of a reference to Soapy's family, then residing at Idaho Springs. Shortly after his arrival in Denver, Smith had married a girl named Annie Nielsen, who bore him several children. He had been so careful to keep his family life and his professional life completely separate that many of his closest associates were not aware that he was married. Now the *News* article touched his family. Straitlaced friends of Mrs. Smith at Idaho Springs, who had believed Annie's husband to be a prosperous but honest and hardworking Denver businessman, began to shun her.

A wrathful Soapy Smith moved fast. He went to Idaho Springs, gathered up his wife and children, and put them on a train for Saint Louis. Returning to Denver, he enlisted the 250-pound Banjo Parker and headed for the *News* building. He and Parker both carried heavy walking sticks, and when Colonel John Arkins, president of the News Printing Company, appeared, Soapy proceeded to give him a severe pummeling, as Parker stood by, cane upraised, to prevent interference by Arkins's friends.

Smith was arrested later at the Jockey Club Saloon on a warrant charging him with attempted murder. Arkins had suffered a fractured skull, but he recovered. At a preliminary hearing, Soapy insisted that he had no intention of killing the publisher and argued that if murder had been his object, he would have chosen a weapon other than a walking stick. He made it clear that the mention of his family had infuriated him and that his purpose was to chastise Arkins. Soapy was bound over for trial on $1,000 bond but was never tried on the charge. Before the trial date he decided Denver was no longer hospitable, and, gathering up a quartet of his closest associates, the Reverend Bowers, Troublesome Tom Cady, Fatty Gray, and Tom Crippen, moved on.

The gang stopped briefly at Cheyenne, Salt Lake City, and Ogden. When they attempted to move into Pocatello, Idaho, they were met at the depot by a committee of hard-eyed gamblers headed by "Rincon Kid" Kelly, a skin-game artist who had been banished from Denver earlier by Smith. Kelly informed Soapy that Pocatello was his domain and new competition was not welcome. Angry words were exchanged and epithets were flung. Someone pulled a gun and soon bullets were flying. When the smoke lifted it was found that the only casualty was Sam Beecher, a lieutenant of Kelly, who had been hit in the leg. Soapy Smith was arrested and locked in the hoosegow. The Pocatello officials, alarmed by the prospect of their town becoming a battleground for rival grifters, put the Rincon Kid and his followers on a train for Portland. Soapy's gang was dispatched southward to Ogden.

Soapy was acquitted on a plea of self-defense and rejoined his cohorts at Ogden. He then led the gang on a tour of the cities of the Northwest, searching for a new base. At every stop he found that his notoriety had preceded him and he was repulsed by both the local authorities and the incumbent swindling gangs.

In the spring of 1891, Soapy returned to Denver. During his absence the city had experienced a wave of violent lawlessness that made his homecoming almost a cause for jubilation among local law enforcement officials. Despite his occasional slips, Soapy was still considered a cool and calculating sort, a man who resorted to violence only under extreme provocation.

He opened the Tivoli Saloon at the corner of Seventeenth and Market streets in the heart of the sporting district. His gambling rooms were on the second floor, and over the stairway was posted the *caveat emptor* sign that he later cited in court as proof that he provided a public service by skinning compulsive gamblers in his crooked games. Later he opened the White Front Saloon at Edgewater, on the city's outskirts.

The big excitement in Denver the winter of 1891–92 was news of the rich silver strike in the San Juan Mountains, and after a few months Smith turned over operation of the Tivoli and White Front saloons to underlings and departed for the new boom camp of Creede. He found upon arrival that Bob Ford, still trading on his notoriety as the slayer of Jesse James, was already on hand and had proclaimed himself chief. Ford had disposed of a gambling room in Walsenburg, Colorado, and had scurried to the new bonanza to open Ford's Exchange, the biggest saloon and gambling hall in Creede. His mistress, a woman named Nell Watson, had moved a bevy of whores into rooms above the saloon, and business on both levels was humming.

Soapy Smith recognized at once that Ford had neither the brains nor organization to overlord crooked work in a camp as rich as Creede promised to be, and he went about establishing

Bob Ford, who was no match for Soapy Smith in the struggle to control vice in Creede. Courtesy Western History Collections, University of Oklahoma Library.

himself and ignored Ford's grumblings. As a base of operations he opened the Orleans Club in competition with Ford's
Exchange. When the leading businessmen of the town met to
organize a government, Soapy was on hand and offered to
assume responsibility for controlling the gunmen and toughs
who always congregated at a new boom camp. He sent to
Texas for John Light, a coldly efficient gunfighter, whom he
named as town marshal. Light just happened to be Soapy's
brother-in-law. With Light from Texas came Soapy's boyhood
chum, Joe Simons, who became manager of the Orleans Club,
and Bascomb Smith, Soapy's brother. John Light pinned deputy marshal badges on Simons, Bascomb, Smith lieutenant
Joe Palmer, and Soapy himself; the bears were guarding the
honey.

Infuriated at this turn of events, Bob Ford went on a mon-
umental drunk and shot up the town. When he had sobered
up, he was told to make himself scarce in Creede. Ford was
not the brightest gambler in the West, but he had sense enough
to know when the cards were stacked against him. He and Nell
Watson hied themselves to Pueblo. A few months later Ford
petitioned the powers at Creede for permission to return to his
Exchange and promised to behave himself. Soapy Smith, his
position as kingpin secure, magnanimously allowed him to
come back.

Ford's decision to return proved disastrous. On June 5,
1892, a fire swept through the town, devastating an area a half
mile long and a quarter mile wide. Soapy's Orleans Club was
one of the few buildings untouched by the flames, but Ford's
Exchange was burned to the ground. Ford managed to rescue
a piano, his most prized possession, before the conflagration
reached it. As soon as the ashes cooled he put up a tent over
the piano and opened a new place he called the Leadville
Dancehall.

On June 8, just three days after the fire, a woman entered
the dancehall. She was taking up a collection, she said, to
cover the burial expenses of a soiled dove known as Slanting
Annie, who had recently died. Bob Ford glanced over the list
of contributors, saw that Soapy Smith had donated five dollars, and snorted contemptuously. "I'll raise him five," he said.

Taking a pencil, he wrote: "Bob Ford—Ten Dollars—Charity covereth a multitude of sins."

Seconds later, a nondescript drifter named Ed O'Kelly walked into the tent and blasted the life out of Bob Ford with a shotgun. The motive for the killing was never determined, but it was generally assumed that O'Kelly simply sought the fame that would attach to the man who had killed the slayer of Jesse James.

With the death of Bob Ford, Soapy Smith's domination of Creede was unchallenged. It was said that of the forty saloons in town, only the Denver Exchange, managed by Bat Masterson, did not pay tribute to the gang leader. As busy as he was in Creede, however, Smith still found time to return to Denver frequently. He kept a careful check on his operations there and cracked down hard on interlopers. One such visit in October, 1892, led to a shooting in Murphy's Exchange.

Smith was advised that a gambler and bunco man from Saint Louis named Cliff Sparks had moved into Denver in Soapy's absence and was chiseling into the gang's rackets. Backing his play was a hard customer named Jim Jordan, alias Henry Gilmore. Two local gambling house operators, Jeff Argyle of the Missouri Club and Johnny Murphy of the notorious Murphy's Exchange, were reported to be friendly to Sparks and Jordan.

Tom Cady, who had accompanied his boss from Creede, paid a call on Jordan at the Missouri Club and in the row that followed, Troublesome Tom rapped Jordan over the head with the loaded end of his sword cane. Cady was arrested and Jordan retired to Murphy's to lick his wounds and confer with his partner Sparks. Soapy soon had Cady out on bail and the two headed immediately for Murphy's Exchange.

Ranged along the bar of that unfriendly place they found Jim Jordan, a scowl on his face and a knot on his head; Cliff Sparks, a $2,500 headlight diamond sparkling at his bosom; Bill Crooks, a tinhorn who was Sparks's shadow; Cort Thompson, foot racer, gambler, lover of Madam Mattie Silks, and enemy of Soapy Smith; and Johnny Murphy, onetime railroad engineer who bragged that he ran the toughest saloon in Denver. Few words were spoken. Witnesses later said that they saw Cady brandish his cane and then a shot was fired. Cliff Sparks sank to the floor.

Murphy lifted the head of the dying gambler. "Cliff, old man," he said, "they're off at Sheepshead, and you're last."

"I'm last," whispered Sparks, and expired.

Bill Crooks screamed in anguish: "They've killed Cliff! They've killed my dear old pal!" Falling to his knees, he gathered the body in his arms and, sobbing, pressed his face to the still chest. No one noticed when they pulled him away that the headlight diamond was missing from the dead gambler's boiled shirt. Bill Crooks had bitten it off.

Several arrests were made in connection with the death of Cliff Sparks, but a desultory inquiry into the affair got nowhere. Satisfied that he was still in firm control at Denver, Soapy Smith headed back to Creede.

The spirited days of the camp were about over, though. With the repeal of the Sherman Silver Act, the price of silver plummeted from $1.29 to 50 cents an ounce. Creede, the silver town, did not fold up overnight, but the great influx of new arrivals, the source of the major portion of the Smith gang's profits, fell off substantially and Soapy knew it was time to move on. He had also lost much of his enthusiasm for the town after the death in June, 1892, of his oldest friend, Joe Simons, a victim of pneumonia.

Soapy went back to Denver in early 1893. With him came brother Bascomb, who was soon involved in a shooting that had its genesis in the Soapy Smith–Bob Ford power struggle in Creede the year before. From Walsenburg with Ford had come Dick Hawkins and Harry ("Shotgun") Smith. Hawkins had partnered Ford in his Walsenburg saloon, and Shotgun Smith (no relation to Soapy and Bascomb) had been a booster in the place. During Ford's exile from Creede, Hawkins and Bascomb tangled. Hawkins tried to pull a gun but was leveled by a blow from Bascomb's cane.

The affair still rankled Shotgun, and a year later in Denver he braced Bascomb in the Tivoli Saloon. Both men drew revolvers and grappled. They were still locked in a deadly embrace, each gripping the gun hand of the other, when they crashed through the doors out onto the sidewalk. Finally, Bascomb tore free and fired three shots into the other Smith. Taken to Saint Luke's Hospital, Shotgun Smith clung to life for a time but died at last with a smile on his lips; in his delirium he believed that he had killed his adversary. Bascomb had been unhurt in the duel, however, and was released on a plea of self-defense.

This kind of activity did not enhance Soapy's prestige in Denver, and it tarnished his image as a man who deplored gunplay and controlled his gang with a hand of iron. The clever gambler soon saw an opportunity to raise his stock with the city officials. Operating in Denver at the time was a company known as the Glasson Detective Agency, which was in fact a blackmail operation. Many influential citizens of the city had been victimized by the Glasson Agency, but the police had not been able to build a successful case against the company because of unwillingness on the part of victims to file formal complaints. When Soapy learned that a young servant girl had been dragged into the offices of the agency and roughed up in an effort to obtain a confession concerning the theft of jewelry from the home of a socially prominent couple, he moved fast.

Rounding up a platoon of his gang members that included Jimmy Thornton, Fatty Gray, Yankee Hank Fewclothes, Dolly Brooks, and Ice Box Murphy, he led a raid on the agency. Without warning, the Soap Gang burst into the Glasson offices and laid out the startled detectives right and left with slung shots, brass knuckles, and loaded canes. They forced open locked desks and files with crowbars and dumped papers and pictures out on the street. When riot police arrived in horse-drawn Black Marias, Soapy was putting a match to the pile of material upon which the agency based the blackmail operation. The police stood back and enjoyed the bonfire together with Soapy and his gang.

When questioned by newspapermen about the raid, Soapy assumed the stance of a defender of womanhood. He had been enraged by the atrocities committed by the Glasson agents against the girl, he said, and had decided to put the company out of business. The attack had been a master stroke for Soapy. To the newspaper-reading working people of the city he became a hero-figure, ready and eager to take direct action to protect the downtrodden and oppressed. By destroying embarrassing documents, he endeared himself to many wealthy citizens who had been preyed upon by the Glasson Agency. And by wiping out in a few minutes a resource of difficulty and frustration that had plagued the city's law enforcement officials for months, Soapy earned the gratitude of city hall. That gratitude was, of course, demonstrated best by a hands-off policy with regard to the activities of the Smith gang, and in the ensuing months Soapy reaped his greatest harvest in Denver.

The following year, 1894, featured Denver's City Hall War, a bizarre confrontation between the city and state authorities in which Soapy Smith played a leading role. Populist Davis H. Waite had ridden into the Colorado governor's office on a platform of female suffrage and reform. Soon after his election he was faced with a serious crisis when a miners' strike at Cripple Creek escalated into armed conflict between the miners and strikebreakers employed by the owners. Waite sent in state militia to bring order, thereby alienating both sides. When he remarked that he "would rather see our men riding through the streets through blood to their bridles than surrender our liberties to the corporations," he was immediately dubbed "Blood-to-the-Bridles" Waite and misquoted universally. Backers of both factions concluded that it was *their* blood through which he would ride.

From the governor's mansion in Denver, Waite viewed with dismay the corruption in the city and issued a gubernatorial ukase to the Police and Fire Commission demanding a wholesale cleanup. When the commissioners failed to carry out his edict, Waite charged them with taking bribes from gamblers and demanded their resignations. The commissioners refused and Waite threatened to use state militia to eject them forcibly from city hall. The officials, remembering Waite's "blood-to-the-bridles" statement, turned to the town's underworld chieftain for help.

With the call to battle, Soapy Smith became "Colonel" Smith. Overnight he recruited an army of gamblers, thugs, pickpockets, second-story men, pimps, and saloon bums and deployed them in the city hall with guns, ammunition, and five hundred pounds of dynamite. His orders were to "hold the fort," but, if necessary, to blow it up rather than surrender it to Waite's legions. Standing shoulder-to-shoulder with Colonel Smith's tenderloin troops were most of the police and firemen of the city.

The enraged governor called in his militia and three companies of national guardsmen, supported by two cannon and a pair of Gatling guns, deployed a block from the city hall. General Brooks, in command, sent word to Waite that his men were in position, and he would fire when so ordered. Meanwhile, another force of armed men under Sheriff William Burchinell approached the hall from another direction. No one was sure which side Burchinell would support if shooting commenced. The city was tense, awaiting the impending clash.

A delegation of citizens, appalled by the direction events had taken, called on the governor, pleading with him to call off his troops to prevent a bloodbath. At the last moment Waite relented and ordered the militia to withdraw. The Denver City Hall War was over without a shot being fired.

For a short time after the "war" Soapy Smith's star was at its ascendancy in Denver. The city officials were deeply in his debt, and his part in the successful defiance of the high-handed governor had further heightened his reputation with the citizenry as a popular hero. A realization came to the voters, though, that this unholy coalition of politicos and underworld figures might not be so great for the city after all, and a genuine reform wave set in. Many of the old guard politicians were swept from office, to be replaced by others who owed Soapy Smith nothing. Soapy correctly read the trend and unloaded his saloon interests.

Before departing Denver, he and brother Bascomb went on a drunken spree, shooting up several gambling saloons. At the Arcade they were confronted by Johnny Hughes, a square gambler and partner of Ed Chase. Bascomb flattened Hughes with a blow of his cane, fracturing his skull. The brothers were arrested. Soapy was fined fifty dollars for carrying concealed weapons and three dollars for public drunkenness. Bascomb's

charge was assault with murderous intent. He was convicted
and sentenced to a year in the county jail.

Soapy Smith was now persona non grata in Denver, and
once again he looked to other fields. He had read that the dictator of Mexico, Porfirio Diaz, was having difficulty controlling rebels in remote areas of his country. Smith wrote to Diaz,
offering the services of himself and five hundred hardened
American fighting men to help bring the insurgents under control. Using the title he had conferred upon himself during the
Denver City Hall War, he signed the letter, "Colonel Jefferson
R. Smith."

Diaz answered that he would be pleased to consult with the
distinguished American army officer, Colonel Smith, and invited him to Mexico City. Accompanied by the Reverend
Bowers, his subaltern, Soapy went to the Mexican capital
where he was feted handsomely. Assuring President Diaz that
he had five hundred seasoned frontiersmen ready and willing
to join him at a moment's notice, Smith mentioned, almost
parenthetically, that all that was required to bring this prodi-
gious force into action was a small matter of equipment ex-
penditure, some eighty thousand dollars. The president agreed
that this was a mere pittance and suggested that the colonel
return to the States and gather his army. An emissary from the
Mexican government would later contact him with the funds.
The colonel remarked that a stipend to cover initial costs, say
ten thousand dollars, would be in order. The president de-
murred, insisting that the entire amount would be forthcoming
when Smith's legion had been assembled. It was necessary for
the colonel to employ his finest eloquence finally to secure the
promise of two thousand dollars, payable at once.

Smith returned to the States and actually contacted a number
of brigands of his acquaintance, but Diaz meanwhile did some
checking on the "colonel," learned of his unsavory background and complete lack of military experience, and wired
him that the deal was off.

In the closing months of 1895, Soapy attempted to establish
himself in several Texas towns. He was jailed at Dallas in October on a charge of "quackery." When a Texas sheriff wired

the Denver authorities to inquire if Smith was wanted there, the *Denver Times* made sport of the misfortunes of the former Colorado underworld luminary. "Jeff R. Smith, once king of Colorado bunco steerers and past aide-de-camp to President Diaz of Mexico, is now jailed as a common vagrant. This is all very pathetic. . . . The county authorities hardly believe it is worth while to spend money to bring Jeff Smith back. He is such a pleasant figure at a distance of six hundred miles. . . ."[8]

Soapy went to Houston where, together with Dick Riddle, a Texas gambler with gunfighting credits, he attempted to muscle in on the gambling saloon of J. O. Dalton. When Dalton refused to knuckle under to Smith's demands, guns were drawn. Riddle got off the first shot, but missed, and it cost him his life. Dalton's answering shot dropped him with a mortal wound. Soapy, happy to have escaped the wrath of Dalton unscathed, quickly departed Houston.

He went to Los Angeles and San Francisco, checking out the California cities as possible operational bases. Finding no opportunities to his liking, he crossed the continent to Washington, D. C., and visited his cousin, Edwin Bobo Smith, a respected newsman in that city. Edwin Smith introduced him to many Washington notables, including Senators Vest, Stewart, and Shoup, editor Henry Watterson, Colonel Tom Ochiltree, and renowned foreign correspondent Richard Harding Davis. "They were all charmed with him. . . . and never seemed to tire of his company," wrote Edwin Smith.

He told them stories of his life in the West by the hour. . . . He made friends, all of them influential, through his agreeable personality, regardless of the life he led or of the disreputable character of his associates. Jeff possessed an engaging manner and never had the least difficulty ingratiating himself with persons with whom he came in contact. He had only to get access to a man to win his favorable opinion, and this notwithstanding his reputation. This characteristic accounts for his success as a confidence man, and I might add that if his talents had been employed in legitimate walks of life, it would have assured his success in almost any calling. . . .[9]

Newspaperman W. F. Hynes, who spent an evening with

Soapy, Edwin Smith, and Richard Harding Davis at the Raleigh Hotel in Washington, later wrote:

The one great quality which [Soapy] unwittingly displayed that evening and which doubtless proved his great ally in every game, was his profound knowledge of human nature, which, by the way, greatly impressed Davis. In short, it was clear that Soapy Smith was a man of parts, and evidently was not obliged through any sort of intellectual equipment to take up the business of gambling. He had qualities that made for executive ability, backed by a more than ordinary education.[10]

In 1896, Soapy Smith returned to Denver once more. He soon learned that during his absence a new regime had gained control of crooked gambling and confidence work in the Colorado capital. Top dogs now were the Blonger brothers, Lou and Sam, who had operated a second-rate dance hall and gambling saloon in Denver for sixteen years. French-Canadians by birth, the brothers had come to the American West as youths and had learned the ins-and-outs of the sporting life in the Kansas cattle towns and Colorado mining camps. They had operated briefly in Salt Lake City before opening their modest establishment in Denver in 1880.

Lou Blonger, a short, heavy-set man with bloodhound eyes and a bulbous nose, was the brains of the team. Lou had imagination and ambition, but he was an exceedingly patient man who was content to operate for years as a saloonkeeper and minor grifter until he felt the time was ripe for his power grab. Brother Sam was a large, powerful man with mean eyes, partially hidden behind blue-tinted glasses. Sam lacked his brother's brains and patience, and was further cursed with a quick temper and a penchant for brutally mauling those who incurred his anger, especially women.

During Smith's reign in Denver, Lou Blonger had contributed a percentage of his saloon profits to the crime lord with never a murmur of protest. After Soapy's forced departure, Blonger had taken over. For years he had gathered bits and pieces of information on the secret vices and foibles of officeholders and aspirants for political office. By judicious use of this intelligence and direct outlays of bribe money, he quickly

Mug shot of Lou Blonger when he was finally brought to justice. Courtesy Denver Public Library, Western History Department.

managed to attain favored status with city hall, especially the police department. For years he maintained a direct telephone line from his office to that of the police chief, and a call from him could result in the arrest of a rival or the release of a friend within minutes.

Thwarted in his bid to move back into Denver by the powerful Blonger forces in 1896, Soapy Smith gathered around him a coterie of loyal followers and left town for the last time. He still searched for a favorite locale in which his peculiar talents could flourish and he would once again recapture the glory he had tasted for a short time in Denver and in Creede. With him went veteran gang members Charles Bowers, Syd Dixon, W. H. Jackson, and George Wilder. They were joined by a pair of recent newcomers, "Slim Jim" Foster and "Red" Gibbs.

The gang stopped at the prosperous new mining town of Cripple Creek but were met at the station by "Three-Fingered Jim" Marshall wearing a town marshal's badge and heading a platoon of tough-looking deputies. Marshall told Soapy in polite but direct language to move on. The scene was remarkably reminiscent of the Smith gang's confrontation with the minions of Rincon Kid Kelly at Pocatello seven years before. This time Soapy did not force the issue; with the bemused half-smile of the gambler who knows when the cards are running against him, he tipped his hat to the stern-faced Marshall and led his followers back onto the train.

He made another brief appearance at Butte, Montana, where he tangled with another town marshal, Jack Jolly, and put a bullet in the lawman before hurriedly leaving town. He checked out the possibilities at San Francisco's famous Barbary Coast, but found the local vice lords too well entrenched. At Seattle he remained long enough to incur the enmity of the local skin-game and short-con fraternity. In October, 1897, a delegation of local toughs, led by Johnny Maybell and Eddie Gaffer, served notice in the Horse Shoe Saloon that the Soap Gang was unwelcome in Seattle. A battle royal erupted from which a number of participants on both sides emerged with aching heads, misshapen noses, and gap-toothed smiles. The most serious injury was sustained by Maybell who suffered a knife wound during the melee.

A few days later Soapy led his crew up the gangplank of a northbound steamer, destination Skagway, Alaska, doorway to the Klondike. At Skagway, Soapy found what he had been searching for, a city ripe for plunder. It was a natural, a mushrooming town in a remote location, with little or no established legal authority, where *cheechakos* poured off every ship from the States, gold fever dancing in their eyes and their life's savings bulging their money belts, and where sourdoughs from the ice-locked interior came, toting their bags of yellow dust. All had to spend some time in Skagway, the new arrivals to outfit for the long arduous trip inland to the goldfields, the

Soapy Smith with some of his henchmen in his saloon at Skagway. Courtesy Photography Collection, University of Washington Library.

lucky departees to wait for a berth on a steamship States-bound. Lying in wait for well-heeled suckers on the docks and trails were Soapy's steerers and boosters.

His headquarters was a combination oyster parlor, saloon, and gambling house called Jeff's Place, from which he spun his Skagway net to entrap the gullible. He was aided and abetted by a cadre that included the Reverend Bowers, W. H. Jackson, Syd Dixon, Big Ed Burns, George Wilder, and the fresh-faced youngsters of innocent mien, Red Gibbs and Slim Jim Foster. New Soap Gang recruits were Van B. Triplett, better known as "Old Man Tripp," a white-bearded patriarch with the look of a saint and the heart of a scoundrel, and "Yeah Mow" Hopkins, a veteran of the San Francisco Chinatown tong wars who had a proclivity for violence matched only by the brutal Ed Burns. Allied with the gang were others known only by nickname, Kid Jimmy Fresh, the Moonfaced Kid, and the like, who came from the dregs of the criminal world and drew the line at nothing in their lust for loot. Where once Soapy and his cohorts had confined their activities to crooked gambling games and confidence schemes and had been considered among the aristocrats of the underworld, in Skagway the barriers were down and no crime, including murder, was too foul for them.

A news dispatch from Seattle on February 25, 1898, set forth the deplorable state of affairs at the Alaskan port: "Officers of the steamer *Noyo* from Skagway today reported conditions of lawlessness at Skagway as beyond description. Soapy Smith and his gang are in full control. Law-abiding people do not dare say a word against them. Hold-ups, robberies, and shootings are a part of the daily routine. Eight dead bodies were picked up on White Pass on February 15."[11]

The responsible citizens of Skagway, alarmed at the depredations of Smith and his gang, finally got together and formed a vigilance committee. A notice appeared on the streets of Skagway:

WARNING

A WORD TO THE WISE SHOULD BE SUFFICIENT. ALL CONFIDENCE SHARKS, BUNCO MEN, SURE-THING MEN, AND ALL OTHER OBJECTIONABLE CHARACTERS ARE NOTIFIED TO LEAVE SKAGWAY AND THE WHITE PASS. FAILURE TO COMPLY WITH THIS WARNING WILL BE FOLLOWED BY PROMPT ACTION! SIGNED—COMMITTEE OF ONE HUNDRED AND ONE.

If the members of this committee harbored any illusions that such a notice would intimidate Soapy Smith, they grossly underestimated the man who had in a few months established himself as the criminal dictator of the town. His reaction was swift and typically audacious. Wrapping himself in a cloak of respectability, he called the committee's bet and raised. His minions scurried about the town, tacking up a new notice:

PUBLIC WARNING!
THE BODY OF MEN CALLING THEMSELVES THE COMMITTEE OF ONE HUNDRED AND ONE ARE HEREBY NOTIFIED THAT ANY OVERT ACT COMMITTED BY THEM WILL BE MET PROMPTLY BY THE LAWABIDING CITIZENS OF SKAGWAY AND EACH MEMBER AND THEIR PROPERTY WILL BE HELD RESPONSIBLE FOR ANY UNLAWFUL ACT ON THEIR PART. THE LAW AND ORDER COMMITTEE OF THREE HUNDRED AND THREE WILL SEE THAT JUSTICE IS DEALT OUT TO THE FULLEST EXTENT AND NO BLACKMAILERS OR VIGILANTES WILL BE TOLERATED. (SIGNED) LAW AND ORDER COMMITTEE OF THREE HUNDRED AND THREE.

Soapy had thrown the challenge right back and if he was bluffing, the bluff worked. For several months no more was heard from the Committee of One Hundred and One, and the Smith wolves went about their work unmolested.

When word reached the Far North that the battleship *Maine* had been blown up in Havana Harbor and the United States was at war with Spain, Soapy Smith, fired with patriotism, dusted off his title of "Colonel," organized a company called the "Skagway Volunteers," and sent notice to President McKinley that he was ready to lead his unit into battle against the enemy. The War Department declined his offer but sent a letter of appreciation to "Colonel" Smith, congratulating him on his patriotic fervor. Soapy had the letter framed and conspicuously displayed in his saloon.

On the Fourth of July, 1898, a parade was held at Skagway, led by the grand marshal, Colonel Jefferson Randolph Smith, dressed in his best suit and widest-brimmed Texas hat and mounted on a beautiful dappled gray. Behind the grand marshal marched a brass band, followed by the Skagway Volunteers. Bringing up the rear were any others who wished to join in the parade. Each wore a badge of red, white, and blue bunting, on which was printed in prominent letters: "Courtesy of Jefferson R. Smith." It was a great day, undoubtedly Soapy Smith's proudest hour. He was undisputed cock of the walk, lord of all he surveyed.

Four days later he was dead.

Appalled by Smith's open flaunting of power, the Committee of One Hundred and One called for a mass meeting of concerned citizens to be held at a dockside warehouse the night of July 8. Soapy chuckled when he learned of these plans, telling his followers that he would take care of this minor annoyance. Declining all offers of help, he announced that he would attend the meeting alone and straighten out this little group of troublemakers.

Confident in his power as boss of Skagway, he strapped on a brace of six-shooters and picked up a Winchester rifle. At the approach to the warehouse his way was blocked by surveyor Frank Reid, one of the original organizers of the Committee of One Hundred and One and a severe critic of the Soap Gang and its leader. Smith advanced steadily on the plank sidewalk. He gripped the rifle in his right hand, his finger on the trigger. The barrel rested on his shoulder, the muzzle to the rear. Reid, his right hand in his coat pocket, stood squarely in his path.

A step or two away from Reid, Soapy swung the rifle down. Reid pushed the barrel away with his left hand and pulled a pistol with his right. He squeezed the trigger, but the weapon misfired. Smith, grasping his rifle now with both hands, forced the muzzle against Reid's body and pulled the trigger just as Reid cocked and released the hammer of his six-gun.

Rifle and revolver fired simultaneously. Both men staggered back and collapsed on the boardwalk. As he was falling, Reid got off another shot, hitting Smith in the leg, but this bullet was wasted on a dead man; Reid's first .45 slug had torn Soapy Smith's heart asunder.

Frank Reid, with Soapy's bullet in his groin, lingered in excruciating pain for twelve days before dying. He was buried close to Smith's grave in the Skagway cemetery. Friends erected a large monument on his gravesite bearing the inscription: "He gave his life for the honor of Skagway."

Soapy's grave nearby was marked only by a rough board with the legend:

JEFFERSON R. SMITH

AGED 38

DIED JULY 8, 1898

Their leader gone, the Soap gangsters scattered in panic. The isolation of Skagway, which had worked to their advantage in the entrapment of suckers, now served to ensnare the gang members. Armed vigilantes flushed frightened hoodlums from hiding places along the wharves and at entrances to the mountain passes. Bowers, Foster, and Old Man Tripp hid out in the woods, but after two days of eating nothing but roots and berries, came into town to surrender. The dragnet produced twenty-six prisoners who were lodged in jail. There were calls for stretched hemp justice, but the vigilante leaders managed to control the hotter heads and a mass lynching was averted.

Several of those considered in the higher echelons of Soapy's gang, including Bowers, Foster, Wilder, Jackson, and Triplett, were charged with an assortment of felonies and taken to Juneau, where they were convicted and given sentences ranging from one to ten years. Most of the gang members, however, were marched to the docks, placed upon the steamship *Tartar*, bound for the States, and warned never to show up in Skagway again on pain of death.

HOCK

The century turned and the frontier retreated at an acceler-
ated pace before the relentless march of the true town tamers,
the permanent settlers and their families. The towns rang with
the sounds of carpenters' hammers as churches and schools
sprang up. On the sidewalks where only a few years before
miners and cowpokes had roistered, now children played and
housewives chatted. YMCA buildings replaced dance halls
and deserted saloons reopened as ice cream parlors. In the
council chambers and statehouses a new breed of politician,
put there by the votes of newly arrived shopkeepers and farmers, decried the wild and woolly reputation of the western
country and strove to create a new image for the region. Here
was a country, they said, where God-fearing men and women,
by dint of honest toil and frugality, could build a good life for
themselves and their children. The day of the get-rich-quick
boomers and something-for-nothing speculators was over.
They were to be banished from this new society and with them
the denizens of the sporting world who for half a century had
catered to the vices of the westerner.

For years most of the states had carried antigambling laws
on their books that had been pulled out and dusted off during
periods of reform but then returned to the shelves when the
reformers quieted down. Texas, for example, had a statute
prohibiting gambling that dated back to the original state penal
code written in 1856. Many municipalities enacted similar or-
dinances and collected from the gamblers periodic fines that
were in effect licensing fees. As bones thrown to the reform
elements, some towns restricted gambling to certain blocks or
required that games be played behind screened doors or in the
back rooms of saloons. In Sacramento, for instance, faro
games were relegated to second-floor rooms. It was thought,

389

perhaps, that forcing a man to climb a flight of stairs might deter him from losing house and home at the tables.

The professional gamblers had stoically suffered these inanities and written off the fees and fines as business expenses. With the coming of the new constituencies and new morality, however, the new civil servants dragged out the statutes and came down hard, causing an exodus of gamblers from the established states to the remaining pockets of the frontier. The Klondike drew them for a few years, but the three Southwest territories of Arizona, New Mexico, and Nevada, where frontier values were still prized, became their final stamping grounds.

Shortly after the turn of the century, statehood movements gathered strength in the territories and agitation for the suppression of gambling followed. To demonstrate that they were modern, civilized, and ready for statehood, territorial leaders attacked open gambling, a practice uniquely identifiable with the frontier image they wished to dispel.

On April 1, 1907, a tough antigambling measure went into effect in Arizona. As they closed their games, gambling house operators across the territory were aware of the irony of the date—All Fool's Day. Many Arizonans rejoiced, of course, but in the editorial pages of the newspapers could be detected a note of sadness at the passing of an era and the men who had contributed to the romance and excitement.

"For forty years gambling has had full sway in Arizona," said the *Phoenix Gazette*,

but now the die is cast, both the city and the Territory have refused the gamblers any further privileges, and, like the Wandering Jew, they were told to move on. . . . The men who operated these games in Phoenix are, as a rule, good men; probably the squarest games in Arizona were those operated in this city. This can be said to their credit. . . . Gambling is a thing of the past in Phoenix, and the man who looks to the whims of the Goddess of Chance for his livelihood has folded his tent, and, like the Arab, silently stolen away.[1]

"He will not be forgotten, nor will he be maligned," said the *Tombstone Prospector*:

Since Tombstone's inception the most noted sporting men of the United States came and went and returned; this was a veritable mecca for them. They prospered and lent valuable aid in opening up the country; in wresting the land from savagery and subduing that element of whites who made unenviable history for Arizona. True, he often used his "trusty gun," and to his unerring aim may be attributed the noticeable absence of the "bad man" who, a quarter of a century ago, essayed to run the country. . . . But conditions have changed, the undesirable element has "crossed the range," . . . and now the gambler is told to "move on."[2]

"The Tiger is dying!" announced the *Prescott Journal-Miner*:

On the stroke of twelve tonight he will have breathed his last, and the "Tiger" in Prescott will have become but a memory. . . . But whatever may be said . . . of his power for good or greater evil, there is no gainsaying that in Prescott, those who groomed him, who have looked after his daily wants, who were his closest associates, were, on the whole, "good fellows;" good citizens, who made their living in Prescott; who spent their money with Prescott merchants; who took a pride in the upbuilding of the "city a mile high;" and what more does any public spirited citizen? [They] will be serenely missed by many who knew them best; men who were all that the term "honest gambler" implies. . . . Unscrupulous ones there were among them, 'tis true, e'en as there are in every walk of life, but the majority, in Prescott, at least, were and are men with the making of good citizens; man who, on the whole, lived good, clean lives; men whom but few were ashamed to extend the right hand of fellowship.[3]

New Mexico followed nine months later, on January 1, 1908, with a stringent antigambling law. Owners of premises upon which gambling games were conducted, the dealers and operators, and the players themselves, were subject to five hundred dollar fines and six-month jail sentences. Finally, on October 1, 1910, Nevada joined her sister territories in the ban on public gambling.

The frontier gamblers had been obsoleted; they were now walking anachronisms. Some accepted their fate with the stoicism for which they were renowned. "If decent reformers who think they are doing the right thing try to stop gambling I don't kick," one old-timer was quoted in a national magazine. "They think it is wrong; they're square and entitled to think what they please. I've gambled all my life, and I don't see anything wrong in what I've done."[4]

More typical of the western sporting man's reaction to the turn of events was the caustic comment of one Arizona gambler: "This place is dead now. Every man, woman, and beast goes to bed at eight o'clock. Sleeping has become one of our principal industries."[5]

An Arizona gambling veteran identified only as "the Deacon" best articulated the embittered feelings of those of his class to an eastern magazine correspondent in 1908. The writer found the old gambler morosely leaning against the bar in an Ash Fork, Arizona, saloon. In broaching the subject of outlawed gambling, the journalist mentioned "Old Speedy," a well-known sport who had retired with the law change and was now raising fox terriers. The Deacon fixed the writer with a cold stare. "Yes," he said, "and he made a mistake at that. Should have taken up kittens. That's what the people of Arizona want now—tabby-cats and balls of yarn. When the boys come down from the mines and ranches we should be ready to take them to a knitting-bee."

Warming to his theme, the Deacon jabbed a finger in the correspondent's chest.

Yes, Mr. Tenderfoot, you can go home and tell the folks in the *enlightened* East that the sister Territories of Arizona and New Mexico are now as tame as a Quaker reservation. The accursed evil of gambling has been lifted; the gambler is no longer a *decent* citizen, whether or no he pays his bills and taxes, gives to the poor, and supports the public schools. Although only yesterday he had a voice in the community, today he must remain dumb. He is an outlaw, a social outcast. His old friends and pals, who once valued him so highly that they followed his guidance in politics and honored him by borrowing his money, now pity him. . . .

Will there be gambling in spite of the law? Of course . . . but what is there in it? You've got to give up more than half you make to the graft; you've got to take all sorts of insults from the tenderfoots without even pulling a gun and watching their hair rise on their high brows. You're no more than a pickpocket or a sneak-thief in the eye of the law. If anybody gets killed in your place, you go to a hothouse jail and melt for seven years or more.

Young man, the buttermilk boys have driven us into the ditch. There's nothing left for us but to go to work for a living or play penuckle [*sic*] with the alfalfa-growers in the back room of a saloon. And they've become receiving-vaults, with the roulette-wheels serving as free-lunch counters and the faro-tables covered with the bartenders' fancy work. They'll be taking down the pictures pretty soon and hanging up worsted mottoes. Yes, it's a milksop frontier now. . . .[6]

With which acerbic observation the old gambler swung back to the bar, dismissing his listener. He resembled nothing so much as an angry bull buffalo and the simile was apt, for, like the buffalo, he had become a victim of onrushing history. The buffalo, once the mighty lord of the Plains, had escaped extermination to survive as a curious leftover from a dead past. The western frontier gambler, however, was doomed to extinction, his only progeny a caricature of himself firmly implanted in the popular imagination.

NOTES

ACES

Chapter 1

1. Without question, faro was the foremost gambling game of nineteenth-century America. It was brought to the New World by the French, who called it *Pharao* or *Pharaon* because the backs of the early cards depicted an Egyptian ruler.

The accouterments of faro were an oilcloth "layout" upon which had been painted the thirteen cards of one suit, usually spades; an abacus-like contraption called the "casekeeper" by which a record was kept of the cards that had been played in each deal; and a dealer's box to hold a spring-loaded deck.

Bets were placed by the players on any of the cards or combination of cards on the layout. The dealer, after shuffling the deck, placed it face up in the box. The top card, the "soda," had no part in the betting. The dealer then drew the cards from a slot in the side of the box in a series of "turns." The first card of a turn was a loser, and won for the banker any wager on that card on the layout; the second was a winner and won for any player who had placed his bet on that particular card. If a "split" appeared, a pair on the turn, the banker took half the wagers on that card. The game was complicated by betting on combinations of cards, parlaying bets, and "coppering" bets, that is, betting that a card would be a loser rather than a winner. After twenty-four turns there were three cards remaining in the box—a loser, a winner, and the last card, the hock. Players could bet on the order of these last three cards and the bank paid odds, usually four to one, for correct guesses.

Honestly played, faro gave the player a fair chance to win, the dealer's edge being only the money he won from splits. However, a deft card manipulator could, while shuffling, increase the normal incidence of splits by stacking pairs. A number of "gaffed" or crooked faro boxes were introduced by which unscrupulous dealers fleeced players.

2. Quoted in Herbert Asbury, *The Barbary Coast*, 18.

3. J. D. Borthwick, *The Gold Hunters*, 67.

4. Robert K. Bruner, *A Treasury of Gambling Stories*, 330.

5. Quoted in Owen Cochran Coy, *Gold Days*, 279.

6. *San Francisco Tri-Weekly*, January 4, 1850.

7. Quoted in Curt Gentry, *The Madams of San Francisco*, 39.

8. Chuck-a-luck operators, who tumbled dice through a cone-shaped device of tin placed on a table and invited players to bet on the numbers of the dice before lifting the cone, were called "tinhorn gamblers" in the West. Since practitioners of this game required little investment or skill, the term "tinhorn" was later attached deprecatingly to any individual of limited means, ability, or stature.

9. "Monte," sometimes called "Spanish monte" or "Montebank," came from Spain and was popular in western territories where the Mexican influence was strong. It contained many elements of faro and may have derived from an ancient common ancestor. The dealer dealt "layouts" from a hand-held Spanish deck of forty cards, and then turned the deck over, exposing a card called the "gate." If the gate matched

a card in the layout, the dealer paid all bets made on that card. In some cases, payoffs were made for the simple matching of suits. Odds heavily favored the dealer in this game, but crooked gamblers often reduced the players' slim chances of winning to absolute zero by manipulation of the deck. The game finally fell into such ill repute that the word "mountebank," meaning any kind of charlatan or fraud, came into common usage.

10. Faro was sometimes called "Tiger," and many gambling houses displayed paintings of Bengal tigers behind their faro tables. "Bucking the tiger" was a commonly used expression meaning to play faro against the house.

11. Gentry, *Madams of San Francisco*, 77.

12. Ibid., 79.

13. Chauncey L. Canfield, *The Diary of a Forty-Niner*, 159.

14. G. Ezra Dane, *Ghost Town*, 11.

15. Ibid., 48.

16. Quoted in Gentry, *Madams of San Francisco*, 88–89.

17. Ibid., 88.

18. Asbury, *Barbary Coast*, 80–81.

Chapter 2

1. The French introduced this casino game into the New World. It was called "Van John" in England, but in America it came to be known as "21" or "blackjack."

2. Leroy Hafen, ed., *Colorado Gold Rush*, 207.

3. Ibid., 246.

4. Ibid., 333.

5. George F. Willison, *Here They Dug The Gold*, 85.

6. Ibid., 86.

7. *The Rocky Mountain News*, July 25, 1860.

8. Stanley W. Zamonski and Teddy Keller, *The Fifty-Niners*, 191.

9. Ibid.

10. Ibid.

11. Ibid., 209.

12. Ibid., 210–11.

13. *Leavenworth Daily Times*, November 20, 1861.

14. Stanley W. Zamonski, "Colorado Gold and the Confederacy," *Brand Book of the Denver Westerners*, 1956.

Chapter 3

1. Quoted in Richard O'Connor, *Wild Bill Hickok*, 86.

2. *Topeka Daily Commonwealth*, September 17, 1872.

3. Keno, which evolved from the English game of lotto and was the forerunner of bingo, is still popular in Nevada gambling casinos. Perhaps the largest keno house in the Old West was Congress Hall in San Francisco, where fifty tables, each seating twenty-one players, were available. A houseman, called "the roller," presided over each table, selling cards to the players and releasing numbered balls one by one from the neck of the keno "goose." During its heyday Congress Hall was filled night and day with more than a thousand enthusiasts.

4. Harry Sinclair Drago, *Wild, Woolly and Wicked*, 209.

5. *Dodge City Times*, March 24, 1877.

6. William M. Walton., *Life and Adventures of Ben Thompson*, 36–37.

7. Ibid., 33.

8. Floyd B. Streeter, *Ben Thompson: Man With a Gun*, 128.

9. Robert M. Wright, *Dodge City, The Cowboy Capital, and the Great Southwest*, 272.

Chapter 4
1. *Tombstone Epitaph*, July 22, 1880.
2. Most gambling houses employed an assistant to the faro dealer who paid and collected bets and watched for skulduggery by the players. This man, called the "lookout," usually sat to the dealer's right, and, as part of his duties, periodically spelled the dealer. Some houses also provided another employee, called the "case keeper," after his tool of trade, who maintained the record of cards played.
3. W. B. Masterson, "Wyatt Earp," *Human Life* (February, 1907), 9.
4. W. B. Masterson, "Luke Short," *Human Life* (April, 1907), 10.
5. *Dodge City Times*, October 23, 1884.
6. *New York Times*, October 26, 1921.
7. Robert K. DeArment, *Bat Masterson: The Man and the Legend*, 293.
8. Neill C. Wilson, *Silver Stampede*, 265.
9. Ed Bartholomew, *The Biographical Album of Western Gunfighters*.
10. Captain John G. Bourke, *On the Border with Crook*, 83.
11. *Silver City* (New Mexico) *Herald*, July 18, 1875.
12. Albert D. Richardson, *Beyond the Mississippi*.
13. Herbert Ashbury, *Sucker's Progress: An Informal History of Gambling in America From the Colonies to Canfield*, 338.
14. Ibid.

KINGS
Chapter 5
1. Horace Bell, *Reminiscences of a Ranger*, 12.
2. Ibid.
3. Ibid.
4. Horace Bell, *On the Old West Coast*, 246.
5. Bell, *Reminiscences*, 44.
6. Samuel Dickson, *Tales of San Francisco*, 33.
7. Quoted in Lucius Beebe and Charles Clegg, *The American West*, 268.
8. Dickson, *Tales of San Francisco*.

Chapter 6
1. George F. Willison, *Here They Dug the Gold*, 81.
2. Quoted in Stephen Longstreet, *War Cries on Horseback*, 148.
3. Willison, *Here They Dug the Gold*.
4. Quoted in Scott Dial, *Saloons of Denver*, 28.
5. *Denver Times*, July 9, 1878.
6. G. N. Scamehorn, *Behind the Scenes, Or, Denver by Gaslight*.

Chapter 7
1. Quoted in Charles Samuels, *The Magnificent Rube*, 45.
2. Ibid., 51.
3. Jed Jordan, *Fool's Gold*, 65.
4. Ibid., 199–201.
5. Ibid., 203.
6. Samuels, *Magnificent Rube*, 79.
7. Ibid., 78.
8. Glenn Chesney Quiett, *Pay Dirt: A Panorama of American Gold-Rushes*, 23.

Chapter 8
1. Glenn Chesney Quiett, *Pay Dirt: A Panorama of American Gold-Rushes*, 437.
2. Lucius Beebe and Charles Clegg, *U. S. West: The Saga of Wells Fargo*, 265–66.
3. Max Evans, *Long John Dunn of Taos*, 83.
4. Ibid., 127.
5. In the jargon of the West, faro players "bucked the tiger"; monte players "piked" the game, and were therefore "pikers." As monte fell into disrepute, bankers were forced to open their games to lesser fry, players who would only risk small change, and "piker" came to be a derisive term applied to any timid bettor.
6. Anonymous, "Playing the Gold Camps," *Saturday Evening Post*, (July 7, 1923).
7. Charles Samuels, *The Magnificent Rube*, 93.
8. Ibid., 130.
9. Ibid., 296.

QUEENS

Chapter 9
1. Duncan Aikman, *Calamity Jane and the Lady Wildcats*, 280–81.
2. Grace Ernestine Ray, *Wily Women of the West*, 62–63.
3. Josiah Gregg, *Commerce of the Prairies*, 168–69.
4. Matthew Field, *Matt Field on the Santa Fe Trail*, 205–208.
5. George Douglas Brewerton, *Overland With Kit Carson*, 189–91.
6. George Douglas Brewerton, "Incidents of Travel in New Mexico," *Harper's New Monthly Magazine* (April, 1854), 588.
7. Lois Cheney, "La Tules of Old Santa Fe," *Golden West* (January, 1967), 8.
8. Field, *Matt Field*, 209–13.
9. Diary of Philip Gooch Ferguson, 1847–48, From Ralph P. Bieher, ed., *Marching With the Army of the West*, 321.

Chapter 10
1. Quoted in Bob and Jan Young, "Madame Moustache," *True West* (June, 1956), 12.
2. Robert A. Hereford, *Old Man River: The Memories of Captain Louis Rosche, Pioneer Steamboatman*, 120–12.
3. Quoted in Curt Gentry, *The Madams of San Francisco*, 143.
4. Quoted in Harry Sinclair Drago, *Notorious Ladies of the Frontier*, 86.
5. Ibid.
6. Young, "Madame Moustache," 33.
7. *New York Tribune*, January 3, 1878.
8. Quoted in Forbes Parkhill, *The Wildest of the West*, 8.
9. Charles L. Martin, *A Sketch of Sam Bass, the Bandit*, 22.
10. Ibid., 20–21.
11. John F. Finerty, *War-Path and Bivouac*, 212.
12. Henry F. Hoyt, *A Frontier Doctor*, 39.

Chapter 11
1. J. Marvin Hunter, *The Story of Lottie Deno: Her Life and Times*, 17.
2. Ibid., 37–38.
3. "Dinero" is Spanish for "money."
4. Hunter, *Story of Lottie Deno*, 41.
5. Sallie Reynolds Matthews, *Interwoven, A Pioneer Chronicle*, 109–110.
6. Edgar Rye, *The Quirt and the Spur*, 70.

7. Hunter, *Story of Lottie Deno*, 39.
8. Ibid., 39–40.

Chapter 12
1. Colonel Bailey C. Hanes, *Bill Doolin: Outlaw*, O.T., 160.
2. Quoted in Joseph Miller, ed., *Arizona Cavalcade*, 192.
3. James D. Horan, *Desperate Women*, 321.

KNAVES

Chapter 13
1. Horace Bell, *Reminiscences of a Ranger*, 453.
2. Evelyn Wells, *The '49ers*, 192.
3. Granville Stuart, *Forty Years on the Frontier*, 218.
4. Ibid.
5. Nathaniel P. Langford, *Vigilante Days and Ways*, 81.
6. Stuart, *Forty Years on the Frontier*.
7. Ibid.
8. Wells Drury, *An Editor on the Comstock Lode*, 159.
9. Herman Francis Reinhart, The Golden Frontier, 242.
10. Langford, *Vigilante Days and Ways*, 61.
11. Reinhart, *Golden Frontier*, 244.
12. Langford, *Vigilante Days and Ways*, 75.

Chapter 14
1. Myron Angel, ed., *History of Nevada*.
2. Charles D. Greenfield, "There Was Something About Him," *The West* (February, 1967), 32.
3. *Gold Hill News*, January 2, 1877.
4. Greenfield, "There Was Something About Him," 50.
5. Helen Fitzgerald Sanders, ed., X. *Beidler: Vigilante*, 140–44.
6. Nathaniel P. Langford, *Vigilante Days and Ways*, 358.

Chapter 15
1. David W. Maurer, *The Big Con*, 6–7.
2. Mary Lou Pence and Lola M. Homsher, *The Ghost Towns of Wyoming*, 80.
3. James Chisholm, *South Pass, 1868*, 100–101.
4. Thomas A. McNeal, *When Kansas Was Young*, 138.
5. Quoted in the *Trinidad* (Colorado) *Daily News*, January 25, 1882.
6. George Jean Nathan, "The Old-Time Train Gambler," *Harper's Weekly* (May 21, 1910).
7. George H. Devol, *Forty Years a Gambler on the Mississippi*, 267–69.
8. Ibid., 190.
9. Ibid., 285.
10. Donald Henderson Clarke, *The Autobiography of Frank Tarbeaux*, 85–93.
11. Devol, *Forty Years a Gambler*, 181.
12. Clark, *Autobiography of Frank Tarbeaux*, 34–35.
13. Ibid., x.
14. Richard B. Hughes, *Pioneer Days in the Black Hills*, 159.
15. Henry F. Hoyt, *A Frontier Doctor*, 24–33.
16. January 4, 1879.
17. September 17, 1872.

18. *Rocky Mountain News*, November 30, 1880.
19. *Trinidad* (Colorado) *Daily News*, January 25, 1882.
20. May 5, 1881.
21. Quoted in the *Trinidad Daily News*, January 25, 1882.
22. May 2, 1882.
23. Forbes Parkhill, *The Law Goes West*, 89.
24. Ibid., 37.
25. February 12, 1876.
26. Anonymous, "Playing the Gold Camps," *Saturday Evening Post* (July 7, 1923).
27. Quoted in Helen Fitzgerald Sanders, ed., *X. Beidler: Vigilante*, 146.
28. Anonymous, "Playing the Gold Camps."

Chapter 16
1. Frank C. Robertson and Beth Kay Harris, *Soapy Smith: King of the Frontier Con Men*, 231.
2. Pierre Berton, *Klondike Fever*, 335.
3. Ibid.
4. Ibid.
5. William R. Collier and Edwin V. Westrate, *The Reign of Soapy Smith*, 17.
6. Ibid., 32.
7. July 29, 1889.
8. October 12, 1895.
9. Robertson and Harris, *Soapy Smith*, 160.
10. Ibid., 156.
11. Collier and Westrate, *Reign of Soapy Smith*, 233.

                                  HOCK
1. Joseph Miller, ed., *Arizona Cavalcade*, 195–96.
2. Ibid., 203–204.
3. Ibid., 200–201.
4. Hugh S. Fullerton, "American Gambling and Gamblers," *American Magazine* (March, 1914).
5. Barton Wood Currie, "The Transformation of the Southwest Through the Legal Abolition of Gambling," *Century Magazine* (April, 1908), at 905.
6. Ibid., 907.

BIBLIOGRAPHY

Books

Aikman, Duncan. *Calamity Jane and the Lady Wildcats*. New York: Henry Holt & Co., 1927.

————. (ed.). *The Taming of the Frontier*. New York: Minton, Balch & Co., 1925.

Amory, Cleveland. *The Last Resorts*. New York: Harper & Brothers, 1948.

Angel, Myron, ed. *History of Nevada*. Oakland: Thompson & West, 1881.

Asbury, Herbert. *The Barbary Coast*. New York: Alfred A. Knopf, 1933.

————. *The French Quarter*. New York: Alfred A. Knopf, 1936.

————. *Gem of the Prairie*. New York: Alfred A. Knopf, 1940.

————. *Sucker's Progress: An Informal History of Gambling in America From the Colonies to Canfield*. New York: Dodd, Mead & Co., 1938.

Ashbaugh, Don. *Nevada's Turbulent Yesterday*. Los Angeles: Westernlore Press, 1963.

Bancroft, Carolyn. *Denver's Lively Past*. Boulder, Colo.: Johnson Publishing Co., 1959.

Barnard, Evan C. *A Rider of the Cherokee Strip*. Boston, New York: Houghton Mifflin Co., 1936.

Bartholomew, Ed. *The Biographical Album of Western Gunfighters*. Houston: Frontier Press of Texas, 1958.

————. *Wyatt Earp: The Man and the Myth*. Toyahville, Texas, Frontier Book Co., 1964.

————. *Wyatt Earp: The Untold Story*. Toyahville, Texas, Frontier Book Co., 1963.

Beebe, Lucius. *Comstock Commotion: The Story of the Territorial Enterprise*. Stanford, Calif.: Stanford University Press, 1954.

Beebe, Lucius, and Charles Clegg. *The American West*. New York: E. P. Dutton & Co., 1955.

————. *U. S. West: The Saga of Wells Fargo*. New York: E. P. Dutton & Co., 1949.

Bell, Horace. *On the Old West Coast*. New York: William Morrow & Co., 1930.

————. *Reminiscences of a Ranger*. Los Angeles: Yarnell, Caystile & Mathes, Printers, 1881.

Berton, Pierre. *Klondike Fever*. New York: Alfred A. Knopf, 1958.

Bieber, Ralph P., ed. *Marching with the Army of the West, 1846–1848*. Glendale: Arthur H. Clark Co., 1936.

Borthwick, J. D. *The Gold Hunters*. New York, 1924.

Bourke, Captain John G. *On the Border With Crook*. New York: Charles Scribner's Sons, 1891.

Boyer, Glenn G., ed. *I Married Wyatt Earp: The Recollections of Josephine Sarah Marcus Earp*. Tucson: University of Arizona Press, 1976.

Breihan, Carl. *Badmen of the Frontier Days*. New York: McBride, 1957.

Brewerton, George Douglas. *Overland With Kit Carson*. New York: Coward-McCann, Inc., 1930.

Briggs, Harold E. *Frontiers of the Northwest*. New York, London: D. Appleton-Century Co., Inc., 1940.

Brolaski, Harry. *Easy Money: Being the Experiences of a Reformed Gambler*. Cleveland: Searchlight Press, 1911.

Brown, Dee. *The Gentle Tamers: Women of the Old West*. New York: G. P. Putnam's Sons, 1958.

Bruce, John. *Gaudy Century*. New York: Random House, 1948.

Bruner, Robert K. *A Treasury of Gambling Stories*. Chicago: Ziff-Davis Co., 1946.

Canfield, Chauncey L. *The Diary of a Forty-Niner*. New York, San Francisco: M. Shephard Co., 1906.

Chafetz, Henry. *Play the Devil: A History of Gambling in the United States From 1492 to 1955*. New York: Clarkson N. Potter, Inc., 1960.

Chisholm, James. *South Pass, 1868*. Lincoln: University of Nebraska Press, 1960.

Clarke, Donald Henderson. *The Autobiography of Frank Tarbeaux*. New York: The Vanguard Press, 1930.

Collier, William R., and Edwin V. Westrate. *Dave Cook of the Rockies*. New York: Rufus Rockwell Wilson, Inc., 1936.

———. *The Reign of Soapy Smith*. Garden City, N.Y.: Doubleday, Doran & Co., 1935.

Collinson, Frank. *Life in the Saddle*. Norman: University of Oklahoma Press, 1963.

Coolidge, Dane. *Fighting Men of the West*. New York: E. P. Dutton & Co., 1932.

Cox, William R. *Luke Short and His Era*. New York: Doubleday & Co., 1961.

Coy, Owen Cochran. *Gold Days*. San Francisco: Powell Publishing Co., 1929.

Cross, Ralph Herbert. *The Early Inns of California*. San Francisco: n.p., 1954.

Dane, G. Ezra. *Ghost Town*. New York: Alfred A. Knopf, 1941.

Davis, Clyde B. *Something for Nothing*. Philadelphia: L. P. Lippincott Co., 1955.

DeArment, Robert K. *Bat Masterson: The Man and the Legend*. Norman: University of Oklahoma Press, 1979.

Devol, George H. *Forty Years a Gambler on the Mississippi*. New York: 1892.

DeVoto, Bernard. *The Year of Decision, 1846*. Boston: Little, Brown & Co., 1943.

Dial, Scott, *Saloons of Denver*. Fort Collins, Colo.: The Old Army Press, 1973.

Dick, Everett. *Vanguards of the Frontier*. New York, London: D. Appleton-Century Co., Inc., 1941.

Dickson, Samuel. *Tales of San Francisco*. Stanford, Calif.: Stanford University Press, 1957.

Donaldson, Thomas C. *Idaho of Yesterday*. Caldwell, Idaho: The Caxton Printers, Ltd., 1941.

Drago, Harry Sinclair. *Notorious Ladies of the Frontier*. New York: Dodd, Mead & Co., 1969.

———. *Wild, Woolly and Wicked*. New York: Clarkson N. Potter, Inc., 1960.

Drury, Wells. *An Editor on the Comstock Iode*. New York, Toronto: Farrar & Rinehart, Inc., 1936.

Dunham, Sam C. *Riley Grannan's Last Adventure*. Austin, Texas: Packsaddle Press, 1969.

Ellis, Amanda Mae. *The Strange, Uncertain Years*. Hamden, Conn.: Shoe String Press, 1959.

Emrich, Duncan. *Comstock Bonanza*. New York: The Vanguard Press, 1950.

———. *It's An Old Wild West Custom*. New York: The Vanguard Press, 1949.

Evans, Max. *Long John Dunn of Taos*. Los Angeles: Westernlore Press, 1959.

Field, Matthew. *Matt Field of the Santa Fe Trail*. Norman: University of Oklahoma Press, 1960.

Fielder, Mildred. *Wild Bill and Deadwood.* Seattle: Superior Publishing Co., 1965.
Finerty, John F. *War-Path and Bivouac.* Norman: University of Oklahoma Press, 1961.
Frackelton, Will. *Sagebrush Dentist.* Chicago: A. C. McClurg & Co., 1941.
Ganzhorn, Jack. *I've Killed Men.* New York: The Devin-Adair Co., 1959.
Gentry, Curt. *The Madams of San Francisco.* Garden City, N.Y.: Doubleday & Co., 1964.
Gibson, George Rutledge. *Journal of a Soldier Under Kearney and Doniphan, 1846–1847.* Glendale, Calif.: Arthur N. Clark Co., 1935.
Glasscock, Carl B. *The Big Bonanza.* Indianapolis: The Bobbs-Merrill Co., 1931.
Gregg, Josiah. *Commerce of the Prairies.* Norman: University of Oklahoma Press, 1954.
Hafen, LeRoy, ed. *Colorado Gold Rush.* Glendale, Calif.: The Arthur H. Clark Co., 1941.
Hanes, Colonel Bailey C. *Bill Doolin: Outlaw O.T.* Norman: University of Oklahoma Press, 1968.
Hereford, Robert A. *Old Man River: The Memories of Captain Louis Rosche, Pioneer Steamboatman.* Caldwell, Idaho: The Caxton Printers, Ltd., 1943.
Hicks, John Edward. *Adventures of a Tramp Printer, 1880–1890.* Kansas City, Mo.: Midamerican Press, 1950.
Horan, James D. *Desperate Women.* New York: G. P. Putnam's Sons, 1952.
Hoyt, Henry F. *A Frontier Doctor.* Boston, New York: Houghton Mifflin Co., 1929.
Hughes, Richard B. *Pioneer Days in the Black Hills.* Glendale, Calif.: Arthur H. Clark Co., 1957.
Hunt, William R. *North of 53: The Wild Days of the Alaska-Yukon Mining Frontier, 1870–1914.* New York: McMillan Publishing Co., 1974.
Hunter, J. Marvin. *The Story of Lottie Deno: Her Life and Times.* Bandera, Texas: The 4 Hunters, 1959.
Jackson, Joseph H. *Anybody's Gold.* New York, London: D. Appleton-Century Co., Ltd., 1941.
————. *Bad Company.* New York: Harcourt, Brace & Co., 1949.
Jahns, Pat. *The Frontier World of Doc Holliday.* New York: Hastings House, 1957.
Johnston, Abraham Robinson; Marcellus Ball Edwards; and Philip Gooch Ferguson. *Marching With the Army of the West, 1846–1848.* Edited by Ralph P. Beiber. Glendale, Calif.: The Arthur H. Clark Co., 1936.
Jordan, Jed. *Fool's Gold.* New York: The John Day Co., 1960.
Knight, Oliver. *Fort Worth: Outpost on the Trinity.* Norman: University of Oklahoma Press, 1953.
Lake, Stuart N. *Wyatt Earp: Frontier Marshal.* Boston, New York: Houghton Mifflin Co., 1931.
Langford, Nathaniel P. *Vigilante Days and Ways.* Boston: J. G. Cupples Co., Publishers, 1890.
Laughlin, Ruth. *The Wind Leaves No Shadow.* New York, Toronto: McGraw-Hill Book Co., Inc., 1948.
Lewis, Oscar. *Sagebrush Casinos.* Garden City, N.Y.: Doubleday & Co., 1953.
Lilienthal, Jesse. *Gambler's Wife.* Boston, New York: Houghton Mifflin Co., 1933.
Lillard, Richard G. *Desert Challenge.* New York: Alfred A. Knopf, 1942.
Lindsey, Benjamin B., and Harvey J. O'Higgins. *The Beast.* Garden City, N.Y.: Doubleday, Page & Co., 1917.
Longstreet, Stephen. *War Cries on Horseback.* Garden City, N.Y.: Doubleday & Co., 1970.

————. *Win or Lose: A Social History of Gambling in America*. Indianapolis, New York: Bobbs-Merrill Co., 1977.

Lyman, George D. *The Saga of the Comstock Lode*. New York, London: Charles Scribner's Sons, 1934.

McIntire, James *Early Days in Texas: A Trip to Heaven and Hell*. Kansas City, Mo.: McIntire Publishing Co., 1902.

McNeal, Thomas A. *When Kansas Was Young*. New York: Macmillan Co., 1922.

Marryat, Frank. *Mountains and Molehills*. New York: Harper & Brothers, 1855.

Martin. Charles L. *A Sketch of Sam Bass, the Bandit*. Norman: University of Oklahoma Press, 1956.

Martin, Douglas D. *Tombstone's Epitaph*. Albuquerque: University of New Mexico Press, 1951.

Matthews, Sallie Reynolds. *Interwoven, A Pioneer Chronicle*. Austin, Texas: University of Texas Press, 1977.

Maurer, David W. *The Big Con*. New York: The Bobbs-Merrill Co., 1940.

Miller, Joseph, ed. *Arizona Cavalcade*. New York: Hastings House, 1962.

Miller, Max. *Holliday Street*. New York: Signet Books, 1962.

Miller, Nyle H., and Joseph W. Snell. *Why the West Was Wild*. Topeka: Kansas State Historical Society, 1963.

Mumey, Nolie. *Creede*. Denver: Artcraft Press, 1949.

————. *Poker Alice*. Denver: Artcraft Press, 1951.

Myers, John Myers. *Doc Holliday*. Boston: Little, Brown & Co., 1955.

Nadeau, Remi. *Ghost Towns and Mining Camps of California*. Los Angeles: The Ward Ritchie Press, 1965.

O'Connor, Richard. *High Jinks on the Klondike*. New York: The Bobbs-Merrill Co., 1954.

————. *Wild Bill Hickok*. New York: Doubleday & Co., 1959.

Ostrander, Gilman M. *Nevada: The Great Rotten Borough, 1859–1964*. New York: Alfred A. Knopf, 1966.

Otero, Miguel A. *My Life on the Frontier. Vol. I*. New York: Press of the Pioneers, 1935.

Parker, Gilbert. *Tarboe, The Story of a Life*. New York: Harper & Brothers, 1927.

Parkhill, Forbes. *The Law Goes West*. Denver: Sage Books, 1956.

————. *The Wildest of the West*. New York: Henry Holt & Co., 1951.

Pence, Mary Lou, and Lola M. Homsher. *The Ghost Towns of Wyoming*. New York: Hastings House, 1956.

Perkin, Robert L. *The First One Hundred Years*. Garden City, N.Y.: Doubleday & Co., 1959.

Peyton, Green. *San Antonio: City in the Sun*. New York, London: Whittlesey House, McGraw-Hill Book Co., Inc., 1946.

Quiett, Glenn Chesney. *Pay Dirt: A Panorama of American Gold-Rushes*. New York, London: D. Appleton-Century Co., Inc., 1936.

Quinn, John Philip. *Fools of Fortune, or, Gambling and Gamblers*. Chicago: G. L. Howe & Co., 1890.

Raine, William MacLeod. *Guns of the Frontier*. Boston: Houghton Mifflin Co., 1940.

Ray, Grace Ernestine. *Wily Women of the West*. San Antonio: The Naylor Co., 1972.

Reinhart, Herman Francis. *The Golden Frontier*. Austin: University of Texas Press, 1962.

Richardson, Albert D. *Beyond the Mississippi*. New York: The American Publishing Co., 1867.

Robertson, Frank C., and Beth Kay Harris. *Soapy Smith: King of the Frontier Con Men*. New York: Hastings House, 1961.

Rogers, John William. *The Lusty Texans of Dallas*. New York: E. P. Dutton and Co., 1951.

Rosa, Joseph G. *They Called Him Wild Bill: The Life and Adventures of James Butler Hickok*. Norman: University of Oklahoma Press, 1964.

Ross, Dudley T. *Devil on Horseback*. Fresno: Valley Publishers, 1975.

Rye, Edgar. *The Quirt and the Spur*. Chicago: W. B. Conkey Co., 1909.

Samuels, Charles. *The Magnificent Rube*. New York: McGraw-Hill Book Co., 1957.

Sanders, Helen Fitzgerald, ed. *X. Beidler: Vigilante*. Norman: University of Oklahoma Press, 1957.

Sandoz, Mari. *Son of the Gamblin' Man*. New York: Clarkson N. Potter, Inc., 1960.

Scamehorn, G. N. *Behind the Scenes, or, Denver By Gas Light*. Denver: George A. Shirley, Publisher, 1894.

Schoenberger, Dale T. *The Gunfighters*. Caldwell, Idaho: The Caxton Printers, 1971.

Smith, Duane A. *Rocky Mountain Mining Camps*. Bloomington/London: Indiana University Press, 1967.

Sonnichsen, C. L. *Billy King's Tombstone*. Caldwell, Idaho: The Caxton Printers, Ltd., 1942.

Soule, Frank; John Gihon; and James Nesbit. *The Annals of San Francisco*. New York: n.p., 1855.

Sprague, Marshall. *Money Mountain*. Boston: Little, Brown and Co., 1953.

Spring, Agnes Wright. *Cheyenne and Black Hills Stage and Express Routes*. Glendale, Calif.: The Arthur H. Clark Co., 1949.

Streeter, Floyd B. *Ben Thompson: Man With a Gun*. New York: Frederick Fell Inc., Publishers, 1957.

————. *The Kaw*. New York, Toronto: Farrar & Rinehart, Inc., 1941.

————. *Prairie Trails and Cow Towns*. Boston: Chapman & Grimes, 1936.

Stong, Philip D. *Gold in Them Hills*. Garden City, N.Y.: Doubleday & Co., 1957.

Stuart, Granville. *Forty Years on the Frontier*. Cleveland: The Arthur H. Clark Co., 1925.

Taylor, Bayard. *El Dorado, or, Adventures in the Path of Empire*. New York: Alfred A. Knopf, 1949.

Thane, Eric. *High Border Country*. New York: Sloan & Pearce, 1942.

Townsend, Robert S. *Proud Heritage*. Kansas City, Mo.: n.p., 1957.

Van Cise, Philip S. *Fighting the Underworld*. Boston, New York: Houghton Mifflin Co., 1936.

Walton, William M. *Life and Adventures of Ben Thompson, the Famous Texan*. Houston: The Frontier Press of Texas, 1954.

Watson, Margaret G. *Silver Theater: Amusements of the Mining Frontier in Early Nevada 1850 to 1864*. Glendale, Calif.: The Arthur H. Clark Co., 1964.

Wells, Evelyn. *The 49'ers*. Garden City, N.Y.: Doubleday and Co., 1949.

Wendt, Lloyd, and Herman Kogan. *Bet a Million!* Indianapolis: The Bobbs-Merrill Co., 1948.

Williams, Brad, and Choral Pepper. *The Mysterious West*. Cleveland, New York: The World Publishing Co., 1967.

Willison, George F. *Here They Dug the Gold*. New York: Reynol & Hitchcock Co., 1946.

Wilson, Neill C. *Silver Stampede*. New York: The Macmillan Co., 1937.

Wolle, Muriel Sibell. *Stampede to Timberline: The Ghost Towns and Mining Camps of Colorado.* Denver: The Artcraft Press, 1949.

Wright, Robert M. *Dodge City: The Cowboy Capital, and the Great Southwest.* Wichita: Wichita Eagle Press, 1913.

Zamonski, Stanley W., and Teddy Keller. *The Fifty-Niners.* Denver: Sage Books, 1961.

Articles

Ankeny, Levi. "The Enigmatic Ferd Patterson," *The West* (October, 1965), pp. 18–19, 54–56.

Anonymous. "Playing the Gold Camps," *Saturday Evening Post* (July 7, 1923).

Bailey, Tom. "The Duck That Laid the Golden Eggs," *Frontier Times* (Winter, 1960), pp. 18–19, 36–39.

———. "King of Cards," *See, The New Magazine for Men* (May, 1958), p. 12–15, 72–84.

Brewerton, George Douglas. "Incidents of Travel in New Mexico," *Harper's New Monthly Magazine* (April, 1854).

Cheney, Louis. "La Tules of Old Sante Fe," *Golden West* (January, 1967), pp. 8, 62–64.

Currie, Barton Wood. "The Transformation of the Southwest Through the Legal Abolition of Gambling," *Century Magazine* (April, 1908).

Fullerton, Hugh S. "American Gambling and Gamblers," *American Magazine* (March, 1914).

Greenfield, Charles D. "There was Something About Him," *The West* (February, 1967), pp. 30–32, 49–50.

Howell, Deal. "The Sweet Grass Hills Massacre," *The West* (February, 1965), pp. 20–21, 48.

Lo Bello, Nino. "Poker Alice," *True West* (October, 1956), p. 47.

McKenna, Gail. "Shanghai Hell." *The West* (September, 1965), pp. 38–39, 56–57.

McMillan, Mark. "Lucky Bill Gets the Noose," *True West* (Spring, 1954), pp. 22–23, 33–34.

Masterson, W. B. "Famous Gunfighters of the Western Frontier: Ben Thompson," *Human Life* (January, 1907).

———. "Wyatt Earp," *Human Life* (February, 1907).

———. "Luke Short," *Human Life* (April, 1907).

———. "Doc Holliday," *Human Life* (May, 1907).

Murbarger, Nell. "Ghosts of Gold and Glory," *True West* (July–August, 1955), pp. 4–11, 43–46.

———. "Ring-Tailed Roarer," *True West* (February, 1956), pp. 4–7, 34–35.

Nathan, George Jean. "The Old-Time Train Gambler," *Harper's Weekly* (May 21, 1910).

Pharo, Agnes M. "The Intellectual Con-Man," *Frontier Times* (September, 1965), pp. 25, 54.

Secrest, William B. "Jim Levy, Top-Notch Gunfighter," *True West* (August, 1978), pp. 24–26, 56–58.

Wirt, Sherwood Eliot. "The Man From Eldorado," *Alaska Life* (July–August, 1945), pp. 34–43.

Young, Bob and Jan. "Madame Moustache," *True West* (June, 1956), pp. 12–13, 33.

Zamonski, Stanley W. "Colorado Gold and the Confederacy," *Brand Book of the Denver Westerners* (1956).

Newspapers

Austin Statesman
Denver Post
Denver Republican
Denver Times
Dodge City Times
Gold Hill News
Leavenworth Daily Times
New York Morning Telegraph
New York Times
New York Tribune
San Francisco Morning Call
San Francisco Tri-Weekly
Silver City Herald
Tombstone Epitaph
Topeka Daily Commonwealth
Trinidad Daily News
Trinidad Democrat
Rocky Mountain News
Spokane Daily Chronicle

INDEX